Storytelling
Sociology

Storytelling Sociology

Narrative as Social Inquiry

edited by
Ronald J. Berger
and Richard Quinney

LYNNE
RIENNER
PUBLISHERS

BOULDER
LONDON

Published in the United States of America in 2005 by
Lynne Rienner Publishers, Inc.
1800 30th Street, Boulder, Colorado 80301
www.rienner.com

and in the United Kingdom by
Lynne Rienner Publishers, Inc.
3 Henrietta Street, Covent Garden, London WC2E 8LU

Library of Congress Cataloging-in-Publication Data
Storytelling sociology : narrative as social inquiry / Ronald J. Berger
and Richard Quinney, editors.
          p. cm.
     Includes bibliographical references and index.
     ISBN 1-58826-295-2 (hardcover : alk. paper)
     ISBN 1-58826-271-5 (pbk. : alk. paper)
     1. Sociology—Methodology.   2. Narration (Rhetoric)   I. Berger, Ronald J.
II. Quinney, Richard.
HM511.S76   2004
301'.01—dc22

                                                                2004007780

British Cataloguing in Publication Data
A Cataloguing in Publication record for this book
is available from the British Library.

Printed and bound in the United States of America

The paper used in this publication meets the requirements
of the American National Standard for Permanence of
Paper for Printed Library Materials Z39.48-1992.

5   4   3   2   1

Contents

Preface   vii

1   The Narrative Turn in Social Inquiry
    Ronald J. Berger & Richard Quinney   1

Part 1   Family and Place

Introduction   13

2   Searching for Yellowstone   *Norman K. Denzin*   17

3   Twin Towers   *Nelia Olivencia*   25

4   Remembering George Washington on the Rio Grande
    A. Javier Treviño   35

5   My Ain Folk: Scottish Oral History and
    the Sociological Imagination   *Jean V. L. Hector Faley*   49

6   Everyone Else: Becoming Jewish   *Tony Platt*   63

7   Walking with Lao Tzu at Auschwitz   *DeWitt Clinton*   71

Part 2   The Body

Introduction   87

8   Becoming Quasimodo: The Shaping of a Life
    William E. Powell   91

9   No Body Is Exempt: Beauty Compulsion and
    Resistance in Japan   *Laura Miller*   107

10 Mama's Always on Stage: The Absurdity of the
    Pregnant Academic   *Darcie Vandegrift*   119

v

11   Sexual Boundaries: Trespasses into Chaos   *Marga Ryersbach*   129

12   The Razor's Edge: Narcotics and the
     Embodiment of Trauma   *Diane Schaefer*   139

13   Hoop Dreams on Wheels   *Ronald J. Berger*   153

Part 3   Education and Work

Introduction   167

14   How I Started My Life in Crime   *Sheila Balkan*   171

15   Born Illegal   *Stephen C. Richards*   183

16   Telling Tales: Journey of an Itinerant Storyteller
     Robin A. Mello   195

17   Silence of the Lambs: The Architecture
     of the Abattoir   *Carla Corroto*   207

18   Working-Class Heroes: Rinaldo Cappellini and the
     Anthracite Mineworkers   *Robert P. Wolensky*   215

19   A Road Less Traveled   *John Horton*   231

20   It Means Something: The Ghosts of War   *William B. Brown*   245

Part 4   The Passing of Time

Introduction   265

21   The Glowing of Such Fire   *Richard Quinney*   267

References   283
The Contributors   295
Index   297
About the Book   307

Preface

This book has its origins in a friendship we began in January 2002. Richard had recently moved to Madison, Wisconsin, after retiring from his professorship at Northern Illinois University in DeKalb, and had e-mailed Ron that he was in town. Coincidentally, Ron and his sociology colleagues at the University of Wisconsin–Whitewater had just been talking about inviting Richard to speak to a group of criminology students.[1] The gods of sociology must have been watching.

Our only previous contact had been through a couple of e-mail exchanges we had in 1994 when Ron invited Richard to submit an article to *Sociological Imagination,* the journal of the Wisconsin Sociological Association, which he was coediting with Bruce Wiegand. In the abstract of that *SI* article, Richard wrote, "The wonder of human experience is caught in moments of verbal and visual reflection. We tell our stories and we make our images in the course of everyday life. Meaning is given to the lightness of our being; for the record, a visual sociology of human existence" (1994:130). Bruce, who tragically died from a brain tumor in 2002, wrote the "From the Editors" introduction for that *SI* issue: "Quinney writes in an autobiographical style but never doubt the steel-eyed critique of Western existence that lies just below the surface of the written word."

Richard had been writing autobiography (and about storytelling) for some time. Ron's work had taken a different turn too; he was working on a life history study of his father's and uncle's Holocaust survival that had profound personal meaning in his life, and he was just beginning a project on disability that was inspired by circumstances in his family. After our first chat in the luminous sunroom of Richard's home, we realized how much we had in common. We agreed to get together again soon.

Our conversations often turned to autobiography and biography and to our mutual interest in developing a more self-reflective form of sociology, one that engaged us more fully as human beings rather than as detached theoreticians or researchers. We decided to organize a session for the fall 2002 meeting of the Wisconsin Sociological Association and call it "Memoir as Ethnography." Nelia Olivencia and Amber Ault joined us on a panel that was well received by the group in attendance. After the conference, we started thinking about how many people we knew who were doing this type of work and decided to explore the idea of an anthology of original articles. We realized that memoir was not the concept we were looking for, and after some thought, we landed on the idea of narrative and storytelling—the idea that lived experience is constructed, at least in part, by the stories people tell about it.

We proceeded to tap into our networks of colleagues and friends, among whom were some highly regarded scholars, to inquire about their interest in contributing to the book. We wrote to those who we knew were already doing narrative sociology or who we thought might be interested in taking the narrative turn. We asked them to think about a contribution that would entail writing about their own life experiences or about their location in a research milieu. The response surprised even us. With no more than two degrees of separation from people we already knew, we had more than enough contributors for a book. These writers are primarily sociologists but also include scholars from anthropology, education, literature, social work, and architecture. Researchers who have been involved in class, racial/ethnic, gender, sexual orientation, and disability studies are represented in the book.

The organization of the book emerged inductively, as we sought a flexible, sensitizing scheme within which to tell the collective story of the book. We decided on four interrelated themes—Family and Place, The Body, Education and Work, and The Passing of Time—that tell a story about the life course, about the writers' familial and spatial/temporal roots, about the ways in which the social is embodied in their skin and bones, about their entrances and exits and time spent within various institutional worlds.

We no longer write to further our careers, but seek a sociology that is self-reflective and willing to engage the personal, a sociology that refuses to segregate our professional insights from our own lives. We have discovered that we find meaning and solace in the writing and reading of well-told sociological stories. To this end, we hope to advance our vision of a *storytelling sociology,* our vision of where to take the narrative turn in social inquiry that has engaged many of our colleagues across the disciplinary spectrum of academe. "Seeing our lives as stories is more than a powerful metaphor. It is how experience presents itself to us" (Taylor 2001:4). Tell me a story, the children cry. If we tell them, they will listen.[2]

Notes

1. We must admit to some awkwardness in writing about ourselves in the third person. But the pronoun *we* falters when we speak about the two of us in one voice.

2. We'd like to express our appreciation to Lynne Rienner, Amber Ault, Ruthy Berger, and the anonymous reviewers for constructive suggestions that helped improve the manuscript, as well as to Lesli Athanasoulis, Lisa Tulchin, Ruth Goring, and the rest of the staff at Lynne Rienner Publishers for their support and assistance with this project.

Storytelling
Sociology

CHAPTER 1

The Narrative Turn in Social Inquiry

Ronald J. Berger and Richard Quinney

But in order to make you understand, to tell you my life, I must tell you a story.

—*Virginia Woolf*

The remembering makes it now. And sometimes remembering will lead to a story, which makes it forever. That's what stories are for. Stories are for joining the past to the future. Stories are for those late hours in the night when you can't remember how you got from where you are. Stories are for eternity, when memory is erased, when there is nothing to remember except the story.

—*Tim O'Brien*

What remains of a story after it is finished?
Another story.

—*Elie Wiesel*

Once upon a time, sociology emerged as a field of scholarly inquiry out of a need to understand the social changes that accompanied the industrialization of society in the nineteenth century. It was born in an intellectual space between positivist science and literary representation, alternatively striving for analytical understanding and practical application, on the one hand, and the conveyance of meaning and empathy, on the other (Gubrium and Holstein 1997; Lepenies 1988; Richardson 1998).

Sociology and Its Critique

Positivist sociology advanced a view of the discipline as a value-free enterprise dedicated to the creation of objective, nonideological knowledge derived from scientific observation of empirical reality.[1] In the United

1

States (but not in Europe) this disciplinary quest led to the ascendancy of quantitative methods and the "mathematization" of sociology, to use Ben Agger's (2000) term. Although some of the early classics of American sociology included works in interpretive biography and ethnography,[2] and qualitative studies found a secure foothold in the field, quantitative sociology achieved hegemonic status. Rigor of method demarcated the boundary between "real" sociology and impostors. Economics, not the humanities, became the allied field most admired by professional sociologists as they sought to advance their academic careers and persuade university administrators and grant agencies to fund faculty positions and research projects for sociologists. To some extent, even qualitative methods became subject to such constraints, as witnessed in the development of systematic techniques for the coding and transformation of qualitative data into numerical variables that could be analyzed by means of the latest computer software (Neuman 2003).

In the postmodern era of the late twentieth and early twenty-first centuries, however, a growing number of sociologists have become disenchanted with the project of positivist sociology. Critics within the discipline have observed that sociology has become so dependent on quantitative instrumentation removed from lived experience that its claim of being an empirical science capable of ascertaining social reality seems rather dubious. The apparent objectivity of quantitative data is belied by the fact that the numbers do not speak for themselves. The meaning of these data is in large part a rhetorical accomplishment, as researchers assert relationships among variables with descriptive terms such as "significant," "robust," "stable," and "predictive" (Agger 2000; Maines 1993).

Especially noteworthy for his role in advancing this critique was C. Wright Mills, who observed that sociologists' preoccupation with method, what he called "abstracted empiricism," endangered the disappearance of sociology's subject matter. In *The Sociological Imagination*, Mills (1959) called for a sociology that grappled with the intersection of biography and history in society and the ways in which personal troubles are related to public issues. This famous dictum, as we shall see, underpins the perspective of this book.

Mills was, of course, a man of the political left, and his penetrating analyses of class and power paved the way for an intense engagement with Marxism and socialist ideas among New Left activists and academics in the 1960s. This movement, along with the civil rights, women's, sexual liberation, and anticolonial movements of that period, pushed the critique of positivist sociology further. New voices were heard as members of previously marginalized groups began speaking their own "truths" about their lives and the world as they saw it. Sociologists were challenged to abandon their faith in value neutrality and seek alliance with these advocates of change.

Feminism in particular played a key role in debunking sociology's privileged knowledge claims. Feminist scholars argued that "truth" is contested and polyvocal and that women's social position in society gives them distinctive insights, indeed a different epistemological standpoint, from men's. They advocated a research methodology that would eschew personal detachment and encourage collaboration and empathic connection with research subjects, cross-fertilization among academic disciplines, and involvement in action-oriented research that would facilitate personal and social transformation (Harding 1991; Jaggar 1983; Laslett and Thorne 1997; Reinharz 1992).

In the years that followed, intellectual movements variously called poststructuralist, deconstructionist, and most commonly *postmodernist* launched a provocative philosophical critique of scientific practice as an exercise of power. According to Michel Foucault, a chief figure in this movement, dominant regimes of "truth" construct restrictive criteria for the generation of knowledge and empower institutionalized "experts" with authority to administer knowledge and police heretical practices. In doing so, these regimes also produce a set of inferiorized knowledges, or disciplinary "others," which though subordinated and marginalized remain historically viable and continuously in revolt (Barrett 1991; Lemert 1997; Seidman 1996).

The counterreaction to these critiques and the defense of the status quo have been fierce in some quarters (Huber 1995; see Pierce 2003; Richardson 1996; Sparks 2002). Some consider postmodernism a fad that will eventually pass and are asserting institutionalized authority within doctoral programs, faculty recruitment and retention decisions, and professional publication outlets to police ideas they believe are undermining the legitimacy of sociology. But whatever postmodernism is, and according to Charles Lemert (1997), it may not be what you think, it will not go away. If postmodernism is about anything, it is about the fact that the world has changed in some unmistakable yet ill-defined and unfolding way, and that our conventional ways of thinking about social life may no longer suffice (Denzin 1997).

The Narrative Turn

Amidst all this commotion and strife, one began to hear a cacophony of voices throughout the social sciences and the humanities about *narrative, narrative analysis, stories,* and *storytelling.* This movement is constituted by diverse "analytic languages and growing representational heritages" that often talk around and past each other and do not fully engage (Gubrium and Holstein 1999:564). There is at this moment no central core or standardized set of procedures that can be said to have achieved dominance. The less contentious and more cordial practitioners are content with allowing various avenues of inquiry to grow and are reluctant to enforce a regime of truth that will undermine creative developments.

In general, narrative is about stories and story structure. It is about imbuing "life events with a temporal and logical order," about establishing continuity between the past, present, and as yet unrealized future, about transforming human experience into meaning (Ochs and Capps 2001:2). Narrative turns mere chronology—one thing after another—into "the purposeful action of plot" (Taylor 2001:2). A coherent plot is one that has a beginning, middle, and end. It grows plausibly out of what has come before and points the way to what might reasonably come next. Hayden White calls this *emplotment,* the way in which "a sequence of events fashioned into a story is gradually revealed to be a story of a particular kind" (1973:7).

Narratives, however, are not always orderly accounts and do not invariably have happy endings. In *Lost in the Funhouse,* John Barth self-consciously comments on the failure of his story to cohere: "the plot doesn't rise by meaningful steps but winds upon itself, digresses, retreats, hesitates, sighs, collapses, expires" (1968:96). Such stories are harder to hear, harder to make sense of, because they are stories about disconnectedness, about absurdity and uncertainty. In their telling, however, the sense of chaos may actually be eased, a "healthy disorder" may be unleashed (Mitchell 1981:ix). Even an effectively narrated tragedy will allow us to "take comfort that even the worst life has to offer can be given a shape, can be expressed—enacted—and therefore contemplated and reconciled" (Taylor 2001:75). But while some narratives are about healing, others are about wounds and pain that cannot be cured but only endured (Frank 1995; Zeitlan 1997).

Some analysts make a distinction between *narrative* and *story.* For example, D. Jean Clandinin and F. Michael Connelly (1998) characterize narrative as a *method* of inquiry and story as the *phenomenon* of that inquiry. They write that people "lead storied lives and tell stories of those lives," while "narrative researchers describe such lives, collect and tell stories of them, and write narratives of experience" (p. 155). David Maines (1999) conceptualizes narrative as the cultural "master frame" or structure that prefigures stories and makes storytelling possible. Stories rely on and invoke collective myths, archetypes, symbols, linguistic forms, and vocabularies of motive, without which their meaning "would remain unintelligible and uninterpretable" (Ewick and Silbey 1995:211–212). Arthur Frank, on the other hand, notes that "since narratives only exist in particular stories, and all stories are narratives, the distinction is hard to sustain" (1995:188).

Narrative scholars of various stripes seem to concur with the proposition that lived experience can be understood through the stories people tell about it. Stories are ways not merely of telling others about ourselves but of constructing our identities, of finding purpose and meaning in our lives. Frank observes that "stories of people trying to sort out who they are figure prominently on the landscape of postmodern times" (Frank 1995:xiii). In the telling we remember, we rework and reimagine the past, reflect back upon ourselves, and entertain what we have and could become. What is included or omitted from our stories makes plausible our anticipated futures. Because stories unfold over time, they are provisional and open-ended and contain the possibility for change. At the same time, storytelling does not occur in a social vacuum. It requires listeners who may validate or reject our stories or require us to accommodate our stories to theirs (Clandinin and Connelly 2000; Gubrium and Holstein 1997; Rosenwald and Ochberg 1992; Taylor 2001).

Some analysts are concerned that by acknowledging that everyone has *their own* story, narrative inquiry runs the risks of dissolving into solipsism or the local circumstances of each particular telling and of assuming that people's commonsense accounts are suitable substitutes for sociological analysis. According to this view, people tell stories and use narrative in everyday life, but it generally takes a trained observer to make sociological sense out of all that is told. Thus Jaber Gubrium and James Holstein argue that researchers should allow "indigenous voices [to] have their own say" without abandoning their *authorial* obligation to "complement and contextualize the explication of informants' accounts, or nonaccounts as the case might be" (Gubrium and Holstein 1999:569–570; Rosenwald and Ochberg 1992).

The narrative literature is replete with myriad authorial strategies for narrating people's stories. Gubrium and Holstein are noteworthy for their ethnomethodologically informed inquiries into the *how* questions of "narrative practice," that is, the everyday activities through which "stories about experience are presented, structured, and made to cohere" and thus constitute and sustain the meaningful realities of social life (1997:147). They view stories as incomplete "prior to their telling" and are interested in how people assemble their accounts "to meet situated interpretive demands" and in the process transform "experiential 'chaos' into coherent and decipherable forms" and social identities of the self (1998:166). To this end, they employ a variety of abstract, generalized narrative concepts (e.g., narrative linkage, slippage, editing, options, control, collaboration, coherence) to illuminate "how the meaning of experience is both artfully constructed and circumstantially conditioned" (1998:177; Holstein and Gubrium 2000).

Gubrium and Holstein offer readers a healthy sampling of conversational exchanges derived from a rich source of ethnographic data. Other narrative researchers employ more narrowly construed conversational analyses, examining the microstructural features or rules of conversation that enable people to speak to "one another in an orderly, recognizable fashion" (Gubrium and Holstein 1997:55). These texts may use formal notation devices that take on the appearance of quasi-mathematical verbal formulas. Then there are those who utilize content analysis assisted by the latest computer software or apply semiotic or other linguistic methods to analyze the microstructural properties of symbolic texts. These narrative strategies privilege analyst and method over storyteller and story and distance us from the world of lived experience.[3]

Microlevel narratives also lack a Millsian sensitivity to the interconnection between biography and history in society. In contrast, other narrative analysts examine personal stories as embedded in a field of power and inequality that extends beyond the realm of "pure narrativity" itself (Rosenwald and Ochberg 1992:7). Here the analyst is concerned that storytellers are unable or unwilling to articulate the structures of domination that colonize consciousness and reiterate and elaborate hegemonic frameworks that reinforce the status quo. Personal experience can be too narrow, too idiosyncratic, to shed light on important social debates. Often the most compelling insights come from examining the multiple experiences of others. Thus the imposition of critical social analyses may be necessary for the telling of subversive stories that facilitate personal, spiritual, and political emancipation. According to Patricia Ewick and Susan Silbey, "Subversive stories are narratives that employ the connection between the particular and the general by locating the individual within social organization" (1995:220). The personal is political. Personal troubles are public issues.

A problem with such critical narratives, however, is that they, too, often privilege the analyst over the storyteller. If the past has taught us anything, it is that members of marginalized groups should be afforded the opportunity to speak their own truths. Changing social conditions create cultural openings for the telling of alternative tales, which in turn pave the way for new modes of engagement with the world. Historical reality is a contested terrain. People previously silenced are now giving voice to their stories and imagining better endings for themselves and the communities in which they are enmeshed.

Qualitative Methods and
Self-Reflexive Social Inquiry

The critique of positivist sociology discussed earlier in this introduction gave birth to a "crisis of representation." In the postmodern period, who can lay claims to speak the truth? Nowhere has this crisis been more visible than in the field of qualitative methods (Denzin 1997; Denzin and Lincoln 2003).

Qualitative inquiry, an interdisciplinary endeavor, owes a particular debt to the early anthropologists and Chicago school sociologists who laid the groundwork for the ethnographic fieldwork method in the early twentieth century. In those early years and for several decades thereafter, researchers were assumed capable of authoring objective, truthful accounts of "other" cultures and societies (Adler and Adler 1987; Denzin and Lincoln 2003).

In the 1980s anthropology was at the forefront of a methodological self-reflection that challenged the assumptive separation of the observer from the observed. Qualitative data were now understood as a product of the interpretive work that constructs social reality, that "writes culture" (Clifford and Marcus 1986; Denzin 1997; Frank 2000; Geertz 1988). To some extent, it is noncontroversial that ethnographic research is more dependent than quantitative analysis on the researcher's use of self, for in fieldwork the researcher is the primary instrument for documenting and interpreting the data. Conventionally, however, this truism is viewed as a potential liability. While a range of membership roles is tolerated (e.g., observer-as-participant, participant-as-observer, and complete participant), ethnographers are encouraged to maintain analytic detachment, to cultivate an "attitude of strangeness," and especially to avoid "going native" (Adler and Adler 1987; Neuman 2003:375).

The postmodern challenge, on the other hand, actively eschews the ideal of the trained "social science voyeur" who stands apart from the experience being observed, remembered, or recorded (Denzin 1998:411; Richardson 1998, 2002). There is no separation of the observer and the observed. The writer's voice is always present. The author is part of the story. In this view, researchers no longer have the option of avoiding self-reflection. As Michelle Fine and Lois Weis observe, "It is now acknowledged that we, as critical ethnographers, have a responsibility to talk about our own identities, why we interrogate as we do, what we choose not to report, on whom we train our scholarly gaze, who is protected and *not* protected as we do our work" (2002:284).

In the midst of this epistemological reappraisal, *autoethnography* emerged as an identifiable research strategy. As far as we can tell, the term is attributable to David Hayano (1979), who defined it as the cultural study of one's own people. Under the creative influence of Carolyn Ellis, however, autoethnography came to be understood as a method by which the ethnographer turns her or his gaze inward, while also maintaining the observer's gaze outward and examining the larger social context in which experiences of the self occur (Bochner and Ellis 2002; Ellis 1995, 2004; Ellis and Bochner 1996).

While many of the articles in this book could be described as autoethnographic, the term is too narrow for our purposes. We are interested in both the autobiographical and the biographical, and we understand these two genres as intertwined. One cannot write autobiography without interfacing that story with the stories of others. Neither, as we have seen, can one write biography without recognizing the authorial voice that produces the biographical presence. Thus we seek a narrative sociology that embraces both of these forms, as well as the ethnographic and other qualitative genres (e.g., life history, oral history, life story, case studies) whose boundaries blur in rebellion against the instinct to classify (see Denzin 1989:47–48).

A self-reflexive sociology anticipates the charge of solipsism and self-indulgence that is often brought against it. The rebuttal to this charge lies, in part, in the Millsian recognition of the relationship between the individual and society. Society runs through our blood. We are not separate from it. As Jean-Paul Sartre would have it: "I am the universal singular, universalizing in my singularity the crisis and experiences of my historical epoch" (paraphrased by Denzin 1999:511). Or, in Kathryn Church's words: "My subjectivity is filled with the voices of other[s]. . . . Writing about myself is a way of writing about these others and about the worlds which we create [and] inhabit" (1995:5). At the same time, and this is perhaps the paradox, the writer must have the humility to acknowledge that "I give you the world as experienced by a single individual. And even when I am moved to generalize beyond my own experience, be cautioned that this is just one observer writing to make sense of his own life" (Quinney 1998:xi–xii). There is never a single story that can be told.

Toward a Storytelling Sociology

Storytelling is as ancient as the language it uses. It emerged out of the need to speak and to understand the world. Storytelling secures and increases our consciousness and extends the reality of our experiences. But since the last quarter of the twentieth century, we seem to have undergone a storytelling revival. The writing and reading of autobiography and biography are more popular than ever. Everyone wants to write his or her memoir. Professional storytellers have become more visible. People are researching their family's genealogy and relatives' histories, preserving these stories for future generations. Storytelling is invoked in the art of healing, as a way of defining one's journey through and beyond suffering. Sociologists have become storytellers.[4]

Perhaps this revival reflects a culture that is ill at ease, that lacks compelling myths to bind us all together. Perhaps it has something to do with our sense of rootlessness, of separation from extended family. Perhaps it's the secularization of the world or the vacuousness of television. Perhaps it's a form of nostalgia, a way to resurrect something we never really had. Perhaps it's the condition of postmodernity.

In this book of narrative sociology, we follow Robert Coles's lead. In *The Call of Stories,* Coles (1989) tells of the advice given to him by one of his supervisors, Dr. Ludwig, during his residency in a psychiatric ward. Ludwig urged Coles to dispense with the theoretical abstractions of his profession in order to let patients tell him their story. "What ought to be interesting, Dr. Ludwig kept insisting, is the unfolding of a lived life rather than the confirmation such a chronicle provides for some theory. . . . Let the story itself be our discovery" (p. 22).

Norman K. Denzin (1997, 1999) distinguishes two general orientations toward narrative inquiry: the *analytic* and *storied* approaches. The analytic, as we have seen, is more positivist in orientation, maintaining the analyst's neutral stance, silencing the writer's voice, and employing abstract interpretive schemes derived from preexisting theory or deduced from the data itself. The storied approach, on the other hand, is theoretically minimalist, seeking meaning in the stories themselves and encouraging the listener/reader's active engagement with the material (Jackson 1998; Polkinghorne 1995). This is why, in the forthcoming introductions to the four sections of this book—Family and Place, The Body, Education and Work, and The Passing of Time—we avoid overtheorizing the essays. Following Thomas Barone (1995), we understand the artfully persuasive storyteller as one who is willing to relinquish control over the story's meaning and to trust readers to bring their own interpretive and emotional sensibilities to bear on the tale being told.

In this project, which we call *storytelling sociology*, the measure of the "truth" is judged not by conventional scientific standards of validity and reliability but by the power of stories to evoke the vividness of lived experience (Denzin 1997). The aim is verisimilitude, or what Sara Lawrence-Lightfoot and Jessica Hoffmann Davis call "authenticity," the degree to which the narrative captures "the essence and resonance of the actors' experience and perspective through details of action and thought revealed in context" (1997:12). Stories transfuse "the pale abstractions of disembodied reason with the blood and bone of the senses and presents them for inspection" (Taylor 2001:30). They tell a truth that "no amount of theorizing or recitation of statistics" could reveal, a truth that generates empathy, makes it more difficult to marginalize others, helps build social bonds (Duncan 1998:107). Stories help us consider "the conditions under which the moral terms of the self are constituted" (Denzin 1999:513). They make us more "forgiving of moral failure at the same time that they convince us" of the necessity of moral choices and of the need to engage the world in the struggle for peace and justice (Taylor 2001:55).

A compelling story is not simple entertainment, although it can be entertaining. A compelling story "isn't a flight from reality but a vehicle that carries us on our search for reality, [a] best effort to make sense out of the anarchy of existence" (McKee 1997:12). Characters in stories—when they are interesting characters—make choices, exercise agency in the face of structural constraints, attempt "to take control over their lives and the stories about them" (Denzin 1999:512). They are both chosen by and choose their stories. A compelling story connects personal experience to public narratives, allowing society to "speak itself" through each individual.

In storytelling sociology, the writing is recognized as part of the research process. It is not merely a "report" of one's observations, but an integral part of the process of creating meaning. As Laurel Richardson observes, "I write because I want to find something out. I write in order to learn something that I didn't know before I wrote it" (1998:347). It is through the writing that we discover our "voice," as we emerge from silence, in our search to discover or rediscover our selves (Lincoln 2002; Lincoln and Denzin 2003; Lincoln and Guba 2003; Richardson 2002).

Storytelling sociology encourages writing that experiments with different forms of representation and that seeks engagement with the world beyond academe. Much sociological writing is, quite frankly, dull and turgid. Students, if they can manage to muddle through it, find it boring and "are disappointed that sociology is not more interesting" (Richardson 1998:346). We need to cultivate a writing that reaches a broader audience, not just a writing that impresses our colleagues with our ability to master theoretical abstraction or mathematical technique. We need a writing that avoids esoteric language, that informs and enlightens without being pedantic, that appeals to both the intellect and emotions, seeking to inform and inspire and joining "the endeavors of documentation, interpretation, and intervention" (Lawrence-Lightfoot and Davis 1997:xvi).

Lawrence-Lightfoot and Davis, among others, seek an interdisciplinary approach to narrative inquiry that operates at the border of the social sciences and the humanities, that blurs the boundaries of empiricism and aesthetics. This approach is permissive of experimental forms of writing that abandon conventional scientific formats. In the process new narrative genres are being created. We are now hearing more about "sociopoetics" and "performance" texts that span the range of communicative expression with photography, drama, music, and dance (Bochner and Ellis 2002; Ellis and Bochner 1996; Gergen and Gergen 2003; Richardson 1998, 2002).

Relative to these experimental forms, the readings in this book are in many ways more conventional. Our own affinity is for a narrative style that most closely resembles the personal essay. As Phillip Lopate (1995) notes in his wonderful anthology *The Art of the Personal Essay,* this a genre that spans a history of over 400 years. According to Lopate, the "hallmark of the personal essay is its intimacy" (p. xxiii). It is a writing that reveals the process by which the writer has arrived at her thoughts, lets readers in on his doubts, makes the writer vulnerable in the text, reflects on roads taken and not taken. This does not mean that the writer bares all. It is not kiss and tell. The writer is entitled to some privacy.

The writing style of the personal essay is friendly, even conversational, but also literary. The reader should enjoy the "pleasure of knowing that we are in cultivated hands, attending to a well-stocked liberally educated mind" (p. xli). Importantly, according to Lopate, the "personal essayist must above all be a reliable narrator; we must trust his or her core of sincerity. We must . . . feel secure that the [writer] has done a fair amount of introspective homework . . . and is trying to give us the maximum understanding and intelligence of which he or she is capable" (p. xxvi).

This criterion raises the question of narrative truth. We agree with the proposition that there is no such thing as unmediated reality. At the same time, the contributors to this book have made a conscientious effort to describe the world as they see it (or perhaps, we should say, as they *tell* it). They do not deliberately deceive or "make things up" to provoke the reader's attention. We are content to live in the borderland between reality and our perceptions of it, as we marvel at the breadth and depth of the human experience. Let the stories begin!

Notes

1. Critiques of positivist sociology can be found in Denzin (1997), Lemert (1997), Maines (1993), Richardson (1996), and Seidman (1996).

2. Some good examples are Anderson (1923), Shaw (1930), Thomas and Zaniecki (1918–1920), Thrasher (1927), and Whyte (1943).

3. Further comments on such strategies can be found in Denzin (1997), Frey et al. (1992), Manning and Cullum-Swan (1998), Ochs and Capps (2001), Pathas (1995), and Silverman (1991).

4. Storytelling in sociology and in the larger society is celebrated in Denzin (1997, 1999), Frank (1995), Hovey (2003), Quinney (2000), Sobol (1999), Stich (2002), Taylor (2001), and Zinsser (1998).

PART 1

Family and Place

It was C. Wright Mills's contention, as it is ours, that the simultaneous consideration of individual lives and social contexts, the exploration of how they are intermeshed, can yield sociological insight into both those lives and those contexts. The family would seem as good a place to start as any, for the very existence of the "autobiographical and biographical genre is structured by the belief that lives have beginnings in families" (Denzin 1989:19).

It may seem a simplistic observation to say that life begins with a family. But as the contemporary state of family life attests, what constitutes a "family" is very much a social construction. For many people, family constitutes not just a *presence* but an *absence* as well. Missing people. Ghosts of the past. People who live in our heads. Lives once known that have been lost.

Families are also situated in time and place. We live in, and through, historical eras. Our lives are shaped by the time in which we were born into the world and through which we move in successive stages, carrying with us the particular stamp of the generational cohort in which we are enmeshed (Elder 1994). Our lives are situated in a place, or places. A place is not simply an address, a geographical locale. "The meaning of a place . . . depends on the geniuses we locate there" (Bell 1997:813). It is populated by persons, "even when there is no one there." We "live in landscapes filled with ghosts," of people we once knew, who give life to a place even in their absence. Our memory of place is filled with visions of the physical terrain, whether it is the asphalt streets of an urban milieu or the scenic beauty of a mountainous landscape. We experience these physical environments as if they were people, for they are embodied with a soul, the soul of our selves and the lives of others who have made us what we are or hope to be (or not to be).

This section opens with **Norman Denzin**'s "Searching for Yellowstone," a moving familial narrative that unfolds into a critical reading of Wallace Stegner's autobiographical account of his own childhood. Stegner, as Denzin points out, is considered to be the founding father of contemporary literature and history on the American West. He wrote a dozen novels and seven nonfiction works, won numerous prestigious awards, and was a national figure in the environmental movement. Denzin reads Stegner as a way back to his own family's history, as a way to dream himself back into the mid-twentieth-century midwestern landscape of his roots.

Stegner's father was a salesman, as were Denzin's grandfather and father. Denzin sees many parallels between his own feelings and those of one of Willy Loman's sons in Arthur Miller's *Death of a Salesman*, a feeling of shame over what constituted the white male middle-class American dream of that era, a dream of making fast money but never being unscrupulous enough to get it. This sad story of America was written upon the backs of the northern plains Indians, whose history, Stegner (mistakenly) says, stopped in 1890.

It is in Yellowstone, however, where Denzin searches for the answer to his life. Yellowstone, the oldest national park in the world, famous for its natural wonders, its geysers and hot springs, is perhaps another embodiment of the American dream. Denzin is searching for a spot where his grandfather fished for trout many years ago. Stegner's father had passed through those parts too. Denzin's grandfather wanted to take him there, to experience a place where he could find fulfillment. But Denzin will have to take the trip on his own.

Nelia Olivencia takes another American landmark, the Twin Towers in New York City, as the point of departure for her understanding of family and place. Prior to the infamous September 11, 2001, attack on the World Trade Center, Olivencia had not really thought of herself as a New Yorker, as being part of the Lower East Side of that city, even though this is where she grew up. In her essay, "Twin Towers," Olivencia reflects on her conflictual feelings of being a child of Puerto Rican immigrants, a woman who grew up under difficult conditions and who experienced rejection by the Anglo world, a woman who persevered in the face of difficulty to forge a life of accomplishment. September 11 hit her with a jolt, as it did the rest of the nation (indeed the world) and caused her to reassess her feeling of alienation from the United States. She was no longer a Nuyorican but a New Yorker *and* a Puerto Rican.

Like the Twin Towers, Olivencia was half of a twin pair. In 1989 the two of them had ascended to the top of the Twin Towers. She could never have imagined the demolition of these structures. It was a metaphor for what had happened to her formerly tight-knit family, which was crumbling under the weight of her overbearing and aging mother. September 11, however, was an opportunity for a reconciliation not only of Olivencia's ethnic identity but of her relationship with her mother as well, as she came "full circle to the trust of a newborn for her mother."

Ethnic identity is also the theme of **A. Javier Treviño**'s "Remembering George Washington on the Rio Grande." Treviño writes about growing up in the U.S.-Mexican border town of Laredo, Texas, and more specifically about his experiences with his high school marching band and the band's participation in a particular celebration of George Washington's birthday. This annual tradition, which began in 1898, might seem peculiar given that Laredo is over 90 percent Hispanic (mostly of Mexican descent) and that Mexican nationals from across the border are invited to join in the festivities.

Treviño notes that the event has come to symbolize "an organic solidarity of continued cooperation" between the United States and Mexico as well as a "bicultural way of life." But while blurring traditional social boundaries, this "invented tradition" produces new ones as well, a fragmented integration fraught with paradoxes and contradictions, especially in a post–September 11 context involving U.S. leaders' increased suspicion of open borders. Still, Treviño remains intrigued about living on "the border," as he remains spiritually and existentially connected to his roots, which he now views from a spatial and temporal distance. He remains "umbilically bound" to Laredo and its celebratory tradition. "It's eccentric," he writes. "It's the border. But it's ours."

Like some of the other contributors to this book, **Jean Hector Faley** lived her life with a feeling of ambivalence about ethnic identity, having reluctantly immigrated from Glasgow, Scotland, to the United States in her teens. But it was not ambivalence about being an American that troubled Faley. Rather it was remorse about the life she has lost by being severed from her homeland. When she returned to Glasgow in her later years, she stood in the place she had stood as a young child decades earlier. The community had been decimated by the decline of industrial jobs. Familiar landmarks had been demolished. The old tenement structures were gone, as was the vibrant tenement culture of her youth.

Faley's "My Ain Folk: Scottish Oral History and the Sociological Imagination" is not an essay of romantic nostalgia for a day gone by but recounts an experience of self-discovery through the lives of others: "my ain folk, my own people." As she embarked on an oral history project with older Glaswegians who had lived through that earlier era, Faley found herself not only preserving for posterity a lost way of life but also coming to understand her own angst as a reluctant immigrant, which she had experienced as a personal trouble but which was in fact a commonly shared public issue.

Tony Platt, too, was a European immigrant to the United States. But for secular Jews like Platt, America was not exile, not the abyss of the Diaspora, but in fact the "promised land." Platt was a product of the post–World War II decline in anti-Semitism, when being Jewish became a matter more of choice than of social proscription. In fact, in Manchester, England, the land of his birth, many of Platt's relatives seemed to care about everyone else but Jews. Platt's essay, "Everyone Else: Becoming Jewish," takes us into this world of secular Judaism and the progressive leftist politics it entailed.

After his arrival in Berkeley, California, in 1963, Platt involved himself in the political struggles of the day, hanging out with Jews "for whom anti-Semitism was our lowest priority" and who sided with Palestinians and not Israelis in the politics of the Middle East. But something curious started to happen to Platt many years later, in 1999, while he was doing research on California history at the Huntington Library. He learned of an original copy of the 1935 Nazi Nuremberg Laws that the library administrators had kept secret for over five decades. Platt wondered why. His ensuing and persistent inquiry into this issue led one library employee to comment, "You're becoming really Jewish." Platt was taken aback, but he realized "she was on to something." As he concludes his essay, we get the sense that Platt is not quite sure what that something might be. Is it nothing more than an uncanny reminder of his past? What does it mean to be a Jew when one has more interest in politics than in religious faith?

Reading Platt's essay along with **DeWitt Clinton**'s "Walking with Lao Tzu at Auschwitz" makes for an uncanny connection as well. Clinton, a son of a Methodist minister, had always been fascinated with the people of the Old Testament, which propelled him (perhaps subconsciously) on a lifelong quest in search of the Hebrews. When he finally found them, he converted and became close friends with a Jewish refugee from Nazi Germany. He started to hear the ghosts of the Holocaust calling out to him. Can one be a Jew without thinking about Auschwitz?

Clinton, a literature professor and poet, had also become fascinated with other religions of the world. He was especially drawn to Eastern philosophers—the Buddha, the Dalai Lama, and especially Lao Tzu. As he read the works of these great thinkers alongside literature of the Holocaust, a poem took shape in his mind. An old Chinese sage was giving voice to those who were silenced, taking the poet on a spiritual journey into a tumultuous past. Clinton's epic poem "Reading the *Tao* at Auschwitz" concludes his essay: "In Time to Come This will be / A Place where Tourists come / To weep, or finish what was started . . . / Some will wander through, amazed / A Place like This was ever Here . . . / Let the living start to come back / Let it be a place of memory / A place where some had hope / We'd all rise & float away / From this place."

CHAPTER 2

Searching for Yellowstone

Norman K. Denzin

I am now ready for the Yellowstone Park, and look forward to the trip
with intense pleasure.

—General William Strong, 1876

Native American writer Elizabeth Cook-Lynn says she can no longer read
Wallace Stegner, the founding father of contemporary literature and history
on the American West.[1] She refuses to accept Stegner's view that history
for northern plains Indians "sort of stopped at 1890" (Cook-Lynn 1996:29–
30; Stegner 1962:66). To read Stegner, she contends, is to endorse his view
that Native Americans occupy a marginal place at best in the history of the
American West. I agree with Cook-Lynn.

Cook-Lynn explicitly criticizes Stegner's view of Native Americans as
given in *Wolf Willow* (1962), his autoethnographic account of his childhood
in Cypress Hills in southern Saskatchewan, where his family homesteaded
from 1914 to 1920. In *Wolf Willow* Stegner speaks of the plains Indians'
destroying "the world that nourished them" (p. 66). He describes the home-
stead setting of his childhood as a semicivilized world and writes of living
on the "disappearing edge of nowhere," "growing up as a sensuous little
savage" in a new country that had no history (pp. 24–25, 28, 57). Cook-
Lynn's point, of course, is that the plains Indians' world was drenched in
history, culture, and tradition, a history that fourth-generation European
immigrants, including Stegner's family, could not see but helped to destroy.

But today I read Stegner anyway, and this is because his autoethnography and his family history help me find my way back to my father, my
grandfather, and my mother (see Stegner 1943, 1962, 1979, 1992).
Dreaming my way into a midcentury landscape, I seek to understand my
family's middle-class version of the American dream. Yellowstone Park is
as good a place as any to start.[2]

In 1932, about the same time Stegner's father was taking a shortcut through Yellowstone Park on a bootleg whiskey run to Cody, Wyoming (Stegner 1943), my grandfather was fishing for brown and rainbow trout in the Firehole River near Old Faithful Lodge. I have a picture of Grandpa smiling, standing beside a Lincoln roadster, wearing a white shirt, a tie, and a gray fedora, proudly pointing to a string of over twenty trout. Today I search for the spot in Yellowstone where Grandpa caught those trout, wondering if he and Stegner's father may have been in the same place at the same time.[3]

Stegner's father was a salesman; so was Grandpa, and so was my father. Grandpa made his money in the Depression. He invented a mechanical device somewhat like a slide rule or today's hand calculator. Used properly, it allowed persons to instantly compute sums, fractions, decibels, or ratios. The slender bronze-colored metal device was in the shape of a monkey suspended in midair. Trapped in a metal cage, the monkey wore a red hat. The monkey's arms and feet could be moved back and forth and up and down, across a sliding metric. If you divided 30 by 2, the monkey's hands pointed to the number 15. Grandpa talked small-town store owners into buying the franchise rights to his calculating monkey. For $10,000 a store owner could have the sales rights to an entire county. Grandpa then showed owners how they could use trading stamps, which would give customers discounts on purchases at their store, if they bought a monkey. Grandpa printed and sold these stamps. In his Lincoln roadster Grandpa toured the Middle West, the West, and the South, selling this system. He got rich and retired to the farm at the age of forty, taking hundreds of boxes of monkeys with him. One version of family legend holds that he was chased out of Kansas City by the mob, the same mob that helped Truman gain the White House in 1945.

My father sold hardware, John Deere tractors and plows, Farm Bureau life and car insurance, Ramblers, Dodges, Pontiacs, used cars, sunken treasure from pirate ships, antiques and collectibles, and fake brass doorknobs. He could sell anything. My junior year in high school we read Arthur Miller's *Death of a Salesman* (1949). I saw too many parallels between Dad and Willy Loman. Like one of Willy's sons, I was ashamed to have a father who was a salesman. My girlfriend at the time, whose father was a physician, said I had nothing to be ashamed of. I cried anyway, reading Willy Loman's disgrace and death as if they were my father's.

When I was sixteen my father sold me a $5,000 life insurance policy. The premium has stayed the same for forty-five years, $44.80 payable June 1 and November 1. Every time I write out the check I think of that night when he sold me the policy, telling me that this sale helped him make his quota for that month, maybe even qualify him for a ten-day company fishing trip to Canada and a Hudson Bay Wool blanket.

My father never got rich. He was a devout conservative, a Reagan-Bush Republican; over his desk in Small Stuff, his antique shop in the Amana Colonies, hung a photo of him and George Bush shaking hands. Across the top, Bush wrote, "Thanks to my good friend Ken Denzin." My father believed in the U.S. of A. and in the American dream, no social security or affirmative action; he held to hard work, handcrafted bookcases, dark blue serge suits, gray sweaters, close-cut hair, women in the kitchen, Camel cigarettes, home-cooked meals, community theater, learning from your mistakes, and after sobriety, kindness, generosity, and fierce loyalty to family.

When he died he left a few clothes, three broken Timex watches, two pocketknives, a woodworking shop full of hand-oiled tools, awls, files, screwdrivers, little planes, saws, drills, bits, levels, hammers, and pliers. I gathered them up and took them home. I bought a sheet of pegboard and some hooks. I hung the pegboard on the wall in my basement shop and neatly arrayed the awls, hammers, and screwdrivers. It looks like a display in a museum, my father's legacy, three wood boxes and a handful of tools. We spread his ashes on the Mississippi River.

Stegner says his father "was born with the itch in his bones. . . . He was always telling stories of men who had gone over the hill to some new place . . . made their pile, got to be big men" (1943:83). By the time I was eight my family had moved ten times. The next sales job was always going to be the best, somewhere, "if you knew where to find it, someplace where money could be made like drawing money from a well, some Big Rock Candy Mountain where life was effortless and rich . . . but not in Chicago, or Milwaukee, or Terre Haute, or the Wisconsin woods, or Dakota. . . . Twelve houses at least in the first four years" (pp. 83, 374).

> On the Big Rock Candy Mountain
> Where the cops have wooden legs,
> And the handouts grow on bushes,
> And the hens lay soft-boiled eggs,
> Where the bulldogs all have rubber teeth
> And the cinder dicks are blind—
> I'm a-gonna go
> Where there ain't any snow,
> Where the rain don't fall
> And the wind don't blow
> On the Big Rock Candy Mountain (Stegner 1943:461)

And the bluebird sings to the lemonade springs (Stegner 1992). When Stegner's father died, the final sum was "One dented silver mug . . . One pair of worn shoes, one worn suit, a dozen spotted neckties, a third interest in a worthless mine" (Stegner 1943:556).

The Big Rock Candy Mountain was always just around the corner, and my father, like Stegner's, never seemed to have the nerve, or resolve, to get there. Perhaps it was the fear of really getting on top of the mountain—or was it pride, or restlessness, or an arrogance born of a natural talent never fully realized? To paraphrase Stegner (1943:437), my father was haunted off and on throughout his life by the dream of quick money, but he was never quite unscrupulous enough to make his dream come true. He was a gambler of sorts, but not quite gambler enough. He had "a kind of dull Dutch caution." He would "gamble with one hand and hold back a stake with the other." My father was self-centered, stubborn, an egotist dependent on women, stern-voiced, quick to anger, with two years of college, a childhood of poverty and illness, three wives, and three divorces. My grandfather did not have these characteristics.

Men like Willy Loman, my father, and Stegner's father are victims of the post–World War II version of the American dream: work hard, listen to your government, save your money, and you will succeed; do your own thinking but keep it defined in narrow terms, good versus evil. This is a dream that chews up little people and spits them back out. Men like my grandfather escaped this version of the dream. They learned how to get to the top of the Big Rock Candy Mountain, no dull Dutch caution in them, no self-doubt, no crippling addiction, always self-controlled, good humored, never showing anger except to family.

Grandpa left Yellowstone with a pocketful of memories and one photograph. Stegner's father drove through the park and made a bundle on the whiskey he sold to bootleggers in Cody. Surely the two men never met, but the memories of them come together in my mind, opposites, each man seeking something in this sacred site called Yellowstone.

By the time he had his picture taken Grandpa was a man of leisure, a man of wealth. In those days such men were tourists, travelers to places of natural wonder, places like Yellowstone (see Dorst 1999; Pomeroy 1957; Rothman 1998; Shaffer 2001). Male tourists in those days wore suits, white shirts, gray fedoras, and drove Lincoln roadsters. Grandpa fit this model to a T. Old Faithful became the place where he performed his version of this identity. In his mind's eye, that picture represented in a timeless way what his version of the American dream had allowed him to become, a tourist from the Midwest, a man of means occupying a position of authority in nature.

Stegner's father, like mine, never had time to be a tourist. There are no pictures of Dad in a park. Parks like Yellowstone were places to drive through on the way to somewhere else where money could be made. And when he found himself in nature, it was when he won a trip from the Farm

Bureau Life Insurance Company. One million dollars in premiums bought ten days in a Canadian fishing camp with a group of salesmen who were strangers to one another. But there are no pictures from those camps, just a story or two, and an old faded Hudson Bay blanket. Peanuts, he said, "One day we'll go to Canada on a fishing trip, catch walleyes and pike." But we never went. And then, on another day, Grandpa said, "One day we'll get to Yellowstone, and I'll take you to Old Faithful." And we never went.

As a child and a young man I grew up with these two stories and this picture. Somehow they were sandwiched between and around that photograph of Grandpa and his trout. When Grandpa died and we took his belongings from the nursing home, I got the Yellowstone picture. I feel like Terry Tempest Williams (2000), who also grew up with a picture hanging over her head. My question is hers, "What do I make of this legacy, of this picture?"

> As a child I grew up with Hieronymus Bosch's painting . . . El jardin de las delicias . . . hanging over my head. My grandmother had thumbtacked the wings of Paradise and Hell to the bulletin board over the bed where I slept. The prints were . . . part of the Metropolitan Museum of Art's series of discussions designed for home education. . . . Whenever my siblings and I stayed overnight, we fell asleep in the "grandchildren's room" beneath Truth and Evil.
>
> —*Terry Tempest Williams (2000:5–6)*

Whenever I stayed overnight with my grandparents, I fell asleep in the guest bedroom, which had Grandpa's Yellowstone picture sitting on the dresser. I awakened each morning to the picture of Grandpa and his fish. I have followed that picture into the heart of Yellowstone Park, to the inn at Old Faithful. I have walked along the banks of the Madison and Firehole rivers, where he surely fished. I have stood, as he surely did, with other tourists and waited for Old Faithful to erupt skyward. I have hiked past Upper Geyser Basin to the campground at Fountain Paint Pot, wondering if Grandpa camped here. I drove to West Thumb, Grant Village, and Geyser Basin, looking for his footprints.

> We say that Yellowstone National Park was established on March 1, 1872, but in fact we have never stopped establishing Yellowstone. Whether as first-time visitors or as world-famous biologists we continue to discover and explore it, and we also continue to create it. That is why I call this book *Searching for Yellowstone*. Our continuing attempt to understand the park and fit it into our national and international life is the most important and certainly the most exciting thing we do here. . . . The search for Yellowstone is . . . a search for ourselves . . . a search for . . . understand-

> ing . . . these emotional, subjective and shared portrayals [that] enable us
> to communicate that search without . . . analytical filters.
>
> —*Paul Schullery (1997:2–3, 261–262)*

Like Schullery, I search Yellowstone Park for meanings, for answers, and I find them in my reflections in the clear evening waters of the Yellowstone River itself. Rod and reel in hand, gray-haired, wearing baggy khaki shorts, faded blue shirt, and Birkenstocks, I stand at water's edge. I stand not in the image of my father or my grandfather. I have become someone else, a sixty-one-year-old college professor who writes books and stories about whom he might have been.

The meaning of the picture is now evident: my grandfather's smile was an invitation to come to this site. Like others in his generation, he searched for meaning in his life. He was drawn to and found Yellowstone, and in this site he felt fulfilled and complete, fulfilled in a way that he never felt anywhere else. This is why he wanted to take me to Yellowstone, so I could experience this feeling for myself, so I could find myself in the fast-running waters of this river.

And I am finding myself. I use this river as a bridge between two landscapes, the plains of the Midwest and the mountains of Montana and Wyoming. On this bridge I look in two directions at the same time. I see two reflections: my father on the one side, my grandfather on the other. In this moment, as these two reflections come together, I see myself more clearly than ever before. There has always been too much of my father in me for me to have become someone like my grandfather, a man who would wear a suit into the park. And there has been too much of my grandfather in me for me to be like my father, a restless man of quick schemes who would race through a park to get somewhere else.

But I'm always pulled in both directions at the same time. Their memories flow through me as I stand and look into this river. I am proud of who I have become, my father's son, my grandfather's grandson, a man who has grown up. Now I smile back at my grandfather's photograph and thank him for this gift.

And Mother? When Grandpa was staying in Old Faithful Lodge and fishing for trout, Mother and Grandmother were visiting Aunt Elizabeth in her summer home in the Berkeley Hills above Oakland, California. Grandma did not like to travel with Grandpa, so they took separate vacations. She did not like his line of work, and she did not like the women he met on the road. So she and Mother never went to Yellowstone.

I suppose, then, this is why I still read Stegner, for reading him helps me continue my search for Yellowstone, its meanings in my life, and my place in my family's history. Working through Stegner's treatment of Native Americans also helps me better understand cowboys and Indians, redskins and chiefs, and their contradictory places in our national imagination. For this understanding I thank Elizabeth Cook-Lynn.

Notes

1. Wallace Stegner wrote twelve novels and seven nonfiction works and won numerous prestigious awards, including the Pulitzer Prize in 1971. He was a national figure in the environmental movement and a major Western historian (Benson 1996).

2. I take this essay's title, in part, from Schullery (1997). I thank Laurel Richardson for her comments on an earlier version of the essay.

3. My grandfather was Waldo William Townsley. John Townsley, whose relationship to my grandfather is uncertain, was a midcentury Yellowstone Park superintendent. John had a son named Forest. When I was ten years old Grandma Townsley invited Uncle Forest and Aunt Elizabeth to visit the farm. They came from Milwaukee. Aunt Elizabeth was an interior decorator. She decorated Grandma's living room. The Victorian walnut loveseat she picked out in 1950 sits in our balcony today. In searching for Yellowstone, I claim my place in this version of Townsley family history.

CHAPTER 3

Twin Towers

Nelia Olivencia

It would never be the same again. The veil lifted from my eyes to reveal the devastation wreaked on September 11, 2001, on a neighborhood that had been the setting of some of the most formative years of my life. Until that moment I had not thought of myself as a New Yorker and as part of the Lower East Side of the city. I was shocked by the pain I felt as I saw the fortress of my life become vulnerable.

As a child, I was exposed to the brute force of nuns who punished children harshly for real or imagined infractions and to a world full of destruction: condemned buildings with broken windows, gutted insides, and backyards littered with broken liquor bottles, used condoms, chunks of rock, and scraps of paper. It was ugly, but to a child the broken glass of the liquor bottles shone like jewels, and the backyards served as the backdrop for imaginative games in which I leaped around hills made of trash and played stickball and kick the box.

The years I spent growing up in the Lower East Side prepared me to confront, survive, and overcome the many obstacles that were yet to come. As a nine-year-old, I made a conscious decision to be an outsider rather than suffer humiliation and hurt. As a teenager, I was victimized by but survived within rival gang turfs, lived side by side with drug addicts and prostitutes, criminals and assassins. I was usually the one who escorted friends from bad streets to good streets. As a young woman in college I learned to accept and overcome rejection and denigration of my people and me. I worked at menial jobs in which I was verbally and physically harassed because I was a Puerto Rican and a woman. In graduate school, I survived the intellectually refined mental and verbal abuse of the world of academics.

The place I lived as a child was a village within a village within a metropolis. My contact with the world was in Spanish, with an outside world that was Puerto Rican. This outer world would eventually extend to Brooklyn College, Mexico, St. Louis, California, Wisconsin, and beyond, in solitary travels throughout South America and to many other places such as London, Amsterdam, Munich, Madrid, Granada, Paris, Casablanca, Cairo, Tangiers, and Mexico City. And then there was September 11, 2001.

I knew where everything in the Lower East Side was located and had gone back often to revisit. But the sudden blow of 9/11 to the pattern of my comfortable memories as a child and outsider brought shock, disbelief, utter pain, and sorrow. I felt as if my guts had been ripped open. My feelings were not of loss or revenge; instead I began feeling what America is really about. I gained a new level of insight into this country and of myself as a New Yorker. I had always defined myself as a Puerto Rican, not as a New Yorker. But this identity was uprooted, and I became what I now am— not a Nuyorican but a New Yorker *and* a Puerto Rican.

The people who perished in those towers reflected the vision of this country as the most multicultural and polyglot of nations. They represented a spectrum from the most humble to the richest person. They were from many nations, races, religions, and from every level of society. It was a revelation, albeit a tragic one, of what makes New York City the heart of the United States and the Lower East Side a significant element within it. It is a place to which "visitors are drawn . . . to connect with their heritage in the old neighborhood—to trace family memories, explore legendary streets, discover venerable synagogues and other historical places, visit tiny shops and sample food evoking the past" (Mendelsohn 2001:1). It is a neighborhood that generated the likes of George Gershwin, Cole Porter, Jacob Javits, Irving Berlin, Jimmy Durante, and Rocky Graziano. It had comforted me with a belief that, as an immigrant, I too could transcend the neighborhood and become "somebody." Its streets have played a role in many films and songs: Delancey Street, the Williamsburg Bridge, Pitt Street, Orchard Street, the Henry Street Settlement, the La Guardia projects, the Grand Street Settlement, the Essex Street Market, and Seward Park.

The Twin Towers silhouetted against the sky served as a backdrop to these places. Their destruction left a deep gash, an immeasurable hole, in the fabric of New York. Beginning with immigrants who constitute a tough people, the assault reverberated across the neighborhood, the city, the country, and the world. We would never be the same, and as New Yorkers we gained a new respect and admiration from others for our ability to overcome this blow.

My nuclear family furnished me with an identity and supportive environment from which I was able to exit daily to streets full of danger and garbage, lined with broken windows, cracked sidewalks, and leveled tenement buildings. An early memory is my own insistence at four on being called "Araña Peluda" (Hairy Spider) to shock and amuse my elders. I frankly liked the sound of it, knowing that in some way it described my shiny, kinky black hair. I loved music and dance. At five, I would break into song and dance, a blooming talent later used by my third-grade teacher to beg for donations for the church. People gaped at this "child wonder" with her lyrical voice. For my mother I became the family's hope, a vehicle for the road to riches.

My life was also shaped by my experiences in which we as Puerto Ricans were denied housing, employment, and equal opportunity. I remember my father and mother telling me that finding a landlord who would rent to Puerto Ricans was difficult. I remember as a teenager seeing my closest friend, an Irish/Norwegian, being hired at the same time and place as I was but at much higher pay and working with customers in the front. Meanwhile, I was paid at minimum wage and had to use the freight elevator to go to work in the back upstairs. I discovered at seven or eight years of age that speaking English was essential to survival in a monolingual society that despises accents and foreign tongues. My mother's inability to speak English exposed her to constant ridicule, exploitation, and abuse. I swore to myself that I would fully master English. My mother had a second-grade education; I attained a Ph.D. Rather than emulating the victimizer, as Frantz Fanon so well described in his works (Gordon et al. 1999), I have always identified with the underdog.[1]

My background prepared me to become actively involved in events of the late 1960s and 1970s such as the shaping and implementing of affirmative action, open admissions, and women's rights to fight injustice and inequity. I wore with assurance, determination, and commitment the hats of a minority activist and a woman activist. Three other faculty members at San Jose State College joined with me to sketch out a curriculum that would be called Chicano studies and become part of the race and ethnic cultures program. It was similar to the struggle being waged for Puerto Rican studies at City University of New York by my brother and sister. I was present at Black Panther events, at a seminal workshop for the creation of "el teatro campesino" (the cultural/dialectical theater of Cesar Chavez's United Farm Workers), at dialogues and confrontations regarding Black studies, and at the first antidraft movement march. The resolve carried over into my years in Wisconsin, when I marched for abortion rights and served as chair of the Governor's Committee on Hispanic Affairs and a member of the Governor's Commission on the Status of Women, as well as a founder of the Wisconsin Women's Network. Most recently I served on the national board for Chicano studies, and I am now serving on the national board for Puerto Rican studies. My determination in all of this has been driven by those early years in the Lower East Side.

My experiences prepared me for the global vision I now have and my love for, rather than fear of, differences. This view shaped my reaction to 9/11, for even though the downing of the Twin Towers was a personal catastrophic experience, it was also a statement against the United States' blindness to the plight of many around the world who live without basic necessities such as food, potable water, clothing, and housing. Still, after 9/11 my life would never be the same again. My new sense of identity as a New Yorker and Puerto Rican has not overcome my ambiguous feeling toward the United States, in which I still feel like an outsider. The river runs deep. Only when I am outside of the country do I feel like I am part of it. Only then do I realize that I have internalized many things that are American—but so has the rest of the world. The ambiguity remains.

Like each of the Twin Towers, I am half of a set of twins. Nelson and I were shaped and molded by the common bond of sharing the same womb, being born prematurely four minutes apart, spending the first month of our lives in an incubator, and being visually impaired. It also meant sharing the same birthday cake and birthday celebrations, attending the same school and classes for eight years, participating in the same social activities, and sharing the same friends until college. Only when I went to graduate school at Washington University in St. Louis was the bond broken. To this day I have dreams in which I search for my other half, never feeling complete.

Our Puerto Rican identity manifests itself differently because of gender and geographical differences. While I left New York City for graduate school never to return permanently, my twin remained in the city. While both of us are fluent in Spanish and English and versed in Puerto Rican and U.S. history, politics, and culture, our dual vision of the world is balanced differently—his toward being American, mine toward being Puerto Rican. Our political perspectives differ. I view Puerto Rico as a nation; he views Puerto Rico as part of the United States.

The only way I can make sure that I am communicating with my mother is to speak in Spanish. "Las torres gemelas que se derrumbaron el 11 de septiembre, ¿te recuerdas de este evento?" (The Twin Towers that fell on 9/11, do you remember this event?). My mother nods yes. This is in response to her asking me who is bin Laden, whose picture flashes on screen during the Spanish news show she is watching on TV. So many years of living in the financial world center, but she still lives in a parallel universe. I stand on the line between these two worlds—juggling hers and mine. She, a ninety-year-old Puerto Rican *jibara* (peasant) with a second-grade education, I, her daughter, with a Ph.D. The same bloodline and culture.

From her window in a room on the tenth floor of the Isabella Nursing Home in Upper Manhattan—on the right side, a view of the George Washington Bridge, the Hudson River, and the Westside of Manhattan; on the left side, the Bronx, the East River, and the Eastside of Manhattan. The right view is a spectacular panorama my mother ignores by keeping the windows of the room curtains closed all day. This is the way she has lived her whole life, her body and soul always in Puerto Rico.

My brother and I, my mother's twin towers, born prematurely at six months' gestation after a massive hemorrhage—she claims we plot against her. Although we never waver in our physical, economic, and emotional support, even the twins' devotion is crumbling under her extreme demands.

Two nightmare visits during the 2002 Christmas holidays leave us spent. During the first one she refuses to talk, eat, or open her presents, and she talks about worms promenading across her hands. Her banshee screams make me flee her room on the second visit. My twin, aided by five hospital workers, fights to move this frail eighty-pound woman from the bathroom from which she will not budge to her bed. The forty-five-minute battle concludes with his coming to get me. Distress, anger, and shame struggle within me. Shaking with trepidation, I reenter the room only to be berated by fanatical preaching about how one's mother is to be venerated, cared for and honored, not abandoned as I am doing. The outrage, fury, and humiliation I feel at hearing these reproaches that have been repeated so often during the last twenty years make me almost flee a second time.

My other half, my twin brother, puts a different spin on it. He jokes, drips sarcasm and mockery, imitating my mother's shrieks and her words to him: "Salte; vete sinverguenza" (Get out, go, you shameless person). When she refuses to eat, he sticks the meat-filled fork in her face, and her fury offers an opportunity for a camera snapshot. Negative attention affirms the existence of a son for whom she only appears to show contempt because he is the most like her now deceased husband. Out of four children, only the eldest and first son merit her devotion and unconditional love. The "others," as I baptized the rest of us, are a mere nuisance. But now even her relationship with her favorite son has disintegrated. There is only her all-consuming obsession to manipulate, control, and destroy any opposition.

I ask myself, "Why is she like this? Had she always been like this and I just did not see it before?" But I do know that this same primitive instinct preserved her and her family in the past.

Her own mother relinquished the mother's role to her eight-year-old daughter, charging her with caring for her siblings, who eventually numbered eleven. My mother's childhood, education prospects, and dreams were shattered at this age, never to be regained. This loss made her determined to instill in her children her survival instincts and unfulfilled thirst for education.

Like my father, who was orphaned at age seven, my mother had no childhood. She recalls falling off a stool she used at eight years of age to reach the stovetop to cook. When a spot of scalding water fell on her, her mother responded by beating her. She recalls begging one of her brothers, the brightest one, to teach her the lessons he had learned at school. At night by candlelight, this brother would repeat lessons taught that day. She would hungrily devour the knowledge and the books he shared with her. It was only at forty-five years of age that she completed elementary school in the United States, with other immigrants from places like Italy and Poland. As a teenager I helped her with her homework and attended her graduation ceremony, applauding wildly for her.

I loved, admired, and worshiped this woman. She was our sanctuary and protected us the way a lioness shields her cubs. She chased for blocks an older boy who struck me in the head with a baseball. She threw caldrons of boiling water on members of a gang named the Mayrose, a training group for future Mafia members, who broke my bedroom window playing stickball almost every other week, scattering shards of glass over the furniture and floor. When this same group tried to rape me on the backstairs of our building, my screams brought her immediate response. With the meager allowance my father permitted her, every year she scoured the Orchard Street area bargaining for hours to buy her children new Easter outfits.

My mother's constant refrain to me was "Be proud of being Puerto Rican, and get an education." But she was also proud of sewing a Black Panther insignia pattern onto my older brother's jacket, proud of his manly feats in the streets. She served him American meals specially prepared to his tastes while the "others," the rest of us, were fed typical Puerto Rican meals of rice, beans, and pork chops.

A woman of contradictions and ferocity, my mother endured shame and embarrassment during Abuela's visits from Puerto Rico to the humble three-room apartment that six of us occupied along with small companions—rats, mice, cockroaches, and occasional bedbugs. There was no inside toilet or bathroom, no living room, no heat or hot water. The halls were infested with derelicts and addicts who urinated, defecated, and shot up drugs. My mother and her children lived in such conditions for over ten years. Eventually her mother and other family members from the Island stopped visiting us.

No recriminations against her own mother ever surface now, except for the denial of an education that would have catapulted my mother to the higher social and economic status to which she aspired her whole life. In later years she impersonated a woman of breeding, covering her rough, wrinkled, worker's hands with gloves. She emulated the airs and deeds of a lady of the manor or upper class and, like Florence Nightingale or Mother Teresa, dispensed money for which she had scrimped for years to those she felt were less fortunate. With her return to Puerto Rico after forty years of exile in the United States, she became the understudy for her mother's role.

My matriarchal grandmother commanded her tribe of thirteen children, thirty-two grandchildren, and forty-two great-grandchildren, who provided her with a rent-free house, food and other necessities, and a maid after my grandfather died. Less than five feet tall, weighing ninety pounds, and illiterate, Doña Isa, as she was called by everyone including her children, was a cold and unloving woman who ran the farm in Corozal, Puerto Rico, administering harsh corporal punishment to her children on a regular basis and, except for the act of procreation, ignoring her alcoholic and faithless husband. Out of her large brood, three sons became successful businessmen; three daughters, including my mother, escaped to New York City. The oldest son became an alcoholic, a beautiful daughter was lobotomized to deny her sexuality and maintain her virginity, and another daughter was banished and permanently expelled from Puerto Rico because of her "wildness." The lobotomized Ines, once spirited and lovely, was reduced to the equivalent of a mindless five-year-old child who soiled her underpants, played and sang songs from her youth all day, and at times became physically and uncontrollably violent. Her cruel, heartless fate haunts me and reminds me of the violence that, if prodded, lurks in us all.

But in this telling I find only a partial answer to why Mother is now the way she is, always trying to transcend the obstacles of her childhood, her poverty, and the incongruities between her aspirations and reality. Within two years of her return to Puerto Rico, my father's death ended her short-lived realization of her aspirations for wealth, prestige, social standing, and acceptance. She was left widowed and defenseless, without the necessary tools to maintain her illusions. How could she be the independent woman she thought she was when she could not divide or multiply, comprehend the concepts of fractions and decimals, balance her checkbook, or grasp what interest rates or dividends were? All of these skills are indispensable for economic and social independence.

My mother is a woman who wants all or nothing. She wanted all that her mother had in her advanced years—a gift house, a maid—and the right to inherit the mantle of matriarch after her mother's death, but these never came. In my mother's world, her life in New York, including her husband and children, was a shabby mirage. Her most recent return to the city was forced upon her because of her incessant demands and the burden she had placed on her extended family—sisters, brothers, cousins, nephews, and nieces. And her own children are irrelevant and useless because they could not ensure the fulfillment of her dreams and expectations. This uncompromising, dominating, and independent *varonil* (manly) woman has become an unyielding engine of primitive violence. The veneer of any pretense to be anything other than who she is has been forever stripped away. Her humanity and individuality have given way to the raw instinct for survival and performance of basic bodily functions. Loftier concepts like love and acceptable social behavior have vanished, a possible result of the aging process. But it's also part of her strength and weakness, her unbending will to not conform blindly to the strictures of society in Puerto Rico and the United States, a characteristic inherited by her children.

My twin brother's badgering again prevails over my fear of heights when I give him my involuntary agreement to ascend to the top of the Twin Towers in 1989. As we overlook the city, looming above helicopters, my fear is held at bay by the unnerving yet majestic panorama surrounding me on four sides.

I never imagined that the towers would be gone, just as my vision of my family vanished so long ago. My nuclear family was torn apart piece by piece by my widowed mother. My mother's power emanates from her tightly knit family, where it is expressed to turn son against son, daughter against daughter, son against daughter. This ongoing destruction is as wantonly shocking as the instantaneous disintegration of the towers on September 11.

Why do I write? Perhaps to understand myself and perhaps to keep my sanity. Today I talked to my mother, who just turned ninety-one. Over the phone, her high-pitched, cracked voice and the clacking of her false teeth made it difficult for me to understand what she was saying or decipher what was real, what was fancied, and what lay in the world in between.

We have always been able to communicate because of my ability to comprehend her at different levels of consciousness, without having to censor myself from listening to her. That is what my sister probably means when she says that I really understand our mother. It is not the fact that she speaks only Spanish—except for a few English words sprinkled here and there to make sure I understand her, something I also resort to at times—but that I listen oh-so-very-carefully to what she says and does not say, the nuances of silence and "tu sabes lo que estoy diciendo." I am the only one who believes her when she says that she was in the emergency ward because of a heart attack, or that someone attacked her and stole her walker. She is not paranoid or delusional. No, I am not special, nor do I cater to the idea that I am the only one who knows what she is saying or that I know her better than my siblings. I just know when it is real. It hurts, and I cannot bear it. My heart starts racing a mile a minute and I think I am going to die. Because I am there in the moment and in her mind, in the reality that she lives as a ninety-one-year-old woman with most of her generation long dead and gone.

The Twin Towers have fallen and been covered over. The standoffs, battles, and furious interchanges between mother and daughter are over too, chased off by the specter of her impending death and struggle with living demons. My mother reminisces about her "precocious" and frantically energetic daughter, a child whose unstoppable questioning, curiosity, and physical activity constantly challenged her.

But New York exists and my mother lives on. On my most recent trip to New York City, I approach her with trepidation and anxiety. She is frail, with only a short time to live. She might die tomorrow, or in a few years— that is all we can predict, because death gives no notice. The three visits that my daughter and I pay her, for once, are shockingly tranquil, positive experiences. Is this my mother's response to her own mortality? The indomitable mother-force spins lighthearted tales of her own childhood for her granddaughter, forging the bond between grandmother and granddaughter that had been hindered until now by differences in language, culture, and generations.

I am amazed by my mother's warm reception and by her lucidity in recounting events of our common past and my childhood experiences of want, sadness, and comic tragedy. We recall the *Daily News*'s front-page photo of a four-year-old Puerto Rican neighbor's body pierced through by a jutting two-story-tall stake after she fell from a fourth-floor window; the picture in *El Diario* of the corpse of a young Puerto Rican man lying on the floor of a bar, killed by my second cousin; and the *Daily Mirror*'s spread on the bullet-riddled body of an Italian hit man and cop killer in a 34th Street hotel, a former member of the Mayrose gang, part of the group that attempted to rape me when I was fifteen. Less public memories include the time that Colorado (Red), a Puerto Rican who later became leader of the Dragons gang, was fed by my mother because he was hungry. Later in his teens, one day he came running through our tenement apartment and up the fire escape to escape from police, who were chasing him from tenement to tenement because he had shot a member of an Italian gang. And we remember how the Egyptian Khalil, husband of one of my mother's cousins, brought gifts from his wanderings throughout the world to my mother for her kindness and out of respect.

More personally, my mother remembers caring for two newborn babies at intervals eight years apart, the children of her "wild" younger sister. There were five of us then sleeping in one room containing a crib, a piano, a full-sized bed, a television set, and a bureau; I banged against one or another every day. Shared living, shared experiences. This is the first time in my life that I pepper my mother with endearments like *chiquita* and *preciosa* and hug her with love and gentleness so as not to cause more cracks to her brittle-boned body covered by translucent skin. I can finally give her love without having conditions or stipulations placed on it. And for the first time in her life, she accepts it willingly and warmly.

I leave New York City, for once, with a sense of peace, without guilt or shame, with a feeling of fulfillment at being able to give without being shunted aside, mocked, or berated. I have come full circle, to the trust of a newborn for her mother.

Note

1. My father and mother migrated from Puerto Rico in different years for different reasons. My father came from Mayaguez (a major city on the west coast) with his widowed father in 1925, when he was thirteen years old. They moved to the Bronx, where my grandfather bought a *bodega* (small grocery store) with the money my father's deceased mother had willed to her son. My mother fled to Manhattan in 1934 to escape an arranged marriage and to earn money to send back home to her siblings. She worked in the garment district until 1937, when she married my father, whom she had met through a mutual acquaintance. Their children were born in Flower Hospital in the middle of Spanish Harlem. Our birth certificates placed our address at East 110th Street, in *el barrio*. In the late 1940s the family returned to Puerto Rico, hoping to remain there, but prevented from staying because of my father's inability to find work. The move back to the Lower East Side in 1947 left the family with financial problems that lasted for many years.

CHAPTER 4

Remembering George Washington on the Rio Grande

A. Javier Treviño

There is an old Mexican custom having to do with a newborn's dried-up umbilical cord that, if we take seriously Émile Durkheim's (1912) notion of religion as consisting of beliefs and practices relative to sacred things, could well be regarded as fraught with religious significance. When the shriveled, black-brown life stem falls off a few days after birth, the parents gently, and with a certain degree of reverence, as though it were a sacred object, bury it near the child's birthplace. The practice is the burial; the belief is that the child for the rest of its life will be tied—bound—to that place of its birth. I'm told by my parents that my *ombligo* was buried in the border town of my birth, Laredo, Texas, a city whose character the traveler-writer Paul Theroux has described as "more Mexican than Texan" (1979:39). This is where I spent my formative years. It is also the home I left long ago but to which I periodically return to visit, though never to stay (Treviño 1999).[1]

Writing of his own experiences in the borderland of the Midwest, Richard Quinney (2001) observes that only by truly attending to life—by intimately experiencing a remembered past and an unfolding present—can one go beyond the borderland. For the sociologist who has left the borderland for the mainstream world—the dominant culture—transcendence of that place of origin means seeing it from a different, a more distanced, perspective. It also means that in returning to the frontier—*la frontera*—a perspectival shift occurs so that that place, that home on the margin, can no longer represent the social center. This notwithstanding, I remain spiritually and existentially tethered to that border town, and as I return to it with a certain conversance in sociological theory, its people and its culture now appear to me to be off-center, *eccentric*.

With this awareness I now look back to another time, at that city of my birth on the Texas-Mexico border during a very significant period in my life: my three years in high school, 1972–1975. I consider my experiences as a member of one particular group—the J. W. Nixon High School Band—particularly (though not exclusively) in the context of our band's participation in a unique ceremony: Laredo's annual Washington's Birthday Celebration (WBC).

A city. A band. A ceremony. Today, some thirty years later, I remain inextricably tied to them. And so, as a sociologist whose specialty—indeed, passion—is sociological theory, I endeavor to remember, in autobiographical retrospective, and to explain, if only to myself, this time, this place, these events.

Laredo, Texas, is situated on the banks of the Rio Grande, the murky-brown, watery demarcation it shares with its sister city in Mexico, Nuevo Laredo. In his superb ethnographic study, his "tale" of the two Laredos, Alan Klein aptly describes this border as "a foot-dragging river barely 200 yards across, cut between two very hot and tired-looking towns" (1997:3). While these two towns—*los dos Laredos*—are separated by a river and a political boundary, they are integrally bound by culture, language, kin relations, a bridge, and the WBC.

Begun in 1898, Laredo's annual WBC has continued unabated through good times and bad: the Mexican Revolution, World War I, the Great Depression, World War II, the 1970s oil crisis. But what is perhaps most intriguing to scholars who have considered the event is that it is celebrated in a city whose population is over 90 percent Hispanic (of Mexican descent) and who are joined by thousands of other Mexican nationals (Cigarroa 1991; Dennis 1997). This eccentricity, however, is something that most Laredoans do not think much about; nor, for that matter, did my friends and I back in the mid-1970s when we participated in the WBC events as members of the J. W. Nixon High School Band.

The band was 125 members strong, and we called ourselves La Banda de Animo, the Band with Spirit. And spirited we were. Our pep rallies—those rituals during which we loudly and zealously projected (never blared) our school fight song "Jalisco" (an adaptation of the mariachi song "Ay Jalisco No Te Rajes")—near our totemic mascot (a statue of a green mustang, reared on its hind legs, positioned in the grassy patch next to the band hall) were truly "animated" social gatherings.[2] Long before I had read Durkheim's *The Elementary Forms of Religious Life*, I was experiencing the "collective effervescence"—the shared exaltation and passionate belief—of belonging, truly belonging, to a group: the Mighty Mustang Band. No doubt we believed in ourselves as a performing band, for we had just been awarded Division 1 status in marching, in my freshman year during the fall of 1972. Perhaps more significant, we believed in ourselves as a cohesive in-group with our own folkways, our own *esprit de corps*. We were La Banda de Animo and thus different from other student organizations—Student Council, Slide Rule Club, Speech Club—even while we may have also belonged to some of these groups and pursued various other activities. So too did we *inspire* (breathe the spirit of life?) school spirit at the football games as we played contemporaneous scores such as "Theme from *M*A*S*H*" and "Theme from *Shaft*." During halftime, which was *our* time, we performed eagerly and energetically, with true panache, as we executed our signature march, the Chester Step, evoking, at least to my adolescent mind, Don McLean's enigmatic lyrics in "American Pie":

> Now the halftime air was sweet perfume
> While sergeants played a marching tune
> We all got up to dance
> Oh, but we never got the chance
> 'Cause the players tried to take the field
> The marching band refused to yield
> Do you recall what was revealed
> The day the music died?

With an average annual rainfall of less than nineteen inches and half of its streets unpaved, Laredo is typically hot and, at least until the 1970s, always dusty. The summer of 1972, just prior to the start of high school for me, was a real scorcher for weeks on end, and the lyrics from America's "A Horse with No Name" seemed to strike a resonant chord as we practiced—our marching and our music—on the blistering asphalt of the school's parking lot:

> The first thing I met was a fly with a buzz
> And the sky with no clouds
> The heat was hot and the ground was dry
> But the air was full of sounds

I found it terribly difficult to simultaneously play the cornet, count my marching steps, and pivot and turn, all while attempting to deal with the oppressive heat. After practice one late afternoon during the *canícula*, the dog days of summer, I walked home exhausted, convinced I would be cut out of the marching band even before the school year began. Perhaps I would not belong to this group, this company of comrades with whom I had already bonded, after all.

For some reason I am not aware of, I was kept in the band despite my

lack of marching ability and musical talent, and a few weeks later, as my first year of high school was getting under way, we had our first moment of real excitement. On a bright afternoon, September 22, 1972, we congregated downtown on Convent Avenue and played "Hail to the Chief" as President Richard M. Nixon passed by on his way to visit the U.S. Customs facilities and the International Bridge spanning the Rio Grande and connecting the United States and Mexico. Smiling and waving to the 25,000 or so people gathered along the streets of Laredo, the president, campaigning for reelection, rode on the backseat of an open Oldsmobile Cutlass Supreme, flanked by six Secret Service agents, all wearing their distinctive wraparound sunglasses (Foster Grants, if the agents were cool). Students holding placards lined the avenue—not, as youth at the time were doing in other cities, demonstrating against the Vietnam War, calling for elimination of war research, or decrying campus ownership of stock in Gulf Oil.

Rather, our signs posted such slogans as "We Are Proud of You Mr. President," "Long Live Nixon," and "Welcome Mr. President."

Few of us in Laredo had been radicalized in the early 1970s. We still called ourselves Mexican Americans, not Chicanos. The social activism of protest and dissent, the Black Panthers and Malcolm X, Cesar Chavez and even the Texas-based La Raza Unida Party were worlds away from most of us on the border. Thus much like the rest of the nation about to reelect Nixon in a landslide, on that sunny autumn day we Laredoans put in abeyance what little we knew about the Watergate affair. The televised Senate hearings were still a few months off, and the investigation into the break-in, ongoing at the time, was still a mystery to many of us. Besides, controversy aside, Richard Nixon was the first president to visit the city since Dwight D. Eisenhower some twenty years before, and *that* said something.

Then as now, we in largely neglected and traditionally Democratic south Texas tactfully and courteously, with our "yes sirs" and "no ma'ams," accepted whatever attention we could get from the centers of power, even if it came from a Republican speaking pidgin Spanish. We did not need such an astute observer of everyday life as Erving Goffman to tell us our moral order is affirmed through the interpersonal ritual behaviors—the ceremonial rules and expressions, those "salutations, compliments, and apologies which punctuate social intercourse" (1967:57)—that we exhibited toward each other as a way of showing respect for the sacred self. For those of us on the borderlands, ritual face-work has always been instinctive; a realization I arrived at only in retrospect and after preparing a book on Goffman (Treviño 2003). The most "dissent" we band members could muster that afternoon was to chant, through our giggles, "No more years . . . no more years," after Nixon had passed us and was well out of earshot.

Given that he was campaigning for reelection for four more years, the president took time on his way to the International Bridge to speak briefly with representatives of the Nixon Band and the high school's all-girl precision marching unit, the Golden Spurs. The Spurs invariably stood out, dressed in their impeccable white uniforms of fringed flippy skirts and short jackets, cowgirl hats and boots (complete with spurs), all lined with sparkly gold trim. After his reelection Nixon remembered the Spurs and invited them to perform in his inaugural parade; he did not invite the Mighty Mustang Band.

So on January 20, 1973, we all watched, with a certain measure of pride, the Golden Spurs on television as they paraded down Pennsylvania Avenue waving their pom-poms. We saw them pass the presidential reviewing stand—an enclosed bullet-proof Plexiglas box over which hovered an enormous presidential seal—and perform for Nixon and his controversial vice president, Spiro T. Agnew. The girls—*our* girls—had indeed come a long way, baby.

By early February temperatures had plummeted in south Texas, and Laredo was covered with a rare dusting of snow—up until that time only my second such experience—enough to make miniature snowballs. Searching for an appropriate song with which to celebrate the gently falling flakes, the disc jockey at the local AM radio station, KLAR, opted for the Rolling Stones' "Get Off My Cloud." A week or so after our cloud of snow, with temperatures still low, we marked Laredo's seventy-sixth consecutive Washington's Birthday Celebration (see Green 1999; Young 1998).

As happened every year during the four-day fiesta, Mexican nationals were given *paso libre*—they were permitted to cross the International Bridge to Laredo without papers under a waiver of visas and passports. Over 100,000 visitors from neighboring Texas towns and from northern Mexico communities arrived for the festivities.

We began our participation in the 1973 celebration the evening of Thursday, February 15, as our marching band performed in the Washington's Birthday Youth Parade. We wore our summer band uniform, which consisted of white Levis, white shoes (slapped with multiple layers of liquid shoe polish), and a gold Nixon High School sweatshirt. We were grateful to have our sweatshirts to ward off the chill in the air. We marched along with over seventy other units including high school bands, ROTC battalions and precision drill teams, pep squads, and student clubs and organizations such as the Future Farmers of America and the Student Council. As the *Laredo Times* put it at the time, the Youth Parade featured "the area's most talented and handsome students plus many floats designed by young Laredoans."

At nightfall and following the Youth Parade, about 50,000 people on both sides of the border lined the streets in the riverside section of the two Laredos to watch the annual International Fireworks Display, a star-spangled show more typical of a Fourth of July celebration. The *Laredo Times* proffered its description of the staged pyrotechnics: "Falling stars and other colorful fireworks illuminate the silvery waters of the Rio Grande."

That week, as it did every year during the celebration, the carnival came to town for ten days and opened adjacent to the International Bridge on the banks of the Rio Grande. As it had since 1926, the WBC carnival featured Leonard Martin's Twentieth Century Rides, complete with neon-lit devil rides like the Zipper and the Roundup, as well as tamer ones like the merry-go-round and Ferris wheel. My little brother, Ricky, had a pony ride in a cloud of powdery-white dust, while I enjoyed foot-long hot dogs, heavy on the onions and mustard. A *Laredo Times* article described the carnival and fireworks show as follows: "Multi-colored lighting displays on the grounds reflect the myriad of featherlike, revolving arms, spinning wheels and exploding stars blending in the skies overhead to produce a fantasy world." The rock group Chicago's then-popular tune "Saturday in the Park," which seemed to be playing everywhere, appeared to appropriately characterize the fiesta events:

> Saturday in the park
> You'd think it was the Fourth of July
> People talking, really smiling
> A man playing guitar
> Singing for us all

Two days later, early on the morning of Saturday, February 17, with steady rainfall and 40-degree temperatures, which did little to dampen our excitement, the band members met on the Nixon campus, where, with musical instruments in hand, we boarded school buses—"Yellowhounds," we called them—that would take us to St. Peter's Plaza. This time we wore our "formal" uniforms of hunter green and white, adorned with gold piping and with a wide white stripe running down the side of the trousers. We were to assemble at St. Peter's to take part in what was for us the biggest event of the WBC.

The Grand International Parade has been the centerpiece of the Washington festivities since its inception in 1898, when the procession was a mile long. Three-quarters of a century later, in 1973, the Grand Parade was over three times that length, consisting of thousands of participants from the two Laredos and nearby towns, and some 130 units including drill teams, high school and military bands, Mexico drum and bugle units, military marching units, and U.S. and Mexico student organizations. And, of course, there were scores of floats, several of which carried people dressed in eighteenth-century Colonial-style attire; one of these transported Martha and "Jorge" Washington. At the head of it all, riding on horseback, was the Indian princess Pocahontas—one of the iconic staples of the celebration since 1898—who, upon receiving the key to the city from the mayor, signaled the start of the parade.

On that drizzly, dreary morning the three-mile parade route meant marching from the starting point at St. Peter's Plaza down Houston Street, where we performed before a reviewing stand in front of the County Courthouse and played "Guadalajara," a traditional Mexican favorite and a guaranteed crowd-pleaser. Uniformed soldiers from Monterrey, Mexico, executed intricate maneuvers while a Nuevo Laredo acrobatic team did running handstands on the black, rain-slick streets. We turned north onto San Bernardo before finally disbanding at the Martin High School campus.

Both sides of Houston and San Bernardo Streets were lined with umbrella-sheltered spectators who courageously, or perhaps foolishly, had ventured out into the inclement weather to view the parade. But given that it was the worst parade weather in years, the crowds were relatively sparse. The newly elected Texas governor, Dolph Briscoe, who had been in office barely a month, exclaimed in mock surprise from his parade motorcar, "I thought it *never* rained in Laredo!" A spectator in the bleachers retorted, "It just *snowed* in Laredo last week!"

In any event, that day was too cold and wet for us to really appreciate much of what we were supposed to do. With our mouthpieces nearly freezing, our lips became too numb to play in tune. When Joe Villarreal, who was marching near me, blew into his cornet, no notes were produced. We had no choice but to fake it; besides, the spectators were much too miserable to care how well we played. Three or four blocks from our destination, Richard Rodriguez's tuba began to gurgle as too much rainwater had entered the bell and accumulated inside. Forget the spit valve; Richard had to tip the tuba over to empty it.

Drenched and dog-tired by the time we reached the Martin campus, we were only too happy to get box lunches—the payment for our troubles. Sitting on the bleachers at the Martin gym, we wolfed down our ham and cheese sandwiches engulfed in musty smells—a combination of rainwater and perspiration that had soaked deep into our uniforms, making them feel almost twice as heavy. No one could say that we had not done our best to help celebrate, in grand style, the birthday of "the father of our country."

As the school year came to an end, the Nixon High School yearbook, the *W-Bar*, summed it up in language seemingly reminiscent of what I later, as a social theorist, came to recognize as systems-functionalism: "And in the midst of our [individual] quests, we found each other. United, we became a family; we shared our ideas, our hopes, and our experiences. And, like brothers and sisters, we worked together to make our [social] system survive." Though at the time I knew nothing about the great systems theorists of sociology, such as Talcott Parsons, about whom I would edit a volume many years later (Treviño 2001), I did know that I had come through my first year of high school thanks largely to *my* social system, the Nixon Band.

Since its early beginnings, the Washington's Birthday Celebration has stood for, among other things, goodwill—that is to say, an organic solidarity of continued cooperation between two neighboring countries, the United States and Mexico. In 1974, the seventy-seventh annual border fandango was no exception. As the *Laredo Times* reported, the celebration was "Laredo's favorite way of introducing good neighbors from both sides of the Rio Grande to a uniquely bicultural way of life." Indeed, it may be said that Laredo has two distinctions in regard to its tradition of observing Washington's birthday. First, it has always been the only city in the United States to honor the country's first president in a big way, persistently for many decades, and with the festivities spread over several days. And second, the celebration has a decidedly international flavor with Mexico's active participation in the events. One of those significant "good neighbor" events is the WBC International Bridge Ceremony (IBC).

The IBC is a rite as stately and elaborate as they come. This bicultural gala event dates back to 1898 and involves hundreds of high-ranking government officials and dignitaries from Mexico and the United States who meet, enveloped in a kaleidoscope of sashes and flags, brass and gold, at the midway point of the International Bridge over the Rio Grande—literally, at the border—and exchange *abrazos*, embraces, as a symbol of the reaffirmation of international friendship. It is a major political snub not to be invited, and quite impolitic to refuse an invitation, to the *abrazo* ritual. Among those politicos in attendance in 1974, my sophomore year, were the governors of the Mexican border states of Tamaulipas and Nuevo León as well as, for the second consecutive year, Texas governor Briscoe. From Mexico City came a personal envoy of President Luis Echeverría as well as representatives of several federal ministries, and from Austin, the Texas capital, came a contingent of officials from the executive, legislative, and judicial branches of government. Indeed, once a year during the February holiday the Texas government literally relocates to the border at Laredo.

Shortly after the most august, early-morning IBC, the Grand International Parade was held under sunny skies and balmy temperatures, in sharp contrast to the previous year's cold, rain-drenched affair. Despite the Arab oil embargo, the so-called energy crisis (a few weeks before the price of oil had climbed from $3 to $11.65 a barrel), drill units from as far north as Richmond, Virginia, and drum and bugle corps from as far south as Durango, Mexico, had made the trip to the annual parade. Mexican troops had for many years participated in the parade, but in 1973 an irate general at the Pentagon had phoned WBC president Alberto Magnon to inform him that it was against the law to have an armed foreign military force in the United States. Magnon, in essence, told the general to bug off and slammed down the phone (Green 1999). That year, as they did every year, Mexican troops marched in honor of the first American president. According to the *Laredo Times*, after the Grand Parade one participant noted, "Old George never saw or could imagine a parade such as this one Laredo dedicated to him."

Amid Ronald McDonald riding in a red sports car, the Shriners in their minibikes, and the Budweiser Clydesdales—as well as street vendors hawking twenty-foot multicolored balloons shaped like giant worms, toy *papalotes* (windmills), string puppets, and *bolillos de aguacate* (avocado sandwiches)—the Nixon Band performed with pride and purpose at the Grand Parade. At the end of it I could glance with satisfaction at my friends, Raul Leal on trombone and Ruben Gonzalez on tuba. We had done it again; we had managed once more to play and march in unison while swerving to avoid those steamy, smelly, pasty "landmines" left by the horses in front of us; and we knew, to paraphrase Elton John, that, thank God, our music was still alive.

But as spectacular as the parade was, for most of us in the band, including myself, a more significant event—indeed even more so than the prom—was the annual Band Banquet and dance that took place at the end of the school year. The banquet was uniquely *ours* in a way that the prom was not. In May 1974, the banquet was held at the elegant Red Room of the landmark Hamilton Hotel in downtown Laredo. I took the prettiest and kindest girl I knew, Terry Newbury, whom I had met the previous fall at a band-sponsored dance held at the Nixon gym. Terry wore a formal orange dress; I wore my speckled red-white-and-blue sports coat—not out of any sense of patriotism but because it was the 1970s. The banquet marked the end of another school year and the anticipation of my final year with La Banda de Animo.

Owing to the *paso libre,* the streets of *los dos Laredos* were during February 1975 once again filled to capacity with visitors from north and south of the Rio Grande. With warmer than normal weather, the fiesta was kicked off in radiant sunshine. That year's WBC president, Dennis A. Longoria, with what seemed to be a unique admixture of American democracy and Mexican *amistad*, extended his celebratory welcome to all as he proclaimed, "*Esta es su casa*—this is your house; the two Laredos are honored that you are joining with us to salute the ideals of freedom which the first American president symbolizes."

In the early morning on Saturday, February 15, we members of La Banda de Animo lined up at St. Peter's to march once again—and for me, for the last time—in the Grand International Parade. As always, the parade was a big one, consisting of a cast of more than 10,000 people and 143 entries; these included over forty floats, dozens of decorated cars, horse-drawn vehicles, and a great variety of school and college bands. From north Mexican cities six drum and bugle corps and color guard units passed in review. Decades later I can still vividly recall the piercing, jarring metallic sound of the bugles and the loud rat-tat-tat of the drums from these Mexican battalions, their cadences echoing off the buildings. They marched intensely; they were loud and intimidating. Later that day I heard, or perhaps read, that there had been a knife fight between two rival Mexican units that had participated in the parade.

Doubtless the color and spectacle of the parades, fireworks display, carnival, and other events of those days provided a source of great fun and enjoyment for throngs of people from both sides of the Rio Grande. Most of these activities—whether people-watching, marching, dancing, drinking, or eating *carne asada*—literally took place on the streets of Laredo. There were, however, other ceremonies—ones characterized by greater glamour and poise, ones that included only a certain social set—that were for all intents and purposes off limits to the hundreds of thousands of poor and working-class people, the common folk, *la raza*, of *los dos Laredos*.

Chartered by the state of Texas in 1939, the Society of Martha Washington was formed to select a man and woman of Laredo society to portray George and Martha Washington each year during the February holiday. The society was also charged with sponsoring the annual Colonial Pageant and Ball, where the daughters and granddaughters of society members would be formally introduced as debutantes.

In 1975, with coiffured hair, tiaras, and Colonial-style gowns—intricate affairs replete with sequins and satin, lace and latticework—sixteen debutantes were presented at the pageant, five of whom were senior girls from Nixon High School. Against an elaborate backdrop, set in 1797 Philadelphia, depicting a mansion decorated in the Colonial tradition, the debutantes (called "the Marthas") promenaded and gracefully bowed before an audience of their peers at the Civic Center auditorium. Two people from Laredo's most prominent families, George E. Glassford and Josephine P. Zúñiga, portrayed George and Martha Washington in powdered wigs, knickers, and embroidered velvet gown.

For the majority of Laredoans, life has always been financially difficult. The 1960 Census Bureau declared Laredo the poorest municipality in the United States, and the situation hadn't improved much during the early to mid-1970s when the city had the nation's highest unemployment rate. In 1975, the U.S. Department of Commerce listed Laredo's per capita personal income (annual) as $3,322, which is an especially low figure when compared with income in Laredo's nearest city, San Antonio ($5,126), and in another border town similar in culture and demographics, El Paso ($4,365), for that same year. Thus for most Laredoans, paying the $10 admission fee for the Colonial Pageant to see teenage girls in $10,000 gowns was simply out of the question. Besides, these periwigged Washingtons were high society, or as *la raza* was fond of saying in a bilingual play on words, "high sosiegate" (from the Spanish *sosiego*, roughly meaning good behavior).

Laredo's Washington's Birthday Celebration is an extravaganza to the first American president that in pageantry and size is unrivaled anywhere, this being a great source of pride for Laredoans. What perhaps makes it quite simply the most distinctive event of its kind is that the celebration blurs all sorts of traditional social boundaries while producing new ones. It could, in fact, be seen not only as an "invented tradition" (Hobsbawm and Ranger 1983) but as one that is continuously being reinvented. If postmodernism is characterized by a disconcerting mixture—a fragmentation and integration—of seemingly incompatible viewpoints and lifestyles (Treviño 1996), then the WBC is the exemplar, par excellence, of the postmodern. The iconography of WBC rituals combines nationalisms, cultural identities, and languages (Dennis 1997). What we have, therefore, is a communal ceremony replete with all sorts of paradoxes and contradictions. It's eccentric. It's the border. But it's ours.

I end this account of my early experiences on the borderland as I began it—by returning, always returning, to that far-off time and place and to those off-centered events. But these things have changed, and with change comes a passing, a loss, as well as a longing.

It is no longer the 1970s. The vague sense of wariness of others, the crisis in trust, that Goffman captured so well in *Relations in Public* (1971) and that Watergate epitomized a few years later, has today reached a fevered pitch. After the September 11 tragedy, the *paso libre* was suspended. It seems that Americans can no longer trust an open border.

And Laredo is no longer the sleepy little town it once was. Due largely to the North American Free Trade Agreement, it is now the second-fastest-growing city in the United States and the busiest inland port in the Western Hemisphere. It has a more robust economy for the middle classes than ever before, at the cost of the rich getting richer and the poor poorer.

As for the Washington's Birthday Celebration, it recently marked its 106th consecutive year, with the festivities now consisting of thirty-six separate events spread over sixteen days. If not necessarily better, it's at least bigger.

And I, too, have changed. I remain a son of the southern border, of *la frontera*, umbilically bound, as it were, to that town of my birth. But upon returning there I now feel, with essayist Richard Rodriguez, like "a kind of anthropologist in the family kitchen" (1982:160), unable to keep from analyzing, searching, and researching that eccentric and familiar place to which I have grown closer with distance.

Notes

1. I thank my fellow band members Joe Villarreal, Richard Rodriguez, Ruben Gonzalez, Raul Leal, and Jerry Leal for helping me to remember. I am most grateful

to Julia Casso and Lisa Morales of the Washington's Birthday Celebration Association for making available their historical documents; to Joe Moreno Jr., Special Collections librarian at the Laredo Public Library, for giving me access to the archives; to John Balli and J. J. Rodriguez for providing the yearbook photo; and to Lisa Lebduska for her comments on an earlier draft of this essay.

2. I had recently learned from my Latin teacher, Mr. Dallin, that the word *animate* was derived from *animus*, referring to "spirit."

CHAPTER 5

My Ain Folk: Scottish Oral History and the Sociological Imagination

Jean V. L. Hector Faley

I am a reluctant immigrant. Despite my professional success and my now satisfying life in America, had circumstances been otherwise I would never have chosen to come. Loss of extended family, a close-knit community, and a rich national culture presented me with a persistent and painful loss.[1]

After the birth of my second daughter, my longing for my own culture became intense. The words of the Scottish song "Oh, How I'm Longing for My Ain Folk" came into my mind one day, and I felt a desperation that I had not felt in a very long time. I had visited the place of my birth in England, and various other places in Scotland, but I had yet to muster the courage to revisit my demolished community and face the destruction and loss.

I turned to a long-time friend, who had the good sense to ask me what the words "my ain folk" meant to me. My wise friend sat silently while I responded with a flood of tears. Finally, I was able to say, "I want to be with my own people."

My friend repeated my words thoughtfully. "My own people." I then received some very good advice: "Jean, it's time to go back. Take your daughters and go home!"

I thought long and hard about this. I had often wondered what had happened to other people who had left my community. I also wondered what differences our childhood experiences and values had made in our adult lives. So I decided that not only would I return home, I would also try to find a few childhood friends. Perhaps I would interview them and explore their lives and mine, and while doing so, learn more about the place where I grew up.

As a sociologist, I was well aware of C. Wright Mills's (1959) classic thesis about the sociological imagination. I was very interested to explore the relationship between my own personal biography and the history of my community. However, the discovery that my trauma of having to move away from a dying community had been shared by countless people, each like me, experiencing this as a personal trouble, was a great surprise.

This personal and intellectual journey began on the warm, rainy summer afternoon in 1987 when, after arriving in Glasgow, I was finally standing where my childhood tenement building had once risen majestically overlooking my little school just across the narrow street. Mesmerized by the expanse of rough, glass-strewn ground where once had stood my tenement building, and across the way a dignified sandstone church and my favorite sweet shop, I recalled a similar event. As a young child in the early 1950s I had stood in the shell of a bombed-out church, looking up at what was left of the once majestic windows. I recalled the feeling of devastation and sadness. But this was much, much worse. I felt as if I could not breathe, as if I would suffocate if I didn't get away. I had struggled with this persistent emotion for many years. I had always believed I would feel better if only the building were still there, if I could climb the stairs and ask the occupants if I could come in and see my "wee hoose" just one last time. But it was gone, along with everything in it that I had loved, the beloved books, artwork, childhood dolls, and dollhouse I had been forced to leave behind.

In Scottish cities, tenement communities had sprung up in the industrial era in the mid-nineteenth century. Blocks of stone flats with common open public entrances called "closes" defined these neighborhoods, both physically and socially. These were vital, thriving communities with local color and character. Life was hard, but the people were proud and resilient. They maintained strong kinship ties and friendship networks and banded together to lend each other mutual aid. The women especially helped carry their families through two world wars, depressed economies, and, in many cases, near starvation.

With the widespread unemployment that followed the death of the steam locomotive and related industries in the late 1950s, these neighborhoods deteriorated rapidly, and most were eventually destroyed by "urban renewal" and vandalism. The destruction of community was particularly ruthless in Glasgow. Residents emigrated to find new jobs, leaving blocks of empty and decaying tenements behind. As new buildings, high-rise flats, and towns were constructed, the old tenement culture, a 100-year-old way of life, disappeared forever. These changes, especially the experience of immigration to other countries, was accompanied by trauma: a loss of roots, relatives, friends, culture, and common language that had a rich yet still unrecorded history.

While I stood there trying to decide what to do, suddenly from across the street I heard the voice of an older women calling to me. "It's a right scunner [vomiting sensation], isn't it Hen?" She was returning from the shopping center a couple of miles away with her groceries in a little cart, passing behind me on her way to one of the high-rise flats built in place of the demolished tenements. The familiar colloquialism "Hen," an old Glasgwegian term of endearment, produced in me a sensation of relief and affection and also gave me a chuckle. She had guessed rightly, from not only my bodily stance but the strain in my face, that I had at one time lived in the invisible building I was viewing in my mind's eye. She told me that the small community library, which had been taken over by the National Trust, was still standing and that part of it had been turned into a museum. She encouraged me to go there. "It'll help ye," she said. Her words were prophetic.

The museum was housed in the old library that I had haunted incessantly from the time I was five years old until I left Scotland in my teens, taken by my aunt and uncle, who were my adoptive parents.[2] The library was still in use, but the old spacious high-ceilinged newspaper reading rooms where my grandfather had once stood reading now displayed community treasures in museum cases and exhibits. The Victorian library furnishings, even the book check-out desk, were still there, just the same as when I was younger, and where an elderly women remembered (as did I) a librarian making her show her clean hands before allowing her to check out books thirty years earlier, during World War I.

Since the museum's opening two years earlier, people had contributed hundreds of artifacts and thousands of photos. Some of the younger folks had been collecting the memories of older people who had once lived in surrounding areas. Using some of these narratives and traditional historiographic materials, the curator had written a book on the work experiences of the men who, like my uncle, had worked in the locomotive industries in the area (Hutchison and O'Neill 1989).

My visit was fortuitous and serendipitous. No one had yet compiled a social history using oral narratives of tenement women, children, or family life in this or any other Scottish urban community. I was given access to thousands of pages of museum transcripts, photos, and artifacts such as diaries and church records. The museum curators, pleased to find someone with a unique combination of native and scholarly interest, were willing to locate local narrators for me to interview and reinterview in order to reconstruct a portrait of Glasgow family life.

Eighteen months later, with a year-long sabbatical and leave, I returned to Scotland. Inspired by Paul Thompson's (1986) treatise on oral histories of underrepresented people, I spent the next twenty months in discourse, narrative recording, transcript collation, reading, and archival research. My goal was to recreate through oral histories a description of the ordinary, daily life of working-class women and men inside their homes and closes. I wanted to reveal the daily routines of cooking, cleaning, shopping, washing, child care, and holidays, as well as the experience of illness and death.

My initial idea was to present the museum with a series of essays and photos and to create with the staff an installation depicting the inside of a two-room tenement house. Perhaps I would write a few descriptive oral history pamphlets, which I expected would be tucked away on a shelf for those few students or grandchildren who might like to know about this now vanished way of life. But as the material burgeoned and I became more obsessed with my subject, the museum curator said to me one day, "Why not write a book?"

After my typically Glaswegian self-denigrating response—"Me do a book? I couldn't possibly!"—and after much talk, encouragement, and self-assessment of my abilities, the book became a goal. Even so, I still had in mind a work that would sit on the shelves of libraries and museums, awaiting the rare scholar, and I would feel a great sense of relief and accomplishment that I had preserved a lost way of life before it was too late. I had no inkling that my book would speak to a greater public need. It was indeed a great shock when my publisher called me in January 1991 and told me that the book (launched with the opening of my museum exhibit in mid-October) had sold out by Christmas and was a national bestseller in Scotland (Faley 1990).[3]

Since that time—and after many people wrote me about the book, and after interviewing even more people for a second book that I have yet to complete—I've reflected upon the expected and unexpected learning that took place as I studied my subject, immersed myself in the oral histories, and began to experience the emergence of my sociological imagination. I developed an effective linguistic interviewing method, greatly expanded my understanding of my heritage, and discovered the link between my own "trouble" and an unnamed but very real public "issue."

It is not difficult for a researcher to recount the discoveries resulting from what she set out to learn or to explore the things she knew she didn't know before and during her investigation. After all, this is what research is all about. However, in my reflexive musings I realized that the things I had not consciously known also had a powerful effect on me. Thus there are three areas of experience that constituted the fulfillment of my sociological imagination, which can best described as: *what I knew I didn't know, what I didn't know I knew,* and *what I didn't know I didn't know.*

What I Knew I Didn't Know: Finding Biography in History

Like all researchers, I planned to educate myself and explore what I knew I didn't know. I read extensively in oral history, both substantive literature and methodology. Knowing that I actually knew very little about the history of Glasgow's industry and tenement communities, I looked forward to my reading and writing in this area. I was aware that a large part of my fascination with this subject was the conscious expectation that I would increase my sociological imagination in regard to my own biography. Despite the excellence of Scottish education, working-class history and even industrial history were not taught in primary or secondary school, nor was anything about my own community covered. I certainly didn't know how much I was going to learn about the social circumstances surrounding the troubles and hardships of my narrators.

The major themes that emerged in my study tended to have a dialectical component. On the one hand, there was great hardship and suffering, constant disorder, dirt, and grim physical surroundings, and monotonous industrial and domestic work schedules. On the other hand, there was much communal kindness and helpfulness, pristine standards of cleanliness, orderliness, and thrift, comforting rituals of hospitality, and a "poor but honest" philosophy of life, with an emphasis on refinement and respectability.

In spite of the hardships of tenement life—which ranged from exhausting domestic work, malnutrition, poverty, and overcrowding to abusive family relationships, disease, and death, particularly of infants and children—communality prevailed. This included the physical closeness and helpfulness of grannies and grandpas, aunties and uncles, other kin and neighbors. People helped each other by cooking a communal pot of soup, cleaning the house of a sick woman, going messages (shopping), sick-visiting, offering tea and sympathy, washing a dead body, wet-nursing a baby, informally adopting and raising a family of orphans, or taking in children on a weekend night if a father was inclined to drink and abuse. The honesty and trustworthiness of neighbors were such that doors were left unlocked for people to walk in to care for a sick person or to borrow some loose tea if no one was home.

My narrators frequently recalled happy childhoods and longed for the dependability of the routines, the pleasures of neatness and cleanliness, the coziness of the fire, the hot cup of tea, the stone hot-water bottle wrapped in a towel or flannel pajamas warming every child's bed, the security of visiting with friends and family. I found in these recountings an affirmation of what I felt I had lost but had never articulated. A hard life, yes, but a warm one as well. It was not a feeling of nostalgia but a vague yearning for the times that one recalls in positive ways, a remembrance of good things that were lost. Like my narrators, I missed the friendliness and safety of the close relationships that were unarguably a byproduct of those hard times.

Disorder often accompanied the circumstance of having many children crowded into a small space. Bedding for makeshift beds (two chairs put together, a bed-chair, a trundle bed, a drawer as bed for a baby or a toddler) had to be taken apart every morning and assembled again at night. Then there was the dirt, which came from a variety of sources: several families sharing toilets, dozens of people passing up and down the stairs every day, overcrowding (eleven people living in two rooms, five or six in one room), infected handkerchiefs and bedclothes, soot from the black stove and surrounding industries, dirt on children's clothes from outdoor play, and the literally black clothes, faces, and bodies of the men coming home from "the works."

Cleaning was a constant preoccupation. Mothers are often remembered as *Aye wi' her hans in water,* that is, keeping water constantly boiling on the range, doing hand wash, spending the better part of the day washing clothes. Cooking, shopping, cleaning, ironing, and child care were never-ending activities. The objective was to be "methodical," which meant an ability to iron clothes and linens flat in order to fit everything into very limited drawer and cupboard space. The children were taught to fold and stack their clothes with the trousers or dress on the bottom and the underwear and socks on the top, ready to be put on first and quickly in a cold room. Being methodical meant hanging all the sheets together and the shirts together so that they could be "wheeched doon" (pulled down) quickly at the beginning of a rain. It meant not being derided by references such as "Och she's a shirt 'n' a sheet woman," that is, as someone who didn't know how to organize her wash and who hung the sheets in between the shirts. Methodical meant scrubbing and using pipe clay and having white steps and shining "brasses" (brass letterbox, bell pull, finger plate, and door handle on the front door), which were buffed up every day.

Methodical also meant regularity. Chores and sociability were organized around the horns that blew to let the working men know they had ten minutes to get in before the gate closed, to announce the time to go home for the midday meal, and again for the evening meal. Cleaning was done Friday night, and baking and shopping on Saturday. Saturday night and Sunday afternoon were for visiting friends and relatives.

I now understood more clearly the "stairheid politics" (a semi-derisive, semi-admiring term) that all the women had faced, myself included. I remember the constant admonitions to keep my dress clean, my knickers pulled up, my fingers off the brass letterbox. There were the frequent directives to step over the front step, not on it, which had had seemed rather petty at the time. I now understood better my aunt's almost obsessive preoccupation with how the front door and I looked to others in the community. When she was thirteen her father had died, and a rapid descent into poverty had left her humiliated with a great drive to achieve respectability again. She feared being looked down on and had a great attachment to her image as a house-proud and methodical housewife. People were friendly and they were helpful; they would even help you with the wash if you were sick. But they were also ready to make slighting comments about a woman whose brasses had fingermarks on them, who had a dirty front doorstep, and who didn't boil the sheets to a bright whiteness.

The "respectable" poor would shun the "lazy" woman who couldn't keep up with a withering and damning phrase—"Och her! She's a clarty besom!"—which probably best translates as a "dirty bitch." Most of my narrators, when asked why they thought there were women like that—and there was always one in every back court, sometimes more—said that these women were probably exhausted and depressed. As one woman told me, "Och, we didnae know about depression then! Poor souls." A few narrators with keen sociological insight noted that making an example of dirty housekeepers kept the others in line.

Thus I could now better understand the frequent nagging of my own internal critic, comparing myself to the pristine neatness and cleanliness of the homes of many relatives and friends, a standard I find impossible to maintain. Never mind that the comparison is to women who had only two rooms to scrub and polish, received no junk mail, and didn't have much paperwork. My messy offices at home and at work constantly accuse me.

Before World War II, when there was no national health or unemployment assistance, there was a terrible fear of being so poor that one's family would have to be given parish relief. An ethic of thrift, a philosophy of "waste not, want not," prevailed. There was sympathy but also an underlying belief that if you became indigent, it was somehow your own fault. Thus the great shame of being "on the Parish." An even greater fear was of being put in "the Puir Hoose" (the poorhouse). This was regarded with almost as much dread as death. The children and parents would be split apart, housed in different parts of the institute; and children might even be placed in foster care. This was one of the main reasons that women stayed in abusive relationships. If they left, or their husband deserted them, they stood to lose their children.

After hearing one of my narrator's accounts of her widowed mother scrubbing neighbors' stairs for a sack of cold boiled potatoes, and glad to get it, one of my uncles told me that my grandmother had done the same thing after the death of my grandfather. She had many a time gladly accepted a sack of cold potatoes and, if she was lucky, a small amount of cooked mince (boiled hamburger) for a day of scrubbing stairs or doing a large washing of clothes. People would work themselves almost to death rather than become the indigent poor.

I could now more clearly see why I had internalized such a strong value of hard work. I saw the connection with my family's experience, which I could now identify as an attempt to mitigate the great shame associated with grinding poverty. I saw how my biography, and my psyche, belonged to this great web of social history, and I began to know myself better.

What I Didn't Know I Knew: Partners and Patois in Discourse

Despite the poverty, some people maintained the last vestiges of respectability by use of the spoken word. Many a scantily clad but clean child received a good "skite" (smack) for coming off with a slang word or "low" pronunciation. Having been raised during the days when patois meant not only dialect but inferiority, I had been the ambivalent recipient of elocution lessons. Monitored by what my sociology colleagues would refer to as an "upwardly mobile aunt," I became adept at code-switching, which, for want of better terms, I now call "back-close," "two-up," and "three-up" patois.

"Back-close" patois (referred to as "roon the back talk" by class-conscious parents) means the language that was spoken by many of the children who played in a common "back" (usually concrete) amidst the "middens" (garbage huts) and wash houses. It was the language of play, and of poorer people and older people, thought by some to be a low form of talk, characterized not just by pronunciation but by idiomatic and often combative ranting and "cheeky" banter. It also included a certain amount of rude talk, and among some children a sprinkling of "bad" words. Examples of this common talk (with which I was well versed) would be "Ach, yer bum's oot the windie," which meant your bottom, bare of course, is sticking out of the window. Or "Keep yer haun's aff ma jaikit, glaikit." Use of words such as *jaikit* (jacket) and *glaikit* (a mentally limited person with the classic zinc-deficiency signs of protruding tongue and heavy lidded eyes) could elicit a reprimand from elders.

Class and dialect consciousness was so intense that a favorite game among children was to sing in a very posh (Anglified) voice: "Oh, the brown cow has broken out and eaten all the hay," finishing with a rapid, canting, guttural rendering of Glaswegian patois, "The broon coo's broken oot and eaten aw' the hay!" Making fun of posh people and their speech style was an intrinsic part of Scottish humor.

"Two-up" patois was a "genteel" Glaswegian dialect used by persons in working-class Glasgow who were (or thought they were) what canny folks called "pan breid," or pan bread. This referred to the use of a loaf of bread made of soft white flour and baked in a square-shaped tin that produced square slices with lightly baked crusts. Pan bread was, of course, more expensive than the "plain loaf" (black crusted bread) and was used to make "cut" sandwiches for afternoon tea, a throwback to Victorian tea sandwiches.

"Three-up" patois describes a very Anglified Scots (or Oxford English if you were really facile), attainable either by a middle-class upbringing or through elocution lessons. It was referred to by teachers as the King's or Queen's English, depending on who was on the throne at the time.

There was a definite social and architectural stratification in the tenements. The houses in the close were less desirable. With each successive floor upward (one-up, two-up, or three-up) desirability, and expense, increased. "Close" entryways and one-up houses were invariably inhabited by larger families. The head of house, if a male, worked at one of the lower-paid skilled or unskilled jobs, and if a female, she was usually a "widawoman" (widow woman) or an "auld grannie" (old grandmother). Two-up houses were inhabited by skilled workers and three-up by foremen, shop owners, and office workers. The wives of these workers wore better clothes and were reputed to change their knickers (underpants), and the knickers of their children, more often than those in the cheaper houses.

Close entryway dwellers had a lot to deal with. There was more noise and dirt, as the dark "back close" (the passage into the backcourt) was often a place where men surreptitiously relieved themselves with a "pee up the wal" and where children who didn't want to go home to their own toilet left a steaming "jobbie" (bowel movement) in the corner. And Friday- and Saturday-night drunks often left their spew in the close directly, or over the stair banister, a mess that women would have to clean up later.

Despite the rising status associated with the number of stairs climbed, there was a clannish sense of identity among the residents in regard to living "up oor close" and "roon oor back" (the closes that shared a common backcourt or green where children played and women did the wash in the wash houses and hung clothes out to dry). Most people had relatives up their close and in the closes adjoining the backcourt and could easily talk to each other across the windows.

In retrospect, I now realize that my narrators were sometimes concerned about the social class difference they perceived between us. There were times when liminal moments had to be negotiated and transcended through ameliorating information and variations in our patois. A delightful woman in her nineties, trying to place me in her sphere of reference—both of us being terribly "three-uppy" in our polite beginnings—asked me, "How many up did ye live at 42 Gourlay Street?" My answer was that we were two-up. I added that my uncle was a boilermaker and my aunt an upholstery sewer. This let her know that we needed two incomes to be two-up. I also noted that we used to live at 4 Millerbank Street in a single-end (one-room) in the close. Satisfied, she proceeded to tell me that she had lived "in the close," although her mother had come from a better class of parents. We talked further about the advantages to children of living in the close, where you could literally climb out the bedroom window and play outside until someone "clyped," that is, told on you to your parents.

Working-class people can convey a great deal about someone's social standing in the community with just a couple of choice words or phrases. As one of my favorite narrators said to me about a woman I was planning on interviewing: "Och well, she's a wee bitty pan breid, if ye tak' ma meanin'," which meant that she was "refined," used two-up patois, and probably had the financial means to go with it. Or, as he added in jest with much laughter, "Ye know whit that means, Jean, don't ye? It means she doesnae swear!"

In reference to an old neighbor, another said, "Och well, she fancies hersel'. Oh aye, she thinks she's pan breid, but she's no!" This is a reference to someone who aspires or pretends but who hasn't really made it, a case of "fur coats and nae knickers." This same gentleman, who began working in the coal mines at age fourteen, told me, "Ah wis brought up rough, Jean. So that's how I talk. Ah wis wan o' they low wans. But ah wisnae a midgie-raker [a trash-can rummager]. Naw. I worked hard, hard, Jean."

My facility with dialect and idioms, as well as shared metaphors and metonymy, proved valuable in eliciting stories and descriptions of these daily routines. Later, as I reflected on my use of patois, I realized that I had unconsciously used the two-up patois when requesting interviews on the phone and when first entering a person's home. I wasn't really aware of this until much later when working across tapes. I could hear myself shift from more Anglified speech into the more rapid canting and idiomatic Glaswegian. I didn't know I "knew" when to do this!

This was something well ingrained in me as a child. The Anglified patois was used as a social passport. It showed respect and marked you as respectable. Demonstrating that I could switch, and especially that I was old enough to have learned this old style of language (now passed away among the younger folk), was perhaps one of the most effective passports to older people's precious memories that I had at my disposal.

One example in particular illustrates this process. One woman in her eighties had been a very good informant and quite disclosing. In fact, wonderfully, I discovered that she and I had shared the same close address of 42 Gourlay Street. In the beginning of our interviews, she was usually two-up in her use of dialect. I had interviewed her several times in person and on the phone. One day, after reflecting about her childhood, she drifted off into a bit of back-close patois and said, "Aye we had to sprachle [to flounder about and struggle] and get on." She looked at me shrewdly and said, "That's an old word. Dae ye know whit that means?"

I gave her the correct translation, and with a look of pleasant surprise, she asked me how old I was. "Och, I thocht ye were much younger than that." She had been a disclosing and reflective narrator before, but after this she was even more disclosing with her views, telling me that if she were young now she would never, never, get married. "I'd have children, but I wouldnae bother getting merrit [married]." Quite a radical statement for a woman of her age!

Many people were quite vocal in talking about what school they went to, their involvement in church activities, and where they worked outside the home. But they would be a little stunned when I asked them to describe details about cleaning the house. Women in particular would need to be reassured that I thought this was very important and that other people would really like to know about it. Then the flow of the narrative would become more animated and voluble.

The use of cultural schema, embedded in the idiomatic phrases, was the best way to facilitate the flow of conversation. Asking for details on black-leading a fireplace might be met with "How [why] dae ye want tae know this?" I would eventually get the information, but if I initiated the topic by saying something like "Dae ye mind [remember] the black fire? Dain the brasses?" a typical response was "Oh aye, the brasses! Oh, aye, that wis important." Or "Oh, black-leadin' the fire. It was awfy [awful]." This would easily set off a conversation about hard work, neighbors' judgments, fingerprints, the smell of Brasso, and sometimes reminiscences about the honesty of neighbors who always left their key in the door or on a string inside the letterbox.

My request to a ninety-five-year-old man that he tell me about what he did as a wee boy—like many male informants, he really wanted to talk about his work as a brass maker—was met with "Are ye from the university? Are ye wanting to psychoanalyze me?"

Without conscious reflection about this, I replied by telling him I did teach at a university but that I came from Springburn and "the dugs in ma back were hotchin'" (dogs in my backcourt were infested with fleas). This was an assertion that despite my university education, I had humble origins and had not forgotten them.

Uproarious laughter followed, and he said, "Oh aye, ye are from Springburn!" He smiled, drew his chair up close to mine, leaned over, looked me straight in the eye, and said very kindly and tenderly, "Well, whit dae ye want tae know?"

It was at this moment, when mentally sitting at the feet of this elderly gentleman who reached back in his mind and told me about life during World War I, that I fell absolutely in love with oral history! It was the beginning of my feeling of great reverence toward people's memories. I discovered that the approach that was most comfortable and creative for me was to establish a discourse with my narrator as a partner rather than as an interview subject. I came to truly appreciate Alessandro Portelli's (1991) observation that one must always have respect for what people choose to tell you, because what they tell you is so often beautiful. Oral history at its best, as Michael Frisch (1990) suggests, is a form of "shared authority," an inherently democratic craft.

What I Didn't Know I Didn't Know: Trouble Becomes Issue

I had left my community and my country unwillingly. I had left house, hearth, neighbors, friends, and relatives with a sense of unreality: this could not possibly be happening. The grief that I had borne, sometimes consciously and painfully, sometimes without awareness, pushed back into a dim shadow, affecting me year after year. I had experienced my immigration as a personal trouble. The moving away was something that had happened to me, and I interpreted my enduring grief as a personal difficulty. I perhaps took it as a personal failure. There were others who had immigrated who did not seem to carry such grief and unease. I thought it was because they were securely embedded in a family system with their own mother, father, grandparents, and other relatives. Something unfathomable persisted, regardless of my will that it be otherwise. I had a dual consciousness that haunted me, my marginality operating as a master status. It was at times so painful that as a college freshman I labeled my distress privately to myself as a "refugee complex," something that I would eventually have to face.

Over the years I had frequently scanned in my mind the streets, the stairs, the house, the fireplace, the neighbors "hingin' oot the windie" (leaning out the window) to chat you up as you came up the streets. Not that it was such a wonderful or an exceptionally happy life. It's just that it was suddenly gone, and I couldn't find the traces of it anywhere. This had left me with an indelible yearning for "my ain folk." My own people! Particularly the older people who were bearers of the community culture that is no more.

I wrote about this loss and yearning in the preface of my book, and after its publication I had several book signings. It was at one of these signings that I had my first inkling that my "trouble" was shared by many others. One woman, who had already read my book and had traveled by train all the way from Perth to meet me, told me that ever since the buildings in her community had been pulled down, she had gone over and over in her mind how the inside of the homes looked. She thought incessantly about the daily routines and the general way of life so as not to lose it. As she told me this she began to cry, saying that she was so happy because this whole way of life would now be preserved in my book.

However, it was not until I began to receive letter after letter—usually with diaries, poems, maps, old photos, and biographies enclosed, and all of which I answered—that I came to realize that there are countless people who have been traumatized by forced exodus and destruction of their communities. My first letter was from a man whose mother died when he was sixteen and his father didn't want to take care of him. He joined the Boys Service, a branch of the Royal Air Force, and when he came back, his father had given up the apartment and everything was gone. He wrote in his letter, "I'm writing to you not because of the book, though it was wonderful and I cried through it to finally have my memories preserved, but because of what you said in the preface. I said to my wife, 'This lassie's just like me! She understands.'"

Since then, and hundreds of letters later, from as near as Pennsylvania and as far away as Tasmania, I have discovered the similarities between my grief and emotional struggle and that of others. My trouble, which I endured in isolation, was not a unique experience. In my recent interviews I have found that each person had a similar tale to tell, whether it was leaving to move to a community a few miles away, to a high-rise a mile away, or to another country. It helped them if they had a close family. Nevertheless, many of the adjustment issues were the same. As one man who immigrated to Canada wrote me, "You know, I immigrated with my family at age nine, and I have spent the rest of my life dealing with that." The stories I've been told have commonalities. Many felt a sense of desolation over the realization that they would never live in their home country again. Most talked about years of ambivalent adjustment to, even depression over, their experience of immigration. They live, we live, with a dual consciousness, observing the adopted culture with an outsider's eye. And they experienced a profound sense of awe, relief, and delayed grief when they made their first trip back to Scotland, often after many years of separation.

All of the stories people have told me both for the book and since the book has been published have given me a new perspective on my own biography, helping me see where my own life blends into the larger tapestry of the immigrant experience. For me, this has been a wondrous odyssey into the sociological imagination. The discourses I have had with many people who kindly constructed their personal narratives and gave me the benefit of their reflexive thinking were often beautiful, sometimes tragic, but always meaningful. They not only led me to great insights about the communities in which they and I had lived but also helped me find my own place and my own sense of belonging to those times gone by.

Portelli suggests that "oral history does not begin with one abstract person observing another, reified one, but with two persons meeting on a ground of equality to bring together their different types of knowledge and achieve a new synthesis from which both will be changed" (1991:xii). The sociological imagination has fulfilled its promise, and through the discourse of oral histories and the people who have shared their stories with me, I have been profoundly and positively changed.

Notes

1. This chapter is a substantial revision of an earlier version that appeared in a special issue, *Oral and Life History,* in *Sociological Imagination* 31, no. 2, 1994.

2. When I was a child, my father literally kidnapped me from my mother and home in Dorset, England, and took me to Scotland. After both he and my mother remarried, they gave me up for adoption to my aunt and uncle.

3. The book is currently in its tenth printing.

CHAPTER 6

Everyone Else: Becoming Jewish

Tony Platt

Belief in the power of old wounds to leak into the present was not so easily dismissed.

—*Pat Barker*

If you keep quiet, they'll be nice.

—*Bertolt Brecht*

"The problem with Jews," complains Yossi, my Israeli brother-in-law, "is they care about everyone else but themselves."

"Everyone else," he repeats for my benefit. Yossi never has this problem. He may hate his government, which he does, but he loves his nation. For him, Jewish identity and the struggle for justice are intertwined. He left Iraq with his parents under the gun and with only one possible destination. For me, it's a different immigrant story. I left England to escape an overbearing father, not racial persecution, and to get far away from the provinces, not pogroms. I could choose my destination, and, wisely, I chose California as my Promised Land.[1]

I grew up in the wake of World War II, in the declining capital of industrialization, its chimneys belching out yellow-gray fumes around the clock. "Manchester reminded me of everything I was trying to forget," said the artist Max Ferber when he arrived in 1942, the year of my birth and his exile from Nazism (quoted in Sebald 1996:191). For generations, Manchester had been home to one of the oldest gatherings of Jewish immigrants in England. Jobs in the cotton industry attracted the first Jews in the late eighteenth century, and by 1850 there were enough, mostly Germans, to fill two congregations. My Romanian and Polish grandparents arrived at the turn of the century, tinkers and dealers, trying to get a foot inside the smokestacks before the 1905 Aliens Act closed the door. Grandpa Daniels was one of 89 hawkers, Grandpa Platt one of 1,122 tailors in north

Manchester's mosh pit of Jewish Lithuanians, Romanians, Russians, Poles, Africans, Turks, and Middle Easterners, united only by fear of the pogrom and the lure of commerce (Lipman 1954; Sebald 1986; Taylor, Evans, and Fraser 1996).

The Daniels and Platt families clung for a while to their diminishing Yiddish and struggled with the mysteries of English, which they learned to speak and read but barely to write. My paternal grandmother, Annie, always had trouble with her *v*'s and, unfortunately, liked to wear "a welwet hat with a weil." They all stayed close to home and trusted only their own. "One of ours?" they'd ask each other when trying to verify a stranger's provenance. By American standards, Manchester's ghetto was a very small world: maybe 25,000 by 1900, and not much larger some fifty-five years later when I came of age. But one big happy family it wasn't. My mother's class-savvy parents, convinced that Romanians topped the immigrant pecking order, were stunned when Eileen fell in love with my dad, Monty, a Polish *dripki* who seemed destined for a life of poverty.

My parents, born in the 1920s in Friedrich Engels's city, were materialists who worshiped no icons other than Bertrand Russell's science for peace and progress and Havelock Ellis's sex manuals. To them, every mystery had an answer. They abandoned Yiddish, except for a few phrases, named me after a Catholic saint—Anthony, followed by my brother, Stephen, and sister, Susan, names for looking forward, not back—and as good young commies subordinated the Jewish Question to the proletarian struggle.

My dad decided the big stuff in our household. He made my siblings and me go through the motions "for the grandparents"—bar mitzvahs for the boys, synagogue on the high holidays, Friday-night dinner. But he also made it clear to us that the religious piece of Judaism was all mumbo-jumbo, the leftover rituals of backward peasants. My mother, following Monty's step at every turn, including the one that eventually took her down a blind alley, also abandoned any kind of religious practice. They both remained atheists all their life, even during the last months of miserable deaths from lung cancer, when, against all odds, they persisted in looking to doctors, not rabbis, for a miracle.

In the household of my childhood, Eileen, doing what she knew best and had learned from her mother, maintained a space for traditional Ashkenazy recipes alongside the haute cuisine imported from the Continent. All her life, especially as she moved into the upper middle class, she did good works for Jewish and Zionist charities. She read the *Jewish Chronicle* and was attentive to the successes of Jewish actors, Jewish athletes, and Jewish politicians. All her close and not-so-close friends were Jewish, every one of them. Near the end of her life, she moved into the same Jewish old age home in which her mother, the Romanian immigrant, had lived for many years and died.

My dad, who scoffed at Eileen's soft, philanthropic Zionism, also retained a strong Jewish identity that was rooted in his everyday life. His two oldest friends, his two wives, and his last girlfriend were all Jewish. And of my brother, sister, and I, he was closest to Sue, whom he regularly visited in Israel long after he had given up any hope that a Jewish state could create a better human society than any other place on earth. "Just as fucked up as everywhere else," he'd report after a visit. But he kept going back.

My dad's Jewishness emerged not so much out of an active desire for cultural preservation as out of an appreciation for the necessities of self-preservation. England has a long history of active anti-Semitism, which encouraged Jews—especially ones as successful as my dad was in the rag trade—to stay on their toes and be watchful: keep a getaway bag packed and an accessible account. As a teen, Monty went to a mixed working-class grammar school in Salford, where the lads divided themselves into teams of yids versus yoks for pickup football games at lunchtime. Later his practical paranoia was fueled by the concentration camps, which he visited in 1945 but never discussed with his children, and honed in the mid-1950s by the post-Stalin revelations of Jew-hating in his once beloved Soviet Union. Like my Puerto Rican friend Piri, who always sniffs the air for the *caca* of racial insult, my parents had their antennae permanently circling the atmosphere, searching for enemy signals.

When my mum and dad moved up the class ladder in the early 1950s, they moved us out of the Salford ghetto and leapfrogged over middle-class Didsbury into village life in "the country," with its faux Elizabethan pubs, horsey set, and ever-so-polite anti-Semitism. "How odd / of God / to choose / the Jews," as Hilaire Belloc put it. We were among some of the first Jews to integrate the rural Protestant suburbs of Cheshire. Though many others soon followed us, my parents and their friends were forced to set up their own club for aspiring Jewish golfers. Later the club opened its doors to aspiring Indian and Pakistani golfers and other outcasts from suburban gentility.

For a year or so I crammed at a private prep school, one of a handful of Jews; there I was polished for speeding along the fast track into the meritocracy: first the prestigious Manchester Grammar School (MGS) in 1953, then Oxford in 1960. I benefited from the postwar decline in anti-Semitism, just as American Jews found barriers and quotas removed by the GI Bill. At MGS there was such a sizable minority of Jewish students, mostly "scholarship boys," that we had our own assembly every morning and were exempted from singing "Onward Christian Soldiers." My maternal grandmother continued to worry about my safety when it was no longer justified. After I broke my shoulder at age thirteen playing rugby, she sniffed the air. "Wasn't Jewish?" she asked about the kid who had tackled me, already suspecting the answer.

A few years later, Grandma Daniels would warn me about the danger of *shiksas* on the prowl for Jewish husbands. "Who can blame them?" she'd say. "Jewish men have brains, they're smart, make a good living." You don't hear about Jewish men being taken to court by frustrated wives for loss of consortium. But my brother and I were no match for those wily Christian gold-diggers. My first wife was respectably Protestant, the second a lapsed Catholic who still crosses herself before the plane takes off. For health as much as cultural reasons, I made sure that my son Daniel was circumcised, unlike my brother Steve, who left his Tom's peter intact. There was some rejoicing in the family when our sister Sue immigrated to Israel, more in search of adventure than of the Messiah. Her marriage to a divorced, dark-skinned Iraqi Jew was welcomed as an improvement, albeit slight, on her older brothers' track record of "marrying out."

By the 1960s, with British racial anxieties shifting to rebellions in the colonies and the specter of Caribbean, African, and Asian immigration to the core, I rarely encountered anti-Semitism in high school and college, and then only from individuals, not institutions (Fryer 1984; Paul 1997). Now that there were bigger and better demons to trump the Hebrews, we had our opportunity to prove our loyalty to the Crown. My grandmother had grown up a staunch racist, hating all *schwartzes*, but never knowing one until the Caribbean cooks at her fancy Jewish retirement home adopted her recipe for chicken soup. The last time that I visited her, close to her 100th birthday, she called out a cook to meet me, and there they stood, the Jamaican and the Jew, arms around each other. On the other hand, my Uncle Phil, who moved to New York as a young man, stood firm in his hatred of "niggers" and died a bitter old man with his bigotry unblemished.

My parents did not buy into this double standard, because they understood that Hitler hated blacks as much as he hated Jews. When political exiles from Africa sought refuge in Manchester in the 1940s, Monty and Eileen showed their solidarity with the "Mau Maus" by attending a cocktail party for Jomo Kenyatta. I was brought up to believe that apartheid was as morally wrong as anti-Semitism, even if it meant giving up the family's season ticket to the Lancashire Cricket Club when it invited South Africa to play in violation of the boycott. Among my mother's collection of antiques, now displayed on a shelf in my living room, was an eighteenth-century abolitionist snuffbox, decorated with a slave breaking his shackles and the inscription "Am I not your brother?"

But there were limits to my family's antiracism. The farther away the injustice—Africans terrorized by the Boers, Negroes facing dogs and waterhoses in the U.S. South—the stronger my parents' indignation. Meanwhile, twenty miles from our suburban village was the laager of Moss Side, where immigrants from the Caribbean and Africa huddled in the rooming houses of absentee landlords, waiting for work. My dad never hired black men in his textile factory, and their kids didn't receive scholarships to my school. The closest I got to people in that community was through the top window of a double-decker bus as it made its way past the crumbling terraced houses nonstop to Manchester.

By the time I moved to Berkeley in 1963 to rise with the crème de la crème up through graduate school, anti-Semitism had receded into the background in the United States and Jews were out in academia. The battleground for me shifted to racism and civil rights, free speech and Marxism, feminism and gay rights. "Everyone else," I can hear my brother-in-law saying. I hung out with Jews in the movement, for whom anti-Semitism was our lowest priority. "Never again" was not exactly a slogan that resonated in our lives. My heart was not with the 2,000 Jews who fought with the Confederacy to defend Dixie. Nor with the Jews of New York who supported the teachers' unions against black community control of schools. Nor with the Jews of Miami who hated the godless Cuban revolution. Nor with the Jews of Beverly Hills who live in fear of foreigners swamping the Golden State.

When the Palestinian intifada erupted, I worried about my sister and her family's safety and sanity, but I didn't abandon critical thinking skills and political analysis. And after September 11, 2001, I think that it is even more important to speak out against American unilateralism, Islamic fundamentalism, and Israeli militarism. "Jews, of all people," observes Tony Kushner, "with our history of suffering," should know better than to acquiesce in the "dreadful suffering of the Palestinian people" (2002:147). How can silence be good for the Jews? (Like my grandmother, you may have noticed, I've started to make statements posing as questions.)

I admit that I felt a twinge of unease when my daughter Rebecca decided some ten years ago to embrace Catholicism and give her wedding bouquet to Mary when she married her Mexican boyfriend. But I was bothered more by the religiosity of her decision than by any sense of cultural betrayal. I would have felt worse if she had married an Orthodox Jew and walked behind him with eight kids in tow. Also, it was okay when my son Daniel followed his sister by marrying a Catholic Chicana. He didn't convert but, like the rest of us, is trying to figure out how to live in a hybrid family that celebrates multiple gods. I don't think of my four grandchildren as diluting the race, but rather as getting all these unexpected bonuses in their cultural genes. I hope they will not choose or be forced to choose only one true identity.

"Almost-Jews" is how Howard Zinn describes the straddled identities of people like us, for whom biology is not destiny. My children's names reverberate with the Old Testament, yet many of my closest friends are, as my parents' generation used to say, non-Jews. I love Jewish humor, even

Jackie Mason's, whose politics I despise, and hanging out with people who have a Jewish past similar to mine. Occasionally I'll even go to a Passover seder. But I'm not interested in accompanying Lynn, my atheistic friend, to an inspirational synagogue for the high holidays. And I politely turned down an old comrade when she tried to recruit me to a group of hip feminist Jews who mix mysticism with stretching. She had mistaken my recent interest in yoga as a sign that I was searching for my Jewish roots.

Maybe it's different when ethnicity is imposed on you, as I discovered in the summer of 1999. My wife Cecilia and I were both visiting fellows at the highly selective Huntington Library in San Marino, a part of greater Los Angeles, but a world apart. Spending the summer doing research on California history at The (always-capital-*T*) Huntington was a hot and cold experience. For a professor in the state university system, with a high teaching load and almost no time for research, it was a luxury to get paid to amble through extraordinary documents and take time off for tea in the Rose Garden Room or a walk through the Japanese gardens. And without pressures or expectations other than those that were self-imposed. But The Huntington, located on Oxford and Stratford streets, also triggered a flashback to my undergraduate experience in England in the early 1960s. As the grandson of East European immigrant Jews and the son of nouveau riche entrepreneurs from the provinces, I had felt out of place at Oxford among so many Protestant toffs and gentlemen scholars. Nearly forty years later, despite the surrounding buzz of postmodernity, here I was again in an ever-so-proper institution that longs for the imagined solidity of the Victorian past. I was sure that I had entered the world of period costume dramas so beloved of PBS when The Huntington invited its Junior Fellows to an evening of Cocktails and Croquet: "White attire is suggested" and Pimm's Cups will be served.

A few weeks after my arrival, at the end of June, a meeting was called to brief staff and researchers about one of The Huntington's holdings, a rare original copy of the 1935 Nuremberg Laws. The library's administrators wanted to give us their spin on why they had decided to loan what they called the "Hitler Materials" to a Jewish cultural center in West Los Angeles, after preserving them secretly and off the books since General George Patton stashed them at The Huntington in 1945. The loan was a grand media event, covered around the world in more than 1,000 print and 600 television stories. But rather than greeting this act of interinstitutional generosity as an opening in the Pasadena Wall, some reporters were nosy: they wanted to know why The Huntington had kept the documents so hush-hush for fifty-four years. "The question being asked by many," raised by Jack Ford on NBC's *Today* show, was "Why did the Huntington Library simply hold these documents in a vault for more than fifty years rather than give the public access to them?" Good question, I thought.

But to The Huntington, the past was a closed book. "No good deed goes unpunished," sighed Robert Skotheim, the library's distinguished president, at the June meeting. "The press has tried to make a story where there isn't one," added the curator of rare manuscripts. The briefing concluded with the presentation of a bouquet of flowers to The Huntington's communications director in gratitude for the way she had handled a suspicious media. As the audience politely applauded, she stood smiling on stage in front of a huge blow-up of Hitler's laws for the "safeguarding of German blood and honor," the legislation that put the Reichstag's rubber stamp of approval on what would eventually become the Final Solution.

I left this surreal tableau and wandered around in a daze. The next day I started a new project on the missing fifty-four years. When my research *at* The Huntington turned into research *on* The Huntington, in particular how racism and anti-Semitism permeated the institution after World War II, the atmosphere quickly turned chilly. "You're acting more like a journalist than a researcher," an administrator chided me, as if there couldn't be a worse insult. And all of a sudden certain files were off limits.

For the first time in my academic career I was doing research on anti-Semitism. When a contact tipped me off that General Patton had once admired *Mein Kampf*, I began reading up on Nazi propaganda. "Excuse me," I asked a clerk at the local Barnes and Noble in Pasadena, "do you have anything by Hitler?" "Would that be Adolf?" he asked politely.

My Jewish identity opened doors that otherwise would have been shut. It was as though I had discovered the Jewish equivalent of the Masons' secret handshake. As word got out about my investigation, people came to me with their ex-officio stories. "I'm Jewish," one secretary admitted to me in lowered voice.

"I was never invited to lunch with people in the seventies because of my wife's Jewish accent," confided a long-time researcher.

"I stopped doing research there in the eighties because the place was so anti-Semitic," another told me.

"I don't like going there, too WASP," commented a Jewish librarian from a local university.

"When I first started working here at The Huntington," a curator recalled, "I would get at least one inquiry every year from somebody who wanted to know whether we had any books made from human skin. Now where did that idea come from?"

Another curator led me to a photograph of General Patton holding a presentation copy of *Mein Kampf* that hangs in the corridor of the Rare Book Department. "We pass it every day."

The more I heard these confessions, the more I felt like the protagonist in Nathaniel West's novel, who begins his job as the cynical Agony Aunt columnist for a newspaper and ends up inseparable from the desperate people who send their cries for help to Miss Lonelyhearts. "You're becoming really Jewish," observed Cecilia, the Irish Catholic redhead who likes to put a potpourri of saintly tchotchkes over my desk to ward off evil spirits. "Really Jewish?" I shot back, hunting for innuendo, but I knew she was on to something.

My research on the Nuremberg Laws took me to the other world of Los Angeles, to a four-year-old institution nestled in the Santa Monica Mountains. Unlike The Huntington, the (small-*t*) Skirball is not a museum or library but a cultural center, organized around themes of Jewish life in the New World. It's an optimistic story, presented Hollywood-style in concerts, videos, and star-studded performances, as well as through traditional icons and artifacts. And it's not just for Jews. "We want this to be a surrogate home for everyone," proclaims Uri Herscher, the Skirball's visionary founder and president.

The Skirball may be a place "where cultures connect," but its core is Judaism, and this was the first time in a long time that I had hung out in a Jewish institution. I feel uneasy here too, especially in the main permanent exhibit, "Jewish Life from Antiquity to America." As a child in England I'd fidgeted through pious accounts of heroic tenacity against all odds. The linear story line of an epic journey by The Jewish People from the wilderness of Egypt to the Promised Land of West Los Angeles grates on my analytical sensibilities. I prefer my identity politics much more porous.

I quickly walk past the upbeat story of Jewish progress until I come to the case displaying the Nuremberg Laws, finally on public display after fifty-four years in The Huntington's nuclear-proof basement. The few sheets of typewritten decrees, banal indeed, are dwarfed by the huge vanity copy of *Mein Kampf*, which Patton claimed as a war trophy in April 1945. As I watch elderly visitors linger before the exhibit and peer into the gloomy cabinet, I too become immersed in present absences: my father's silence about his impressions of the concentration camps, my grandparents' nose for whiffs of danger, my brother-in-law's chiding about my ambivalent identity. I stop to chat with volunteers and docents, middle-aged Jewish women with strong opinions and a rooted presence, so much like my mother before her zest turned bitter. The familiarity takes me by surprise.

Note

1. Earlier drafts of this essay benefited from helpful comments by and discussions with Frances Payne Adler, Rina Benmayor, David Edgar, Bob Gould, Ed McCaughan, Cecilia O'Leary, Dennis Sherman, Janet Wolff, and Howard Zinn.

CHAPTER 7

Walking with Lao Tzu at Auschwitz

DeWitt Clinton

Back in the early 1960s my father, a Methodist minister, sometimes offered his parishioners a special program of his Holy Land slides—hundreds it seemed, pictures of rocks, stones, rocks, and more stones. It was a long night of ancient Israel. Was it in that same year that our church, his church, had its first Passover seder, probably in the spring, close to Easter? I vaguely recall wearing a bathrobe and rubber flip-flops and eating olives, probably with pimentos. Did we have hummus and pita? A favorite food now, but I'm not sure what we ate so long ago. The lentil soup wasn't half as good as the soup I now eat regularly at a local Middle Eastern restaurant.

That was the first model seder I can ever recall "reclining" for. Dad talked about the Hebrews of the desert way back in the Book of Exodus. This was in Kansas, Dodge City. What's a kid to think? What's the chance of anyone getting out of the desert alive so long ago? After all, wasn't the book pretty old? No one there is alive today, right? Such was my very poor Sunday school view of Jews in the desert, even though the seder in Dodge City was pretty cool. Despite the neat clothes, Dad's talk, the olives, I still wasn't moved enough to go find any Hebrews. I assumed there were none to be found. Besides, what did I know about the Sinai Peninsula?

I went off to a Methodist undergraduate college with the high aspirations of becoming someone just like my dad, a Methodist minister. By the end of the first year, I had begun to wonder about it all, despite the overly dramatic professor of Old Testament who often would jump onto the front desk and rant at us as if he were Elijah. Somehow the idea of Methodist seminary began to wane. As an emergency strategy, I tried the Peace Corps, but that failed too. So in the summer of 1968, having never found any more Hebrews after all those classes, except in the Book, I trained in Missouri, and later in Oklahoma, for battle tactics in Vietnam. Still no Hebrews. By the time my tour was over, I had completely rejected seminary, thought of

lay work in the church, forgot that, and then, for the next seventeen years or
so, forgot everything and anything religious or spiritual, even though I did
have some hummus and pita, stood under a sukkah, ate a Hillel sandwich,
and actually made friends with a few graduate school classmates who were
Jews, not Hebrews. I'm sure John Wesley read about the Hebrews in the
Old Testament of his Bible, but I'm not sure he invited them to his prayer
sessions when he was preaching out in the English countryside. I'm sure he
didn't see any in the New World either, though quite a few had made it
even before he landed.

It wasn't until I walked sheepishly into a synagogue in Milwaukee in
the late 1980s, accompanying my wife, who was looking into Judaism, that
I ever really found out about living, praying Jews. That Friday night I probably became a Jew, much to the surprise of my dead Methodist father, who
would never know, but it would concern his widow, my mother, who eventually thought I might not get into heaven if I took Naftali ben Abraham as
my new name and identified myself with the "Hebrew people." I had finally found them. They had actually made it out of the Book of Exodus, even
though the ones leaving Egypt all died; their children made it to the
Promised Land with the help of Joshua, or at least that's how the story
goes. It's a long story, and I've been enraptured by story, allegory,
metaphor, symbol, image, and motif most of my life.

My next seder after Dodge City occurred without a bathrobe and flip-
flops. There was no pita and hummus, no olives. There was a frightening
serving of some kind of molded white fish that I slathered in horseradish,
having had neither before, only to surprise myself with the searing of my
nostrils. We never, never, had such gefilte fish back in old Dodge City. This
food was served on white linen tables, there was an "order" to it all, and
over the years as I began to put the different parts of the story together, it
made more and more sense. The part that seemed especially wonderful was
when the rabbi opened the front doors of the synagogue and in great anticipation of Elijah's arriving *finally* said, if he should arrive, class will be canceled tomorrow. Cool. No more Old Testament classes. Just Hebrew Bible
classes.

Before all that happened, though, my wife would come home from the
synagogue on Sundays and tell me about all the stories she was told, and
now they all sounded so much more interesting, intriguing, than what I
remembered from college lectures about the Old Testament and even earlier, when I was prepping for a license to preach. I don't even remember
Abraham ever coming up much in Dad's sermons, nor did I ever hear anything about Torah or *Nevi'im* or *Ketuvim*. Now I was beginning to feel like
one of those weary travelers joining up with Abraham's small tribe, not a
straggler, but someone at the rear. Slowly, page by page, I made my way
further back toward those Hebrews, for now they were talking about sto-

ries and rituals that seemed astoundingly beautiful and incomparably spiritual.

Then I met the person my wife spoke so much about, a retired psychology professor from the University of Wisconsin–Milwaukee, the one teaching adult classes at the synagogue on Sundays, who had left Germany just before the 1938 Kristallnacht pogrom. But then I didn't even know what Kristallnacht was, because I had no understanding of the Shoah. Like any kid in eleventh grade, I guess, I had read William Schirer's *The Rise and Fall of the Third Reich*, but for the life of me I couldn't remember, all through college or Vietnam or grad school, anything he wrote about the Holocaust. I'm afraid to go back and look, which would only confirm either my poor memory of reading or Schirer's disinterest in talking about death camps and Zyklon-B. Little did I know then, on first meeting this Herman Weil from Frankfurt, a student of Martin Buber and the *I and Thou*, that he would take me into his home and his heart, where my wife and I would come to know him and his wife as our own parents, the ones who made it out.

Several times I've looked at photographs of prisoners at Buchenwald in the glass cases at the United States Memorial Holocaust Museum in Washington, D.C. It was only after Herman died that I tried to see if I could find him there. Was he standing at *achtung* for hours and hours each day? Did he see what I saw in the photograph of ten Jews hanging from a gallows? The more I looked, the closer I moved to the glass, the more I would see my own reflection peering out. Herman's wife, Berta, saved his life in Buchenwald by reporting to officials in Hamburg that he was French born, a son of Alsace Lorraine. She walked into Nazi headquarters, presented Herman's birth documents to a desk sergeant, and pleaded for his release.

Herman never spoke of Buchenwald. Why should he? He only described the quiet walk home, with him worrying that he would be rearrested as an escapee because he was still in prison garb. In a matter of days he, his wife, and their child were at Bremen, then New York, then Iowa, then Milwaukee, where he would read about Germany's battles and the Holocaust. Much as he tried, he and Berta were unable to bring their parents out of Germany.

Years later, standing outside a bookstore in Lodz, Poland, I found an edition of Art Spiegelman's *Maus*, and though I couldn't read a word of Polish, I had a very clear sense of the graphic panels since I had to some degree been introduced to the Holocaust through *Maus* upon the recommendation of a Jewish friend and colleague at my university. Though a seventh-grader could pick it up and understand it, I found the college students I taught as stunned as I was when I first read it, just a few years before my teacher and mentor Herman died.

Little did I know then that I was preparing to stand in a women's barracks in Auschwitz-Birkenau (or Auschwitz II) on a cold June day by myself, listening to rain on the roof, looking into the shadows, running my hand back and forth across the wood bunks, wondering if I would hear even a whisper of Yiddish or Greek or Romanian, or anything Vladek Spiegelman might have seen at Birkenau as his son Art tried to imagine in his graphic novel. Nothing but the rain. The barracks had been swept clean. No fecal smells. No cacophony. No mournful wails. It was more like an empty barn, abandoned years earlier. Whoever was once here is now dead, in ashes that drifted over Poland long ago. I didn't know, even as a young adult, how many had come here, how many Jews had been brought to all these places of incineration and hard labor. I had no idea how many.

Sometimes I'm still back in Dodge City with the bathrobe and flip-flops, pretending to imagine the early seders in Jerusalem. Sometimes I see myself in Holocaust stories, in the poems, in the plays, in the memoirs—the association and identification so powerful, I sometimes can barely comprehend that I am sitting on the sofa in our safe home, protected, for the most part, from frightening knocks on our front door in the middle of the night.

After our conversions to Judaism, long after our "Jewish" second wedding ceremony in Liberty Park in Jerusalem, long after climbing Masada, or standing on the Golan Heights, long after a bar mitzvah where I froze in the middle of a Haftarah blessing, long after studies with the rabbis, long after aspiring to become even a rabbinic aide, or an outreach fellow helping others to understand Judaism and possible conversion, I started reading in Eastern religions, at first in preparation for teaching a course at the university where I work, but later simply wanting to learn more about the Buddha or the Dalai Lama or Thich Nhat Hanh. At the end of the road, barely in sight, was an old Chinese sage, bending over his horse with a bad case of back pain, almost on the edge of the universe, when the border guard asked him to write down his wisdom. And there I was, picking it up, astounded with the paradoxes of wu-wei and yin-yang.

For weeks, months, I found myself slowed down to a crawl with these writings of Lao Tzu, the *Tao Te Ching*. At first I wanted to clear my calendar, stop interfering in anyone else's life, get out of the meddling business, and for once live moment by moment, experience by experience. I found the best way to do this was to continue my classes in Hatha Yoga in a walk-up studio in the Third Ward of old Milwaukee. In part, I had been consumed with the Holocaust, mainly through the creative artists who could remember, or imagine it. And as a professor, I not only had taken to introducing the Book of Exodus to my undergraduate students but had also taken them to India, Tibet, and now China through study of Asian religions.

Was it in the middle of a Triangle Pose, Virabbhadrasana II, that it all coalesced into a perplexing title? Stepping out of the pose, I walked over to my coat, took out a small writing pad, and wrote down something that made no sense but in time would take me into places as a poet I never had traveled to and never will again. But for the moment, the most intriguing thing was simply this odd title that appeared to me, and I knew, given my poor memory, that I should write it down, even if it made no sense: "title for a poem? Reading the *Tao* at Auschwitz."

For weeks I didn't know what to make of it. I even asked my Internet writing group if they had any suggestions. One of them said, get back to the *Tao*. Of course; how stupid could I be? Take the *Tao* to Starbucks, take the journal, and see what happens. In the months to come, while on sabbatical to prepare a course on the literature of the Holocaust, I began to shape a poem that seemed to be the apotheosis of everything I had learned as a poet, and as a reader of the Holocaust, and as a novice to the *Tao*. I had to unlearn everything I knew as a poet, I had to remember everything I knew as a poet, I had to draw upon nothing of the Holocaust, I had to draw upon everything I'd ever read, seen, wondered about, imagined, thought, taught, puzzled over regarding the Holocaust. Where would I begin? With Starbucks coffee of the day pouring into my body, I opened the *Tao*.

As a poet, I've often written about history and place without ever standing in the place I'm envisioning. In the 1970s I pored over a Mayan holy book, *The Chilam Balam of Chumayel,* and becoming so engrossed in the images, the metaphors, the sweep of history, that I began writing my own version, somewhat jazzier than the original. During the writing of those conquistador narratives, I simply felt my way through the history of the Mayans, the Incas, and their first contact with the European gods who rode on horses. It was only years later that I found myself walking toward the Mayan cenote at Chichen Itza. Gazing into the almost dry well hole, I wondered how I was ever able to visualize years before this place, the capital of the Mayas, simply by reading their holy texts. The day with my wife at Chichen Itza stays with me now, even if I forget the lines of the narrative poems I once wrote.

The same was true for writing about the Incas and Pizarro and Atahualpa. Someday I will climb the last steps to Machu Picchu, but then, back in the 1970s, my journey was to rewrite, improvise even, the grand histories of the Incas from their first history, *The Royal Commentaries* by Garcilaso de la Vega. The mediator I invented for these ancient stories was the Native American trickster Coyote. In years to come, this mediator would become an old Chinese sage gazing into the horror of Auschwitz-Birkenau.

So even though my wife and I had paid our tickets to join a group of college students in their journey to see the places of the Holocaust in

Lithuania and Poland, as I began writing "Reading the *Tao* at Auschwitz" it never occurred to me that I wasn't there already, walking amidst all the suffering, disease, and death of the early 1940s. I could never explain properly to friends and colleagues why Lao Tzu was there. All I knew is that I found it incredibly interesting that I could fast-forward this Chinese hermit to Oswiecim, Poland, and through his mediation, as I wrote from the eastside of Milwaukee, perhaps we could find something that had not been said before about the worst place in the world.

In time to come, I realized that I did not want to write an eighty-one-section poem about Auschwitz, for there was no point in drawing on every chapter of Lao Tzu's text. But quite a few drew my attention—the ones that seemed to read like odd juxtapositions—something out of order, something impossible to see, something unimaginable. Each day, hovering over the *Tao* with a *grande* Flavor of the Day and a yellow pad, I began walking through the camp. I didn't know the exact layout, but in my mind's eye I began to envision it, having read about it for several years in a variety of forms, narrative memoirs and poems, even a few plays and short stories.

Through the two months of writing this poem, I somehow felt this was what I was destined to write, after all the years, after the hundreds of poems that had been written earlier. I had felt this way only once before, when after reading, then writing, about the death of the Inca king Atahualpa, I began weeping at my writing table, deeply saddened by his death and the European invasion. Now it wasn't Peru, nor China, but a death camp that I still find hard to comprehend.

I wrote as if in a séance, as if in a trance, hardly noticing anything of the world in March and April of just a few years ago. In some ways, it is fair to say I didn't know what I was doing. In other ways, I knew this poem was what I was called to write; how else could I explain how the words poured out in response to just a hint of a text from Lao Tzu? I believe I entered into a state of mind I have never been in before, deeper than simply attending a worship service, more humbling than reading aloud Tefillah, something close to communion with the goddess Poetry herself, and Lao Tzu, and all the dead who commanded me to remember what had happened at this place. By the time I had written twelve or so sections of the poem, I knew that I had found the magic number: in Hebrew, *chai*. I would write eighteen sections, to leave readers with a sense of being cleansed by the rains and snowstorms and heat of this place.

I had hoped to read the poem aloud at the Auschwitz-Birkenau memorial where the crematorium once stood. But June of that year was chilly with constant drizzles in Poland, so I only asked if the Archives Office of the Auschwitz-Birkenau Museum would accept it as a gift. Perhaps I will read it the next time I visit.

How famished we all were after spending several hours at Auschwitz I and II. The sweet Polish chocolate cookies sold at the museum offices

were the most extraordinary cookies I've ever tasted. I ate one after another after another. That evening we ate dinner in the Old Jewish Quarter of Krakow.

Somehow I had found the Hebrews I had always heard about. Somehow they found me. Somehow Lao Tzu's simple instructions had allowed me to hear the empty silence that even he could never have imagined, even if he had crossed the old China border into unknown lands.

Reading the *Tao* at Auschwitz
A Sequence of Poems by DeWitt Clinton

I
In the Beginning we saw Nothing
From Nothing came Something
Something made All of us
Turn into ash only to
Float onto those just Arrived,

Or on farmers, nearby,
Turning us into Soil & Food

II

    "When I no longer have a body
    what trouble have I?" —I, xiii[1]

Having Nothing
We gave away Nothing
Flesh which we Had
Was not ours to keep

III

Imagine, go ahead Imagine
Undressing in a place
Where signs direct
Everyone to Remember your number
To be efficient, your number is used again

IV

    "When the task is accomplished and his work is done
    The people will say, 'It happened to us naturally.'" —I, xvii

Sign to remind us
Of the Work before us
"Arbeit macht frei"

V

    "Between good and evil
    How great is the distance?" —I, xx

What is Good for All
Is not good for All
What is Evil for Some
Is Evil for All
A train bound for Auschwitz
Is a train that's on Time

VI

In Antiquity
We were moved from place to place
Always in the Eye of God
In more recent times
An efficient rail system

Sees to our wandering ways
Always Delivered
Always on Time

VII

>   "When there is not enough faith,
>   There is a lack of good faith." —I, xxiii

Prayer is said Standing
A *Barechu,* a call to Worship
We have not bathed, we are weak
We are too weak to even Speak
Everyday is our Yom Kippur

VIII

>   "One who excels in traveling leaves no wheel
>   tracks." —I, xxvii

In Time to Come This will be
A Place where Tourists come
To weep, or finish what was started
When we all get back to the Bus
On the hottest days
Some will come with Pepsi cans
Some will come bearing bottles of Evian
Some will crave their Swiss chocolat
Some will belch from their late lunch
Some will wander through, amazed
A Place like This was ever Here
Some will stand next to old ovens
Some will look into the lens
In time to come, Uncle Morty will say
You showed us those already

IX

>   "Hence, some things lead and some follow;
>   Some breathe gently and some breathe hard;
>   Some are strong and some are weak;
>   Some destroy and some are destroyed." —I, xxix

Who is the guest? Who is the host?
Clearly we are the bad guests
Who have stayed far too long
Even if we call this our home

The air left in the trains rises
Like the air rises in the showers
Too little, and all of us breathe too hard,
Breathe hard and all will be gone

The strongest scooped in what was there
The weakest sipped what was not there
Only the weakest were there at the Gates
Mouths open, feeding on the foulest air

A dog and a stick in one world is not
A dog and a stick in this world
In this world, a dog and a stick insist:
"Everyone please, please, stay in line"

X

    "The way never acts yet nothing is left undone."
    —I, xxxvii

We needed soup
We needed clothes
We needed penicillin
We needed cots
We needed mothers
We needed water
We needed more soup
We needed flannels
We needed air
We needed guns
We needed prayer
We needed Benji
We needed Marla
We needed all we ever knew
We needed law
We needed time
We needed home
We needed stew
We needed health
We needed Moses
We needed bombs
We needed meals
We needed You

XI

> "Thus a thing is sometimes added to by being
> diminished and diminished by being added to." —II, xlii

This is the way we define each day
Ours with the distinguished face
Scientifically a meager race
Some know the music has begun
Some stand in line until we're all done
Some seek life on the path to the right
Some seek life on the path to the left
This is the way we define each day
At roll call, we face the Book of Life
At roll call, we face the Book of Death
Without a stitch, we stand for *selektion*
Selektion defines our every day
Skin & bones is what we wear
This is who we've all become
Day by day, this is the Way

XII

> "Without looking out the window
> one can see the way of heaven." —II, xlvii

We push as hard as we can everyone in
We pull as hard as we can everyone out
This is our life, until we can do it no more
This is the life of the *sonderkommando*
Now we have pliers to pull out the gold
Now we have scissors to cut the dead hair
Push and pull, pull and poke this is our life
Some of us must move all our kith and kin
Some of us must move all from a putrid room
Into the ovens for baking corpses to ashes
Ashes to ashes dust to dust we never
Thought this is the way to say *kaddish*
Sometimes it is our wives we push
Sometimes it is our children we push
Soon it will be we who will be pushed
No longer able to push ourselves
Soon we all rise a plume so high
We will soon see all there is to see

XIII
Outside our small town
Is our very own dump
Every week we're instructed
To set out our rot & waste
For our very own dump
Every week it goes away
When winds come from the east
All of us close our windows
The stench of our very own dump
Ruins almost every evening event
Certainly no one can (calmly)
Garden when rains bring back
What we once had set out
This is the price for the efficiency
Of having our very own dump

XIV
> "What is firmly rooted cannot be pulled out;
> What is tightly held in the arms will not slip loose;
> Through this the offering of sacrifice by descendants
> will never come to an end." —II, liv

In the desert
We became holy
Guided by God
Guided by a Code
We knew the world was holy
Everything even our
Quiet breath of sleep
Was *kadosh* even the
Air even the fire
We made for all our
Sacrifice—winged, hoofed,
Grains, oil, wine—
All we sacrificed
All we offered whole
Now we are the offering
We are what rises
From this foul place
A rising plume a
Constantly rising
Kaddish of the dead

Never ending
Day and Night
Night and Day
Month by Month
Year by Year

XV

"Do that which consists in taking no action;
pursue that which is not meddlesome;
savour that which has no flavour." —II, lxiii

Each day we hear
The high whine
Each day we feel
The ground tremble
Each day we see
Factories blown sky high
We pray for the President
We pray for the Prime Minister
Each day someone tells
Them about us
Some of us
On no diet
Help with the war effort
Making parts, giving parts
Each day we pray
To be somewhere
In those crosshairs

XVI

"The whole world says that my way is vast and resembles
nothing. It is because it is vast that it resembles nothing.
If it resembled anything, it would, long before now,
have become small." —II, lxvii

Before what we knew as Is
The Nameless One, The One
Who thought of all This,
In order to make what was Thought
Made space for all This
A *tzim tzum* a Space for Space
From what once was Not
A *Bereshit* kind of place

& all that was what once
Resembles nothing of what now Is
Though all who lived in this Place
This place of Labor and Bones
Say Whoever made what This Is
Could not have made what This Is

XVII

    "He who is fearless in being bold will meet with
    his own death; He who is fearless in being timid will
    stay alive." —II, lxxiii

We are the last lot
A lonely lot
A labored lot
We are who you
Cannot see
We are skin & bones
We move slowly
About the place
We hardly
Take up space
We are a corpse
A flickering breath
We can hardly
Hold a spoon
Pictures go right
Through us
We are what you
Can't believe
We are what
Cannot be
In spring in Pesach time
In liberation time
We are the record
Of what was here
We who can hardly walk
We who can hardly talk
We are the ones left
We are the *muselmann*
We barely know we're free

XVIII   *Chai*

"In the world there is nothing more submissive and
weak than water. Yet for attacking that which is hard and
strong, nothing can surpass it." —II, lxxviii

In the World to Come make it rain
Make it snow make it sleet
Make the heat rise up
Let the evening cool the ground
Let the grasses grow
Let the wildflowers grow
Let the bones remain
Beneath all this
Let the rains come
Pouring rains
Howling rains
Sweet rains
Let the snow pile up against the stones
Let the snow sink deep into the ground
Let the dew cleanse each summer day
Let the sun bake the place
Let the moon & the stars
Make evening light of the place
Let the ice thicken all that was here
Let the icicles drip from every roof
Make the skies darken
Make the skies brighten
Let the living start to come back
Let it be a place of memory
A place where some had hoped
We'd all rise & float away
From this place
Ashes rising from this place
Ashes circling as far as one could see
Ashes circling over All
Over Everyone over Everything
Circling a constant circling
A ring forever circling
A constant ringing *S'hma Israel*

Glossary

IV. *Arbeit macht frei:* German for "Work will make you free."

VII. *Barechu:* a portion of the Jewish worship service.

XI. *selektion:* German for random selections to the gas chambers.

XII. *sonderkommando:* German for prisoners forced to work in the gas chambers and crematorium; *kaddish:* Aramaic, closing prayer of the Jewish worship service.

XIV. *kadosh:* Hebrew for holy; holiness.

XVI. *tzim tzum:* Jewish mystical term for God's contraction in order to make room for the creation of the cosmos; *Bereshit:* first word in Hebrew Bible, "In the beginning" or "At the beginning."

XVII. *muselmann:* Arabic, later German, used in the camps for the walking dead.

XVIII. *chai:* Hebrew letter and number 18 designating life; *S'hma Israel:* Hebrew, "Hear O Israel"; the Jewish central affirmation, prayer.

Note

1. Selected readings excerpted in the poem are from the *Tao Te Ching*, a collection of ethical sayings ascribed to a Chinese sage, Lao Tzu, fourth century B.C.E.

PART 2

The Body

The contemporary aphorism "You are what you eat" expresses
not only a cultural preoccupation with bodily health and fitness but also a
historical retreat from the body-mind dualism that was postulated by the
seventeenth-century French philosopher René Descartes. We live our life in
our body, and our sense of self, our identity, is embodied in our skin and
bones, our blood and guts, our heart and sinews. This truism, however, is
often made problematic, as contemporary standards of physical attractiveness and ability impinge on our consciousness to nag at our sense of self-
worth, making us feel forever inadequate, keeping us in pursuit of some
ideal most of us can never achieve (Murphy 1987; Wolf 1992).

There was a time when the "ideal" body was distinguished from the
"normal" body, the latter being an invention of the nineteenth century.
Previously, as Leonard Davis observes, the ideal body, as exemplified in
the tradition of the nude Venus, presented itself as a "mytho-poetic body"
linked to the gods (1997:10). This body was not viewed as attainable by
humans; it was understood that the ideal could never be found in the real
world. In a culture with an ideal body form, Davis argues, everyone is
"below the ideal."

In contrast to the ideal, the concept of the "norm" or "average"—and
eventually of the "normal" as an imperative—began with the collection of
medical and criminal statistics in nineteenth-century France. Sociological
positivist Adolphe Quetelet argued that *l'homme moyen*, or average man,
"was the average of all human attributes in a given country," both a physical average and a moral average (Davis 1997:11). By inference, and more
directly in works such as Victor Hugo's classic historical novel *The
Hunchback of Notre Dame* (1831), the notion of the normal entailed the
construction of its opposite, the physically and morally abnormal.

Hugo's novel, of course, was not an endorsement of the view of his day
but a powerful and provocative critique of the existing social order. As
William Powell points out in his essay, "Becoming Quasimodo: The
Shaping of a Life," Hugo's novel was a critique of "the Catholic church,
the sexual predilections of the priesthood, the dimness of the monarchy and

the body politic, social systems that foment the creation of underclasses, biogtry, mob mentality, and uncaring and unthinking people in general."

Powell has lived his life with a feeling of affinity with the main character of Hugo's novel, Quasimodo. In his teens Powell was diagnosed with "Scheuerman's disease, a hereditary condition of the spine in which growing children . . . develop vertebrae in wedges that bend and curve the whole spine, particularly the upper back and neck." Powell resists defining himself by this condition but finds that he must unavoidably take his back into account when thinking about who is and what he does. This is Powell's story—or at least as much as he chooses to tell—of the pain, both physical and emotional, he has endured. It is a story about what it is like to live with a stigma, to live as an outsider. However, Powell's is also a story of courage, of perseverance in the face of adversity, a story that would have made Quasimodo proud.

The theme of the body as stigmatized outsider is also explored in **Laura Miller**'s "No Body Is Exempt: Beauty Compulsion and Resistance in Japan." When Miller first began her anthropological research on Japanese beauty salons, she felt like an outsider to this experience. But she soon found it impossible to remain disengaged. Miller initially thought that Japanese culture, unlike American culture, was marked by enduring respect and appreciation for the elderly. She hadn't anticipated the globalization of the cult of youth, in which all women are judged by comparable standards of beauty. Miller discovered that Japanese women, too, were worried about their breast size, weight, body hair, hairstyle, and facial features and were seeking remedies for their culturally constructed (albeit internalized) inadequacies. In the course of Miller's research, the salon workers she interviewed insisted that her body was also in need of treatments. Miller, who had previously been quite comfortable with her "artsy hippie professor" look, started to wonder whether her appearance was "grossing people out" and whether her own aging "body was still not absolved of the female duty to be beautiful."

The pregnant woman as outsider is the subject of **Darcie Vandegrift**'s essay on the body. In "Mama's Always on Stage: The Absurdity of the Pregnant Academic," Vandegrift describes the reaction of graduate students and professorial colleagues to her first pregnancy, to the symbolic meanings of her changing shape, as her "body became an on-site Rorschach exam reflecting others' projections about how gender, sexuality, and economy intersected in the workplace." Vandegrift's experiences demonstrate both continued ambivalence toward and supportive acceptance for women who perform productive and reproductive labor simultaneously. She interprets these reactions, and the position of pregnant women in academe, as interconnected with a broader array of transgressive identities that are provoking universities to "acknowledge our multiplicitous humanness."

Marga Ryersbach, too, finds that her body doesn't quite fit in with the social order around her. However, it is not the shape of her body but how she expresses it sexually that is the theme of her essay. In "Sexual Boundaries: Trespasses into Chaos," Ryersbach writes about her bisexuality and "plays with gendered power and [her] assertions and submissions in the arena of sexuality." It has not been easy for Ryersbach to live in the borderlands of sexuality, and she has incurred many wounds for her trespasses, especially because those who "adhere to sexual practices that are unintelligible to others" have their identities invalidated. But for Ryersbach, sexuality is part of a project of making her life art. It is the essence of her freedom, a freedom found in "the chaos that refuses closure and denies solidification," that defies society's impulse to define, to limit the type of person she chooses to be.

While life as chaos is a theme of **Diane Schaefer**'s essay, hers is a chaos that is not of her own choosing. Schaefer's life has been haunted by internal demons, demons that she believes have roots in the socioeconomic conditions of her family, demons that for years usurped her claims to a better life. In "The Razor's Edge: Narcotics and the Embodiment of Trauma," Schaefer writes of the internalization of socially structured trauma and of her experience of abuse that ate away at her soul, her sense of self-esteem. She turned to narcotics, and the people who used them, to redeem herself, to find comfort. But she knew all along she was living on a razor's edge, poised to fall into the abyss of a bodily anesthetized existence that could ultimately lead to death. Pulling herself out of this trap required an internal fortitude that is indicative of our species' inherent will to survive, of our need to free our spirit so that we may embrace the "possibility of glorious joy" that life can offer.

Perseverance in the face of adversity is a theme of several essays in this book. In "Hoop Dreams on Wheels," the concluding piece in this section on the body, **Ronald Berger** tells "a story that hinges on the question of how one rises to the occasion and that exhibits an 'ethic of inspiration' rooted in woundedness but that refuses to give in to despair." Berger's essay is about disabled bodies, a subject that presented itself to him through his daughter's condition of cerebral palsy. He was "searching for role models, for people who possessed insight about living with a disability," to help face this challenge in his life.

Berger describes the circumstances that led to his involvement with dedicated wheelchair basketball players, individuals whose stories of accomplishment he finds inspiring. He writes about the lives of three of these athletes and, in doing so, questions the critique of the "supercrip" that is prevalent in the disability community. "Supercrips" are individuals whose inspirational stories of courage, dedication, and hard work prove that one can defy the odds and accomplish the impossible. The concern is that these stories foster unrealistic expectations about what people with dis-abilities could achieve if only they tried hard enough. It fosters the myth of the self-made person that mitigates society's responsibility to change, to accommodate itself to the needs of people whose bodies are different. However, as Berger suggests, the stories of the athletes he knows indicate that they did not make it on their own. Their lives must be understood in social context: their successes were enabled by the actions of others. Berger writes that he has learned that disability, like illness, can present itself as an opportunity to become what Arthur Frank calls a *dyadic* or *communicative* body, a body that teaches by being "a body *for* other bodies," a body that turns fate and contingency into agency and that reflects "confidence in what is waiting to emerge" (Frank 1995:37, 171).

CHAPTER 8

Becoming Quasimodo: The Shaping of a Life

William E. Powell

Once upon a time, I was a little boy who began to grow up crooked. Perhaps god suggested that I "get bent" and I took it literally. Most boys grow straight upward as they age, but as I grew older my back began to bend and hurt. As I began bending, my sense of being and looking different from my peers grew more pronounced. Now as I write this recollection I am a white-haired man on the cusp of old age, a man who still takes "my back" into account when I think about who I am and what I do.

For more than forty years my back has had a hump and my head and neck have bent forward. I have to recline my seat in automobiles so that my head is straight up and I can see ahead clearly. Back spasms, headaches, and the painful grating of my neck vertebrae on each other have become a condition of life, and there is no comfortable position in which to sit or stand for more than a minute or two. When I walk I must constantly monitor my balance and my feet—they wobble and drag and I am prone to frequent stumbling. I have grown accustomed to the person I am, though I confess to constant frowning from the effort to appear and function normally. Things could be a lot worse, and I am grateful for what I can and have accomplished.

For the past decade and a half I have carried around in my mind and heart a novel that I have begun to write, a novel about the heirs of Quasimodo. The vicissitudes of life sensitize us to story lines that we come across, and I recall stumbling across Victor Hugo's *The Hunchback of Notre Dame* (1831) in my childhood. That novel's story line, though fraught with complex plot devices, resonated with my life and became a subtle framework for weaving together my observations about the foibles of humankind. The story line and characters have evolved, in my adult years, into a garden for cultivating aspects of my life and imagination.

Before I discuss the progression and effects of my physical malady on my life course, it would be helpful to remind readers of the story that brought the character Quasimodo into being. In a nutshell, the story line of *The Hunchback* is this.

In the early fifteenth century in Paris, a malformed baby boy is abandoned on the doorstep of Notre Dame. His mother then abducts a more beautiful baby to replace the one she just abandoned. The baby with the grotesque face and humped back is raised by a priest and ultimately becomes the bell ringer of Notre Dame. That duty and his appearance socially isolate him, but he earns his keep at the expense of his hearing. The bells' noise deafens him. As a deaf, disfigured, and rather grotesque young person, Quasimodo the feral bell ringer becomes the central character in the novel.

All of the other characters in the book respond only to his physical appearance. None see beyond the outer trappings to his intelligence or his ability to care and love. In his childhood he develops a strong, one-sided attachment to the priest who took him in, but the priest is uncaring, calculating, overly critical, and eventually lustful over an object of Quasimodo's affection. In the course of a local celebration, Quasimodo becomes the butt of people's scorn without realizing the humiliating role he is serving, and after a minor transgression he is lashed with a whip in a public flogging. A young gypsy woman (actually the infant his mother had replaced him with, now grown) takes some mercy on him and gives him water when he cries out in thirst and pain. He experiences the first touch of kindness in his life and is enchanted by the young woman. The gypsy girl, Esmeralda, is a self-absorbed adolescent, however, who is oblivious to the effect she has had on Quasimodo.

Esmeralda, in turn, is smitten with a dashing officer in the local militia. He responds to her beauty but is troubled by her low social status and doesn't respond to her as a viable candidate for a relationship. Later, a rumor is heard that something dire has happened to the officer, and local officials assume that the gypsy girl Esmeralda has done him harm (the fifteenth-century version of "let's find a scapegoat" when bad things happen). In lynch mob fashion they quickly sentence her to death. Quasimodo sees the crowd's intentions and rescues her in dramatic fashion. He carries her off to the church seeking sanctuary. The priest feels stirrings in his loins and begins to lust after Esmeralda.

Meanwhile, the rabble and constabulary attempt to storm the church to lynch her. Keeping her safe in the bell tower, Quasimodo protects her by flinging down heavy objects on the crowd below. Political pressure is applied to the priest to give her up; when she rebuffs his advances he blames her for enchanting him and gives her over to the crowd. She is summarily and grotesquely hanged. Quasimodo is understandably distraught by the treachery of the priest, his ersatz father, and flings him to his death from atop the cathedral. Some years later, in a building in which the hanged and the indigent of Paris are left to rot, a skeleton of a hunchbacked man is found holding and embracing the remains of a young woman with a broken neck. Quasimodo is loyally united in death with the object of his love.

The potboiler that is *The Hunchback* served as a vehicle for Hugo to lampoon the Catholic Church, the sexual predilections of the priesthood, the dimness of the monarchy and the body politic, social systems that foment the creation of underclasses, bigotry, mob mentality, and uncaring and unthinking people in general. Quasimodo, an innocent without guile, is the only character in the novel capable of love and caring. But the goodness of his heart is obscured by his appearance.

For the "me" that began to bend as a teen, Hugo's *The Hunchback* became a story line that metaphorically resonated with my own experience and upon which I could hook personal observations about the world. In a very personal sense, it became a literary precursor to the underlying message of David Rosenhan's "Being Sane in Insane Places" (1973): we are so accustomed to insanity that we become oblivious to sanity itself. Further, when we consent to insanity as normality, we cease to care about what sanity is.

The thread of events I describe in this attempt at a narrative about "growing up" happened in the context of a much fuller and richer life story. I stored the memories that form the substance of my narrative many years ago in rural Indiana, and the winnowing of what was to be stored and what was to be ignored was done by my much younger self. Had I the ability to go back and rerecord minutiae of my life, I would try to remember more, but that younger self was not an academic and not selective or objective about information. The words attached to my memories as I call them up were recorded in a "voice" with a dialect different from the one I speak now. That former, younger voice will seep into my narrative. There are many things that occurred in my youth that I will never discuss. That caveat notwithstanding, this is a narrative of the effects of Scheuerman's Kyphosis on my development and the course of my life.

I was born at the tail end of World War II between the surrenders of Germany and Japan. My father was more than twice my mother's age, and they married shortly before I was born. We lived in a series of apartments in a soot-blanketed, low-rent, working-class neighborhood next to a large railroad yard in a medium-sized Indiana city. The soot from the coal-fired steam locomotives was so thick that little grass grew and everything that didn't move acquired a dark coat.

Siblings came along in my first six years, and a family grew. I was a precocious kid with an early and well-developed memory. My mother was very imaginative, bright, and humorous. My father was quiet, moody, reserved, caring, and rather clueless about the demands of being a parent and spouse. If my parents had been birds they would have made a rather lopsided nest. In my early years we moved to a small rural Indiana town from the city in which I was born. My mother's large extended family lived in that area, and I found myself immersed in a family of which I had previously been only vaguely aware. The move entailed moving away from frequent contact with my father's small extended family to equally frequent contact with my mother's much larger one. My parents had no automobile, so I lost contact with my father's family.

I enrolled in school in that small town, but during our first year we had to move from our house. We were grudgingly taken in by relatives. The six of us lived in one upstairs room. We lived there for well over a year, and I intensely recall the realization that our presence was resented. It was unpleasant being where you were not wanted, and that was a particularly unhappy period of my life. I began to be tardy and miss school—it was difficult to be self-conscious, fearful, and unhappy around others. I learned firsthand the imprint of depression and shame and anger on a young life.

Fortunately, I also discovered the power of compassion, humor, simple kindness and caring, and mattering to people. There were occasional teachers and townspeople who noticed me and were more aware of me than I knew. One teacher especially took an interest in my artistic endeavors, while others encouraged my penchant for reading. One even appreciated my cynical sense of humor. An ancient great-aunt talked with me often and treated me as a treasure of great value in her solitude. My mother helped me find refuge in the town library, and between the first and second grades I discovered good novels and began reading incessantly. Early on I learned that while some people can shame and resent you, the kindness of others can save you. An experience of mattering or counting, to some extent, balances exclusion. Or, to paraphrase Shakespeare, those who plumb sullen ground to find bright metal are creation's grace notes.

In time we found another house—the only house in town without an indoor toilet and proper heat. It was a decrepit old place with a tin roof and broken windows, sandwiched between a railroad track and a grain elevator. We learned to sleep in freezing rooms and go to the bathroom in an outdoor toilet that stank in the summer and froze your butt in the winter. The starkness of our daily existence was broken by my mother's imagination, sense of humor, and inclination to play, and by my father's quiet presence. We played imaginative games and listened to soap operas on the radio at night—a darkened room added to the suspense and intrigue and also saved electricity. My mother made life interesting and tolerable, taught us games, and gave us great freedom to roam and explore. We became more than a bit feral. My father was not one to mince words, and we kids all began to speak a pronounced lower-class, rural, Hoosier dialect and could swear like troopers. The coarseness and bluntness of our language aside, we were never permitted to lose our tempers or resort to violence. Other than kindness, little else was sacred.

We also acquired the subtle wry humor that laced the local Hoosier dialect—a little-recognized national treasure, the double-speak of the downtrodden. Spoken well, that regional "mother tongue" is still old familiar music to my ears. The dialect, however, didn't cause us to be confused with "properly bred people" or Rhodes scholars. As a kid I was tacitly aware of the linkage of language to class and place and how language distinguished and embedded people in distinct places in our culture. As I write this now, the words and phrases that come from my memory are those fashioned and stored by the voice of that child I was then. The language of home was the language with which I learned to joke, soften the world with humor, dream, and converse with like-minded souls.

When we moved to the decrepit house on the opposite side of town, we acquired a new landlord who behaved like a total jerk. We hated his princely visits to collect his forty dollars per month, his insults and hostility, and his constant inspections of the house. Years later he died in Guyana, having mutated into "the Reverend Jim Jones." Strange, the lives of others with which our own lives intersect. More's the pity that he took so many other souls with him.

Getting adequate food and clothing in those years was very problematic—the town pharmacist once commented that I was so skinny that I "looked like I had worms." My parents were proud, but we kids became increasingly aware that our lives weren't like those of most others. We didn't have a car, didn't have money for school functions, got cheap Christmas gifts donated by a local church, didn't get routine health or dental care, didn't eat at school with the other kids (nor did we eat much at all), weren't involved in the social life of the community, and certainly didn't have much in the way of material possessions. We learned that for the sake of trying to fit in, however, it was best to put on a good front, go to church regularly, and keep things on the home front private. Keeping up appearances, it was then called.

One thing that my burgeoning social awareness did was make the lines of distinction between my family and others more apparent. We were treated as outsiders, and I sought reasons to explain why we weren't like other people, why there seemed to be a wall between us and them. I learned to resent what I saw as others' inclusion in the community and our exclusion and wanted to understand why we lived as we did. That search for explanation and understanding modified the lens through which I viewed the world and the possibilities I perceived as open to me. It shaped how I conceived myself.

We learned that we weren't "poor" or excluded purely because of income—there were other factors as well. In that community such differences remained implicit rather than explicit. I do recall references to "your kind," though I didn't know what that meant. I learned that being poor came with some causal attribution. In the world of that time and place the reason usually came down to character or laziness or moral defect or inadequacy, or all of those combined. The world wasn't conceived as a place in which people had different odds for success; you or your folks simply weren't up to it or were inherently of "lesser stock." Perhaps adults then knew better, but the message for kids was that advantage was largely a matter of innate human worth. If you had less you were worth less. While I knew that other families did more things together and socialized more, it just didn't occur to me that we could actually expect more. Most certainly, the social order became deeply ingrained in us—we knew our place and were mired in it.

While I learned to question the fairness of people's opportunities and standard of living vis-à-vis our own, I somehow also accepted that inequalities were "just the way things are." "Know your place and don't beat your head against the wall" was a tacit motto that we absorbed but also, more important, saw enacted. I learned to hear and internalize opposites without reconciling them. Unreconciled contradictions are a good breeding ground for softly seething anger.

As I began to be more aware of social inequities, other issues began presenting themselves. Changing events and circumstances and awareness became intertwined in my life's narrative, and its thread became a rope. Life did not become more simple, it simply became more complex.

That we rarely socialized with others seemed vaguely connected to who we were and somehow correlated to my father's estrangement from the community. I recognized that my parents were both bright, caring people, albeit temperamentally unsuited to one another. Neither of them had marketable skills. My mother had graduated from high school, but my father had gone only through the eighth grade. Both had grown up in difficult circumstances and learned to "make do." I perceived no commanding flaws in them that served as an explanation for their being stuck on the lower rung of the social ladder. I came to realize that life was simply giving us the short end of the stick for reasons I could not clearly discern. In short, I developed an early but puzzled social awareness as well as powerful feelings about unfairness and inequality and social justice. I also became readily angered by mistreatment and realized no correlation between human promise and economic well-being. But anger and resentment and disinclination to back down from anything did little to help my social skills or to show a viable way out of the fix we were in. The slow, seeping realization that you don't matter to society is more subtly corrosive than most people know.

I went regularly to school, did reasonably well, and cultivated my creativity, imagination, and humor. I had the freedom in my late grade- and middle-school years to venture far and wide, exploring and looking for rocks for my rock collection, gathering woods violets in every shade and hue between white and purple, building models, and working on charity drives because I was allowed to sort through the coins and exchange Indianhead pennies for money I got from cashing in returnable pop bottles. I learned to camp in the woods for days at a time and to make gas balloons from dry-cleaner bags and attach messages to them. I even made friends with the town's hobo or tramp. The latter became a lengthy and significant relationship, in which I first discovered that I could matter to others for my own ability to notice and care.

That free lifestyle resulted in a bit of eccentricity, and I became a cynical and private young man. My rather solitary lifestyle, while interesting, also didn't enhance my adolescent social and romantic skills or help me cultivate a circle of close friends. Lone wolves rarely dance in cotillions.

I evolved into the scrawny, invisible kid with the chronically runny nose and allergies. Much of my substantial vocabulary could have rendered a sailor speechless, and eloquence was reserved for matters of the heart. My first bloom of noticeable physical growth began in my early teens. I began getting taller and thinner just as things began to decay at home. My father's health began to deteriorate markedly, and he could no longer work as a printer. He became the town's night watchman—an even lower-paying though physically undemanding job. My mother also began getting tired more easily and ultimately developed myasthenia gravis, a disease of progressive muscle weakness that particularly affects one's breathing and endurance.

My father became a sick old man who withdrew more and more into his shell. He and I rarely talked deeply, and he was rather secretive about his past life and his family background. I knew that he had "ridden the rails for a while" and had worked in a traveling circus, as a bootlegger during Prohibition, as a printer, and at sundry other jobs. I also discovered at that time that his grandmother, who helped raise him, was "dark skinned" and that the name by which we knew him wasn't his true name. At different points in his life he had assumed different pseudonyms. It was difficult relating to an older, physically ill, remote father who was private and very mysterious. I developed a lifelong yearning to learn my family's secrets. Weighty stuff for an adolescent to grapple with.

My physical growth as an adolescent began to accelerate at the same time that my parents' health and our family finances crashed. I became lanky and gawky and skinny and malnourished. I retreated into books and began to read nonstop and do little homework, having learned that I could get acceptable grades in spite of not studying. Scholarship was not a passion, just a bare necessity. At that point in life I started having constant backaches and vague visceral stirrings—twinges and cramps.

I began overhearing comments about my bony back. It began to curve in a bit of an S shape, and I was developing a "hunch" (kyphosis) at the top and a swayback (lordosis) near my belt line. The change was simply attributed to poor posture. After a year or two of "bad posture" attributions and more pain and becoming more bent over, I was taken to a physician. He referred us to a specialist, and my parents became anxious because of the anticipated costs. After x-rays, history taking, and a physical examination, the specialist announced that I had Scheuerman's disease, a hereditary condition of the spine in which growing children, usually male, develop vertebrae in wedge shapes that bend and curve the whole spine, most particularly the upper back and neck. By the time of that diagnosis I had developed a noticeably humped back, and my neck and head leaned forward and down. Holding my head back so I could look straight ahead became an effort. I discovered, however, that I was well suited for spotting loose change on the sidewalk.

The physician's suggestion for reducing the probability of further curvature was to put me in a plaster body cast for several months, followed by a corset with steel rods to shape my back for two years. His thought was that it was too late to undo the changes that had already taken place but that treatment might slow the progression of the disease. In short order, at the end of a school year I went to a hospital to have the plaster cast made and was told to strip naked in a room with several other people in it. My body image was not good, and I was acutely self-conscious about my appearance. It was unpleasant to suddenly become the kid whose medical problem reshaped part of his identity and made him the center of attention. I remember the focus on my physical self as being threatening and having to have a cast applied as particularly traumatic. It was necessary to lie naked on a wide sling of folded cloth stretched between two tables. The cloth was bowed like a narrow hammock, and I was pushed down into it so that my lower back would curve out a little. Thick felt was wrapped and tied around me, starting at my groin (acute embarrassment), and then when the wrapping proceeded to my upper back, my shoulders and neck were forced back to straighten them. I was then wrapped mummylike, and thick layers of wet plaster cloth were applied and let dry. I looked like an albino corn dog.

When the casting was done and we were ready to leave, my pants wouldn't close around me. I found it necessary to walk through the lobby of the hospital to my grandparents' car with my hands cupped over my open fly. Feeling suddenly visible and vulnerable can imprint some harshly vivid memories. Having my back forced into a straighter position hurt for several weeks and created sores where the cast rubbed against the thin flesh over my hip and tailbones.

The night I returned home from having the cast applied, my parents thought going on a church hayride would cheer me up. I put on a T-shirt and shorts with elastic in the waistband and bounced on the hay bales, trying to feel and act normal. Of course everyone noticed the bulge around my midsection, and it generated a lot of questions. I didn't like the attention, because I had suddenly become visibly abnormal and different rather than fitting in.

I also had not thought about the possibility of getting straw and dust down the inside of my cast and soon found myself in a several-months-long bout of extremely unpleasant itchiness. The itchiness was compounded by hot weather and sweating inside the cast. Unable to wash inside the cast, I found that one could develop quite a body odor after a while. The more I wore the thing, the more I found reason to be embarrassed and to shy away from others.

I returned to school in the fall still wearing the cast. It smelled and bulged out at the top and clunked on desks. I just looked weird and felt increasingly self-conscious. While my male peers were caught up in their own physical growth and were preening for the girls, I tried to melt into the woodwork.

Midautumn of that year I went back to see the physician, to have the cast cut off and be fitted for the stiff canvas corset with metal rods. After the cast was cut off I tried to stand up but fell over. I had become even thinner and had little muscle remaining in my abdomen and lower back. My midsection had become Silly Putty and was covered with flaky, gross-looking skin. My upper back and neck still wanted to lean forward.

I was sentenced to wearing the uncomfortable corset for two years, and it became a continuous source of ribbing from others. Jibes about wearing "a girdle" are not the sort of jokes a young male wants to hear. I was also quite aware that the bills for my physical problem had severely strained my parents' already precarious financial situation. My father's illness (emphysema and lead poisoning) had become so bad that he could no longer work for lack of oxygen. While I was self-conscious about my body image and had constant backaches, I also felt guilty for straining our family resources.

I found it easier to further withdraw socially at that time and began reading even more voraciously. By happenstance I reread Hugo's *The Hunchback*, identified with parts of the story line, and felt that it metaphorically related to aspects of my life to which I was hypersensitive—failings at love, being the butt of jokes, being hunchbacked, and having fear of deafness. (I was losing some hearing in one ear.) We often identify with someone. I didn't choose a sports hero or an academic but an imaginary humpbacked character who wanted to belong and be seen for what he was on the inside.

In that time period, my last two years of high school, our family finances finally hit rock bottom. My father couldn't work at all, my mother could only get occasional small jobs as she developed more obvious physical weaknesses, and I worked an assortment of part-time jobs. We often went without food except for vegetables we had frozen the previous summer. There was not a welfare system that we qualified for in Indiana, though we could occasionally get small amounts of barely palatable government surplus food. I went from skinny to gaunt and recall periods when I did not eat for two or three weeks at a stretch. I can now rightly recall my state of mind as being quite depressed, resentful for having to endure things others did not, and anxiety-ridden.

We hid our living condition from others out of shame. I also had episodes of numbness from the waist down and moments when I was unable to stand. There were never-ending backaches. My social skills declined, and I was becoming clumsier and started to stumble a lot. At an age when I wanted to blend in with everyone else, I found it necessary to hide my appearance, mask my awkwardness, and disguise our family's financial plight. My tolerance for emotional and physical pain increased with the need to mask it. And mask it I angrily did.

I fell into an emotional and psychological state common to people who see no way out of their life, who become unable to dream or imagine that anything in their life will ever be different. It is rather like looking into the distance and seeing no horizon. We have no language in our professional literature for the mental state of people for whom hope is unimaginable. To survive in the moment, they learn to "know their place," to lower their expectations and guard against false hopes, and to maintain some smattering of dignity in spite of knowing that they don't matter one iota to the functioning of society.

My cynicism increased, as did my sense of alienation. It was not the confronting of a single problem that vexed me but the synergy of multiple problems. Though I knew, and had often been told, that I was bright, I quit trying to achieve academically. I couldn't conceive of how academic achievements could matter, and I felt that I needed to stay at home to help with the family. I discovered the cognitive myopia that plagues people when they get close to hitting the bottom. This myopia constricts the vision to things in one's immediate surroundings and magnifies them to proportionally fill one's entire worldview. As some things are magnified out of proportion, any greater perspective on the world fades away.

Because I drew well and had designed a small building for my high school, I was offered help at the end of my senior year if I would agree to go to college and major in architecture. The offer included a job and financial help in some nebulous place down the line but nothing to address immediate needs. I said no to the offer because at the time my wardrobe consisted of one shirt, one pair of pants, one change of underwear, a pair of glasses held together by tape, two or three pairs of tube socks, and one broken-down pair of shoes with cardboard stuffed in them to cover the holes in the soles. Also, I felt enormously responsible for helping to raise my younger siblings and be there for my parents. How the hell was I going to college with only those clothes and no money; and who would watch over the others? Further, I had no clue about how to manage independently in the larger world. Relationships too were an unknown quantity. How was I going to acquire the capital to engage in a relationship with a woman as my male peers did? One needed self-assurance and something to offer, a future to aim for. I secretly resented the fact that some people could seemingly get help up the ladder while others got no mentoring or helping hand. Why some people counted and others didn't matter ate at me; fairness had been preached to me as a virtue, but I saw little of it. I had learned how to survive the moment but at the expense of the social knowledge I needed to solve longer-term problems.

I graduated from high school and found a low-paying job in a dry goods store in a neighboring city. It was physically undemanding work, which helped with the back pain but did force me to meet and work with others. My shyness diminished a little, and I was successful in sales because I made a point of treating customers fairly and considerately. After I had worked at the store for about a year, a high school classmate happened to stop in to make a purchase and seemed amazed that I wasn't in college. I told him that I didn't have the money to go and had no way to commute to school. He told me about his own last-minute decision to go (his parents had wanted him to stay on the farm and raise hogs) and offered the opportunity to ride to school free if I registered for classes. I did so "on a whim and a prayer" two days later and started college the following week. It took me quite some time to imagine myself as a college student and to act the part. Some time later the dry goods store in which I had worked was destroyed in an explosion, killing all my former coworkers. Dumb luck or divine intervention is part of life's equation.

I quit physically growing by the end of my teens and had learned that slouching when sitting effectively hid the hump on my back and lessened my pain. When I walked I had to force my head and neck back so that I could look ahead, though at the expense of headaches and constant neck pain. I continued to feel conspicuous in college, particularly when taking the required physical education courses. To pay my way, I took a night job in a factory stamping sheet metal to make wheelbarrows and lawn mowers.

I worked after school and slept one or two hours each night before driving to school the following day. The work was physically demanding, and I was chronically tired and sore; my hands became so scarred from cuts that I couldn't fully close them. During my college years my parents both became increasingly ill, and in my senior year my father died.

I had no particular career goal in college and changed my major about five times. After an extended stay, and having accumulated a large number of credits and a low grade point average, I graduated with a degree in secondary education. Teaching jobs were scarce, and my poor grades worked against me. Our old house had been torn down in my junior year, and we had been forced to move again. At the end of my senior year I went on my first date and quickly married the woman and inherited a stepson. My younger brother was drafted into the army that year, and both sisters married without finishing high school. My mother moved back to the city in which I was born so that she could find work.

It was 1969 when I graduated, and the war in Vietnam was going full tilt. I had long been exposed to the teachings of the Religious Society of Friends (Quakers) and was totally opposed to war. My mother's forebears had been Quakers who came to this country with William Penn, and though my father was not religious, he instilled in us a lifelong dislike of violence. Two close male friends had already been killed in the war, and I began to focus on dislike for the military and moral opposition to war. I registered as a conscientious objector and was later "drafted" to perform two years of mandatory alternative service in a large state hospital in northern Indiana. Since I had a college degree, the hospital assigned me to the social work department. I became the only person I know who was actually drafted into social work.

After my two years of required service were up, I remained at the mental hospital in a supervisory capacity. But by that time, in a phenomenon of nagging worry eloquently described by the naturalist Loren Eiseley (1975), I had developed an unspoken fear that I might pass on some "defect" like my back to a birth child and so arranged to adopt a second son. My youngest son is biracial, and I elected such an adoption because my mother had by then confided in me that my father's family of origin was racially mixed. That revelation helped explain some of my family's behavior patterns and helped my self-concept. Having two young sons to love was a godsend, and I found that I liked being a father.

My colleagues began encouraging me to go to graduate school, and after some time I finally applied. In spite of very high examination scores, I found it difficult to get accepted due to the stigma of my low undergraduate grade point average.

Old photographs from that period of my life show me with a very curved back, and indeed it continued to be a source of pain and discomfort.

In spite of it, I endeavored to live a normal life. But while diving from a diving board in those early years of my marriage, I struck my head on the bottom of a swimming pool. Given the angle at which I had to hold my head back to see ahead, I hit the bottom bending my neck back. My body went numb from the neck down. Fortunately I floated to the surface and was able to breathe until some bodily sensation returned and I regained movement.

The injury to my neck, however, has been an additional source of pain and discomfort since that time, and I have developed arthritis of the spine that has aggravated its curvature and my back and neck pain. Even as I write this narrative I have constant back pain—I cannot sit in one position for very long without discomfort, and I find that I have to cross and recross my legs to compensate for the curvature while sitting. I have, to some extent, learned to live with it but am still self-conscious about my appearance and my increasingly awkward and clumsy gait. I suspect my stumbling will get worse as I age. Though I have a fairly high pain threshold, I find that my physical discomfort makes it increasingly difficult to concentrate.

To bring events in my life's narrative more up to date, I did eventually get into graduate school and received my master's degree in social work. I then worked as a social worker in a mental health setting, with the aged in a medical setting, and as a sexual assault counselor. My social conscience developed a sharper edge, and I became even more acutely aware of racial injustice and social inequality. At the same time, however, I learned to see the decency of the human heart and to love learning, hybridize flowers, engage in photography, and do glass blowing.

In my forties I went back to school for my doctorate while working full time. The subject of my dissertation was an application of Max Weber's notion of open and closed social relationships as "social closure" to an effort to change the licensing requirements and career advancement pathways of nurses. Weber suggested that occupational groups restrict entry into the practice of their craft as a way of increasing the benefits for members and that as a result of such activity other members of society are disadvantaged. My selection of the topic was motivated by my desire to better understand ways that the deck is stacked for and against some people and ways that social exclusion serves to limit the life chances of people. I had intuitively learned all too well that social exclusion results in an inexpressible but very real pain, the pain of nonbelonging and disconnection. Sometimes pain is graced by the elegiac subtext in an otherwise dry dissertation.

I divorced and ultimately remarried while working on my doctorate. I convinced my enormously talented new wife to work on her doctorate, and she too went back to school and completed her Ph.D. After completing my doctorate I began teaching full time and in the intervening years have become a full professor and the editor of a premier journal in my field. I must admit, though, that I do not socially feel quite at home in a university setting—a bit of a pretender perhaps. Many of my academic peers come from families that were better educated than mine, seem more at home in academia, and have readier command of the argot and demeanor of academia. I have learned to "pass" as an academic but frankly miss the familiar music of my old Hoosier voice. I'm not sure how my back will ultimately bend the thread of my life—the curvature is made more problematic by the advanced arthritic changes in my spine and increasing tiredness from the constant muscle guarding to control pain. Nonetheless, life goes on.

I was recently reminded that Scheuerman's Kyphosis has a genetic component when I discovered an old picture of my paternal grandfather; he had a similar curve to his back. His tiny "dark-skinned" mother is sitting primly beside him, and her back looks similarly curved and arthritic. Seeing them, I wonder whether the effect of social stigma is woven into a family's fabric and passed from generation to generation like the genes for Scheuerman's. I look at the few remaining pictures of my forebears with new appreciation for what they struggled with and endured so that I could have a chance to be here.

Our worldview, our vantage point for apprehending the world, is shaped by the place where life plants us. If we're planted in a poor place, it's hard to visualize greener pastures and find the paths to them. Moving up also makes it necessary for some people to un-become themselves, that is, to lose their childhood language, sense of belonging, dialect, history and the microculture they were embedded in, and to learn to affect new manner-isms, speech, and dress. When I think of my drive to fit in, I recall "We Wear the Mask" by the African American poet Paul Laurence Dunbar (1913). The first five lines of that poem read:

> We wear the mask that grins and lies,
> It hides our cheeks and shades our eyes.
> This debt we pay to human guile,
> With torn and bleeding hearts we smile,
> And mouth myriad subtleties.

Like Dunbar, many people, for many reasons, find it necessary to adopt a mask and mouth words to socially fit in, to count, to matter, to maintain the hope that they truly belong.

If there's anything that I've learned from my childhood and my prob-lems with Scheuerman's disease, it's that we are more likely to see the minimums of a person's potential rather than what their optimum performance could be if they were nurtured and made full members of the human family. Like Quasimodo, we are all too often seen as objects; rarely does anyone search for the soul of another.

This narrative, then, is the recollection of some memories from my earlier years—memories stored with the unconscious editing of the youth I once was. Had I the chance to go back in time and store my memories again, I would do so more comprehensively, but as we age each of us must make the best, truest story we can out of what was collected and stored in another time for other purposes. The particulars of our life create our mind's lens, and our lens gives us a grasp of the evolving narrative of our life. At the close of this narrative I still survive though having grown heavier and more bent. I have endured the pain of losing children and the sting of loneliness, yet have known love and peace and have found life to be a gift. Quasimodo should have been so fortunate.

CHAPTER 9

No Body Is Exempt: Beauty Compulsion and Resistance in Japan

Laura Miller

Fumiko asked me to get on the scale. Surprised at what she saw, and frowning in displeasure, she told me I was overweight. I suggested that for a woman my age it wasn't that bad. She responded with a distinctive Japanese sound linguists call the inbreathed fricative, a sort of inverse hiss, followed by "Even so."[1]

Fumiko was a purveyor of beauty, an aesthetician in a Japanese aesthetic salon, a place much like an American day spa. Leaving the scale, she ushered me over to an area where there was a spacesuit-style apparatus waiting. I was asked to place my legs inside two blue cylinders lined with plastic and was strapped in around the waist. This machine was one of many in the salon that were used to rid the body of excess inches. It was turned on, and I felt intense air pressure begin to generate from where my feet were secured. A timer was set for ten minutes, and Fumiko walked away. As I lay mummified in latex, I began to seriously question my decision to do fieldwork on the Japanese beauty industry. Why hadn't I anticipated this discomfort, this absurdity, this humiliation? How had I fooled myself into thinking I could even do research like this?

For one thing, the project was outside the realm of my usual scholarly interests. Since I was trained in linguistic anthropology, my normal pattern of data collection involved the use of audiocassette players and video cameras. Although present, I was not a participant in the interactions I taped and analyzed, and had never projected myself into a project in this manner. Once the recordings were made, I could comfortably transcribe the tapes back home, locating interesting linguistic phenomena like the inbreathed fricative. I liked the way research on language generated data that wasn't filtered through my memory. Although transcription also involves theoretical judgment calls, I found transcribed words, hesitations, self-repairs, and glitches reassuringly solid and seemingly less subjective. So what had happened to make me think that doing research in which I would have a more active role was a good idea?

It began simply, by reading Japanese women's magazines. I first read them to locate new slang and neologisms but gradually became intrigued by the images they carried. The Japanese women in these pages looked different from those in the past. Gone was the naïve, ultra-cute aesthetic so pervasive in the 1980s; it was replaced by women who had engaged in obvious encounters with drastic forms of body sculpting and cosmetic retooling. Media images of cheeky models, pop music stars, and everyday girls embodied new ideas about female presentation of self (Miller 2000). Big glossy monthlies—such as *CanCam*, *More*, and *Say*, which target university-aged women or the OL ("office lady," i.e., unmarried office clerk)—featured young, perky, and slim girls who testified to the efficacy of beauty treatments called "face slimming aesthetics," "yin-yang five elements treatment," or more astonishing, "bust up," maneuvers intended to enhance the size and shape of the breasts. Reading the names and descriptions of some of these treatments, I was consumed with curiosity. Although having no doubt that these beauty services were spurious, no different from trends in North America and Europe—consider: "Raul mud ceremony, an Oriental skin exfoliation using medicinal earths" at the Celtic Manor resort—I still had questions. What did they actually do to you? What kind of Japanese woman would pay to have this stuff done to her? How much did it cost? When had Japanese begun to worry about things like breast size, an attribute not traditionally part of their beauty ideology (Miller 2003a)? And given the Japanese reputation for reserve and modesty, how did women deal with strangers' touching their bodies in novel ways?

Having periodically lived, worked, studied, or taught in Japan over a span of almost three decades, I believed I could find out the answers to some of these questions by visiting a few aesthetic salons for treatments, assuming the stance of an unaffected participant-observer, someone not "really" subject to another culture's standards of beauty. But as my experiences with aestheticians and beauty workers like Fumiko illustrated, this proved to be wrong. A seemingly impersonal research project unexpectedly became quite personal, and I was reinserted into a world shared by all women, young or old, Japanese or American, in which female bodies are constantly scrutinized and evaluated against increasingly similar, and narrower, beauty norms.

I began thinking about doing research on Japanese body aesthetics (*esute*) in the mid-1990s, and the opportunity to do fieldwork for it came about in 1997. I had accepted an appointment as a summertime visiting professor at a university in Kanazawa, a modern city located on Japan's main island, Honshu, on the coast between the mountains and the sea. As soon as I arrived, I hunted for aesthetic salons I could visit to interview people who worked there and to receive treatments.

These salons are quite distinct from the equally popular aesthetic surgery clinics, where Japanese were installing new nose and eye shapes. There are usually fifty or more different services offered at an aesthetic salon, but most of them can be grouped into one of three categories: hair removal treatments (e.g., electrolysis and waxing), body treatments (e.g., weight loss using "scientific" apparatuses), and facials.

When I arrived for my first session at the felicitously titled Slim Beauty House, I was processed through "counseling" with a hard-nosed manager/saleswoman named Mie, whose job it was to sell me as many of the expensive treatments as possible. After the completion of various forms and questionnaires, including the essential financial information statement (which asked for job, salary, and bank account status), Mie gave me a handful of the salon's glossy brochures and PR materials. One of them was devoted to an annual "Aesthetic Cinderella Contest" in which the woman who loses the most weight in the shortest time becomes the winner of prizes and beauty prestige. My heart sank as soon as I looked inside the colorful booklet: the "contestants" were not all perky young women. Instead, there were some my own age, and one fifty-nine-year-old Cinderella in a tight pink bathing suit, accompanied by exact measurements of all her body sections. "Oh no," I thought, "being middle-aged is not going to make me exempt from pressure to conform to these ideals."

"Look," said Mie, pointing to one of the aging beauty queens, "any woman can be beautiful." Yes, I nodded, of course. Before my treatment I'd assumed that not only as someone over forty but also as a foreigner, I would be absolved from this expectation. As everyone who has ever lived or worked in Japan knows, foreigners are not subject to the same rules. But I also knew there were widespread ideas about the foreign body to contend with.

For anyone interested in the nature of Japanese national identity and ethnicity, both popular and scholarly writing documents native beliefs about what is thought to distinguish "Japanese" from others (Befu 2001; Dale 1986). In many cases the foreigner serves as a reflexive symbol against which Japanese ethnicity is constructed and evaluated, so discourse on the Japanese–non-Japanese dichotomy is pervasive. The native folk model in which the foreigner as "Other" becomes an object of attention and debate is a form of "occidentalism" that is the obverse of Edward Said's (1979) notion of Western "orientalism." Brian Moeran sees this objectification as a "Japanese attempt to set themselves apart from, restructure, and thus gain authority over, the West" (1990:2).

Whatever it was, my first encounter with it had occurred in 1972, when

I spent time in the northern city of Sendai. While there, I got herded into some outdoor festival dancing called *obon odori*. A journalist picked up the story of a foreigner in town and ran a photo of me in the local newspaper, with a caption underneath that said "Blue-eyed foreigner does *obon odori*." I remember being puzzled by this, not because my eyes aren't blue (they're hazel) but because I didn't see why "blue eyes" were considered my most noteworthy attribute. But a description like that made perfect sense in the Japanese scheme of things.

The word *gaijin* or *gaikokujin* (foreign person) is the label commonly used for non-Japanese. In the past it was primarily reserved for Anglo foreigners, but it has broadened to include other non-Japanese people.[2] Japan's long-standing ideology of racial distinctness and purity includes a presumption that *gaijin* are opposite to and physically different from Japanese. Despite the fact that the majority of Japanese women and a large proportion of young men dye their hair, the opposite of the presumed natural black or brown hair of a Japanese person is blond hair; therefore, proper foreigners should be blond.

Brown-haired Bruce Feiler, author of a book recounting a year spent teaching in Japan, recalls sitting in a bar with friends deliberating over his lack of success in dating Japanese women, when the bartender yelled out, "You have a distinct advantage. . . . Japanese girls love blondes" (1991:203). In some cases foreigners will try to accommodate this expectation. Long-time Japan resident and celebrity Dave Spector, a favorite on Japanese TV, has curly bleached-blond hair and a spirited, ebullient manner that correspond to a popular stereotype of the bumbling and bombastic foreigner. Spector's antics and hair are carefully engineered facets of his *gaijin* persona. He was once asked by a journalist why he had dark brown roots in his curly mop. "This?" said Spector. "It's bleached. How could I possibly be a real *gaijin* if it wasn't?" (Bornoff 1986:36).

People in the Japanese beauty industry often asked me why I didn't dye my hair lighter. Because the majority of Japanese women were doing it, they thought it strange that I didn't as well. Women and men in Japan began dyeing their hair in mass numbers in the 1990s, when it became ordinary for both genders. These days more Japanese high school students color their hair than American high schoolers. In a survey of high school–aged boys and girls, 38.2 percent of the Japanese had dyed their hair, compared to 24.8 percent of the American students (Shôgakukan 2001). Various surveys of Japanese women of all ages who dye their hair may give an estimate as high as 90 percent, and even the lowest survey results are always over 65 percent. Beauty workers thought it odd that I didn't take advantage of hair-coloring technology to turn myself into an authentic blond foreigner.

In addition to "blond" hair, physical differences in the foreign body that are thought to announce themselves to the Japanese onlooker include bodily hairiness and big noses. Fanciful physiologies of those outside one's ethnic group are nothing new, of course. For ages humans have universally held beliefs in the existence of bizarre and misshapen tribes beyond their borders. And it was only in the nineteenth century that the Linnean classification system whittled humanity down to one lineage, *Homo sapiens*. Before that, it included the category *Homo monstrosus* (De Waal Malefijt 1968). A focus on the physical differences of foreigners has a long history in Japan. Painted images of "southern barbarians" appear on Muromachi era (1338–1573) folding-panel screens. These show pictorial exaggerations of Dutch, Portuguese, and Spanish merchants, sailors, and missionaries, in some cases almost caricatured representations of faces with enormous noses and weirdly cavernous eyes under bushy eyebrows. When I lived in Japan in the late 1970s and early 1980s, I often overheard other commuters on subways and trains, who assumed I didn't understand Japanese, say things about my nose being "too high," and I always thought of those paintings of big-nosed traders and ship captains. Although Japanese attitudes about my nose never bothered me, either before or after doing research on beauty culture, body hair was different.

Body hair is not a good thing in Japan. Body hair indexes the savage, the wild, the non-Japanese. For women, even the soft, indiscernible hair that covers all human faces must be done away with. For many centuries Japanese have held hairy bodies in some disfavor. In earlier times hairiness was exemplary of the uncivilized barbarian, as illustrated by the pejorative label for a white person, *ketô*, literally "hairy Chinese." Excessive body hair came to symbolically represent ethnic or racial boundaries. The hairy body might index the outside foreigner, or else the domestic "Other," such as native Ainu or Okinawans. The Japanese term for "antipathy" or "prejudice" is *kegirai*, literally "hair hatred." Hairiness is spurned by many contemporary young men, who engage in various beauty practices to rid themselves of chest, leg, and arm hair (Miller 2003b). So important is keeping hair and beards trimmed that an Osaka advocacy group once demanded that immigration authorities provide individual electric shavers to detainee foreigners who share a communal shaver ("Shavers Demanded" 2002).

All body hair is strictly taboo for women. The female face must be absolutely smooth without even the nearly invisible hair called *ubuge* that covers everyone's skin. Female face shaving is ancient beauty work in Japan, and many woodblock prints from the sixteenth century on depict women using long, thin razors to plane their faces. Delicate pastel razors for women intended for use on the face are still available in any Japanese drugstore. A bride's face and neck are always shaved for her wedding, before thick white makeup is applied. Targets for hair removal include not only the face but also the underarms, arms, back, legs, bellybutton, breasts, crotch area, fingers, and toes.

My body is not particularly hairy. My California ancestors probably didn't have much body hair, either. I have a photograph of grandmother Martina Felicidad Valdez and great-grandmother Maria Antonia Cota Valdez on my office wall at school, and students have looked at it and asked, more than once, "Who are the Indians?" I never need to spend much time on leg or underarm hair removal; it's something I do once every few months if I remember. Despite this, within the context of the Japanese aesthetic salon, I suddenly felt much closer to my primate cousin Pongidae Pan Paniscus. Mie at Slim Beauty House insisted that I would like the results of a treatment to remove the *ubuge*, and when I declined, saying we didn't do that sort of thing in my country, she just looked at me with disbelief.

Later, as I sat in my university-supplied apartment in Kanazawa, I squinted at the microscopic hair on my arms. I wondered what the aestheticians at Slim Beauty House, Takano Yuri Beauty Clinic, and other salons had thought as they applied cremes and packs to my body. Did they go home and tell boyfriends and husbands about the "hairy foreigner"? Looking in a hand mirror, I found the *ubuge*, once invisible to me, now glaringly obvious. I vaguely remembered a novel by the famous Japanese writer Shusaku Endo that describes someone's German wife and how hairy her arms are. I worried about this, even as I acknowledged that my newfound concern derived mainly from my study of beauty industry advertising and contact with pushy saleswomen like Mie. Advertisements for hair removal products and services were often accompanied by illustrations of the perils of ignoring this regimen: depictions of women with thick black hairs sprouting out all over. I learned that female face hairs grow at a rate of 0.35 millimeters in one day, arm hairs at 0.20 millimeters. Perhaps I was really grossing people out? Not only was it aesthetically déclassé, but according to what I'd been reading, it was bad manners. The Japanese beauty industry had reformulated hair removal as an aspect of "etiquette," so that failure to remove body hair wasn't only a matter of beauty, it was downright rude and an affront to others.

While I wasn't about to go running around Kanazawa in search of hair removal products like Silky Body Epilat or Super BeOff, I did consider the advisability of wearing long-sleeved shirts, even in the humid heat of summer, so as not to offend people. My arms, so normal in the United States, had become a source of anxiety.

Each time I have been in Japan I've surprised or confused Japanese expectations about the foreign body. One time I was walking in the Umeda subway station in Osaka, and a granny came up from behind to ask directions. Thinking I was Japanese because of my dark hair and short stature, she hollered, "Older Sister, just a minute, can I ask you . . . ?" When I turned around, she screamed and ran away. Japanese ideas about the foreign body are ambivalent, but more important, they are gendered. In post-war Japan the sexy Western woman made her appearance. Dichotomous representations of the sensual white woman and the decent and healthy Japanese woman were common in postwar women's magazines. As Emiko Ochiai says, "Japanese women had to camouflage themselves as white to become sexy" (1997:157). So being "sexy" meant doing things to the body to bring one's appearance closer to that of the Anglo foreigners seen in Hollywood movies and American television and print media. In addition to body hair and nose size, I had to contend with the disappointment Japanese aestheticians exhibited when my foreigner's body didn't live up to their positive stereotypes. While they weren't quite expecting Barbie or Britney Spears, they believed that I should at least have been a little taller and slim-mer, with larger breasts. Well aware that my short and stocky *mestiza* body was a beauty failure in my own culture, I was constantly reminded of this in another. The aestheticians were always complimenting me on my eyes, and except for the wrinkles, my face passed muster. But the two primary foci of current beauty work in Japan are weight loss and hair removal, and it was in these areas that I disappointed them most.

Attitudes about body hair were linked to long-standing cultural beliefs, but other aspects of the beauty industry pointed to recent changes in social attitudes and thinking. One such change was the new focus on the breasts as an attribute of female beauty. In prewar Japan breasts were main-ly associated with motherhood and were never the focus of the extreme eroticization seen in post-1940s American culture. Japanese clothing styles had produced a tubular female body form that deemphasized the breasts and waist. But recently, in addition to extreme thinness and smooth hair-lessness, the size and shape of the breasts have become an important index of female attractiveness. Consequently, aesthetic salons began offering a menu of "bust up" treatments that ostensibly make the breasts bigger or better shaped. These often involve application of a variety of cremes, packs, and lotions, as well as mechanical stimulation with some type of appliance or apparatus. Often suction cups or metal wands, which are hooked up by cable to an electromassage machine, are placed on or manip-ulated over the breasts. The photographs and text that described these treat-ments were so peculiar that I decided I should arrange to have a bust up treatment to find out what magical science would be called on to do the job.

Several of the treatments I received in the course of my research proj-ect can only be described as bogus, but the bust up session stood out as spectacularly fraudulent. The aesthetician who handled the bust up session at Socie de Esute salon was named Maeda. She had a badge with only her last name pinned to her nurselike uniform. Maeda looked to be in her fifties, and I got the impression that she had been transferred into the body aesthetics business from one of the sex-for-sale industries, given the perfunctory and no-nonsense way she dealt with my body. She was exceedingly formal, and I sensed that she didn't really believe in what she was doing to me. We got along great as long as I didn't ask too many questions or try to watch what she was doing. She measured me before and after the session, applied special mud packs and exfoliation masks, and used metal wands connected to an electromassage machine as part of the treatment. She placed a towel over my eyes while I was lying on the treatment table getting zapped with the wands, and whenever I tried to peek out to see what she was doing, she firmly replaced the towel as if I were getting in the way of her doing her job.

Maeda bowed when I left and didn't try to sell me additional treatments, but the salon manager Hiromi did. She was young, slim, and elegant and resembled Japanese pop star Amuro Namie, who had long light brown hair. I received several telephone calls from Hiromi at my office at the university, as well as a beautifully handwritten letter, inviting me to return for more treatments. "You really got results with the bust up course," she wrote. "If you have time, please come back for a facial and a full-body oil massage."

Kyoko, an aesthetician at Takano Yuri Beauty Clinic, advised me to go get a haircut. (Unlike the American spa, the majority of Japanese salons do not provide this service.) She assured me that I'd look 100 percent better. I knew this already, and friends, family, and even strangers in the United States had told me the same thing. Of course Kyoko was right, but I wasn't willing to spend time and money on something like that. A legacy of being a hippie is that decades before reading Naomi Wolf's *The Beauty Myth* (1992), I had considered hair styling and fashion trends a drain on valuable time and resources, methods for ensuring conformity and consumption. I also suspected that beauty styles were really efforts to homogenize beauty, to turn everyone into blond Anglo wannabes. So until 1987 I still wore the frizzy tresses I had in the 1960s and 1970s and had never once been to a hair salon for a cut or styling. While I was in graduate school at UCLA, a friend somehow convinced me that it was time to change, and I accompanied her to the Vidal Sassoon salon on Rodeo Drive to get a $15 haircut from a student hairdresser. Not having any idea of what sort of hair I ought to have, I told the stylist to do whatever he saw fit. He cut off most of my dark hair and applied a permanent that left small tight curls on all sides, transforming me into an adorable French poodle. Although the world loved this look, after it grew out I never patronized a hair salon again. But this was my personal logic, and it didn't translate. In interviews I held with students learning to be hairdressers and aestheticians at the Hollywood Beauty School in Tokyo's Roppongi district, they were confused that my interest in their subject was coupled with a complete failure to display it on my body.

It was clear that I had an unusual way of thinking, although it was one shared by many other feminists and academic women in the United States. My refusal to purchase trendy fashions, to read American women's magazines, or to visit hair salons may have been a common choice in my own small universe, but it made no sense in Japan. Salon workers constantly tried to sell me expensive beauty treatments or take-home products and seemed confounded that I wasn't interested. The aestheticians and I sometimes squabbled. Presented with the perfidy of my own body as documented in salon measurements and treatment data, I refused to schedule additional treatment sessions or purchase the necessary products to fix my imperfections. Although I told all the salon workers I met with that I was an anthropologist visiting Japan to learn about something new, and not for self-improvement, they didn't believe me. They accepted that I was a professor—why else, after all, would I have known how to speak Japanese?—but they were convinced that every woman spends massive amounts of time and money on beauty. The problem, from their perspective, wasn't philosophical difference or feminist ideology but that I was too cheap or too busy to do the necessary beauty work.

In many ways doing this research project was much less labor-intensive than any I'd ever done in the past, but it emotionally drained me like no other. When I did research on language and interaction, my own language errors were always excused. After all, as a nonnative speaker I wasn't really responsible for not knowing certain words or expressions—like the phrase *ashi ga deru*, literally "feet stick out," which I discovered meant "to run over the budget." Just getting to the point where I could make linguistic mistakes like this was something of an achievement. But beauty was different, and failure to be slim, young, and conventionally pretty was viewed as a personal shortcoming or character flaw.

As part of my research program, I visited the Socie de Esute salon a number of times not only for treatments but to talk to the aestheticians or receptionists. I often spoke with the salon manager, Hiromi, who, although polite and cheerful, left no doubt in my mind that she was a calculating businessperson who was shrewdly estimating exactly how much yen she might extract from me. One time I was waiting in the reception area after a treatment so I could ask her a few more questions. A young woman sat near me on an adjacent loveseat, while Hiromi squatted next to her. A calculator displaying the price of a treatment was set before them, and the customer kept repeating how costly it seemed: "But isn't it a little expensive for a bank worker like me?"

Hiromi's voice went up to a high-pitched, wheedling level and assumed a nasal quality as she replied, "But you're still young, right?"

They both examined the customer's legs (she was wearing a miniskirt), noting both good and bad points. In between giggles, Hiromi said over and over again that the customer was "still young" and that this was her big opportunity to really be beautiful.

I observed many scenes involving high-pressure sales tactics like this, and I knew that young women and their insecurities were the primary target of the beauty business. Even so, the same techniques and logic were applied to any women who entered the salon doors, and no matter what one's state of mind, having focused attention directed to putative body flaws is a debilitating experience.

There weren't exactly revelatory findings from my study of the Japanese beauty industry, but I think I acquired a greater understanding of the concept of "global culture." In spite of ideologies of national, ethnic, and racial difference, the contemporary beauty industry was obliterating many differences. I had thought the idea that women over forty should still strive to look ageless—like Jane Fonda or Farrah Fawcett, who posed for *Playboy* magazine in 1995 when she was forty-eight—was an American problem, part of our obsession with youth. Weren't Japanese supposed to revere age and wisdom? Every textbook on "Japanese culture" always lauds the way Japanese have increasing respect for people as they get older and wiser, a trait always contrasted with an American fetishization of youth. Old folks in Japan even have their own national holiday, Respect for Elders Day, when octogenarians and centenarians are awarded medals for reaching old age. But recently the age at which a woman can stop worrying about presenting a youthful and attractive appearance has been extended. As Brian McVeigh (2000) notes, married women have traditionally worn a frumpy dress style, almost a uniform of sorts, that strips them of all sexuality and, as a material marker of the life cycle, denotes their primary status as family caretakers. But like women in the United States, all Japanese women are now judged by comparable beauty norms, and married women are pressured to still aspire to Cinderella beauty, monitoring themselves decades longer than they did in the past.

Although certain aspects of Japan's beauty culture are unique, many body "problems" Japanese aestheticians earnestly wanted to address—breast size, weight, and dry, wrinkled skin—were no different from the defects American women are taught they must hide or correct. I was trying to understand their beauty culture, and they were trying to save me from being ugly. The strategies of resistance to beauty ideals I had developed in my own society offered no protection in this new setting. I was no longer cocooned in a feminist-academic milieu where my dowdy persona of "artsy hippie professor" provided safe refuge from participation in demanding beauty work and consumption. By getting nude in front of strangers who worked their beauty science upon me, and by having my imperfections meticulously measured, charted, and discussed, I learned that my menopausal body was still not absolved of the female duty to be beautiful.

Notes

1. All my conversations with aestheticians and other beauty workers were in Japanese. The names of the aesthetic salons and treatments are real, but Japanese beauty workers are identified with pseudonyms.

2. Although Japanese treatment of non-Anglo foreigners may be qualitatively different, the *gaijin* designation nevertheless has a saliency that suggests that gaijin-ness might profitably be looked at as a phenomenon that subsumes both ethnicity and nationality.

CHAPTER 10

Mama's Always on Stage: The Absurdity of the Pregnant Academic

Darcie Vandegrift

I got pregnant the month after I filed my master's thesis. I felt I was embarking on an adventure that I was extremely privileged to have, doing so under the best of circumstances. I was healthy, in my late twenties, in a wonderful marriage. I was doing well in my graduate program and had enjoyed tremendous support from my advisers throughout my thesis work. Our careful planning and unexpected luck would bring our child into the world five months before my dissertation research abroad was to begin. The three of us would have a year to be together during my fieldwork in Costa Rica. My progress fit within the defined limits of our graduate division's "normative time," which created possibilities for fellowships and stipends. I was exuberant.

I was also terrified. I wondered what life would be like as both a mother and an academic. But in the first days after the test came back positive, I gave little thought to the months *before* the baby came. I had never met a pregnant woman my age in the university. In my everyday experience before becoming "a Woman with a Due Date," I had yet to know personally a woman in any white-collar job who had procreated early in her career. And in my years as a twenty-something graduate student—one of the very few married, heterosexual women in the department—the closest I'd been to pregnancy as an adult was through movies. In some films the character faints unexpectedly, revealing her frail condition. In other scenes an actor wearing a prosthetic belly under her shirt walks into the hospital, screams a few times on a hospital bed, and is handed a baby. These examples did not really provide me with much of a role model. I had to read Lenin for my area exams. I needed to grasp the finer points of dependency theory for my graduate seminar. Fainting would not help me reach these goals, and a lot of reading, typing, and lecturing would have to transpire before I was to be "handed my baby."

I had no idea how to "do pregnancy" or how I would be perceived as a pregnant person. I certainly had no anticipation of how my body would change or be "read" by everyone I encountered. People doing the reading would include those whose opinions mattered to my future, including advisers who sized up whether I could one day become serious professorial material. In turn, my readings of how others perceived me gave me the earliest evidence on which to plan how I would negotiate the identities of mother and academic simultaneously. On the more treacherous days, I received messages from my institution and from powerful individuals within it that these two subject positions should not even be attempted simultaneously. On better days, these readings and my own emergent sense of embodied motherhood created a different set of understandings, one in which this new terrain could be traversed, perhaps reshaping the institution in the process.

Whether my future multiple identities felt possible or implausible depended on the given day's interaction between external responses and internal ruminations. This interaction often occurred in the moments when the eyes of others met or avoided my growing belly. Regardless of that day's outcome, of which side prevailed in the battle between competence and absurdity, I began to cling to the refrain of that 1992 Arrested Development song "Mama's Always on Stage." As the mama on stage, my body became an on-site Rorschach exam reflecting others' projections about how gender, sexuality, and economy intersected in the academic workplace.

Even before I negotiated a professional life as an obviously pregnant academic, I had to evaluate my self-identity in light of the ongoing physical changes I experienced. In the first trimester, when the life inside of me was unobservable to the uninformed outsider's eye, pregnancy made me aware of my body as never before. I could no longer take for granted a vessel that, with basic maintenance, would carry me through the day. In the first weeks of pregnancy I had to plan ahead to meet its needs lest it turn on me. Presentation of self had never before required so many precautions; I had to make sure my stomach was full and I was near a bathroom at all times. These requirements limited which computer labs I could work in, where I could sit at department meetings, and how long I could stay out of the house. I nibbled food discreetly all day to avoid the nausea misnamed "morning sickness." I fielded phone calls from an adviser with one eye at the toilet, hoping the conversation would end before he heard me retching. I was amazed at the chasm between the body that cooperated to perform my duties as a teaching assistant and the one that drove me to the department bathroom immediately after a class ended.

During the first trimester the pregnant body grows a placenta while experiencing rapid changes in hormone levels and metabolism. This has been described in popular pregnancy texts as the equivalent of running a marathon, except that it happens for about two months. Combine this with a tendency toward low blood sugar, and a better recipe for exhaustion could not be created. My body formed the home for my future fetus while I tried to stay awake. *Tired* could not adequately describe what I felt any more than *hungry* could describe the sensation after a seven-day juice fast. I was lucky enough to have an office as a research assistant. I would often lock the door, create a makeshift pillow from a sweater, and curl up on the carpeted floor to sleep. More than once I remained asleep for an hour. I would practically fall asleep at the dinner table when I got home at night.

I had never before considered how to incorporate the restorative or mindful pause into working life. The culture of my department appeared to favor people who worked all the time. At department social functions people discussed how very much work they had to do and how hard they worked. In this context my exhausted, nauseated state caused me to panic. How would I ever get work done? I would chastise myself as I lay down to sleep at 9:00 on a weeknight. For the first time, I could not will my body to do something that I felt necessary to avoid extreme discomfort. I could not work, at least not as I felt I should be able to.

In hindsight, my application of these standards to myself was a result of an institutional culture, perhaps even a national culture, that fetishizes hard work. But I internalized these values, as they had allowed me to progress in my career. At twenty-seven, I had not interrogated these values to any great extent. The richness of my embodied experiences in the first trimester, in which I experienced my body as one reality and my mind as another, contradictory one, lay in their preparing me for the contradictory subjectivities that awaited me as I became an outwardly pregnant woman and later a mother.

When I returned from winter break that year, I entered the university with three months left until my baby was due. I no longer felt queasy or excessively tired. No one could look at me and think I was just gaining weight; I looked *pregnant*. The difference in treatment was astonishing. I told one of the senior faculty members that arriving back from break was like being pregnant for the first time because my status was now obvious to even the most casual observer. A young woman stopped me on campus and invited me to a single-mothers' support group, perhaps imagining that anyone my age with child on a college campus must be going through parenthood alone. She stopped me as an act of kindness, one of many that I would receive in the next three months.

The astounding part was that under no circumstances could I "pass" as part of the vast majority of women who demonstrated no interest in sexual reproduction. I got noticed wherever I went. I quickly learned to negotiate having my body more noticeable to the outside world. As my pregnancy became more apparent, I learned that my body enacted transgression against the dominant expectations of the academy, a social fact that I could not conceal.

In my feminist theory seminar I had studied writers who posited the body as text. But these ideas in the abstract did not prepare me for the experience of being read on a daily basis as a pregnant woman by faculty, graduate students, and undergraduates. Feminist theorists demonstrate an array of feelings toward the body as a site for study of power and resistance, encompassing a spectrum that somewhat mirrored people's responses to my pregnant self. Reactions varied from "unease and ambivalence to passion and fascination" (K. Davis 1997:11). Because of my pregnancy, my sexuality was up for display, analysis, and comment. Some students endeavored to place my growing family in the context in which they knew me. The rumor circulated in the fall class in which I was a teaching assistant that I was the lover of the course's professor and we would raise the baby together. Graduate students I barely knew asked if I had planned to get pregnant. I take both of these incidents to mean that people were puzzled by my presence, starting rumors and asking questions that would make my strange state fit into what they knew the university to be. The open display of my sexuality as a white woman was met with titillation or disbelief but not scorn; women students of color described to me how during their pregnancy they encountered outright hostility from students who apparently felt that they should not be "bringing another baby into the world."

I am not the first to note that both the university and the corporation have been structured for workers with, as Arlie Hochschild (2002) wrote, "zero drag," or the illusion of no limitations on his or her time or attention. As my pregnancy progressed, I began to develop a waddling gait that most women acquire when their center of gravity is shifted by the growing fetus—the drag became literal. My violation of the category of academic worker with no external obligations was something I carried with me wherever I appeared in my department. My pregnant body violated the private-public split that defines academic labor (as well as many other kinds of labor in a patriarchal capitalist society).

Academics who also do reproductive labor transgress the professorial subject position in a way that threatens to upset the entire structure of the university. The Western model of academic labor was created for men of the cloth to do their thinking. The implicit assumption existed that all time would be dedicated to the holy pursuit of knowledge. Later this institution created for all-consuming study was handed down to men of tweed jackets. The intellectual writes, teaches, and reads. There is no room for Braxton-Hicks contractions or shitty diapers.

But not only does the model academic abstain from reproductive labor for others; he also requires that someone else be doing his reproductive labor for him. Years after my first pregnancy, I picked up Wallace Stegner's highly recommended book *Crossing to Safety* (1987). The first chapter, describing the last days of the couples Lang and Morgan, moved me tremendously. I eagerly continued, particularly anticipating the descriptions of academic life set before World War II. In the chapters that followed, Stegner describes how Larry Morgan works in the basement of his tiny dwelling, fervently writing the days away, while wife Sally copes with and enjoys her pregnancy with their first child. Larry's day is filled with work; Sally's days are filled with her budding friendship with also-pregnant Charity and caring for Larry's every need.

Readers across the nation describe this novel as beautifully written with compelling, memorable characters. But the descriptions of these men's work lives angered and pained me to a level of distraction that prevented me from finishing the book. I admit that the reaction was not entirely mature. Part of my feelings was sheer sour grapes, an outright envy of the days that Larry, even in the poverty of a dank basement, would spend luxuriating in ideas while someone else tended to his needs. But the final straw that caused me to put down the book, for the time being, was the realization that *this* was the ideal worker of my profession. Given this model, I understand much better the reactions I received as a woman in the university about to give birth.

During my pregnancy I came to understand that women (and men) were accepted in the academy largely because they could "pass" as masculine subjects. Zero drag was a part of this traditional masculinity. My growing belly and articulated plans to "take some time off" revealed that I was not a masculine graduate student subject who just happened to be female, a way that I believe many (but not all) faculty sometimes preferred to understand the growing ranks of women studying in the department. My pregnant body provided vivid evidence that I violated what a graduate student (and intellectual) was supposed to be. I felt scrutinized when many faculty and graduate students saw my six-, seven-, or eight-month pregnant body lumbering down the hall: *What could she be doing here?*

This response was not monolithic. Some faculty raised their hands toward my enormous belly with a desire to touch, but held back to avoid breaking the norms of professionalism. Staff, graduate, and undergraduate students frequently asked how I was feeling (a joyful question that much of the world asks pregnant women); most professors did not. Perhaps their awkwardness stemmed from my unusual combination of embodied subjectivities, violating the notion that academic bodies are to be used for thinking and that vessels that grew children belong elsewhere.

I could not rely on the institution created for a masculine intellectual to protect me or the time with my baby after the birth. The accommodations that my department made were due to individual goodwill, not structural changes that would protect all pregnant graduate students. But I was still immensely grateful for them. I list them here to give ideas to pregnant women about what kinds of things they might need to ask of their department. In many ways I was extremely lucky. The staff was exceedingly kind, granting me teaching assistantships that would not require me to be on my feet. My committee agreed to look at my work in an extremely timely manner so I could advance to candidacy before I gave birth. My department chair, who at that time was embarking on her own journey into parenthood by adoption, looked out for my welfare and offered me moral support.

I treasured these people as I would anything of value. Like money or a rare jewel, they gave me both a set of material benefits and the capability to imagine the future. In the moments of the bewildered stares or odd probing questions, I would sometimes doubt myself. I wanted to combine two demanding identities. I found few role models. At the time of my pregnancy, I did not know even one woman who had (a) given birth during graduate school, (b) finished her degree, and (c) negotiated this without divorcing her partner. So I found encouragement under the flimsiest of pretenses: professors who continued to express faith in my ability to finish and faculty who had added children to their family at any point in their career. Responses to my body that acknowledged my whole personhood, that considered both my intellect and my belly, gave me hope that I could realize my dreams of parenthood and a tenure-track job after the baby was born.

At my school the pregnant graduate student occupied a liminal position within the institution designated to educate her. At the time of my pregnancy, our graduate division did not have any kind of maternity leave for students. I was fortunate to have no serious pregnancy complications; had I experienced any of the many possible complications that require bed rest, I might not be writing this essay from the comfort of my tenure-track position. A close friend lost a year of her normative time while on bed rest and caring for her premature baby. This kind of setback, inconvenient and frightening to any white-collar woman, makes the graduate student vulnerable to lost health insurance, reduced or eliminated income, housing eviction, and potentially expulsion for surpassing normative time to completion. My body's more textbook pregnancy cost me "only" several thousand dollars in tuition. To be considered for fellowships the following academic year, I had to enroll during the only quarter I was eligible for disability leave. I sent in my tuition check the week before I gave birth, even though I knew I would do no academic work.

It is not exactly fair to cast the graduate division as the villain in this story. True, the graduate division provided pregnant women in its purview with far fewer protections than faculty or staff received. This was no different from the way graduate students were treated in regard to most employment benefits. The lack of institutional support, the stares or averted eyes in the hallway, the disbelief that I was choosing to have a baby—these obstacles were merely local manifestations of a national phenomenon. Anne Crittendon writes in her book *The Price of Motherhood* (2001) about the confining structures that face college-educated women who have children. The policies facing working parents in the university and the boardroom are the negative reactions to my pregnant body writ large. Crittendon notes that the United States is one of only six industrialized countries in the world that do not require paid maternity leave; only eight U.S. states outlaw discrimination against employed parents. As we do not value the huge contribution that parents make to society, our institutions and the people in power in them marginalize those of us whose bodies evidence an effort to simultaneously perform reproductive and productive labor.

As the months progressed, the split between productive and reproductive labor housed in my pregnant body ambling the halls also provided me a quiet joy, one that I have never articulated before writing this essay. It is a cliché that parenthood reshapes one's priorities; I think it keeps getting repeated because no one can believe its utter truth until they experience it for themselves. I could not conceptualize this myself until after my baby came, but in hindsight, the beginnings of the lesson emerged giddily during the final weeks of my first pregnancy. As a teaching assistant, I worked grading papers and holding office hours for a social theory course. I measured the baby's growth according to my increasing difficulty at sliding into the desk I occupied during class. I listened to twice-weekly lectures on the classical theorists as the students, disinterested in this required course and attuned to the approaching springtime, shifted restlessly. As I sat among the students whose grades I would file just one day before I gave birth, my baby's aliveness and humanity called out to me. My concentration was happily interrupted by the child's almost daily hiccupping. The movements would last for several minutes, reminding me of the tectonic shifts soon to reshape my life. This tiny but persistent announcement felt all the more amazing to me because of its invisibility to those around me. That this little life would hail me in the middle of a discussion on anomie felt impossibly delicious. In these moments I allowed myself to believe that just as I could simultaneously contemplate Durkheim and motherhood, I could give birth to a child and a dissertation.

Some would think this made me a less committed intellectual. Like the naps on the floor early in the pregnancy, the revelry in hiccups might be condemned as an indulgence that distracts the parent from her vocation. I suggest instead that we should be concerned with those sociologists who work without distraction. How can we study the social world if we are not actively immersed in it? I am of the sociological mind that we all live as fractured subjects and that generally this is not a bad thing. Our hearts hold multiple loyalties; we occupy more than one social location. To others, and sometimes even to ourselves, these identities do not appear able to sit together around one psychic table. As I washed my face and looked in the mirror after yet another unexpected nausea-induced rush to the bathroom, I reeled at how my identities of pregnant woman, worker, and developing intellectual did not seem capable of occupying the same body. As I grew (literally) into my temporary place in the world as a pregnant academic, I came to observe how much of this jostling among the subjectivities I claimed arose from the structure of the university itself. The absurdity lay not in my body but in the institution that could not fathom its participants' giving birth to *both* new ideas and new babies.

Of course many kinds of academics besides pregnant women transgress academic subjectivity in myriad ways: men who actively parent, academics of color, queer academics, activists, faculty with aging parents, disabled academics, and working-class intellectuals. Many of us live inside more than one problematic category, creating the possibility that the exclusive men-in-tweed intellectual subject and, more to my concern, the institution that was built for it will be replaced by identities and universities that acknowledge our multiplicitous humanness. This step will allow more of us to survive and even flourish within the academy. For sociologists this reconfiguration can only strengthen the discipline, as we expand the possibilities of a diversity of situated knowledges, offering a more complete picture of the social world (Haraway 1988).

My baby was good to me, waiting until the day after I turned in my final grades to enter the world. The months of pregnancy, in a sense, provided me with an extreme version of the awkwardness I still feel at leading the double life of work and parenting. The split between the productive and reproductive labor processes remains acute, and most parents participate in both by enduring years of sleep deprivation. One of the biggest predictors of achieving a tenure-track job for women in sociology, after prestige of graduate institution, is the absence of children (Spalter-Roth 2001). Academic coworkers in most institutions, like some of my more demonstratively befuddled professors, want children and the pregnant bodies that produce them to remain out of sight. They do not want us to disturb the neat arrangements that have operated so well, demanding that women uphold their bargain to be masculine workers if they expect to strive for a degree or tenure-track position. Fortunately, this dominant agreement was rebuked by a now beloved segment of my graduate community. From these people I learned that the way to survive structures of domination is to lean on allies, speak up as much as possible, and honor myself. As of 2003, three other women have had pregnancies (and babies!) in my graduate department. As our numbers grow, the academy will have to reconsider present understandings regarding acceptable embodiment of intellectual practice.

CHAPTER 11

Sexual Boundaries: Trespasses into Chaos

Marga Ryersbach

> You will come to a place where the streets are not marked.
> Some windows are lighted. But mostly they're darked.
> A place could sprain both your elbow and chin!
> Do you dare to stay out? Do you dare to go in?
> How much can you lose? How much can you win?
>
> —*Dr. Seuss*

I have a memory of Dr. Seuss's writing about the difference between here and there. One may never be there but only here, since once you get there, you are here. In a more academically recognized source, "The Transcendent Character of Life," Georg Simmel describes how a person's "position in the world is defined by the fact that in every dimension of his [or her] being and . . . behavior he [or she] stands at every moment *between two boundaries*" (1971:353). Although Simmel's concept goes beyond definitions on positioning, there is a similarity that can be drawn in regard to sexual identity as being either mainstream or marginal, as either here or there. To me, Simmel's work on the transcendental quality of boundaries suggests that we are not *either* here *or* there, but *both* here *and* there.

Simmel notes how we are immersed in our boundaries as we define ourselves while simultaneously transcending these boundaries as we try to figure out the very boundaries that define us. Melissa Orlie rejects the idea of transcendence. Rather, she says, "we can transgress, but not transcend, the limits of our being; we can exceed given ways of being, but only when we recognize that we always accede to another, limited way of being" (1997:6). Thus Orlie builds on Simmel's work on how we negotiate these transient ways of being as well as how these ways of being shape our ethical selves. We can transgress our boundaries, and in doing so we may trespass upon others. We can be in but never above, and it is not a matter of *whether* we trespass upon others but of *how*.

I claim bisexuality as one boundary of my sexual identity. I do not claim this place only recently, at a time when the voices of bisexuals are finally being heard. Neither do I claim this place lightly, as bisexuality is still far from acquiring "acceptability." But I do claim it and have claimed it ever since I was seventeen and got into a fight with my father. My father had found some pornography hidden in my room. Because of the nature of this pornography (or maybe just because I had pornography at all), my father accused me of being a lesbian. (He says now that his accusation was merely teasing and he never meant it in a derisive manner.) My retort was that I was bisexual. I would like to believe I said this merely as a matter of clarification, but it could be that somehow I felt this wouldn't be "as bad."

Thus begins this story about my trespasses and transgressions. It is about my plays with gendered power and my assertions and submissions in the arena of sexuality—my journeys in the here, in the there, and in the between. Despite the work of Simmel, Orlie, and many other theorists, identity—especially sexual identity—tends to be experienced as a fixed, unchanging aspect that is constructed and maintained within binaries; that is, heterosexual or homosexual, male or female, normal or deviant. My lived experience, as well as my theoretical work, wholly rejects identity of any sort as a fixed and static thing. That it is treated and worked with as such may be an indication that empowerment through identity development is not all that it is cracked up to be.

A recent experience demonstrated for me some of the problematic aspects of identity as a site of both empowerment and constraint. I was engaged in a conversation with a friend of mine about her brother's use of the term *too many things* for people who do not fit neatly within male-female and hetero-homo binaries. We laughed as she told me he remembered me only as "the girl who is too many things." I found this attribution interesting because, on the one hand, it is a way to rhetorically silence and vanquish those who do not conform and, on the other hand, it can be indicative of the possibilities that may be derived from refusing to be pegged too easily. If I am "too many things," I am, of course, not one essential thing. But, again, the "too" implies that I cannot embody *all* these things simultaneously. Funny, too, all the while I was no more than a mere "girl" to this person.

Judith Butler (1999), among others, suggests that these binary designations are constructed through behavioral performances; that is, we "do gender." And since gender is intimately connected to sexuality, I also "do (my) sexuality." Judith Lorber describes this constructionist view of sexuality this way: "All sexual desires, practices, and identities not only are gendered but reflect a culture's views of nature, the purpose of life and procreation, good and evil, pleasure and pain; the discourses about them are permeated with power" (1994:56). Sexual identity, intertwined with and contingent upon gender, is central to the way we are constructed as human beings. When we adhere to sexual practices that are unintelligible to others, our identities are invalidated. As Butler notes in *Gender Trouble:* "Inasmuch as 'identity' is assured through the stabilizing concepts of sex, gender, and sexuality, the very notion of 'the person' is called into question by the cultural emergence of those 'incoherent' or 'discontinuous' gendered beings who appear to be persons but who fail to conform to the gendered norms of cultural intelligibility by which persons are defined" (1999:23). By claiming to be sexually "other," I jeopardize, at the very least, my status as being fully human: I am there but not here.

Illuminating the normative here and the counternormative there, Gayle Rubin (1993:13) describes the sex hierarchy that mirrors hegemonic practices of privilege and stigmatization. These practices comprise the following values that constitute the "charmed circle" and the "outer limits."

Charmed Circle	*Outer Limits*
Good, normal, natural, blessed sexuality	Bad, abnormal, unnatural, damned sexuality
Heterosexual	Homosexual
Monogamous	Unmarried
Procreative	Nonprocreative
Commercial	Noncommercial
In pairs	Alone or in groups
In a relationship	Casual
Same generation	Cross-generational
In private	In public
No pornography	Pornography
Bodies only	With manufactured objects
Vanilla	Sadomasochistic

That these values function in our everyday experience is evident in the mainstream gay and lesbian movement's efforts to move "homosexual" into the charmed circle by dissociating homosexuality from the other outer-limits practices. One of the dilemmas of this effort entails the questions of whether and how to include bisexuals, transsexuals, and transgendered people in this movement.[1] The attempt by those in the outer limits to stand firmly both here and there threatens to dissolve the boundaries that support the charmed circle.

It is from the vantage of the charmed circle that the "matrix of intelligibility" is constructed and maintained (Butler 1999). Sexual identities and practices that do not fit into this matrix run the risk not only of being "deviant" but of *not being*. Yet because culture is not fixed or static, those labeled deviant or dismissed as impossible may eventually challenge and sometimes transform what is deemed possible (if not still problematic). These disruptions and subversions do not necessarily alter the sex hierarchy, for they are constrained by the values that alternative sexualities are permitted to own. Thus homosexuality might be marginally allowed into the charmed circle but only if it can be construed as possessing at least some mainstream values (e.g., monogamous, married, bodies only[2]). It is highly doubtful, however, that homosexuals can fully move into the charmed circle as long as certain values (e.g., procreative) remain definitive. The "normal" and the "deviant" are not simply diametrically opposed; they shape each other. Between here and there, then, are the nowhere lands of sexuality.

Another problematic aspect of "who am I?" involves that way in which I frame the telling. According to Ladelle McWhorter (1999), Michel Foucault was suspicious of how we speak of our sexualities and identities because they are shaped by the discourse of *confession*. Foucault "believed that whereas in the past biography might have been aggrandizing, nowadays it is belittling, because it turns its subject into nothing more than a collection of specific deviations from the norm" (McWhorter 1999:xviii). I can describe how I identify, but in doing so I reduce myself; I become nothing more than another one of "those." The easiest path, it seems, might be to avoid confession. After all, sexuality is considered by many to be a private matter and as such is none of anyone's business. Perhaps regrettably, however, this is by no means the case. Historically, within Western culture since at least the latter part of the nineteenth century, knowledge disciplines such as psychology have constructed sexuality as "our most fundamental truth," a truth whose knowledges and practices are not primarily ours to create (p. 10). Given the inherent power of sexuality as something that cannot be denied without injuring ourselves, as well as the cultural belief that uncontrolled sexuality is dangerous, "sexuality, in the person of the sexual subject, must be made to confess, its confession must be heard, and account be taken" (p. 11). As a friend of mine often says, "It's a trap!" So if I'm not the "norm" typically assumed, then how do I begin to speak of myself without getting sucked into this trap?

The most obvious way to avoid a trap is to go around it. But one problem with the sexuality trap (and similar ones) is that there is no easy way to avoid it. Heterosexuality is an *institution* that is buttressed by other supporting institutions that employ both covert and overt regulatory practices and controls, the most obvious of these being the mental asylum (Rich 1980). Although we have little "free choice" in whether we are heterosexual, homosexual, or something in between, heterosexuality is privileged by a hegemonic cultural discourse about the inherent difference between "male" and "female" biology that has been reified and made unproblematic. Biology is destiny, as is male (heterosexual) superiority. At the same time, there is nothing between man and woman or between heterosexual and homosexual. Thus I am not "really" bisexual; I am just not sure what I "truly" am.

Thus if I admit nothing about my sexuality, I am assumed to be heterosexual, to be "normal." If I follow this path, I can at least remain safely in my closet and exercise the option of revealing nothing—or can I? Speaking about her experiences growing up, McWhorter charges that "we were all being scanned constantly for information regarding our sexuality; we were all constantly scanning ourselves" (1999:27). And while "nobody in particular was in charge of the whole enterprise," there were very real consequences to being found out.

McWhorter relates her story of "hide and seek" as well as the price she paid for discovery—the asylum. She is of course not the only one who has experienced hospital "treatment" for what the American Psychiatric Association diagnoses as "gender identity disorder" (GID) (APA 1994). Daphne Scholinski (1997), who was diagnosed with GID at the age of fourteen and was committed to a mental institution for treatment, tells a similar story. A self-proclaimed lesbian, transman, writer, and artist, Scholinski wrote her memoir in an attempt to make public the suffering she endured at the hands of the mental health profession.

These experiences, as horrific as they are, are not even the worst that can happen to those of us who deviate from the norm. Anne Fausto-Sterling (2000) questions how we "fix" babies born with ambiguous genitalia, a mixture of male and female biological traits. "Why should we care if there are individuals whose 'natural biological equipment' enables them to have sex 'naturally' with both men and women? Why must we amputate or surgically hide that 'offending shaft' found on an especially large clitoris?" (p. 8). No longer are hermaphrodites, or intersexuals as they preferred to be called, allowed to reach maturity unaltered; they are "corrected" either at birth or during early childhood with surgery and/or hormonal therapy.[3]

The mandates of conformity do not dissipate with adulthood, although the stakes may change, along with the enforcers. Joshua Gamson (1998), in his work on tabloid talk shows, demonstrates how some of us who inhabit the "outer limits" publicly confess our sexualities. Yet confession, as McWhorter perceptively notes, "is not the end of the game. You'll go on confessing for the rest of your life. That's what your sexuality becomes, or maybe always was: a thing to be known, an epistemic object. And that is what you are, are desired as, and desire as" (1999:28). Gamson contends that while "trash TV" talk shows are constructed along a range of greater or lesser spectacle, the identities that can be confessed in that milieu are constrained by the discourses shaped around the values of the sex hierarchy. The appeal of these shows is the chaos that often ensues when the identities and their appropriate discourses break down.

Most of us are not in the limelight of television talk shows, but this does not quiet the knocking on our respective closet doors. The rappings are heard at our jobs, with our friends, acquaintances, and family, and from professionals and sexuality experts. The inquisitions are always lurking around the corner if not already apparent. To a certain extent, then, many of us who inhabit the "outer limits" are susceptible to the psychic costs of passing that Erving Goffman explores in his work on stigma. Goffman contends that "there is the practice of 'living on a leash'—the Cinderella syndrome—whereby the discreditable person stays close to the place where he [or she] can refurbish his [or her] disguise, and where he [or she] can rest up from having to wear it" (1963:90).

Whether we choose to be in or out, there is always the potential for paying a great price. Eve Kosofsky Sedgwick's "Epistemology of the Closet" (1993) is a rich source for exploring the complex constructions and manifestations of the closet, not only for gays and lesbians but also for many marginalized others who have to negotiate the perils of passing. This closet, or array of closets, is like many other dualisms in our lives that construct us as marginalized but also gives us places from which to subvert and resist. However, opening up the closet to confession does not disturb the hetero-homo binary. The boundaries are left intact.

For all my protesting, it still seems that there is nothing left for me to do but to confess. As I said earlier, I am a traitor to both sides. My boundaries refuse to solidify, and now that I've reached the age of forty, many of my acquaintances and (thankfully) only a few of my friends still find it difficult to reassure themselves that sooner or later I will choose the side I'm supposed to be on, find that one true love, and commit myself to that final relationship. Worse than this, I inhabit not only the space between homosexual and heterosexual but also engage in relationships where power is played out in ways not explicitly dependent on gender or any other societal marking of privilege but instead on the "position" each person finds pleasurable. I violate quite a few "charmed circle" values. I do not, however, apologize for these transgressions even as I may keep a few of the more extreme of these in the closet. (In saying this, of course, I have already brought them out, at least for a peek.) I am indeed one of "those," and in being so I've done nothing to destabilize the sexual status quo. However tenuous my own boundaries may seem to me, this claiming is not subversive in and of itself. Foucault viewed confession as a discourse that eventually engulfs us all. The liberation of confession does not change social structures; it only changes the "sinner" who is confessing. The sword of

Damocles hangs above my head. *If* our sexualities are the defining truths by which we are known, then my "being" deviant does not, as such, challenge the norm. It can in fact be used to reinforce the norm.

So where can I go from here? If our desires and our identities can only condemn us, silence us, make us into a "case" to be dissected and maybe cured, how can we empower ourselves through our transgressive identities? It is at this dead end that McWhorter believes Foucault becomes crucial. She cites his insisting that "the rallying point for the counterattack against the deployment of sexuality ought not be sex-desire, but bodies and pleasures" (McWhorter 1999:107; see Foucault 1978:175). One reason we must move from desire to bodies concerns the current historical construction of the Cartesian mind-body split. Historically, discipline shifted from body to mind not because the body didn't need to be disciplined but because the mind is constructed as the owner of the body. Given this, once the mind is disciplined then the body as possession also becomes controlled. As McWhorter puts it, "many of us, as we grow older, learn a hard truth: Our physical and emotional control, our so-called 'self-control,' doesn't empower us; it just plays into the hands of others who turn it against us" (1999:143). As long as we are embodied as owners of our physical shells, both our bodies and our desires are controlled by our current practices of normalization and the disciplines and discourses that shape these. If, however, we can learn to be bodies, to experience pleasure as bodies, we have a place to grow new disciplines and, thus, new discourses.

According to McWhorter's reading of Foucault, "If it's freedom we want, we'll have to embrace rather than reject the developmental, normalized bodies that we have become" (1999:161). Through the practice of my sexuality, quite accidentally actually, I found ways to be *in* my body that did not entail being *owner* of my body. I have found that engaging in particular physical practices was no longer about my mind controlling my body; in fact, I surrendered my control to the other person. By purposefully giving control to another, however momentarily, I was in my body more than I had ever remembered. I found that it wasn't really about the "I" at all. I am not speaking here of an adrenaline rush and certainly not of an experience where I rose above or transcended my body. To be honest, I find it very difficult to find the words to describe these experiences. My point is that it had nothing to do with leaving my body behind, nor was it a chemical reaction to given circumstances. Foucault calls for the project of making our lives art, and I had found a way to do just that. I was immersed in a process rather than working toward a goal.

McWhorter demonstrates the possibilities of such an effort with two stories, one about composting that she entitles "Becoming Dirt" and the other, "Becoming White." The poignant part of her story for me happened in the telling of the second story, when she tried to continue the composting that she had found transforming when she moved to a different place, living in an apartment instead of a home with tillable land. She succeeded in making not dirt but a can of maggots. I moved from New York City to a smaller city in the Southeast. The community that I was a part of up north does not exist here. I cannot be the body that I could be there. I've been looking for another way to be dirt but, thus far, have only succeeded in breeding maggots. I use this metaphor because of its disgusting imagery. Without new ways of making my life art, of being dirt, of embracing bodies and pleasures, I am left with the battle of self-loathing and struggling for voice that so many of us who identify as queer and other face each day.

McWhorter argues that "freedom exists only in its practice" (p. 223). It is not simply a place or a set of rights. This does not mean that safe places and rights are unimportant, far from that. It is to say that these are products of the practices of freedom. I must, then, continue to find ways to be queer, to be an activist, a student, a teacher, a daughter, and a woman. As Orlie argues, "Every way of being trespasses against others, albeit to varying degrees. . . . When we respond to trespasses, we recognize that what the world and we have been made to be are not necessarily so" (1997:8). If I'm going to insist on having feet, however transitionally, in the here and the there, then perhaps I must learn to navigate the in-between nowhere lands as borderlands.

As a bisexual woman I resonate with Gloria Anzaldúa's (1987) "mestiza" caught in the borderland between homosexuality and heterosexuality. As the "Third World grates against the first and bleeds," I, too, pick at the scabs I have gotten when trying to move from one to the other (p. 3). While boundaries and borders are not interchangeable, boundaries are often policed by borders, and these borders "are set up to define the places that are safe and unsafe, to distinguish *us* from *them*." I will continue to find ways to dance between these borders despite the wounds I may incur for my trespasses. I will continue to live my life with boundaries that are there to be trodden upon. My art is the chaos that refuses closure and denies solidification.

Notes

1. The term *transsexual* is commonly used to refer to someone who traverses the boundary of the biological sex they were *assigned* at birth. A female-to-male transsexual, for example, is one who believes himself to be male although he was born in a female body. Transsexuals usually cross-dress and commonly use hormones and/or surgery to alter their bodies. The term *transgender* is used to denote someone who may cross-dress, and even shape his/her body hormonally or surgical-

ly, but who does not think of himself or herself as the "other sex." *Transgender* is also used as an "umbrella term to include everyone who challenges the boundaries of sex and gender" (Feinberg 1996:x).

2. "Bodies only" refers to sexual acts that exclude the use of manufactured objects such as dildos.

3. About 1.7 percent of all births can be diagnosed as intersexual (Fausto-Sterling 2000).

CHAPTER 12

The Razor's Edge: Narcotics and the Embodiment of Trauma

Diane Schaefer

When the enemy lies within, it stalks without pursuing, attacks without approach, and murders without killing. Its lethal hand is not succeeded by the deliverance of the grave. Speak of hell on earth—the ghastly presence of this internal demon uproots all faith in the divine.

—*Personal journal, April 5, 1973, age twenty-three*

A gurgling sound rode each breath the man took and seeped through my open window. Shot by the police, the man had sought surgery from friends rather than physicians. Friends would not report the gunshot wound. I had remained behind when my roommate Bill went to assist the heroin users across the hall as they tried to operate.

I never learned what became of the man whose labored breath I heard. My roommate never talked about him, just as he never talked about the night he and another man, who tucked a revolver into his waistband, tried to score drugs. To have talked about trying to remove a bullet from a friend or enforcing a drug deal with a gun would have made hauntingly real the possibility that he too could soon have a bullet lodged within, desperately asking fellow addicts to remove it. In the narcotics world of doped ecstasy and spiderweb pain, the nightmares happening to others all too readily became your own living reality.

When you were caught in heroin's trap, peace was achieved by ignoring what must be done in order to shoot up the illegal substance. I distanced myself from the roughest aspects of that lifestyle by letting Bill inject me, by not copping (buying) the drugs myself, and by working as an executive secretary for a Fortune 500 company during the week. As much as the pain in my life had driven me to the pleasures harbored in a syringe, I could not, at least not yet, submerge myself completely in that subculture.

Like my roommate and the other users, I had not been born craving narcotics, although my background, like theirs, created a need so vast that I would resort to just about anything to quench it. A college transcript reminded me that I had once tried quieting that need in other ways. Instead of using street drugs and hepatitis-laden needles, I had sought knowledge, appeared regularly on the dean's list, tutored, wrote freelance articles for the student newspaper, and worked with a public interest action group ultimately under the direction of Ralph Nader. Academic success led to my induction into an academic honor society and my inclusion in *Who's Who Among Students in American Junior Colleges, 1972–73.* The socioeconomic circumstances of my birth, however, meant that I was not supposed to be college material.

In order to understand the source of the internal demon that usurped my claims for a better life, it is necessary to understand the social structural conditions that wore down any hopes and dreams my parents and their parents may have had. My mother's parents and my parents were born in West Virginia. My father's parents were immigrants from Czechoslovakia, as far as I can tell. Each of my mother's parents experienced work and daily survival in different ways that affected their parenting. My mother's mother was distant and cold to her four surviving daughters (one died twenty-one days after birth). Instead of providing psychological warmth to her children, she alleviated their hunger by cleaning the homes of affluent women and scrubbing their families' clothing on a washboard. As a result of her mother's daily drudgery, my mother did not experience hunger. She did experience the embarrassment of being sent to local charities asking for clothing and, sometimes, for food.

Warmth and affection came from my mother's father, who creatively skirted work's drudgery whenever he could. Mother walked the railroad tracks with him as a child looking for coal that fell (or was thrown by sympathetic railroad workers) off passing trains. My grandfather stole chickens on these walks for the family dinner. Although he was never caught for chicken theft, he was arrested for taking some copper wire. Legitimate work included the Works Progress Administration, where he worked on a road crew and did custodial tasks for a building owned by the local newspaper. At times he used acid, acquired from a glass factory as a byproduct of glass etching, to clean buildings around downtown Wheeling. My grandfather escaped the drudgery that hardened my grandmother's spirit by avoiding long-term, demeaning work and by combining legitimate with illegal opportunities in support of his family. Mother was lucky that her mother's hard work allowed her father a measure of freedom that nurtured his spirit enough to express love and creativity, at least to my mother. Still, as a teen my mother's youngest sister sometimes suffered brutal beatings from the buckle end of my grandfather's belt when she tried to bathe.

My father's experience with poverty was much harsher than my mother's. His mother did not work, but his father worked in the coal mines of West Virginia. As a child, my father had been present when his father was on strike. Father remembers how business leaders hired people to attack the striking coal miners with clubs and dogs. He also saw law enforcement officials team up with business owners during these disputes. As police officers unleashed tear gas against striking miners, my father saw his father and other striking coal miners cast as criminals for endangering business as usual.

A coal miner's income did not go far. My father's six siblings (four from a previous marriage) were always hungry. Father called the hunger he experienced "hunger tantrums" and described meals as having only one food—the one that happened to be available at the time. My father failed a couple of grades in elementary school, something he attributes to being dumb rather than to being distracted by hunger, poverty, and family violence. At the age of nine, he began work as a caddy for affluent golfers. Eager for income, he slept outside the clubhouse on Friday nights with other boys who wanted to be assured an assignment the next morning. At the age of twelve, my father dropped out of school to set pins in a bowling alley from 5:00 P.M. to 7:00 A.M. for 3.5 cents a line. Little boys provided this service before the invention of automatic pinsetters. My father earned $1.75 to $2.25 per fourteen-hour shift. Child labor laws had been in effect for about two years, but many employers ignored those laws. My father's mother was physically and emotionally abusive. She beat her boys, if she could catch them, with leather straps nailed to a sawed-off broomstick. Sometimes she accused my father of gambling some of his earnings rather than giving them all to her. My father still protests that he gave her all of his earnings.

In 1938, at the age of fifteen, my father lied about his age in order to join the Civilian Conservation Corps. Each month he received five dollars while the government sent twenty-one dollars directly to his parents. He was well fed for his labors, the first time in his life that he ate adequately. He worked hard blasting boulders loose and then loading them onto trucks. The large rocks that Father helped gather went into building foundations and bridge supports. Some of these structures remain in Lost River State Park near Mathias, West Virginia.

During World War II my father served in the Pacific, where his ship's mission was to search out minefields. When my father returned, he went into the mines with his father. In those days, the company did not provide training. Instead, a man who wanted to work in the mines had to find an experienced miner to take him down and teach him how to work safely. Since the work was dangerous and the men carried explosives, each miner carefully considered if, and who, they would take into the mines: an inexperienced miner could cause them injury or death.

Both of my parents had learned early, too early, to work hard in order to survive physically. Work, only once and all too briefly, provided them with a glimpse that labor could also provide psychological sustenance and self-esteem. My father and mother met at the Wonder Bar, a bar somehow acquired by my father's half brother. Father worked there and thrived on bartending. The success of the bar, at least in terms of throngs of customers, led my father to think of himself and his brothers as "kingpins." He loved the work and did not take any wages, living off his GI benefits instead.

Unfortunately, the bank would not renew the contract my father's brother had obtained, probably due to some illegal whiskey sales and lack of business skills. My father's brief glimpse of a larger and more pleasant life via the Wonder Bar clamped shut hard. He found employment with the railroads, but his chaotic, on-call, out-of-town assignments were hard on his relationship with my mother. After a railroad mishap that almost killed him, he went back to the mines. He was working in the mines when I was born in 1949, ten months after he and my mother married; my brother was born one year later.

My family lived in a rental apartment near the coal mines. The property consisted of one large room with a kitchen area in the back. My parents divided the room in half, creating a bedroom near the kitchen and a living room in front. Instead of central heating, the apartment had a coal-burning stove. As infants, my brother and I were frequently ill. The family doctor took one look at the moisture built up on the inside walls of our apartment and the poor ventilation of the coal stove and discovered the major cause of all our illnesses.

Northern industry was flourishing in the 1950s but lacked enough workers. Desperate for laborers, employers posted ads near the coalfields and promised a better way of life even for those, like my father, who had not finished school. Father found employment on a General Motors assembly line in Cleveland, Ohio. For a year he made a long drive each weekend back to West Virginia, where the rest of us remained. After obtaining a low-interest loan from the Veterans Administration, my father bought a house and moved the family north. I was three years old.

The house my father purchased was located directly across from a large industrial area on a street heavily traveled by semi-trailer trucks. Nearby plants included a greeting-card plant, a paint and spice manufacturer, a tool and die plant, the large presses of a book-publishing company, and a steel mill. Chemical odors and the noise of machines, trains, and trucks filled the air. Two taverns, one just fifty yards away, served blue-collar workers and contributed to the nonresidential atmosphere. We lived next to a weed-filled lot containing a V-shaped double billboard with advertisements displayed on both sides. My brother and I explored the interior girders of this billboard and became so adept at climbing its internal structure that we could scramble to the top, peer out over the advertisements, and wave to the truckers passing by.

America in the 1950s seemed economically strong and morally intact. My family appeared that way too. After all, we owned a house and purchased a car. Furthermore, my parents never separated or divorced. We always smiled to neighbors and acquaintances, although we rarely invited them into our house. If they had been invited inside, they might have been exposed to a micro–cold war between my parents. They might have been exposed to my father's McCarthy-like need for scapegoats, his fascist tendencies, and the concentration-camp atmosphere he created within the walls of our home.

Father worked evenings and slept during the day. This schedule produced a dark, morguelike atmosphere in the house. If happy childhood play interfered with his sleep, he would explode angrily from his bedroom with savage verbal attacks and beatings in which his face transformed into the face of an angry, snarling beast, fangs exposed. My brother and I labeled Father's room "the crypt" and Father "the creature": when he awoke his swearing and moaning warned us that the creature was aroused and would be leaving the crypt. Father's unpredictable temper turned the somber house into a tense and brooding arena. Angrily he fumed about the house, his violent explosions occurring at random. Anything we said or did, or did not say or do, was potential fuel for his fuse.

My mother remained silent about Father's abuse. At a time when many mothers did not work, she began work after my brother and I entered the Cleveland public school system. The economic opportunities for women in the middle 1950s were low-wage jobs. In order to obtain one of these, Mother lied to potential employers, saying that she had no children. She became a full-time bookkeeper at the local five-and-dime store and feared losing her job whenever she had to stay home with sick children. Mother worked days, and my brother and I let ourselves into the house after school, where we took care of ourselves for two hours until she returned home. My latchkey status and the financial fears that drove my parents made me vulnerable to abuse at home and to trauma from predators outside.

In the elementary school I attended, I soon fell under the predatory gaze of my gym teacher and two custodians. The gym teacher took advantage of my love for sports when I was nine by singling me out for special attention. In the gym, located in the basement of the school, I sat at the gym teacher's desk near the boiler room. He showed me card tricks and played games with me. Soon two custodians joined us. They invited me to join them on a Saturday morning. I arrived expecting more games, but the games they wanted to play that morning no longer contained harmless fun. I emerged from that sublevel gym and boiler room into a chilling rain feeling stunned, frightened, and unsure about what those adults had done. A teacher found me curled up against the brick wall of the building. I have some sense that she told me to stay in her car until she returned. Confused and scared, I got out of her car and walked home, where I hid my blood-stained underwear in the back of my closet under some toys.

When I returned to school on Monday morning, I went to the gym, where it was my privilege to pump up the volleyballs and basketballs in preparation for the week. But I was rejected by the gym teacher. He said not to come there anymore. Sometime later I overheard two teachers talking in the hallway. They were discussing the custodians who had been fired. It made me happy to know that the custodians would no longer be there, but I heard nothing further about the incident. No one talked to me. In the 1950s no one thought to provide further help to the child victim. So I acted like the adults around me, as if nothing had happened.

But something *had* happened, and my psyche protected me by shutting down. I successfully closed out the world around me and do not remember much from my childhood, adolescence, or teen years. Although I spent three years at John Marshall High School, I cannot describe the inside of that building and recall few of the 500 students in my graduating class.

In high school I was quiet and reserved, yet I successfully fended off the advice of high school advisers and eschewed college preparatory courses in favor of secretarial training. Activities at school and college-bound dates felt foreign to me. In contrast, the turbulence I had experienced led me to the streets, where I embraced the hippies' subculture of the late 1960s. Out on the streets I could not, however, distinguish the losers and the drug users from those earnestly endeavoring to promote harmony, peace, and a holistic lifestyle. The boys I connected with were high school dropouts who used drugs.

Once I tried to date a boy I met in school instead of the streets, a boy who was quiet and gentle as well as college-bound. He had an older brother in college who was active in the civil rights movement, and his parents were kind and caring, but I did not understand any of them. I did not understand why they cooperated with each other and treated each other with consideration. When their kindness was directed toward me, I did not know how to respond. One week prior to graduation, this boy's family assisted him in putting together a romantic picnic of French bread, cheese, and wine. We found a quiet, secluded spot along a river and talked as sunlight turned into dusk. Kindness and quietness such as I experienced on that peaceful evening struck an unsettling chord deep within me. As much as I felt special at being the target of their kindnesses, it was so unlike anything I had ever experienced that I could not relax and enjoy myself. I eventually stopped dating this boy because I could not tolerate those disquieting experiences. I ran back to the streets, where I embraced the familiarity of troubled friends and activities.

Ironically, my life expanded a bit when my high school placed me with a Fortune 500 company upon graduation. As a secretary there, I worked with college-educated managers who liked me and provided glimpses into a larger, more interesting world. I became apprenticed to the graphics arts director and assisted the chairman of the board. I typed captions for photographs of the chair's family mansion as well as polo and fox-and-hound hunt club activities. The chairman called me Sunshine, my first positive nickname from someone old enough to be my father. As a result of the kindnesses and encouragement garnered from friends and bosses, I achieved some positive self-esteem that did not come from the streets and did not provoke unpleasant reactions by being too personal or close. A company program encouraged higher education by providing tuition reimbursement, so I enrolled in night classes at a community college. Hopeful that I too might pursue a more interesting life, I quit my position after a few years in order to go to college full time.

In college I achieved academic success and honors. But I had been socialized in chaos, and internal turmoil, the product of traumas, dominated my existence. As turbulence continued at home, I struggled to establish and maintain some personal integrity and values. Higher education had begun to expose me to other ways of viewing life. I admired the nineteenth-century Transcendentalists, Ralph Waldo Emerson and Henry David Thoreau. Their spiritual views and insistence on self-reliance and scholarly activities especially appealed to me. At home, on a more intimate level, my search for personal values was thwarted by the barbaric negativity of my father and the withdrawn, depressed silence of my mother.

Although I was successful academically, I continued associating with drug users and other losers. Although my low self-esteem drove me to those social peers, I remained optimistic about my future until my sophomore year. On a December morning in 1972, while studying in my attic room, I heard yelling and swearing downstairs between my father and brother. Abruptly, my brother left the house, leaving me alone with this brutal man. Almost immediately he yelled out for me to go outside and help him with his dead car battery. He needed someone to assist in fetching a replacement battery, so I pulled my car from the street into the driveway. There, Father rushed at my car carrying the dead battery and ordered me to open the trunk. But ice had sealed it shut, and a volley of verbal abuse highlighted my inadequacies as I pounded around the edges of the trunk until the ice shattered. Father dropped the battery inside and slammed the trunk down as I yanked my arms out of the way. Fearfully, I asked, "Would you mind driving?" A barrage of foul language about my uselessness left me dazed as he grabbed my car keys and drove off.

I had done everything a person could do to help him. Instead of receiving thanks, or even just being left alone, I had been savagely attacked. Some two decades of abusive lessons had taught me that I was not good enough, or fast enough, or clever enough, or pretty enough, or worthy enough. This latest assault on my identity sent my defenses tumbling, and I suffered what could probably be called a nervous breakdown.

I had learned not to let my hurt show. I had learned not to give Father the pleasure of seeing me cry. I had learned to tune him out. None of these mechanisms were working, and I screamed and cried and pounded and kicked at the walls of the house until I was exhausted. When I called Mother at work looking for sympathy, she took his side as always. I hung up. I was confused, hurt, and alone. No one cared. This latest link on a long chain of what Merton Schatzman (1973) calls "soul murder" violated my human dignity at a time when I was struggling in college to reconcile my right to exist in a world I was taught I could not have. Internal demons and their attendant pain gushed forth and began a dark and dominating grip on each hour of my life.

> Life is a cat who plays with its captured mouse before making it admit defeat.
> —*Personal journal, March 1, 1970, age twenty*

In many respects, I began a new life. My defenses had been destroyed on that cold December day, and I became fearfully aware of my surroundings. I acted like one of those abandoned and starving domestic animals sometimes seen slinking about the streets, tail between legs, fearful of human contact. I preferred doing without contact with others. I trembled. I sweated. I began dropping classes, especially those requiring active participation, like my French class. I managed to remain in two classes, but I sat in the back, where my perspiring hands left puddles as I took notes. I sensed that complete self-annihilation awaited if I dropped all my classes, if I gave in entirely to my fears. Mentally I dropped to the bottom of a deep and vile pit, so far down that I could not see any light at the top.

When spring quarter ended in 1973, I returned, as I had in the past, to the company that had hired me after high school. It was a summer job, and I anxiously pondered what I would do to keep self-annihilation away when that job ended. I could not return to school. My hands shook violently and perspired excessively, which convinced me that I could not find employment on my own. The completion of my summer job meant the total absence of options in life, the end of the road. I knew I could not live without options, but fate intervened and opened a door.

I was assigned to work for a newly hired, Dartmouth-educated executive to work on a special project for the company. Driven by the awful fear of having no alternatives in life, I had to fulfill this assignment somehow. When I took dictation from this man, I pulled my chair up close to his desk so that, with my stenographer's notepad in my lap, he could not see my shaking and sweaty hands. As I sat alone in my office afterward, no one could see my trembling, sweaty hands on the typewriter's keyboard. I went to work each day with a sick, brooding feeling, knowing that if I failed I had nowhere else to go and nothing else to do. I could not allow such complete nothingness to creep in.

Although I had no confidence in my secretarial skills, my boss proclaimed those skills top-notch and asked if I would work for him after the summer. Having no other options, I took the job, and my life became confined to that stenographer's notepad and typewriter. My demolished psyche would not allow me to join the other secretaries at lunch or in conversations during breaks. I ate alone, although I ached to join coworkers and develop friendships. For two years my evenings and weekends also found me isolated in pain.

> I went to the woods because I wished to live deliberately, to front only the essential facts of life, and see if I could not learn what it had to teach, and not, when I came to die, discover that I had not lived. . . . I wanted to live deep and suck out all the marrow of life, to live so sturdily and Spartanlike as to put to rout all that was not life, to cut a broad swath and shave close, to drive life into a corner, and reduce it to its lowest terms, and, if it proved to be mean, why then to get the whole and genuine meanness of it . . . or if it were sublime, to know it by experience, and be able to give a true account of it in my next excursion.
>
> —*Henry David Thoreau*

The three-story building where I had an apartment contained a wide mix of people, and I needed companionship. Some of the people in my building attended Case Western Reserve University, but my low self-esteem led me to associate with the drug dealers and junkies who also lived there. I became friends with the drug-dealing custodian, his wife, and their drug-using friends, including Bill, who used heroin. Their friendship seemed like a step up from my family, because they all liked me. They talked with me as if I mattered to them. We shared a common hurt. We hurt ourselves, and we hurt each other, but we were not all bad. We shared the positive along with the negative and formed a family of mutual aid that was maintained by drugs.

I drew on my understanding of Thoreau's deliberate choice to go into the woods when I decided to allow Bill and his lifestyle to move in with me. On some level I knew I had to go into my own type of woods with Bill in order to confront the raw facts of life and to learn what that "razor's edge" might teach (Maugham 1944). My decision to partner up with Bill paid off almost immediately. As a refugee from the upper middle class, Bill displayed a nature that was not always dark and addicted. My first impressions of him included how he sang and whistled in happy abandonment while going about mundane tasks in our apartment. I had never seen anyone in private life who expressed joy and delight in daily living. I had to know more.

Bill opened up a sense of hope. He delighted in and encouraged my musical endeavors on his piano, and I glowed in his praise as I mastered beginning piano. He also showed me how to enjoy daily activities and introduced me to other pleasures like 35mm photography and gourmet cooking. Bill was always eager to do things and to go places. His attitude toward the discovery of new places was remarkable and bold. He acted as though the whole world was his, and he freely explored what it had to offer. I enjoyed our travels and vacations while learning from Bill how to actively explore new places, people, and ideas. Most important, Bill helped me translate the love of nature I gained from my Transcendental heroes into action. Although I had always loved the outdoors, I had been only a visitor there until Bill introduced me to camping. We bought field guides and began identifying trees and wildflowers. I learned how to enjoy the woods in a spiritually profound way.

My life expanded enormously through companionship with this heroin user from the middle class. Most of all, I learned how to feel good, but unfortunately the barriers to positive feelings were removed through use of drugs. Everything about my life with Bill was intertwined with narcotics. All my negative emotions, all my fears, depression, insecurities, and basic unhappiness disappeared because I was anesthetizing my body and soul. Narcotics created a temporary sense of well-being, happiness, and inner peace that opened the doors for exploration of the world around me, whether through music, nature, travel, or photography.

The drug-induced euphoria did not last, however, for there were all the raw feelings of being pushed to physical and emotional limits by the narcotic itself and the chaotic drug lifestyle. Powerful, raw-edged, animal-like instincts arise when one deals with life through drug use. Those drug-related edgy feelings were alleviated by another injection. Heroin was missed and craved, and vicious drug-use cycles were established. For me those cycles never included physical addiction, since I relegated narcotics use to weekends. As a result, I never became used to heroin's unpleasant side effects.

The dark narcotics side of my life with Bill threw me into a tempestuous world of emotions with no control over them. The good feelings associated with drug use were parasitically attached to the bad. I ignored, for a time, those negative emotions as the price I had to pay to feel good, and I focused on the artificial sense of well-being. At least I had feelings and was not always in pain.

Sometimes I yearned for a lifestyle free of drugs and Bill. Bill was not easy to live with. He lied and took advantage of me. One night he borrowed my car and did not return. Without my knowledge he had injected himself with some contaminated drugs before leaving. The police found him wandering about confused and babbling. They held him in jail until he was coherent enough to give them directions home. No one knew where my car was. Luckily, neighbors helped, and I found it before it was towed, vandalized, or stolen. Bill had abandoned it near the middle of a busy intersection, leaving the keys in place.

When Bill stole my television, electric guitar, and amplifier to pawn for drug money, I threw him out of my apartment. Bill, however, kept his key, so I hired a young locksmith to change the locks. The locksmith liked me and spent some time with me the evening he changed the locks. We made a dinner date that I knew I could not keep. My fears were so extreme and my hands trembled so nervously that I could not embarrass myself by attempting a dinner date where I would have to use eating utensils and drinking glasses. As much as I wanted to date this polite young man and get away from Bill and drugs, I could not.

On another occasion when I tried separating from Bill and drugs, I met a young man who was studying to become a pediatrician. He also asked me out on a date. I accepted his invitation to the theater but canceled later when anxiety and fear overwhelmed me. I feared the simple act of talking with him before and after the play.

At times I longed for a more normal lifestyle, but whenever I tried to change, I was painfully confronted with my inability to do so. Thus I remained with Bill and continued using drugs. I maintained some distance from this lifestyle by letting Bill procure the drugs and syringes as well as inject the narcotics into my arms. In this way I considered my drug behavior noncommittal and passive, because I did not actively seek out the drugs, buy them, prepare them in a spoon, filter them through cotton, or inject them into my veins.

I felt doomed to continue my self-destructive existence with people like Bill. I knew it would not be a long life. One time I discovered how close death was linked to the syringe when, seconds after a particularly potent injection, I quickly slipped into unconsciousness. When I struggled back to awareness, I realized that in the darkness of lost consciousness there was a mysteriously fine line between recovery and death. I also felt trapped in a secretarial job that had become ever so boring. I wanted to return to school but had no real hope of picking up where I had left off, nor of finding any normalcy in my life. I felt trapped in my present self-destructive and meaningless existence.

On Friday, June 22, 1979, I crossed the line separating passive drug use from approaching addiction. Abruptly I left work to cook heroin in a spoon, filter it through cotton, and inject it into a vein I pumped up for myself. I watched my blood enter the syringe—evidence that I had successfully found the vein. Frightened of myself and the line I had crossed, I saw my hand shake as I pushed the narcotic up my arm. That injection ripped away the last strongholds of dignity and self-worth I had—my normal work life and a passive use of drugs. I could no longer reconcile my illegal and taboo use of narcotics with any self-concept of personal worth. I plummeted quickly away from the drug's high into an abyss of cognitive dissonance.

My family could not help. A call to home led to an invitation to go drinking with my father. My friends could only offer more of the same—drugs. Alone, I turned to the haunted, frightened eyes reflecting back to me from a mirror hanging in the living room. The wild eyes I saw belonged to the only person I could turn to for help. I stood on what felt like a wide precipice offering only options that would lead to death, my death, either physically or mentally via addiction. Surely there must be another way to live than the ways my family and the drug users had showed me.

Fortunately, Bill's upbringing role modeled the acceptability of calling on therapeutic counselors, and my Fortune 500 job provided very good benefits. I called the Academy of Medicine for a referral and held back tears as the counselor asked questions over the telephone. When he asked if I felt I was going to lose control, I answered yes as my voice quivered and the tears fell. Although I mentioned my drug use, I said nothing about my recent compulsion to inject myself for the first time. I did not want to think about that. There were many things I did not want to think about. It seemed that everything was closing in around me and narrowing my lifestyle into a limited, grimly unacceptable existence. I plunged into a suicidal abyss armed only with the survival thought that if I was capable of pushing life to the edge, of feeling and doing my worst, then it seemed plausible that I might be capable of moving in the opposite direction, in the direction of salvation and hope. I realized that I could rewrite my story (Kiesinger 2002).

> I left the woods for as good a reason as I went there. I learned . . . that if one advances confidently in the direction of his dreams, and endeavors to live the life which he has imagined, he will meet with a success unexpected in common hours.
>
> —*Henry David Thoreau*

The transformation I eventually made from social isolation to social integration, from a world of crime to the professorate, and from being close to death to living fully was a long, tortuous, and vastly difficult journey. The instant transformation that I anticipated, the Eureka-like insight, never occurred. My transformation involved long-term, persistent, Herculean efforts that I know I could not live over again.

The enemy I wrote about in the journal excerpt at the opening of this essay does not, of course, lie within any individual. That enemy is created within a social structure of hierarchies and inequalities that harms many of us by putting the sustaining and enriching resources of life into the hands of the few. My life has been about the embodiment of *socially structured* trauma. I am not alone is this regard, whatever form this embodiment may take, be it drug addiction, alcoholism, child abuse, teen pregnancy, homicide, or self-inflicted death.

I believe we were born for a better world than the one that we have now. The transformation we require is not simply a transformation of the individual but a transformation of society. Life is not mean; somehow we have made it so. Life offers the possibility of glorious joy. The human spirit was meant to fly and to connect with the wonders that abound around us. I am inspired by the democratic ideal, which provides the tools we need to make things better. "The spirit of democracy is the idea of importance and worth in the individual, and faith in the kind of world where the individual can achieve as much of his [or her] potential as possible" (Alinsky 1971:xxiv). Affluence of human spirit can occur only when the material affluence of our world is shared so that the "minor details of life" that create subjection that "crosses [people] at each turn, till they are led to surrender the exercise of their will," no longer destroy our spirit and our capacity to act democratically in the interests of our human community (Alexis de Tocqueville, quoted in Alinsky 1971:xxv).

CHAPTER 13

Hoop Dreams on Wheels

Ronald J. Berger

I became interested in disability issues because my daughter has cerebral palsy, or "CP" as it is called in the shorthand vernacular used by those who are familiar with this impairment. As disabilities go, Sarah's condition is relatively moderate, though this consolation is a sentiment I might not have held had life not taken this turn for our family. Her diagnosis is referred to as spastic diplegia. For the most part it affects only her lower extremities, her ability to walk as the able-bodied do. After many years of therapy and hard work, she is able to walk independently with a cane if the terrain she is traversing is not too demanding and the distance is fairly short. There is always the wheelchair waiting in reserve, pulled out primarily when we are on holiday, when the experience of tourism places greater demands on our need to be mobile.

Sarah is ten years old at the time of this writing and has just undergone several major surgical procedures to both improve her ambulatory ability and mitigate the prospects of degenerative arthritis. The decision to go forward with this surgery did not come easy. My wife and I were confronted with conflicting medical advice and technical terms such as *proximal femoral derotational osteotomy, rectus femoras transfer, strayer gastrocnemius recession*, and *psoas and os calcius lengthenings*. Telling the full story of this medical journey and its aftermath will have to wait for another time and place. In this space I want to tell a different but related story, a story about my involvement with dedicated wheelchair basketball players, a story about individuals who exhibit what Arthur Frank refers to as "mundane charisma" (2002:358).[1] It is a story about perseverance and accomplishment in the face of adversity, about individuals who have reframed their disability as a challenge rather than as a catastrophe. It is a story that hinges on the question of how one rises to the occasion and that exhibits an "ethic of inspiration" rooted in woundedness but that refuses to give in to despair (Frank 1995:133; May 1991).

That I should find wheelchair basketball an arena through which I pursue my family's engagement with disability is not really surprising. I grew up in Los Angeles, with Chamberlain, Baylor, and West. Then came Kareem and Magic, and now Kobe and Shaq.[2] Enjoying their superhuman feats has been one of my guilty pleasures; among academics, spectator sport is not high art. It was not these all-star athletes, however, that piqued my interest in wheelchair basketball. After all, these men do not play in chairs. They can reach the rim of the hoop by catapulting themselves through the air or simply standing tall. My story of wheelchair basketball began with a young man named Melvin Juette (born 1969), whom I first met three years before my daughter was born, when he was enrolled in one of my courses at the University of Wisconsin–Whitewater (UWW).

Melvin is a four-time member of the United States national wheelchair basketball team, winner of two gold and two bronze medals in international competitions. He is, in the game of wheelchair basketball, one of the best in the world. His inspirational story led me to embark on a (still ongoing) research project about wheelchair basketball. I was searching for role models, for people who possessed insight about living with a disability, for those who might offer guidance to help my daughter—help my wife and me—face this challenge in our lives.

I first met Melvin in 1990, when he was enrolled in my criminology course at UWW. He seemed a quiet youth at the time, unlike the vivacious man I later came to know. But of course, like many students, he did not reveal much of himself to me. He would not have stood out among his classmates had he not been one of the relatively few black students at that university, and one of even fewer black students in wheelchairs.

I became reacquainted with Melvin a few years later. Amy Bleile, another student who uses a wheelchair, was taking my criminology course. We were reading an autobiography of a Los Angeles gang member (Shakur 1993). Amy told me she knew Melvin and suggested I invite him to speak to our class. Melvin had been a Chicago gang member and was shot in a gang dispute. A bullet lodged in his lower spine. The doctors said removing it would have caused him more harm than good. He was sixteen years old. A paraplegic, paralyzed for life.

I did not have much of a disability consciousness at the time. The full implications of Sarah's diagnosis and prognosis were not yet clear to me. I was more interested in Melvin's story for its relevance to criminology. He graciously agreed to be a guest speaker. It was then that I learned of his involvement in, his passion for, wheelchair basketball.

Melvin is a remarkable young man. His paralysis from the shooting, he has told me, was both the worst and best thing that has happened to him. If he hadn't been shot, he'd probably be in prison now, or dead, like many of his former gang associates, friends and enemies alike. It was the reason he'd gone on to college, made the United States national wheelchair basketball team, traveled throughout the world to places I have never been.

Melvin had decided early on, when he was still recuperating in the hospital, that he wasn't going to sit around and feel sorry for himself. He remembers how he and his friends had reacted to James, a neighborhood youth with muscular dystrophy. Although James used a power chair, the other boys tried to include him in everything they did. They even changed the rules for touch football to accommodate him. If the passer hit James with the ball, it was counted as a catch. But James was a mope. It wasn't his disability that made him unpleasant to be around; it was his negative attitude. So Melvin and his friends stopped including him. When they made plans to do something, they'd say, "Naw, let's forget about James." Melvin didn't want that to happen to him. He would not get mired in self-pity.

Although sports are an ancient human endeavor, sports for people with disabilities are a mid-twentieth-century phenomenon. World War II was a turning point in the development of wheelchair sports. Improved battlefield evacuation methods and medical technology dramatically increased the survival rate of the wounded. These soldiers, including those with spinal cord injuries, would have died in previous wars. Now they survived, warehoused in veterans hospitals throughout the United States (DePauw and Gavron 1995; Hedrick, Byrnes, and Shaver 1994).

Many of the survivors had previously enjoyed participation in competitive sports and would not tolerate inactivity. They started playing pool, table tennis, and catch, then progressed to swimming and bowling, and eventually to water polo, softball, touch football, and basketball. Today people with disabilities participate in the full gamut of sports, including bicycling, skiing, tennis, track and field, rugby, volleyball, and horseback riding.

It is now widely recognized that participation in sports provides an array of benefits for people with disabilities (see Berger 2004). For many, the primary benefit is the intrinsic satisfaction, the reward felt for playing the game, accomplishing the task itself. Others enjoy the camaraderie, recognition, and social approval from teammates and peers. Participants gain improved physical conditioning and a sense of bodily mastery, along with a heightened sense of self-esteem and personal empowerment that spills over into other social pursuits. One learns to view "challenges as possibilities rather than as obstacles," to deal with defeat not as failure but as incentive to do better (Blinde, Taub, and Han 2001:163). These enhancements are not simply "rehabilitative" or "therapeutic," for they are the same ones often enjoyed by the able-bodied who participate in athletics.

Among all the sports currently available for people with disabilities, wheelchair basketball is arguably the most popular. In the United States, the National Wheelchair Basketball Association (NWBA), organized in 1949, boasts a membership of some 2,000 athletes. It organizes men's, women's, and youth divisions, and sponsors about 190 teams and a score of conferences. Although the NWBA is an amateur organization, a number of its teams receive financial support from and bear the names of professional National Basketball Association (NBA) teams. In addition, there is a U.S. national team that competes every four years in the international Paralympics that are held in the same venue as the regular Olympic games. This team also competes in the international Gold Cup championships, which are held every four years in the off years between the Paralympics.

Even those who love basketball may not appreciate the special skills involved in this sport if they have never seen a wheelchair game. The game is for the most part played according to NCAA or NBA rules, on a full-size court, with the basket ten feet above the ground. Imagine accurately shooting at a ten-foot basket from the three-point line, the free-throw line, or even closer, while sitting in a chair! Imagine moving a wheelchair with speed and agility, maintaining your stamina for the duration of a forty- or forty-eight-minute game.

I once viewed a video of a game that captured the action from the top of the arena. The movement of the chairs pivoting and circling around each other reminded me of the inner workings of an intricate Swiss watch. Then there's the physical contact, chairs banging against chairs, tipping over as players fall to the ground, then pull themselves back up without assistance from others. The game might be described as a combination of bumper cars, speed racing, and a finely choreographed dance. During the course of watching a game, one begins to forget that these are people with disabilities. What one sees are incredible athletes doing things that an untrained able-bodied person simply could not do. The game facilitates the transcendence of disability, moves one beyond pity, beyond the image of the cute yet pitiable "poster child," like the Jerry's Kids featured on Jerry Lewis's annual muscular dystrophy telethon (Shapiro 1993).[3]

People with disabilities no longer wish to be viewed with pity or as objects of charitable goodwill. They want to be seen as individuals with *rights* (Potok 2002; Shapiro 1993). Building on the accomplishments of the civil rights, women's, and consumer movements, they have demanded access to the public sphere and have advanced a "social model" of disability, a revolutionary approach that claims it is not an individual's impairment but the socially constructed barriers—the inaccessible buildings, the limited modes of transportation and communication, the prejudicial attitudes—that create "disability" (Oliver 1990; Tregasis 2002). They have challenged the view that disability is "a perversion of the human condition," an unrelenting tragedy that propels victims into the depths of despair (Camilleri 1999:849). While disabling conditions may never be wished for and are often the source of great suffering, people with disabilities differ quite dramatically in the nature of their impairment, and their condition is not always as "wholly disastrous" as one might imagine (Fine and Asch 1988: 11; Scotch 1988).

In addition to the Jerry's Kids critique, people in the disability community often complain about the media's (and by inference my own) preoccupation with the "supercrip" (Duncan 1998; Shapiro 1993; Wendell 1995). "Supercrips" are those individuals whose inspirational stories of courage, dedication, and hard work prove that it can be done, that one can defy the odds and accomplish the impossible. The concern is that these stories will foster unrealistic expectations about what people with disabilities can achieve, what they *should* be able to achieve, if only they "tried hard enough." The myth of the self-made person implies that society does not need to change.

I understand this concern quite well. As a sociologist I have long been familiar with the blaming-the-victim ideology that works against progressive social change (Ryan 1971). Yet I remain dissatisfied with sociology's frequent neglect of human agency, our capacity to make choices, to transform the structural (and in the case of disability, physical) constraints in our lives. I do not want my daughter to think of herself as a victim. I view the athletes I have met as role models who are facilitating, rather than hindering, her chances for success in life. But neither do I view them as "supercrips." Their stories indicate that they did not make it on their own. They deserve credit for their perseverance and accomplishments, for the agency they displayed in overcoming personal and structural adversity. But their lives must be understood in social context. The choices they made were enabled by the actions of others.

In Melvin's case it began with the therapy he received from the professionals at the Rehabilitation Institute of Chicago (RIC). Melvin remains grateful to them for what they taught him about living as a person with a disability. From the crotchety, straight-talking nurse who told him to "dress [his] own damn self" to the basketball coach who introduced him to the RIC juniors basketball team, they played their part in his resocialization.

Melvin arrived at his first wheelchair basketball game in one of those heavy hospital wheelchairs. With the other players in lightweight sports chairs, he trailed behind them the entire time he was in the game. By the time he got to one end of the court, everyone else was back at the opposite end. No one would pass him the ball. When one teammate finally did, Melvin threw up a shot as he fell backwards in his chair. Miraculously the ball went in.

"You play pretty good," the coach told him. "I bet if you got a sports chair you'd play even better." To entice him to join the team, the coach lent him a sports chair. Melvin thought it was cool riding around and popping wheelies to impress the other RIC patients. A few weeks later the coach took Melvin to see a game played by the Chicago Sidewinders, one of the best wheelchair teams in the country at that time. By now Melvin had been playing regularly with the RIC juniors team. He played mainly for fun, for therapeutic recreation. But the Sidewinders were something else. How quickly these men propelled their chairs up and down the court as Melvin's head ping-ponged back and forth in disbelief. On a fast break a player would throw a behind-the-back pass to a teammate, who'd lay it up into the basket with an underhand scoop or over-the-head shot. How skillfully they maneuvered their chairs, stopping and pivoting on a dime and then shooting or passing the ball to the open man.

It was at that moment that Melvin knew what he wanted to do—to be as good as these men, to be like Mike, one of the best in the world. Although this dream was to carry Melvin far, he had yet to realize what it would demand of him. To excel at wheelchair basketball would mean not just hard work developing his skills but a total transformation of his mindset. Still, the challenge appealed to him. He had never backed away from a fight.

In 1988 Melvin was recruited to enroll at UWW by Ron Lykins, the wheelchair basketball coach, and John Truesdale, the director of the university's Disabled Student Services (DSS). Truesdale, who served as DSS director from 1971 to 2000, began the now nationally recognized UWW wheelchair basketball program in 1973. With some grant money from the Wisconsin Division of Vocational Rehabilitation, he bought fifteen sports model chairs, which by today's standards were still rather large and heavy. He also invested some of the grant money into remodeling the locker room so that the players had accessible showers, toilet facilities, and gym lockers.

Truesdale was the team's first coach. Although he knew something about coaching basketball, he knew nothing about the wheelchair game per se. In fact, coaching strategy for wheelchair basketball had yet to be developed (see Hedrick, Byrnes, and Shaver 1994). Truesdale managed to attract only five students to play that first year. Today UWW boasts one of the premier wheelchair basketball programs in the country. Many of the best players and coaches, pioneers of the game, have come through this institution.

Young players across the United States, Canada, and even Australia have come here to learn and develop their game.

Prior to enrolling at UWW, Melvin considered himself a fairly good student. Unfortunately, all too many good students coming out of the Chicago public school system remain unprepared for college. During his first year on campus, Melvin returned to Chicago almost every weekend to hang out with his old gang friends. He did not do well in some of his classes and was on the verge of dropping out of school.

Allen Einerson, a counselor in the university's Academic Support Services, intervened. He persuaded Melvin to stay on campus that summer to work on his study skills. Einerson taught Melvin various learning strategies and time-management techniques. Melvin admitted he had never read a book from cover to cover in his entire life. Einerson took Melvin over to the university library and asked him what he might like to read. Melvin picked out Mario Puzo's *The Godfather* and after that another Mafia novel. For the first time in his life, Melvin was starting to enjoy reading, and the next semester he started to do well in school.

Melvin also began working harder on his basketball game, spending hours in the gym lifting weights, shooting baskets, and practicing fundamentals. In the 1990–1991 season the UWW team made it to the collegiate championship game. Although UWW lost, Melvin's play that year attracted national attention. He was invited to try out for the U.S. national team, the team that was to play in the Paralympics in Barcelona, Spain, in 1992. It was an honor just to be invited. Melvin had been working really hard and thought he was good enough to make the team. He didn't make the cut.

At first Melvin thought the selection process was rigged. None of the rookies invited to the tryout camp were selected. It must have been a done deal. But then he thought, maybe that wasn't the problem. He had to take responsibility for his own actions. He hadn't really prepared as hard as he could have. His shooting and ball handling still needed work. His physical conditioning could have been better. Mentally he had not yet become a true student of the game.

Paraphrasing Goethe, Melvin is fond of saying, "It's not doing what you like to do but liking what you have to do that makes a world of difference." To this he adds a poetic twist: "Good things come to those who wait, but here's a rule that's slicker. It's what you do while you wait that gets you there much quicker." Simple, perhaps even corny, but this is the kind of inspirational motto that helps drive Melvin to succeed.

In 1994 Melvin tried out for the U.S. team again. The coach that year was Brad Hedrick, one of the most respected and innovative coaches in the game (see Hedrick, Byrnes, and Shaver 1994). Melvin had met Hedrick years earlier when he was coaching the University of Illinois collegiate team and had been scouting players at RIC. Melvin knew what Hedrick wanted from his athletes. He liked those who were quick, those who hustled and were tenacious on defense.

This time Melvin made the team and was on his way to establishing himself as a defensive specialist. He's not the go-to glory guy who scores all the points. But when the coach needs someone to "lock down" an opposing player, Melvin is the one he turns to. To this day Hedrick describes Melvin as one of the most fundamentally sound players he has ever seen.

Melvin was in awe of his U.S. teammates. Trooper Johnson. Darryl "Tree" Waller. Reggie Colton. All of them legends of the game. Melvin had read about them in *Sports 'N Spokes* magazine. Now he was going to the world championship tournament with them!

The Gold Cup was played in Edmonton, Canada, that year. The U.S.

Copyright © 2001 Paralyzed Veterans of America, by permission of *Sports 'N Spokes*.

wheelchair team, like the "Dream Team" of stand-up basketball, was the perennial favorite. Canadian fans have a love-hate relationship with the United States, and during the tournament Canadian kids would come up to the U.S. players and ask for their autographs, then quip, "Thanks. I hope you lose today."

Melvin got a good amount of playing time. And the United States won the gold medal. A mistake in the tournament brochure listed Melvin as the U.S. team captain. When his name was called to accept the gold medal trophy for the United States, he seized the opportunity. He pushed his chair forward and triumphantly accepted the prize. The trophy was huge. It must have weighed about twenty pounds. Melvin grinned from ear to ear as he held it high before the cheering crowd.

Melvin went on to become a member of the U.S. national team in 1996, 1998, and 2000, winning another gold and two bronze medals. An injury kept him out of the Gold Cup tournament that was held in Japan in 2002, but he hopes to play in future international tournaments. Melvin has also been instrumental in forming the NWBA Milwaukee Bucks, a team sponsored by the NBA team of the same name. In 2001–2002 the Bucks won the NWBA national championship. Melvin also received his bachelor's degree in social work and has been working as a probation officer in Madison while continuing to train at the Whitewater campus.

One of Melvin's teammates on the Bucks is Eric Barber (born 1970), a man who is arguably one of the premier shooters in the game. Eric is a three-time member of the U.S. national team and one of the key players who led the team to its gold medal victory in the 2002 games. Melvin and Eric's relationship goes back to the mid-1980s, when they were both playing for the RIC juniors team in Chicago. Unlike Melvin, who has an acquired disability, Eric was born with his condition, scoliosis, a severe curvature of the spine. When he was three, his doctors became concerned about fluid buildup in his spinal column that could cause his brain to hemorrhage. They decided it would be best to operate to correct the problem. They knew the risk could be paralysis. The alternative could have very well been death. As a result of the surgery, Eric has had to rely on a wheelchair ever since.

Like Melvin, Eric is an impressive individual. His diminutive stature belies the fortitude of his presence, both on and off the court. He too was first introduced to wheelchair basketball by the coach at RIC. But unlike Melvin, Eric was not initially enamored with the sport. At thirteen years old, he couldn't get the ball to reach the bottom of the rim. He couldn't imagine how he could ever make a basket, and he turned to wheelchair softball and track racing instead.

About a year later, Eric and his mother moved to a neighborhood with a park just down the street from their home. The park had an asphalt basketball court. After his mother bought him a basketball for Christmas, Eric started hanging out at the court for seven or eight hours a day. Although he played pickup games with whoever came along, he soon realized that basketball was a sport he could practice and become better at just playing by himself.

Eric was competing regularly with the RIC juniors team when he had one of the most delightful experiences of his life. There was a television series airing at the time called *NBC Sports Fantasies*, and people could write in and ask to live out their greatest sports fantasy. Eric's fantasy was to play Michael Jordan in a game of wheelchair basketball. The producers thought it was a great idea, and Jordan agreed to the match.

This was in 1986, just as Jordan was starting to establish himself as an international sports icon. For kids growing up in the city of Chicago, he was already an idol. Eric was given the opportunity to sit down and talk with Jordan for about forty-five minutes before the game. This conversation alone constituted the greatest thrill of his young life. But Jordan told Eric he would show him no mercy; he was too competitive to allow anyone to beat him.

The first player to reach twenty points, at two points a basket, would win the match. To everyone but Eric's surprise, Eric jumped out to a 14–2 lead. It took awhile for Jordan to get used to maneuvering in the wheelchair. After Jordan would miss a shot, Eric would get to the ball and shoot so quickly that Jordan didn't have a chance to react. It didn't take long, however, for Jordan to figure out how to manipulate the chair. Eric's lead began to evaporate. The score was now 14–10.

Eric didn't panic under the pressure. He had already gained a reputation at RIC as a steady and reliable shooter. His teammates had given him the nickname E-Money because his shot was like money in the bank. Eric continued to make his shots and won the game 20–14. He is perhaps the only person on the face of the earth who has beaten Michael Jordan in a game of one-on-one basketball since the days when Jordan's older brother beat him when they were youths.

Upon graduation from high school, Eric decided to join Melvin at UWW. He remembers being persuaded about going to Whitewater when he saw how much Melvin's basketball skills had improved in just one semester. At Whitewater the players practiced at least five days a week. They had great facilities to train in and great coaching. Before Melvin had gone there he was a pretty good player. Now he was an *athlete*.

Eric went on to receive his undergraduate degree in communications and is currently completing his MBA degree with an emphasis in human resources and management computer systems. He credits his success in life to the people around him—his mother and extended family, the professionals at RIC, his coaches, and others. He is particularly grateful to his many cousins, who always included him in the sports they played. He does not think that they treated him any differently because he had a disability. He played baseball with them in a wheelchair. He played *tackle* football in a chair! They went after him as if he were any other player who was trying to beat them. "I'm nothing more than the byproduct of the people in my life," Eric says. "They have made me who I am."

My interviews with the people associated with UWW wheelchair basketball led me to the University of Illinois at Urbana-Champaign to talk to Mike Frogley (born 1963), currently the head coach of the men's and women's teams at U of I. Mike had gone on to Illinois to work on his doctorate in kinesiology after receiving bachelor's and master's degrees at UWW, where he also played and coached wheelchair basketball. Born in Canada, Mike has won several international gold medals as both a player and a coach on the Canadian national team, and he has led the U of I men's and women's teams to several intercollegiate championships as well. Many people in the sport today consider him to be the best wheelchair basketball coach in the world!

Mike's disability stems from a car accident he had when he was seventeen years old. He was driving his Fiat Spider convertible, speeding, to see how fast he could get from his home in Ottawa, Ontario, to his family's country cabin. Around a bend he lost control of the car. He wasn't wearing his seatbelt, and as he fell partway out of the car, his body was twisted around and the vehicle rolled over his back. Mike was paralyzed from the chest down, and a twelve-inch, pencil-like stainless steel rod was surgically inserted on each side of his spine to enable him to sit erect in his wheelchair.

Mike was raised by his parents to thrive on competition and to strive for excellence. His father graduated from military college with a degree in electrical engineering. His mother was an economist and a licensed pilot, at a time when there were few women involved in either of these pursuits. They instilled in Mike conventional values of hard work. His father taught him that there were three things he needed in order to be successful in life, and particular amounts of each: "a pinch of luck, a cupful of talent, and a bucketful of hard work." It was fortunate, his father added, that the one thing Mike had the greatest control over was the bucketful of hard work.

At an early age, Mike would stop off daily at the neighborhood asphalt court on his way home from school. He played with older kids who beat him on a regular basis. Rather than become discouraged, however, Mike was determined to try harder to overcome his deficits. He would analyze the weaknesses in his game and work on those skills. If his opponents were overplaying him to his right, because he dribbled to the basket with his right hand, he would work on his left-handed layup. If they were playing him to drive to the basket, he would work on his outside shot. He'd do whatever it took for him to get better. His thinking was "Okay, you might beat me today. But I'm going to keep working, and one day I'm going to beat you."

Sociologists of sport and gender are often critical of this type of competitive drive, for it can sometimes devolve into a hypermasculinity of sorts, leading to a desire to humiliate and berate an opponent or even unleash untoward brutality on the court or playing field (McKay, Messner, and Sabo 2000; Pollack 1998). But there is a reservoir of inner strength that can be derived from this ethic as well. And when one is faced with the challenge of living with a disability, it can be a resource that helps one move forward with a sense of determination.

Mike tells me that when he first learned that he would not be able to walk again, he "took a deep breath, literally for a moment, and got [himself] together." "Life is too short," he believes, "to feel sorry for oneself." He said to the hospital staff, "Okay, now tell me what I need to do to be as good as I can be." If his physical therapist told him he needed to do 500 push-ups a day, he didn't do 300 or 400 or 490. He'd do 500 and then ask if it was all right to do more.

Like Melvin and Eric, Mike was introduced to wheelchair basketball while he was still recuperating in the hospital. He didn't like it at first. Before his accident, he had been the starting shooting guard on his high school varsity team—a solid player, not a superstar but a double-figure a game scorer. He couldn't quite get used to not being able to float through the air while he was finishing a layup. But he still wanted to get back into basketball. So he called up his old high school coach and asked him for an opportunity to coach the team. The coach agreed, and this began Mike's love affair with coaching.

When he arrived at the high school gym for his first practice, he thought about mentioning the obvious fact that here he was, a guy in a wheelchair, coaching a stand-up basketball team. He decided, however, that he wasn't even going to mention it. If someone wanted to ask him about it, he would answer any questions they had. Otherwise, this was just going to be about basketball, about getting the players to be as good as they could possibly be.

One of the most memorable experiences of his early coaching career was the week-long (stand-up) basketball coaching camp he attended at Georgia Institute of Technology in Atlanta. Bobby Cremins, arguably one of the most successful college coaches of all time, was running the camp. Mike was determined to learn as much as he could from one of the masters of the game. He wanted to make a good impression on Cremins too. He'd wake up at 4:00 in the morning, get showered and shaved, and literally be waiting at the gym as the sun came up. Cremins would be the first one to arrive, and this gave Mike the opportunity to chat with him alone for a while. Mike was in awe of Cremins and soaked in everything he had to say. The next year when he returned to the camp, he found himself an insider among some of the best high school and college basketball coaches in the country.

Mike, like Melvin and Eric, recognizes that others have been responsible for his success in life. "Nobody's a self-made man," he says, while crediting his parents as well as the people who gave him opportunities to go to college and to play and coach basketball. He even has positive things to say about the Canadian health care system for providing him with excellent medical and rehabilitation services. Mike understands the complaint about the "supercrip" but does not think it should prevent people from striving for excellence. "You don't have to compare yourself to me or to a Melvin Juette or an Eric Barber," he says. "You define your own dreams. By the same token, don't diminish the accomplishments of those who have chosen to work hard to achieve their goals. They aren't that special, that extraordinary. Everyone has challenges in their life that they've had to overcome."

I was reading a book by A. Manette Ansay (2001), who suffered an illness that put her in a wheelchair at the age of twenty-three. Ansay writes: "It is not that I believe the things that happen to us happen for a reason . . . [or] that things have a way of working out for the best. . . . But I do believe that each of us has the ability to decide how we'll react to the random circumstances of our lives, and that our reactions can shape future circumstances, affect opportunities, open doors" (p. 265). Jan Brunstrom, a pediatric neurologist who works with children who have CP, tells her patients, "It's not fair that you have CP, but you also have two choices: You can crawl into a corner until you die, or you can fight back" (Hales 2003:17).[4]

As I conclude this essay, my daughter is undergoing many hours of postoperative physical therapy to first recover her preoperative abilities and then (hopefully) to surpass them. In many respects she is like an athlete in training, and my wife and I are not only her parents but her coaches and personal trainers.[5] I have been inspired and energized by the stories of Melvin, Eric, Mike, and the other athletes with disabilities I have met. I have learned that disability, like illness, can present itself as an opportunity to become what Frank (1995) calls a *dyadic* or *communicative* body, a body that teaches by being "a body *for* other bodies" (p. 37), a body that turns fate and contingency into agency and reflects "confidence in what is waiting to emerge" (p. 171).

Notes

1. I would like to think Melvin Juette, Eric Barber, and Mike Frogley for the time we spent together recording their life stories, which are recounted in part in this essay.

2. I can no longer read Kobe Bryant's name without thinking about the sexual assault charges that have recently been brought against him.

3. "The handicapped child," writes Evan Kemp Jr., the original Jerry's Kid, "is appealing and huggable . . . [while] the adolescent or mature adult is a cripple to be avoided" (quoted in Shapiro 1993:22). Critics say the telethon raises money for a cure but does little to improve the lives of the already disabled.

4. Brunstrom also has CP.

5. Sarah, perhaps rightfully, objects to this metaphor. She tells my wife and me, "I don't want coaches. I want parents." She is wise beyond her years.

PART 3

Education and Work

The life course is a socially constructed developmental process through which individuals move forward in a series of interconnected stages or trajectories, each containing a distinct set of normative parameters and expectations (Benson 2002; Elder 1985, 1994; Mayer and Muller 1986). In contemporary Western societies, the age-related structures of education and work are two broad institutional realms, which under optimal circumstances entail cumulative advantages and positive life outcomes but which under adverse circumstances entail cumulative disadvantages and negative life outcomes. People's experiences within these institutions, as well as their ability to make transitions between them, are very much influenced by their location in social structures of inequality based on class, race, gender, and other social statuses. However, telling stories about these milieus can help transform the social structures in which people are enmeshed and liberate the human potential in us all.

Sheila Balkan's essay, "How I Started My Life in Crime," opens this section of the book. Like some of the previous contributors, Balkan begins her story with an account of her family, including her father's Willy Lomanesque experience as a door-to-door salesman in the 1950s (see Chapter 2). By the time she entered junior high school, Balkan realized she was not on the same life trajectory as the dedicated "Leave It to Beaver" students who were college-bound. She was ditching school, disrupting class, and routinely "getting sent to the vice principal's office." At age seventeen Balkan found herself married to a demanding working-class husband, with a baby on the way. A turning point came when he broke her nose because he didn't like the soup she cooked. By age twenty-three she had three sons she adored and a husband she feared.

Balkan's story will strike some readers as a familiar tale of feminist liberation of that era. But it is also a story that reminds us that this tale is worth telling again. Against her husband's wishes, Balkan enrolled in junior college, and a new world of understanding opened up to her. For the first time in her life, she realized that "what was wrong" with her life wasn't her. By the time she transferred to the university, she knew her marriage was over. She loaded her sons into her car and never looked back.

Balkan, a single mother struggling to get by, persevered through undergraduate and graduate school. Through her studies, she developed an interest in criminology. After receiving a call from a criminal defense attorney asking for her help with a "miscarriage of justice" case, she embarked on a new career working as a consultant to attorneys. Balkan writes case histories of defendants, on their behalf, which are presented to prosecutors and judges for the purpose of bail, pretrial, and sentencing proceedings. Over the last quarter century, she has helped many deserving defendants whose lives she has found to be uncannily similar to her own.

Like Balkan's, **Stephen Richards**'s life has revolved around crime. In many ways, according to Richards, he was "Born Illegal." He never knew his father and was placed in an orphanage when he was just a young child after his mother died from an illness. But education was his salvation. He "learned to love school," for it was a place where he could prove that he "was as good as or better than anyone, despite having no parents." Richards eventually attended university and became embroiled in the political and cultural climate of the late 1960s and early 1970s. This included a foray into the world of drugs, and eventually to arrest and criminal prosecution for smuggling marijuana.

Richards spent a total of eleven years under correctional supervision, three of them behind bars. His experiences gave him an insider's perspective on the abuses of the criminal justice system, and upon his release he earned a Ph.D., became a university professor, and helped found a reform movement composed of "convict criminologists." This movement includes ex-convict graduate students and university professors whose goal is to use their professionally honed insider perspective to help reform the criminal justice system and prevent the overuse of incarceration as a way to address complex social issues.

Robin Mello has also become a university professor, and like Richards she came to this profession through a rather circuitous route. As she writes in "Telling Tales: Journey of an Itinerant Storyteller," Mello feels that she has lived her life backwards, like Merlin the magician, who "entered Camelot already aware of what the future held." Mello entered academia after a career as a performance artist, a professional storyteller, only to pursue an academic career through teaching and researching storytelling and narrative as a meaning-making process.

In her essay, Mello tells the story of how she came to be involved in storytelling, traveling the hinterlands of New England telling stories and singing songs at "grange halls, old movie theaters, one-room schoolhouses, and library foyers." At times this life on the road could be rather lonely, but she also felt "connected, creative, challenged." Bringing "storytelling curricula to teachers and their students . . . seemed a natural and necessary next step." She discovered that storytelling could empower both tellers and listeners and bridge cultural divides, but it could also threaten the status quo and invoke demands for storytellers to censor their voice. Nevertheless, Mello has been able to find a home in academia, a place where she's been able to combine "the creative and analytical methodologies of performance and research." She now "feels much like Merlin waiting for release and enlightenment within his crystal cave."

Storytelling resists silence. But while silence has its costs, so can speaking out. **Carla Corroto** made a deliberate decision to tell her story, to speak her own truth. And in "Silence of the Lambs: The Architecture of the Abattoir" she also speaks for the animals who cannot represent themselves. Corroto's story takes place in the educational setting of a professional school of architecture. The capstone course of her final semester required students to design a slaughterhouse. Preparation for this assignment included a trip to a hog abattoir.

Corroto found watching (and smelling) the slaughtering of hogs a horrific process. Equally disturbing, however, was the glib attitude of both slaughterhouse workers and fellow students, which entailed a chauvinistic and sexist dimension as well. This experience revealed to her the gendered organization and masculinist culture that was architecture school and the profession itself. Initially Corroto had tried to adapt to this culture, but she found this impossible to do. Architectural training required abandonment of her sense of self, abandonment of everything but "building form." Moreover, as a woman she was "never fully admitted to the club."

Corroto notes that her feminist identity of resistance was fomented as much in the tour of the abattoir as in retelling the story of the tour. Upon graduation from architecture school, she was employed in a number of firms where officemates trivialized her critique of the abattoir experience. After leaving the profession and entering graduate school in sociology, she found that her new colleagues had an entirely different reaction. They were supportive of her feelings and encouraged her to write up her experience as an "autoethnography," thus validating her identity that "had formed through many years of internal conflict."

Speaking one's own truth is in many ways the story line underpinning **Robert Wolensky**'s "Working-Class Heroes: Rinaldo Cappellini and the Anthracite Mineworkers." Growing up in the anthracite (hard coal) region of northeastern Pennsylvania, son and grandson of mineworkers of Italian heritage, Wolensky became inspired by the heroic exploits of working-class labor rebels fighting for their rights against exploitative mining companies in the early days of the labor movement. Wolensky longed to find "good stories" about Italian Americans in the midst of a popular culture and academic tradition that have stereotyped them as criminals and amoral.

Wolensky has been collecting and writing working-class oral histories for many years. He has been able to use his "status as a 'local boy' to gain access to labor tales that were previously untold to outsiders." In this essay he tells the story of Rinaldo Cappellini, a labor leader who has captivated his attention ever since he "met" the man through interviews with his wife in the late 1980s. The time is 1916 to 1936, a period in which Cappellini's heroism during mineworker strike actions catapulted him to the presidency of District 1, the largest branch of the United Mine Workers of America. Wolensky writes of being "moved by the progressive mark these working-class heroes made for democratic participation, economic fairness, and grassroots power." It is a history, he observes, that "workers from all sectors of the contemporary working class might want to examine and learn from."

John Horton also wants to tell a story about social justice, but his is a story of more recent times. Horton came of age in the 1960s, as a professor of sociology who refused to follow the conformist path of professional careerism and status quo theorizing. Horton's "passion was teaching and mentoring of graduate students, especially those who otherwise might have fallen through the cracks because of their radical ideas or minority identities." As a sociologist on the outside, a "commie fag," Horton took "A Road Less Traveled" as he joined with women, people of color, queers, and radicals of all stripes who cared less about filling in narrow gaps in sociological knowledge than about developing the field as a vehicle for liberation.

Horton's essay is a story about those who were (are) searching for ways to link theory with practice, to combine sociology with political activism. It is a story of turbulent times—the civil rights movement, the Vietnam War, the struggles of women and sexual minorities coming out of the closet. At the time, he "was too green to have been part of the old left and too gray to be a trusted member of the under-thirty generation," and he got his "political and cultural education from both sides." As an academic Marxist, revolutionary comrade, and progressive community researcher, Horton followed paths that were both rewarding and problematic. Along the way, he built an extended family of friends who have given meaning to his life—and he has given meaning to theirs—and "found a home in a time and place where difference is no longer 'deviant' but has become the norm."

William Brown's experience of the 1960s arguably lies at the heart of that era. He was in Vietnam. His work was soldiering. He killed for the United States government. The ghost of a young girl he shot haunts him to this day. His life has been an effort, a series of struggles, to come to terms with this ghost and the carnage and futility of war, to disprove the philosophy of the grunts who said, "Fuck it. It don't mean nothing." It was years before Brown was able to reject this admonition, to understand that "it means something." In the concluding essay in this section, "It Means Something: The Ghosts of War," Brown tells his story. We will let the power of his narrative speak for itself.

CHAPTER 14

How I Started My Life in Crime

Sheila Balkan

1950s

I have always felt that I have lived my life backwards. I was born into my mother's mature fear of poverty and gradually grew to adopt my father's childlike, irrational faith that our ship would come in. Our ship never came in. And night after night my mother watched ships sink on the horizon while my father organized landing parties.

My family—my parents, my younger brother, and I—lived from month to month. For my father, fantasizing about living with greater wealth was an endless source of pleasure and diversion. Every weekend we would pile into his 1954 Buick and drive over the hill to the newly developing San Fernando Valley, where we would look at model tract houses and pretend this was the home that we finally were going to purchase. While no one in our family believed that we would actually buy a house, my father always listened to the salespeople pitch the features in the new homes. After he had heard about the all-electric appliances, the choices of wallpaper in the bathrooms, and the whisper-quiet garbage disposal, he always promised to return on Monday with the down payment. Of course, Monday would come and go without any sign of the check. The reality was that we would always live in apartments, and we never stayed in one place for very long.

Just about every year, we'd come up short on our rent, and it would be time to move to a different apartment. To a kid, each move might as well have been to a new country. I attended five different elementary schools in five different communities, and each time I had to make all new friends.

While our unstable circumstances were hard on me, they were torture for my mother, who yearned for a security that with each new move seemed further beyond her reach. My mother was especially conscious of what it meant to be unsafe. She had escaped the pogroms in Eastern Europe with her family only to arrive in this country without the skills on which the survival of most Americans is based. Never educated beyond the sixth grade or taught to drive, she sought security through stability while my father chased windmills. The comfort and safety that my mother sought from my father were the exact things that, by his nature, she would always be denied.

Unlike my mother, my father was extremely well read. He was a self-made philosopher who had studied at the University of Johnnie Walker. Every night, after my mother had gone to sleep, my father would sit down with a bottle of scotch and read to me from Bertrand Russell, Will and Ariel Durant, and Benedict de Spinoza. He would explain the true meaning of life from his own charming but wobbly perspective. And I learned a lot. To this day, I cherish this time I shared with him.

It was through my father that I was exposed to a variety of communities and cultures. I traveled as a passenger in his Buick while my father took his various wares to sell door to door in the diverse neighborhoods of Los Angeles. Inside the car were boxes of men's shirts, furniture catalogs, and women's clothing that hung from a pole across the backseat. We'd go to Watts, Inglewood, South Central and East Los Angeles, offering credit to people who had none. My father made lots of sales but collected few commissions. Only when the rent was due would my mother send him out to collect. But all too often, instead of coming back with cash, he would return with a new puppy. I half expected him to come back with magic beans.

Needless to say, it was my freewheeling father, and not my stressed-out mother, who made the more attractive role model. By the time I was in junior high school, I was ditching, disrupting class, and getting sent to the vice principal's office. All around me were kids with seemingly perfect lives. They were enjoying school and planning for college and had "Leave It to Beaver" families. They were like aliens to me. They lived in houses, their parents had savings, and they had aspirations. What the hell was that about? I thought the kids with the more interesting lives were the ones who didn't have a life handed to them. They were from the projects or living in single-parent homes, and while I never felt a part of that group either, they were a lot more attractive to me.

1960s

I loved my father, but I saw that he drove my mother crazy. Seeing myself as wild and uncontrollable, I thought I needed someone to stabilize me. So when I married, it was to a man who was the opposite of my father. It was 1963, and young men were being drafted into the military. The Vietnam War was looming. Under Kennedy, married men were disqualified from the draft. I was seventeen and still in high school. Thinking I was doing a civil service, and also because I had been recently invited to leave one high school and seek another, I agreed to get married. After all, my choices seemed pretty limited.

After we married, my husband and I moved to Simi Valley, now the home of the Ronald Reagan Library and the same community that acquitted the cops in the Rodney King case. We bought a house for $17,000 in a new tract development. We had a rock roof, wall-to-wall carpeting with a design shaved into it like a tattoo on the back of a gang member's head, and a baby on the way. I thought I had it made when my working-class husband came up with the down payment.

I thought this was how it was supposed to be. I tried to live my mother's dream that security would bring happiness. The kitchen floor in the house was pure white with a purple stripe down the side. My job was to polish that floor every day while my husband worked as a gardener. It was especially important to keep the floor clean because we didn't have any furniture to cover it up. But as hard as I tried, I couldn't fill my day keeping that floor clean. Out of sheer boredom, I decided to get my first diploma—in cake decorating—and my second child was born when I was twenty.

It was the 1960s, but there was no way to tell from my life in sleepy Simi Valley that anything exciting was happening in the world. It was surrounded in some kind of invisible, protective bubble that kept it in the 1950s. Outside, there was an antiwar movement, Jimi Hendrix was smashing guitars, and everybody was on drugs. Inside, I was queen of the bowling alley. I started to question my domestic bliss only when, after four years of marriage, I was pregnant with my third child.

I couldn't shake my lifelong feeling that I was confined in an existence where I did not belong. While my husband was a hard worker who provided, the life we were living was his. It was like when I was a kid and went door to door with my father: I was just along for the ride, only this ride was not nearly as interesting. My husband, the man who wanted the white floors buffed to a point of translucence, would come home late from his work as a manual laborer, eat his home-cooked dinner, and fall asleep. Of course, he had stopped for a beer or two or three on the way home.

In return for being the provider, my husband demanded perfection. Idiot that I was, I tried to deliver. Unfortunately, I always came up short. I didn't cook as well as his mother, didn't appreciate our life enough, and didn't have large enough breasts. I blamed myself. The turning point finally came when my soup wasn't good enough and my husband expressed this to me by breaking my nose. I remember feeling that the doctors in the emergency room must have thought I was a moron when I tried to tell them I'd hurt myself slipping on a spoon. By twenty-three, I had three sons I adored and a husband I feared.

1970s

With three kids, a dog and cat, and no means of support, I knew that the only way I would get out of the marriage was to become independent. To accomplish this, I realized, I would have to give up my career as a cake decorator. For a while I thought that I had the choice to go to beauty school, but when my husband refused to let me accept a scholarship to learn to cut hair, I placed all of my hopes on the local community college. As it turned out, my husband found my announcement that I was going to take a few art classes far less intimidating than the idea of my learning a trade. I guess I did too. It was only after he and his father scoffed at my ability to survive in a "real" class that I secretly signed up for political science and history.

Of course, while I was in school I needed to make sure that my three young sons were taken care of. My husband had made it clear that I could take classes only if it didn't cause him any inconvenience. With my oldest son in kindergarten, the two youngest needed daycare. The daycare center staff, however, were reluctant to take my youngest son, who was only fourteen months old. They explained that they were not equipped to take children who were not yet potty-trained. Fortunately, my son was able to work with me. I told him that if he gave up his diapers, he would be able to go to school with his brothers. He agreed.

With all of my children provided for, I began school at the brand-new campus of Moorpark College. Even though Moorpark was located in a little rural community just next to Simi Valley, it somehow escaped the bubble. The school, in fact, was an example of the liberal experimentation of the time. It had no administration and was run by the faculty. For the first time in years, I could breathe. It also didn't hurt that I could fulfill my English requirements by studying Beatles lyrics and satisfy contemporary American history with a survey of rock and roll since the 1950s.

The campus was very receptive when Jane Fonda and Candice Bergen came to speak about the war in Vietnam and the nascent women's rights movement. I attended the event out of curiosity—and soon found myself mesmerized. For the first time, I realized that what was wrong with my life wasn't me. There was a world outside of Simi Valley, and I wanted to be a part of it.

UCLA

Ever since I took my first sociology class in junior college, I had known I was going to major in sociology. My professor had assigned *One Flew over the Cuckoo's Nest* (Kesey 1963), *Rubyfruit Jungle* (Brown 1973), and *The Autobiography of Malcolm X* (Malcolm X, with Haley 1975). I started to understand the nature of oppression and how racism and sexism developed. For me, sociology was a personal quest, one that helped me understand why, until that time, the world had never worked for me.

As school and learning became more important, polishing the kitchen floor until it blinded you became less so. By the time I started UCLA my marriage was over. One day, while painting the hall apple green, I felt as if I couldn't breathe. I put down the paintbrush, loaded my sons into the old Datsun, threw in the dog and cat, took the drawers out of their dressers to put in the back, and, just as in a movie, drove off into the sunset and never looked back. Sheila doesn't live here anymore.

My sons and I were on our own. I spent the next several years figuring out how to support a family of four and manage to stay in school. Fortunately, I could always count on a professor to hand me a project to work on. As a research assistant, I investigated the early history of the Legal Aid Society, pored over materials in the library for a monogram on the cigar industry in Cuba, and compared the effectiveness of Scientology, EST, and traditional psychotherapy.

Following up on an assignment in a course on deviant behavior, I went undercover in a massage parlor. In the weeks I spent there, I not only interviewed the women who worked there but dressed like them, wearing a clingy leotard, and actually hid under the massage table when they saw clients. It was very important that I develop an ethnographically accurate understanding of the interaction between client and masseuse. Yeah, that was it.

Another way I paid the rent was tutoring the UCLA football and basketball teams. While it might have been a challenge teaching some of these athletes to put down the toilet seat, I found myself charged with bringing them up to speed on sex-role socialization. What made the job a big draw for me was the ring of barbecues that were set out around the playing field after practice. While I tutored, slabs of beef would be sizzling in the background. My sons were always happy to come along, because they got to hang out with the players and we all got a free dinner.

It was out of necessity rather than ideology that my children were raised communally. The first place we lived was a Venice beach house I rented from my cousin. Because I couldn't begin to afford the rent, I took in tenants, lots of them. Almost everyone who lived in the house was a student who, like me, had no money. For the most part, everyone contributed to making the environment a little bit better. But this was not without exceptions. One was a law student with an asthmatic sheepdog. While the student spent day and night at the library, the dog remained home hacking and drooling all over everything. That didn't last long.

Then there was the couple we called "the chickens" because of the noises they made while they were having sex. The chickens were the only tenants who were not students. They were communist entrepreneurs who owned the Mao Bookstore. I knew the chickens had to go when they became personally offended that I was allowing my sons to eat sugarcoated cereal.

It took awhile, but bit by bit the sounds of wheezing dogs and chickens clucking late into the night disappeared. They were replaced by people who became my lifelong friends and aunts and uncles to my sons. Among them were international students, writers, and political activists.

It was also during this time that I began a long-term relationship that worked. I became involved with a union organizer for Cesar Chavez. He fit right in with the political activism in which my sons and I were already immersed. Our weekends were split between Little League games and demonstrations to boycott grapes, Coors beer, and Gallo wine. When I look back, these were the best times of my life. I finally felt I was part of this world.

1980s–1990s

When I began college my goal had been to become a junior high school teacher. Things changed when I became involved in writing a book with two graduate students (Balkan, Berger, and Schmidt 1980). The book challenged how we define crime as a society and questioned the norms that most Americans took for granted. As I became more involved in research for the book, I became increasingly curious about the criminal justice system and who gets caught up in it.

I also began to pay attention to the way that crimes were being punished. At the time, white-collar criminals were treated relatively leniently. Prostitutes, like the women I interviewed in the massage parlors, were prosecuted while their johns were always ignored. And race, more than anything, seemed to define how severely the courts would treat a defendant. However, the concept of crime seemed to be changing. For the first time, studies on crime were being directed at women, mental illness, and sexuality.

It was also during this time that the works of people like Michel Foucault (1973, 1979), R. D. Laing (1964; Laing and Esterson 1964), Thomas Szasz (1970, 1974), and Betty Friedan (1964) were being embraced in academic circles and generating exciting responses. These authors were exposing the assumptions that society took for granted. They confronted institutions, disputed the legitimacy of power structures, and took issue with the labels that were put on mental illness, deviance, and gender roles. I started to realize that the limitations I felt about my own abilities were external rather than internal.

My work on the book about crime led to a master's degree, and as I kept going I found myself completing a Ph.D. Throughout, I had remained interested in the way our culture looks at and treats those people it labels as criminals. I was helped along by work I was doing with a psychiatrist who was studying how mentally ill juvenile delinquents were treated. That led to a grant to evaluate the California juvenile camp system, which became the topic of my dissertation.

I was completing my dissertation when I received a call from a criminal defense attorney who had been referred to me by a friend who knew I was desperate for money. The attorney explained that he had two clients who were being prosecuted for fraud. What made the attorney interested in hiring me was that I was trained as a sociologist and had an instinct for human nature.

The case involved a Hispanic couple who were being investigated by the federal government for misappropriating grants to minority businesses. The attorney felt that they were scapegoats who were misunderstood by the prosecution. The couple, who ran a small art gallery for local Hispanic artists, were representing their community to assist grant recipients. The attorney saw them as ethical people who were being treated as patsies by a more sophisticated organization that was responsible for the fraudulent conduct. He wanted me to investigate their lives, including their value system, employment history, family ties, and relationships with friends and business associates. In short, he wanted me to humanize them so that a judge would see more than the accusations in the indictment.

It turned out that my experience in field study served me well. When I had investigated massage parlors, I didn't just talk to the women; I interviewed owners, listened in on conversations with clients, and spoke with police. I brought the same approach to my new job.

At the time, there was no one bridging the gap between social science and the justice system. While attorneys would often use psychologists to diagnose and test individuals, there was a need to look beyond the defendant and into the structures and relationships that defined his or her life. Although I was studying criminology, I had no experience with the legal process. After starting out by researching the criminal charges against the couple, I set out in the field to conduct my research.

The result was good. I discovered that this husband and wife were not at all the greedy schemers they were accused of being. When I went out into the community to conduct interviews, I learned about two hardworking, highly respected businesspeople who were seen as loving, committed parents. The simple lifestyle that I described in my report called into question the original portrait of two self-dealing con artists. Based on the evidence I collected to back up my conclusions, the prosecutor softened and took a new position. Eventually the case against my clients was dropped, and the government began to investigate the real ringleaders.

And so was born a career. For the next twenty-five years I worked to bridge the social sciences with the criminal justice system, presenting the lives and histories of defendants to the courts and prosecutors. This is a unique role for a criminologist and one that I had to figure out on my own. While I am generally brought in for purposes of assisting with sentencing, I have also been called on to prepare bail reports, investigate capital cases, and present reports for pre-plea negotiations.

Within a few years I found myself in demand, but never so much as when I came in to the office one day and had calls from a half dozen civil rights attorneys and civil liberties organizations. The cause célèbre was a skinny, eighteen-year-old kid named Max, who looked like a farm boy and had decided, almost a decade after Vietnam, that he was going to burn his draft card. Max's problem wasn't that he had simply refused to sign up for the draft. Lots of kids were quietly doing that. Max was traveling around the country urging everyone to do the same. Because the Reagan administration wanted a few high-profile prosecutions, Max became a target.

For both sides, the case was issue driven. The government wanted to prove that it could enforce the draft, while many of the organizations rallying behind this resister wanted to make sure that no one would again fight in a war against their will. In addition, the "burn, don't tell" policy meant that prosecutions were being reserved only for those individuals who exercised their rights to free speech. While the issues were important to me when I decided to take the case, what motivated me was the person facing the charges. When I met him, I discovered that Max was an extremely serious, extremely devout Quaker. He truly believed that he had no choice but to refuse the draft and to speak out against a future war.

What impressed me about Max was that he was sincere, polite, and anything but an arrogant troublemaker. Still, Max had a problem. It wasn't just that he was guilty and admitted his guilt. It was that he was unrepentant and continued to refuse to register. The prosecution argued that Max should go to jail, and the probation officer noted that this was not the kind of defendant who ordinarily receives lenience. Nonetheless, Max was not an ordinary defendant. It was Max's life and the words of people who knew him that enabled me to communicate to the court that he was highly principled and worthy of probation.

At dinner parties there's frequently one guest who, after a couple of glasses of wine, will fix me with an accusing stare and demand to know how I can defend "these criminals." Well, for one thing, I don't defend them, I explain them, or more accurately, help them explain themselves. No matter what you may think of the crimes, people are more than the crimes they commit. The more you dig into a defendant's life, the more complex and mitigating their circumstances appear.

Take Brenda, for example. Her attorney referred her to me as a woman who had been implicated in numerous bank robberies, many of which were on videotape. Although there was no evidence that Brenda was armed, she had handed tellers a note claiming she had a weapon. My expectation was that I would be meeting a bleached-blonde, hard-core biker chick. Instead, Brenda was a very attractive, articulate, and polite young African-American woman.

When Brenda admitted to me that she committed the robberies, her description of how she carried them out matched just what the prosecution claimed it would prove. She went into the banks alone and did whatever she had to do to convince the tellers she was armed and dangerous. But Brenda also told me one other thing. Her former boyfriend had driven her to all the banks, and whenever she was inside he was always just twenty feet from the entrance.

As I got to know her, I learned more about the history of violence in Brenda's life and about how susceptible she was to being victimized. Brenda not only told me that she had never wanted to rob a bank, she also told me how the man waiting in the car outside had forced her to commit the crimes. He relied on an environment of fear that included holding Brenda at gunpoint and beating and raping her. I also learned that as an infant Brenda lost both of her parents when her father killed her mother before turning his gun on himself. It was apparent to me that Brenda had been conditioned to accept violence and felt hopeless to confront it. Brenda was convinced that no one could protect her.

Fortunately, Brenda's story was so compelling that her attorney and I were able to convince the prosecutor that she had acted under duress and an honest fear for her life. Brenda was put on probation and has not reoffended. She also began therapy as a condition of her probation and performed community service at an educational and gang-intervention program, where she proved to be very effective working with young people. She is currently a rap singer.

Bank robbers are uncommon. If my bread-and-butter clients have not been white-collar criminals, they've been drug dealers. Within this class, Derrick was not unusual. Married, with two young children, Derrick had owned a construction business that paid the bills for several years before the family started having problems. As his business began to suffer reversals, Derrick watched while his wife spiraled into serious alcoholism. Quite obviously, Derrick's family and business needed him like never before. Sadly, however, Derrick heeded this call by turning to drugs and then to drug dealing. As he quickly got in over his head, Derrick was arrested.

As unsympathetic as his case seemed, I learned that Derrick's wife's drinking had reached the point where she was no longer functioning or capable of caring for the children. Even after his arrest, Derrick continued to fulfill the role of both parents to his children and worked hard to help his wife recognize and seek help for her alcoholism. Having agreed to cooperate with authorities, Derrick was free to spend time with his family over the several years he spent helping to make arrests and build cases. If there was one reason that Derrick had agreed to put his life at risk as an informant, it was to continue in his role as a family man.

Because both of Derrick's daughters had learning disabilities, it was especially important that they have the constant support of a dedicated parent. Derrick was dedicated to helping his children with homework, athletics, and personal problems. In addition, Derrick cooked the meals and took care of the house. In his business, numerous employees relied on him and credited him with their own recovery from substance abuse.

I recognized that Derrick's criminal activity had been a desperate response to his family situation, and I also saw the remarkable change his life had undergone since his arrest and the important role he played in the lives of others. Although Derrick ultimately had to spend a few years in prison, his sentence was greatly reduced from what it might have been if the court had not understood the nature and quality of the productive life he had lived for the previous few years.

Among the thousands of cases I have worked on for more than twenty years, there is one case that stands out as unusual for me. In this case both the attorney and I donated our services to try to win the compassionate release of a woman who had been convicted of armed robbery and was now dying of AIDS. As much as this might seem to be an easy sell, almost no one is granted a compassionate release in California unless they have only a few days left to live. As sick as Joy was, however, she hadn't been declared terminally ill. Her one desire was to be able to spend her remaining time with her young son before she died.

To try to explain this woman's plight, I wrote a report discussing her life and how drug addiction had been responsible for her criminal conduct. More important, I wrote about what she had been doing since her transfer to the prison hospital. Despite her own failing health, Joy had reached out to other sick prisoners to give them comfort. Writing for a prison newspaper, Joy provided messages of hope and salvation. She even spent time at the bedside of others who were very ill and dying, although this was against the rules and prison officials would penalize her by setting her release date back.

In spite of these facts, the lawyer and I were unable to get results for quite a while. The judge was sympathetic but explained that he lacked jurisdiction. Ordinarily the sentencing judge loses the power to change a sentence once a few months have passed. In this case it had been years. That meant that the application had to be approved by either the state's very conservative governor or by the Department of Corrections, which had never done anything like this before. Remaining true to form, both parties refused to hear the case. The court staff insisted that this was the province of the Department of Corrections. It seemed as if nothing was going to happen until Joy was on her deathbed, at which point the compassionate release would probably come too late.

Unable to sway the bureaucracy, we finally found our break when we sent Joy's report to a journalist who had been following the case. Fortunately, Joy's story moved him, and he used it as the basis for a series of articles. While the governor and the Department of Corrections still refused to take responsibility, the articles created enough pressure to get the department to put Joy's case back before the court. The judge, who had promised to help if given the chance, granted Joy's release. She spent the remaining six months of her life with her son.

2004

It is April 2004. The nation has gone to war with a third world country over weapons of mass destruction that have yet to materialize after more than a year of occupation, Congress has opened the door to rolling back abortion rights, and 35 million Americans still live below the poverty line. Nothing has gotten easier since I first started dealing with the politics of the criminal justice system in 1980. As often as I've succeeded in showing the human issues involved in a sentencing, I've been frustrated when the system has been cold and mechanized.

One of the most chilling examples of sentencing by numbers was the introduction of the Federal Sentencing Guidelines in the mid-1980s. The emphasis of the guidelines is to turn away from the individual who has committed the crime and look instead at the amount of money lost, the quantity of drugs sold, or whether the defendant was willing to plead guilty and save the government the trouble of a costly trial. While the guidelines still allow arguments to be made on a convicted defendant's behalf, they have to fit within the cracks and find expression in a narrow set of exceptions.

Amid the disappointments and the roadblocks, it never would have been worth it if I hadn't seen the lives I wrote about as parallel to my own. While I've met my share of people who are just plain bad, I most often find that individuals caught up in crime come from a troubled background and are desperate and lost. In short, they are people whose lives I was lucky enough to have narrowly missed living.

My reports are, in part, biographies. I try to find and trace coherent themes that emerge out of the disorder of the defendant's everyday life. I have to admit that I seldom take the time to reflect on my own life. It's too much like work. This essay has given me that opportunity. In trying to make sense of the path my career has taken, I've tried to understand what it was that enabled me to break free from the restrictions of my earlier life. In college, investigating massage parlors, I couldn't help but think how very little separated me from the women I was studying. Like me, many were supporting a family on their own and had dreams of a better life. Some were studying to be nurses; others were students or single mothers. The best answer I can give is that I took strength from someone's believing in me at a very early age. My father was in many ways a doomed romantic and, in the eyes of the world, a failure, but his faith in me was unwavering and lifelong. It gave me the strength to push on when nothing looked promising. I was also lucky enough to have been born at a time of social change. As part of a generation that challenged the patriarchal values of the 1950s, I saw opportunities to empower my life. And that has made all the difference.

CHAPTER 15

Born Illegal

Stephen C. Richards

Lately I've been doing a lot of newspaper interviews and appearing on television news programs. The media are curious about how ex-convicts become criminology professors. Newspaper reporters and television commentators want to know, "Are ex-convict criminology professors better than typical professors?" "Are they popular with students?" "Do they know more about the criminal justice system than most professors?" I do my best to answer the questions without offending my academic peers. When the opportunity comes I try to make my points about policy change that will reduce the prison population (see St. John 2003).

It is very strange to pick up the *New York Times* and read about myself and close colleagues. I watch myself on television (CNBC, FOX, MSNBC) and wonder, "Who is that guy? How did I get here? Why am I subjecting myself to this media fascination?" Academics have a difficult time reducing complex answers to sound bites. Then again, maybe it's not real unless you see it on television.

Today there are over 2 million men and women being held in jails and prisons in the United States. Millions of family members await their return home. Every day I receive numerous e-mails from the families of prisoners. They write about their husbands, wives, sons, daughters, brothers, and sisters. Add to this the many letters I receive from convicts and ex-convicts that require my advice on how to apply to college or pursue a new career or request that I appear at their parole hearing. Between media appearances, I do my best to reply. Maybe I should do an Ann Landers newspaper column for convicts and their families.

While no person is "born criminal," they may be "born illegal." Maybe the stork got lost, had the wrong address, or just got confused. In any event, he messed up my birth completely. The "bird of birth" left me at the wrong door. Born in Cleveland, I arrived at the wrong time in the wrong place to a family in turmoil. I opened my eyes to a young mother who was not ready to raise me. She was twenty-one years old, separated from her husband, and already burdened with my older sister. Now she had a second bundle of joy, this one a boy with blond hair and blue eyes.

No one welcomed the stork on my untimely arrival. There was no celebration or father to claim me as his own. I was a bastard born illegal. As a small child I saw the newspaper stories. My mother went to family court to file a paternity case. In those days blood tests and visual inspection were used to determine who the father might be. I was placed in a basket, taken to court, and presented as evidence. A man I would never know got the blame and was ordered to pay child support. Over the next eighteen years he would send the checks but never acknowledge me as his son.

This was all too much grief for a wealthy, socialite Jewish family. My mother, sister, and I were shuffled off to live in a public housing project in east Cleveland. I remember the project was segregated, with white and black families living in different buildings separated by a fence and park.

My mother paid the bills with two child-support checks and worked as a bookkeeper at a downtown hotel. When I was four or five we left Cleveland, and my mother applied for work at hotels in different cities. I remember traveling on the New York Central, an elegant train of the time that traveled between New York City and Chicago. Mother worked for short periods at hotels in Detroit and Chicago, and then we went on to Milwaukee, where she landed a better position with a large hotel chain.

Meanwhile, as the years passed we lived in less expensive hotels down the street from where she worked. As children we slept in one bed with Mom, ate meals in coffee shops and cafeterias, and played in hotel hallways and lobbies. Mom would tuck my sister and me in bed and then work the night shift, operating bookkeeping machines to total the day's receipts.

My fondest memory of my mother is her playing the piano. Late at night she would sneak us into the hotel ballroom and perform for us on the Steinway. She played classical music and popular songs. My favorites were Judy Garland tunes. Mom would sit my sister and me next to her, and together we would sing "Somewhere over the Rainbow": "Somewhere over the rainbow skies are blue, . . . and the dreams that you dare to dream really do come true."

My mother was beautiful, educated, soft-spoken, and gentle. Despite the attention she attracted from men, she displayed no interest. Instead, she worked every day, tended to my sister and me, and somehow managed to keep the truth from us. She was suffering from a terminal illness. I was too young to understand when she would get sick and be hospitalized. She would become too weak to get out of bed, the ambulance would come, and she was gone. My sister and I would wait for her return. She fought bravely to stay alive and fight off the inevitable. I never heard her complain. When I was seven she went to a hospital and did not return. My sister was sent to live with "her" father in Cleveland, and I became a "ward of the state."

I was placed in the Milwaukee Jewish Children's Home, an orphanage for displaced children. The boys and girls were all ages from infants to adolescents. The "home" was kosher, with separate plates and eating utensils for meals with meat or milk. We attended Hebrew school and temple. On the high holidays we were taken to the synagogue that donated tickets. It made no difference whether the congregation was Orthodox, Conservative, or Reformed.

When I first arrived, some of the older children were "Holocaust babies" from Europe. Their parents had perished in the death camps. Others were the children of Holocaust survivors. Most, like myself, were products of broken families. Some of this misfortune was the aftermath of the Holocaust, which nearly obliterated the European Jewish community and traumatized the survivors, who became the postwar diaspora.

I was fortunate—it could have been worse. At least now I had numerous brothers and sisters. After public housing projects and hotel rooms, I was home with my own, for the first time accepted as part of a collective unit. There were three meals a day and other children to play with, and I had my own bed.

Still, we slept as many as five to a room and took our meals at long communal-style tables. As orphans, we wore nametags on our clothes, had no parental protection or family privilege, and were raised to be self-sufficient. To this day I am still close with many of my orphan siblings.

The child-care workers were kind. If they raised a hand or even their voice to discipline us, they were immediately fired. Every eight hours there was a shift change, and we received a fresh crew to wear out. Some of the staff were college students studying social science or social work; others were older folks who enjoyed children. Most of the staff worked a few years, then moved on in their career. A few worked at the children's home throughout my childhood. They were our surrogate parents and were devoted to our needs. I had the advantage of being able to selectively model myself on a collection of diverse adults, from different social, economic, racial, and religious backgrounds. Some of my favorite staff were African American. As an orphan, I am the child of many "parents."

When I first arrived at the children's home, I was so traumatized that I could barely function at home or school. Nevertheless, I was raised in a collective environment where adults read books and shared their ideas and dreams. I learned to love school, as it was a place where I could prove I was as good as or better than anyone, despite having no parents.

We attended two different inner-city public high schools. Many of the children were gifted students, played sports, were involved in social activities, and were popular with many friends. When I was in high school we had two rock-and-roll bands in the home. We threw parties chaperoned by staff that were well attended by friends from both high schools.

Nevertheless, as orphans we were different. We stuck up for each other, looked out for our younger brothers and sisters, and never ran home to cry. We were good kids, a bit rough around the edges but fiercely loyal to one another. No doubt about it, we knew the score. As orphans we would always be considered troubled and incorrigible, children without parental protection.

At age seventeen, I graduated from high school early and left the children's home to attend the University of Wisconsin–Madison (UW). I was tough, self-supportive, and mature beyond my years. I had to be. Once I left the home there was no return. I was on my own with only the clothes on my back and a few bucks in my pocket.

My older sister, who was raised in Cleveland and who entered UW at age sixteen, helped me get registered. Having grown up in different cities, we were nearly strangers. The first year at school I lived off campus with her and three wild female sociology graduate students. My sister would chase me around the apartment saying, "Incest is best." She was just happy to have a little brother to tease again. I would hide out with the other women in their bedrooms. It was a cheerful introduction to the pleasures of sociology.

In 1969 the Madison campus was the place to be. There were "peace and love" and the antiwar movement. I jumped right in, participating in Students for a Democratic Society and marching for welfare mothers' rights, the Black Student Union and Teaching Assistants' Union strikes, and the mass demonstrations against the Vietnam War. "Make love not war" was our motto.

Still, I was unprepared for the disadvantage of my poverty compared to the social-class privilege of many other students. I found most of the undergraduate students to be silly and immature and totally dependent on their parents' financial support and direction. Despite their cool demeanor and assertion of independent thinking, they were still mere children. Meanwhile, I read textbooks in the bookstore because I could not afford books. When I got hungry I would go hustle some overfed suburban female student who had a meal ticket and lived in the dorm. I was determined to be a good student, even if I could not afford the books and food. Finally, I discovered the student aid office. I remember the financial-aid counselor cried when I told her that I could not complete the parent information on the application form because I was an orphan.

Born illegal, I was destined to be a sociology student. UW has the largest and by many accounts the best sociology program in the world. I declared my major and took every sociology course I could handle. I remember our sociology professors leading us from the lecture halls to join peace marches in the streets. The police and National Guard occupied our campus every year and gassed us from helicopters and military vehicles. An important part of our education was learning how to differentiate between tear, blister, and pepper gas. The "mad town" students fought the police with sticks and stones and filled the county jail and hospitals after each demonstration.

Attending an elite public university, a person meets students from all over the world. At UW I remember taking courses about China, Latin America, and Africa and learned that my government opposed liberation movements everywhere. I was struck by the fact that there are, at the very least, three separate worlds existing side by side. I was born of the first world, which is composed of the rich industrial countries. The second world is the so-called developing countries, where the first world has elected to deploy some investment capital. The third world is the countries that are largely seen by American and European bankers as places to extract mineral resources, rather than economies to develop as a means to raise the standard of living for the indigenous populations.

In 1970 I left the land of privilege and traveled to Mexico for the first time. I should have stuck to the tourist destinations, but no, I had to seek adventure, get to know the people, and venture beyond the pale. Mexico is a country that may be characterized as balancing on the edge of the second and third world. This is a large nation, with vast potential but serious economic disparities. The Mexican elite is very rich, and most everybody else is dirt poor. I quickly found myself mesmerized by a country dominated by a ruthless upper class, mired in poverty and a long history of failed revolutions.

Spending months at a time as a guest of left-wing students in the interior of the country, I lived in villages and urban districts, where electric and water services were sporadic (if they existed at all), the daily staple was beans and corn, and the people knew the federal police and military to be bandits. In retrospect, I understood very little of the language or culture, but I still remember the poverty. I was shocked by the economic conditions, not just the beggars who stood on every tourist corner but also the death that came so young and was so common.

Over the next few years I returned to UW, took some more classes, but eventually lost interest in academic studies. Instead my "higher learning" would continue as a gringo gone bad who volunteered to help finance the modest economic development of a few remote Mexican villages. Desperation and youthful idealism are the mother of invention. What was I smoking?

Well, you guessed it. My romantic interest in the plight of the Mexican people introduced me to a strange business, where Yankee greenbacks flowed south and pipe dreams north. Over the next decade I traveled extensively south of the border and repeatedly returned home to the States, indifferent to the inherent risks, an adventurer playing a dangerous game. I played a role that could only end in disaster. By the end of the 1970s and the beginning of the "war on drugs" in the early 1980s, many of my friends were dead or in prison. By 1982 I was a bit worn from living on the lunatic fringe and far outside the law. The years of travel had taken their toll. Still, the work continued, as the Yankee dollars brought hope and relative prosperity to many people who worked the land in quiet desperation. But I shouldn't have been surprised that my own government thought less of my endeavors and decided I was a dangerous criminal.

I was arrested in 1982, and when I refused to cooperate with the Drug Enforcement Agency, I was threatened with and then indicted on ten counts of conspiracy to distribute marijuana. Facing 150 years if convicted on all charges (fifteen years for each count), I stood jury trial in the Federal District Courthouse in Charleston, South Carolina. Upon being convicted of one count and while on bail, in 1983 I appealed the case to the U.S. Court of Appeals and in 1984 to the U.S. Supreme Court. I was sentenced to nine years and assigned to maximum security at the United States Penitentiary Atlanta (USP Atlanta).

Altogether I stood trial in three federal courtrooms and completed two years under close bail supervision, three years of incarceration, and six years on parole, for a total of eleven years in correctional custody. I served time in several jails, penitentiaries, medium-security institutions, minimum-security camps, and a work-release center; and I had a half-dozen different parole officers.

I entered federal prison at the beginning of the drug war. Because I had fought a federal case all the way to the U.S. Supreme Court, I was sentenced to maximum security. The day I arrived at USP Atlanta the penitentiary was on fire. Cuban prisoners had torched a number of buildings. I never entered "general population" there. Instead I was transported along with 200 other men first to FCI Talladega (Alabama), then USP Terre Haute (Indiana), and later to USP Marion (Illinois) and then USP Leavenworth (Kansas).

I spent most of my first federal-prison year in transit "holdover" units in different prisons. I did a lot of time in the Secure Housing units that convicts call "the hole." This meant that for many months I had no mail, phone privileges, commissary, or visits. The federal prison system was so overcrowded (with four men to a two-man cell) that some were sleeping in hallways, in storerooms, and on staircase landings. Meanwhile, I was getting the tour of the federal "American gulag" (Richards 1990, 2003).

Behind the wall life goes on. I passed my time in federal prison getting to know the men I lived with in cellblocks and dormitories. I met a lot of interesting characters in federal prison. My favorites were the professional pot smugglers. Many of them were ex-military grunts and officers who had joined the business after their tour of duty in Vietnam. One of my friends was an ex-marine who before the war worked on lobster boats in Massachusetts. After the war he took to running fishing boats filled with marijuana from the West Indies to New England. Another buddy was a former army officer who was seriously wounded and decorated for valor in Indochina. He specialized in sophisticated operations that featured high-quality Colombian pot sealed in fruit and vegetable cans. He shipped his product port to port in cargo containers. The containers were then loaded on semitrucks and transported all over the country.

Nearly one-third of the federal prison population is composed of foreign citizens. In the early 1980s the system was filled with Cubans, Colombians, and Mexicans. Many of them were members of well-organized smuggling operations that delivered marijuana to the United States and Europe. I found the Colombians to be the most interesting. The upper echelon was serious about their business, well educated in American and European universities, multilingual, and dedicated to the use of marijuana proceeds as "primitive capital" to develop their country. These men talked about how they invested their profits in housing developments and industrial infrastructure back home.

The sad part was that many of the men I became friends with, both Americans and foreign citizens, were major traffickers in marijuana. As the length of federal drug war sentences are determined by the amount of weight (pounds or tons), many of them were given life sentences. Today, as I enjoy my status as a university professor, some of these men are still wasting away in federal prison, and a few have died in custody.

In federal prison I found a lot of men who like myself had been raised in difficult circumstances. Many of them were the products of indifferent parents, broken homes, the foster care system, or children's homes. Few of them received regular family letters or visits. Once a year they received a Christmas card or maybe a visit from their ex-wife. These men were very much like the children I grew up with in the orphanage. They were tough and self-reliant and accustomed to congregate living. In many cell houses they were the more experienced prisoners who set the tune and ruled the tier. This included operating the most lucrative prisoner businesses—gambling, drugs, and homemade liquor.

Despite all the interesting characters and alternative activities in prison, I still managed to catch up on my reading. This was relatively easy considering that in the joint you get three meals and a bed, there is no family to support, and there is little else to do. I always had a book in my coat or pants pocket. I would read at my workstation, on the yard, or in my bunk till lights out. My books were what "was sent in" or I could find in the prison library. My favorites were old college textbooks, nonfiction, and, in the last year or so, sociology.

In 1987 I left federal prison, returned to Wisconsin, and entered graduate school at the University of Wisconsin–Milwaukee. Most men and women encounter serious problems exiting prison and reentering society. Fortunately I'd had a lot of experience with difficult transitions. After foreign adventures and federal penitentiaries, I was happy to be back at school reading books and writing research papers. Still, I found the students at the university to be a bit ill-mannered. It took me awhile to get used to being bumped in the crowded hallways. In the penitentiary a convict would apologize, while at the university the students just crashed into each other and kept on going.

I was also a bit confused by the bright clothing my fellow students wore. Federal prison is a drab world where convicts wear khaki uniforms. My first day at the university I was sitting alone at a table eating lunch in the cafeteria and minding my own business. A group of male students sat down without asking permission. Dressed in pastel-colored T-shirts and shorts, giggling about nothing, they proceeded to eat their lunch without a nod in my direction. I assumed they were gay and moved to another table. It took me awhile to get acquainted with the fashions of the day.

I enjoyed graduate school at UW-Milwaukee and later at Iowa State University. But I was always surprised at the attrition rate, the number of students who lost interest in their studies, failed comprehensive exams, or never completed their dissertation. Then again, these students had other opportunities. They could pursue alternative careers. As a felon, I had more limited options.

What are the odds that a person with no parents and a prison record will become a university professor? Considering my background, it is a miracle I ever finished high school, let alone earned a Ph.D. Today I am a professor of sociology and criminology at Northern Kentucky University. My students have fun and do not get bored. Every semester I begin my classes by quietly studying the faces of my students. I mean no offense. I am simply searching for those few souls who may find the courage to live their lives with their eyes open.

Fortunately, I am a sociologist, which means that my departmental colleagues are expected to give at least lip service to "diversity" and "multiculturalism." Unfortunately, the race, ethnicity, and gender textbooks do not yet discuss or include felons and convicts in their progressive ideas. Nevertheless, my colleagues at the university read, write, and usually think with a relatively open mind. Somehow they have adjusted to the fact that they share workspace with a criminal.

Ex-cons have no protection from discrimination. In fact, by law they are subject to and singled out for exclusion and discrimination. As semicitizens they may be denied employment, housing, credit, and the right to vote, depending on the state. There are numerous states that deny ex-convicts entrance to graduate schools and employment at universities. The most recent example affects thousands of university students who are denied financial aid because of drug convictions.

As one of the few ex-convict tenured criminology professors in the country, I am now relatively safe from overt discrimination. Still, I have learned that becoming a tenured professor means I do not have to suffer fools or foolish books. I have no patience for social scientists who study their subject from a safe distance. I am one of a growing group of "convict criminologists" who have the courage to both do the science and "tell it like it is."

I enjoy being an ex-convict professor. As one of the leaders of the convict criminology (CC) movement, I prefer the company of my "felonious friends," who although they have fancy college degrees have not forgotten from where they came. Like me, CC was "born illegal," but it is now thriving in the university and is beginning to inform and transform the way academics research and write about prisoners and prisons.

CC began in 1997. The idea emerged over a dinner conversation at a San Diego restaurant among James Austin (a "non-con" criminologist who is a highly regarded expert on prison reform) and "ex-cons" John Irwin, Chuck Terry, and myself. The group continues to grow as more and more ex-con and non-con professors are added to our ranks. We do not have a formal leadership structure and operate more like an extended support group, with no one person speaking for all. We have socialized together and drawn large audiences at American Society of Criminology, Academy of Criminal Justice Sciences, and American Correctional Association conferences and have published an impressive body of books and journal articles.[1]

The general message of CC is that the conventional academic discourse about crime and criminal justice has excluded the very people who have been processed through and spent time in the system. Despite the scholarly tone and pretensions, the field of criminology and criminal justice is dominated by scholars who have not taken the time to consult or interview prisoners. Countless books and articles have been published in which authors miss the mark and misrepresent a reality they barely comprehend. The result is a body of research and professional opinion that serves the social control needs of prison administrators and the state and that obfuscates the failure of the criminal justice system to control crime, rehabilitate prisoners, and protect the public. Meanwhile, the socioeconomic problems (poverty, unemployment, racism) that contribute to crime continue to multiply and plague our country. Scarce public resources that should be spent on education, health care, and economic development are squandered on building more prisons. Men and women are cycled to prison, back to the community, and to prison again. The prison population grows, and the victims of both crime and incarceration get more desperate for solutions.

A serious conversation about reducing crime must include convicts and ex-convicts, and now we have convict criminologists sitting at the table. Our first goal is to transform the academic knowledge base on prisons. With some exceptions, most of the existing literature is written from a managerial viewpoint, that of prison administrators, and does not reflect the experience and insights of prisoners and their families. Most academic research and college textbooks do not truthfully convey the conditions of confinement and harm done to prisoners. Students read idealized accounts that mask the reality and horrors of incarceration. They are fed a steady diet of functionalist explanations that portray prisons as imperfect but necessary institutions that require periodic reforms. There is very little discussion of prisons as a politically organized elite effort to manage "deviant" populations and control the "dangerous classes" (Shelden 2001). We are now writing diligently in a concerted effort to remedy this problem.

Our second goal is to use our dual roles as ex-cons and professors to challenge the public's perception of prisoners. We represent the potential of people who are currently warehoused in our nation's prisons. There are many men and women wasting away in penitentiaries and correctional institutions who need immediate access to college courses and advanced training. We know that most prisoners can become productive members of society if they are given the opportunity to do so.

Our third goal as convict criminologists is to participate in and support the social science research, humanitarian, and prison reform organizations that are working to reduce the number of people who are incarcerated in the United States. Currently we have the highest per capita rate of incarceration in the Western world. There are at least a million men and women doing time for *nonviolent* offenses (Irwin, Schiraldi, and Ziedenberg 2000). Many of these prisoners have been locked up for *first-time* convictions. As convict criminologists, we advocate reducing the prison population through fewer admissions, shorter sentences, and early release. Prison should serve as a wake-up call, a place to get straight, not a shabby home for millions of Americans.

Our fourth goal, implied by the first three, is that over time CC will provide the public with a more realistic understanding of prisoners and prisons. We write books, journal articles, and newspaper and magazine pieces. We write for the general public as well as the academic community in an effort to exert our influence over public policy and debate.

Our fifth goal is to change the very language that is conventionally used to discuss prisons. We do not use the words *offenders* or *inmates*, for example. These are managerial terms used by law enforcement and correctional staff. We prefer to use *men, women, prisoners, convicts,* or *a person convicted of a criminal offense.* The point is to remember that a person is not a statistical category and cannot be defined by their crime or residence in prison.

Born illegal, I have told my story as simply and sincerely as I dare. I am an orphan and an ex-convict. I am the child of many parents, an adult assembled from the bits and pieces of many caring people who crossed my path and somehow shared their gifts. The lessons they taught kept me alive in the penitentiary and prepared me to be a professor.

CC was "born illegal" too. Somehow a miracle has occurred, as a few convicts have made it out of the penitentiary through graduate school and are now teaching sociology, criminology, and criminal justice at universities throughout the country. These orphans of incarceration are becoming prominent scholars in their field, adding intellectual rigor and excitement to debates about crime and criminal justice.

As an ex-convict criminologist I live my professional life with one foot still in the penitentiary and the other in the university. Meanwhile, there is another cable news producer on the phone, and the convict mail is piling up on my desk. So I will make yet another television appearance. This will give me a brief reprieve from answering my mail. Maybe it will bring some comfort to the guys behind the wall.

Note

1. This literature began with John Irwin's classic works *The Felon* (1970), *Prisons in Turmoil* (1980), and *The Jail* (1985) and now includes books by James Austin and John Irwin (1994, rev. 2001), Greg Newbold (1989), Barbara Owen (1998), Richard Jones and Thomas Schmidt (2000), Jeffrey Ian Ross and Stephen C. Richards (2002, 2003), and Charles Terry (2003).

CHAPTER 16

Telling Tales: Journey of an Itinerant Storyteller

Robin A. Mello

Storytelling should be viewed as a set of procedures for "life making." And just as it is worthwhile examining in minute detail how physics or history go about their world, might we not be well advised to explore in detail what we do when we construct ourselves through stories?

—*Joseph Bruner*

In the Beginning

"Once upon a time . . ." "Once there was . . ." "I remember a time . . ." "Long before you were born . . ." These phrases serve as verbal markers, or signals, that the listener or reader is about to experience a story. As an itinerant storyteller turned educator and scholar, I have found the use of stories in teaching and research to be a natural and commonsense endeavor. This is because the storied experience (both experiential and analytical) is part of my daily life—and I have come to know narrative as my primary source for making meaning.

Working with tales and narratives is my job as well as avocation, and over the past two decades I've had the good fortune to be offered opportunities that connect storytelling with my other professions of teaching, researching, and acting. This has meant that I've been able to work with creative and educative narrative models that contain a multiplicity of socially constructed information and beliefs. What follows is a series of vignettes that tell the story of how my perception of narrative evolved from a useful *tool* into a way of *knowing*.

1981: Becoming a Teller

Cindy and I are conversing over coffee at an inner-city Dunkin' Donuts café. It is January in Maine, and despite the bright afternoon sunlight, the temperature is well below zero. Wind blows in through the door and chills the air every time a customer leaves or enters. I wrap my sweater around me and breathe in the hot steam coming from my thin cardboard cup.

Cindy is my best friend and the director of a regional children's theater company. She works tirelessly to provide "at risk" children with opportunities to create and experience the performing arts. I have been working as a theater therapist and literacy teacher in an alternative day school for teens who are what state social services call "delinquents."

The discussion, for the last half hour, has centered on our dream of creating a traveling theater project for homeless teens, but the money question has us stumped. Might we qualify for grants and other public funds? Cindy has come up with a brainstorm: I will apply and be accepted to the Maine Touring Artists (MTA) roster—a grant program sponsored by the National Endowment for the Arts and the Maine Arts Commission (MAC). The MTA subsidizes independent artists willing to travel and present community programs in remote and rural areas of New England. For a member of MTA, a theater project for at risk youth might be fundable. There's a glitch, however: the MTA only accepts autonomous performers.

"Sounds perfect, made for you," says Cindy.

"But I'm an actress," I reply. "I need a script, costumes, props. I'm not a solo act."

"Nonsense. You are a storyteller. You just don't know it."

What does a storyteller do exactly? "Do you mean acting out *The Three Little Pigs*?" I ask. The only storyteller I can conjure up is my Uncle Charlie, who would launch into earthy and outrageous narratives after he'd had too much to drink. This probably is not what Cindy has in mind.

"No, it's a lot like dramatic reading, only in storytelling you just let it flow, improvise, participate in the moment, you know—don't worry, I'll help."

That's how it began. Over the next few months I worked with Cindy honing a set of performance tales: Rudyard Kipling's "Just So" stories, Ulysses and the Cyclops, and "The Magic Ravioli" (an Italian folktale I'd heard as a child). As Cindy predicted, I "passed" the audition and found myself listed as a one-woman-show ready to travel to the hinterlands of New England with what the MAC described as "a program of arts and culture."

Although our dream of a theater company for inner-city children never materialized, my life did take an unexpected turn. Bookings and tours for the story-performances expanded until two years and many stories later I quit my day job (as a special education teacher) and went full force into self-employment in the arts. This meant traveling the length and breadth of New England—from the Canadian border to the outer islands off the Atlantic coast. Places where the hillsides were covered with cornfields, pine forests, rock walls, and abandoned factories. Villages with names like Forest City (a town of 150 people), West Paris, Eastport, and Machias Fork. I'd arrive in these far-flung communities, an itinerant teller, narrating for my supper.

Sometimes my hosts would request tangible items along with the folktales: things such as fresh milk for a family of boat builders on North Haven Island (it was a scarce commodity), Chanel perfume for a young couple's anniversary in Height-the-Land, or Chinese take-out carefully packed in a makeshift cooler and delivered to a teacher working in the Alagash Wilderness (she missed the taste of egg rolls).

I told stories and sang songs at grange halls, old movie theaters, one-room schoolhouses, and library foyers. People responded in kind. Audience members would often come up after a show and tell me stories—a narrative transaction, a story swap. From time to time I'd be invited to visit their homes and workplaces, take a boat ride, or share a meal. It was a powerful and exhausting epoch in my life, when I felt connected to the world through my ability to evoke responses from audiences using only language and drama. I felt creative, challenged, and also lonely. After the last story had been told, I'd get in my car and drive away—on to the next storytelling session over the ridge of mountains into the west.

1988: The Voice of the Teacher Is Heard in the Land

There's a problem with combining the roles of storyteller and performance artist. It can promote a false paradigm, placing the act of narration beyond the purview of the "ordinary" person and within the late-twentieth- and early-twenty-first-century Western construct of artist as expert—outside the boundaries of "normal" society (Stone 1998; Zipes 1995). Instead of perceiving storytelling as an innate experience open to all humans, many individuals are left with an impression that narration requires highly specialized and exceptional skills. This in turn encourages listeners to think of their own story as amateur, which flies in the face of what is known about human ability.

Our species strives to make meaning through language and narrative (Coles 1989; Pinker 1994). This is how we create cultural perspectives and social norms. One could argue that civilizations have all been built on shared narratives and that storytelling is not only a creative endeavor but also a survival skill. Therefore, to assume that it is not attainable by the majority is to hold a false assumption about a native and natural process.

Elevating storytelling above the ken of most individuals is to deny the very thing that makes them human. Ironically, this is the type of attitude that often silences those who have traditionally been community storytellers: teachers, librarians, homemakers, parents, and caretakers of children. When MTA opened up its touring program to schools and offered them the opportunity to sponsor artist residencies long term, I jumped at the chance to break down the expert-amateur dichotomy by bringing storytelling curricula to teachers and their students. It seemed a natural and necessary next step.

One particular experience during this phase of my work as a storyteller stands out as an example. The incident took place during a year-long storytelling program sponsored by MTA and the Bayside Consolidated School District. As resident artist for the year, I had the opportunity to work with all teachers and students in the entire Bayside district, at five different sites. Things went well until I met the teachers at Tidewater Elementary School. A majority of faculty members there were extremely reticent to involve themselves in any creative-arts project and for all of the usual reasons: overwork, discomfort with change, devaluation of the arts, suspicion. It was not an easy working relationship.

Teacher workshops in particular were problematic. Struggling to chip away at the diffidence and passive-aggressive attitudes most of the participants displayed during seminar time felt like an uphill battle. Then, quite unexpectedly a change occurred. It was brought on, oddly enough, by the New England weather. A "noreaster" of epic proportions blew in with unexpected force right in the middle of a weekday. Directly in the path of the blizzard, the school took the full brunt of the storm. Power went out, and icy conditions prevented students from being sent home. Teachers had to make do in their classrooms, stranded without light, heat, water, or electricity. I was not there at the time, but when I arrived two days later I was greeted by a group of excited teachers! They gathered around me eager, for the first time, to tell their stories.

One veteran teacher said: "I was just sitting in this dark, cold classroom, and all my students were staring at me, and I was wondering what to do. I didn't want them to know I was scared and I didn't have any ideas. Then suddenly a light went on in my head! I thought to myself, storytelling! So I told my students to pretend that there was a campfire in the middle of the classroom. We moved the desks, put on our coats, and sat around cross-legged on the floor—close for warmth. I began to tell stories. My students didn't make a sound. I was so happy and relieved. After a while the lights came back on, and somehow the plows made it through so we could get the kids on buses—but I will always remember telling stories in the dark."

One of her compatriots chimed in, "Yes! That happened to me too! There I was telling a story—not reading it but telling it! All my students . . . I had their undivided attention; it was so amazing, so great. I said to myself, 'I've got to do this all the time from now on.' And even with the lights out I could keep on teaching."

Most of the teachers at Tidewater had had similar experiences. Telling empowered these educators as they used their voices to guide, focus, and reassure their students. They were able to teach through a tempest in the dark.

Storytelling and Social Change

Through transmission of narrative the storyteller allows the powerless to perceive himself or herself as powerful. The storytellers of South Africa during apartheid, for example, told what seemed (to the dominant white political structure) to be "simple folk stories." Listeners perceived these same tales, however, as liberating acts of social protest (Scheub 1996). This is not a new phenomenon. Familiar and seemingly innocuous stories, such as the Household Tales of the Brothers Grimm, have been told for centuries as a form of social opposition. They may sound like entertainments but feature subplots that challenge authority, oppressive attitudes, and the status quo (Bottigheimer 1987; Dégh 1979; Stone 1998).

A case in point is the Nasrudin group of tales used in the Sufi tradition to confront conformist thinking. The fact that they are still being told, remain culturally and spiritually vital, and continue to evolve is evidence of their value. (Current versions of these stories mention freezers, trains, cars, computers, and even the stock exchange.) Like the Coyote myths of the Lakota Sioux, Aunt Nancy stories of the African slaves, and Jataka tales from the Buddhist tradition(s), these ancient stories provide vital tools that continue to engage listeners, teach values, *and* challenge social norms (Scheub 1998; Shah 1983).

When narrative texts are used to challenge authoritarian perspectives, teachers (and tellers) gain opportunities to creatively explore multiple perspectives from a wide range of social standpoints. Yet this mode of expression can also threaten institutions of power, which in turn retaliate by attempting to limit or prevent such performances. For instance, a few years ago after I completed a storytelling workshop for high school students, the principal took me aside. He complained that one of the participating teachers regarded my "material" as offensive; I would not be "allowed" to tell a particular Mayan creation myth again. If I did I would be summarily dismissed from the residency program. He observed that the story contained descriptions of deities that were "not in keeping with the beliefs of the local school community." It was not permitted to refer to "a god" or mention the word *god,* or *goddess,* in that school. Ironically I inquired if I might relate a Tibetan story mentioning Buddha.

"Of course," replied the principal.

"What about Krishna? Could I say the words 'Great Mother Earth' or mention Allah?"

"Oh yes, we just can't say the word *god* in school. Please remember that."

This presented me with a dilemma: How could I respond to censorship while maintaining an inclusive repertoire so that students might be exposed to multicultural perspectives? Rather than quit, I altered my story selection, telling a Buddhist Jataka tale and a Nasrudin story from the Sufi tradition. But the incident did prompt me to take a deeper look at the issue of censorship in my own work and generate more material inclusive of multiple beliefs and contexts.

Not all experiences of censorship result in such positive and straightforward outcomes. Most do not. The arts, in general, often seem threatening to those forces that strive to control society, and artists as well as academics are commonly among the first to suffer repression during political conflicts (Scheub 1996). Sijie Dai (2001), for instance, tells the story of watching his father being tortured at a political rally—accused of the crime of teaching school. Who could be so threatened by a teacher's voice? To answer this question and to give an example of how stories function in creating shared perceptions of social experience, I'd like to "tell" a story that is derived from North African and Celtic sources.

Bread for the Mind, Meat for the Ear, and Water for the Heart

Once upon a time, a long time ago, after the war was over and the people had been defeated, the new King decided to make a victory tour of his recently acquired lands. To assert his power, he forbade any commoner to read or write. Schools were outlawed and the practice of teaching forbidden—on pain of death. The poetry and great epics of the people were banned. Many scholars fled into exile.

Early in the King's tour the Crown Prince fell ill. As a result, court was established at a small country castle far away from the royal city. The best physicians and tutors were sent for to tend to the Prince's needs, and all waited anxiously for the boy's recovery. To while away the worrisome hours, the King would climb up to the tallest tower and walk along the battlements. This became a habit with him at sunrise and sunset.

It was during one of these solitary promenades that the King began to notice something unusual. Every morning he saw children disappear into the hedgerows that lined the countryside below. Each evening this ritual was repeated in reverse order. Children would emerge from the bushes and run back to their cottages and farms. In spite of their poverty, the King saw that these children were healthy, full of laughter and life.

The mystery soon was put out of the King's mind, however, as he received news that the Prince's condition had worsened. In desperation he sent out a proclamation promising great rewards to anyone who could cure the Prince. In response to this decree, an old village woman appeared. Hobbling up to the King, she addressed him in a quavering voice.

"Your majesty," she said, "I can cure your son. What he needs is 'bread for the mind, meat for the ear, and water for his heart.' I know where these are to be found. But as my reward I claim your solemn promise that you will rescind the laws that forbid us to speak our language, sing our tales, and teach our children."

The King was desperate and agreed. Smiling, she took him by the hand and led him to a broad meadow outside the town.

"Now listen."

All of a sudden the King heard a strange music filling the air. It was made up of children's voices, bits of alphabets, histories, and epic sagas all rising on the wind in a magical cacophony. The entire countryside was full of recitation and laughter.

"You are listening to our teachers in their hedgerow schools, who, in defiance of your laws, feed our children 'bread for the mind, meat for the ear, and water for the heart.' Our stories are bread that provides knowledge. Our history is meat that strengthens our understanding, and our poetry is the water that slakes our thirsty hearts. This is why our children are healthy and happy. Bring the Prince to our hedgerow school so that he may be cured and grow as our children do. A people without knowledge cannot strengthen, a country without stories does not prosper, and a Prince without connection to his people and their history can never become wise."

How does this story affect the reader/listener? Its meaning will depend on the individual's physical well-being, social position, political beliefs, age, past experience, education, and so forth. No story has a single authoritative meaning. This is what makes methodology difficult for the social scientist who wants to know the reasons and purposes within the narrative and how it functions for certain populations.

Joseph Campbell (1990) claims that folktales, such as the one above, are understood at the intrapersonal, sociocultural, macrosystemic levels. In other words, their meaning can be interpreted in specific as well as universal ways at the same time. No one, be they storyteller, teacher, or scholar, can really know what a story will mean to any other individual listener. However, we can make some connections within our social groups as well as cross-culturally. The multiplicity of interpretations, in fact, can be a source of strength in the storytelling world.

1990: Telling Stories in the USSR

Storytelling has functioned within my personal experience as a conduit for community interaction, education, and creating cultural bridges—making it possible for me to travel past the borders of my own experience to that of others. In 1990, for example, on a "goodwill tour" arranged through the U.S. State Department, Sister-City Exchange Program, and National Endowment for the Arts, I, along with a group of other New England "folk" performers, had the opportunity to perform my storytelling for audiences in the former Union of Soviet Socialist Republics.

One afternoon toward the middle of the tour, leaving the apparatchiks and politicians to their meetings and formalities, I asked our interpreter if I could spend some time telling stories in the schools (as opposed to the theaters and festivals where we'd been working). Although the request was unexpected, it was met with enthusiasm. The next morning I was whisked away from official proceedings and taken to a large elementary school in the middle of Archangel City. There I wandered around to my heart's content, talking with teachers, telling stories to groups of children, and swapping anecdotes. I spent the day going from classroom to classroom performing the world tales I knew best. Every time I told a story I felt at home. When Tia Strega (Italian for "Auntie Witch") tried to cast a spell on the heroine of my Italian-American version of "Snow White," the Russian children gasped in horror. When the old man won a bet with Satan in "Duffy and the Devil," they laughed aloud. With the exception of the interpreter's presence, there was no real qualitative difference for me between telling stories in a Soviet school and telling them in an American one. Students participated in the same way audiences did in the United States. I took this as a sign that my storyteller identity seemed to confer a license to speak, one that rose above boundaries and ethnic identities. This interaction transcended the barriers constructed by our respective governments, connecting us on a significant human level.

This experience taught me that the act of telling is a type of social contact that connects as it communicates. Standing in that school building on the banks of the Divina River, telling stories, I knew that what I was doing not only was part of a long tradition but was also a radical social act that had telling at its core.

1993: Stories Go to College

Arthurian myth tells us that Merlin lived life backwards.[1] He entered Camelot already aware of what the future held. While his ability to foretell the future was perceived by others as magical and wise, Merlin knew he was merely retelling history from his memory, describing the future as he had lived it before. Imagine the confusion he must have felt watching everyone else going into the future while he was growing back toward their past.

In 1993 I was accepted into a doctoral studies program at Lesley University, Cambridge, Massachusetts. Entering the academic world in my mid-thirties after almost twenty years as a traveling performer and artist, I was disoriented. The first semester of graduate school felt like Merlin's dilemma: in a constant state of confusion, I perceived myself as working backwards. As a teacher-artist I had learned to *do*, perform, and explore text, to know my stories through experiencing them first and asking questions about larger theories and prior knowledge later. As a novice academic I was required to turn the model around, putting theory (aka the literature review) before action (aka method). Added to this was the fact that most of my colleagues in the qualitative field were discovering stories for the first time while I had been living with narrative data for years.

This was Merlin's predicament, in a sense, and his story—along with that of Sisyphus, the Titan who kept rolling a stone up a mountain only to see it slip from the top and roll down again—helped me gain a sense of perspective and keep my sense of humor. I discovered that I was passionately interested in doing qualitative work and that through the process of inquiry and scholarly investigation more nuances, understandings, and "ah-ha" experiences were discovered.

Researching stories made them more useful and expanded their importance. The scholarship of story required me to reevaluate my assumptions about performance, art, teaching, and telling. It forced me to create theories, write analytically, and weave the threads of my life experience in a new paradigm. Thinking, producing, examining, and evaluating narratives also helped me focus some unanswered questions about stories and their educative function in learning environments. In the end, after the dissertation was officially approved and the degree granted, the presence of story as a meaning-making was more significant and richer (Mello 2001, 2002).

2003: The Present

It is 9:30 on a Tuesday morning. I am telling a Portuguese folktale to thirty people, all under the age of twenty. They are students, newly enrolled in my university course on storytelling (aka THRBA 460.01), and are listening with intensity as well as apprehension. Over the next fifteen weeks we will read about, create, research, improvise, and tell each other stories. They know that soon it will be their turn to tell—in the same way most of their ancestors did over thousands of years. Storytelling is, after all, humankind's first literacy. In this course we perpetuate a long-standing tradition, yet we also reinterpret it through our multiple twenty-first-century lenses, which have been influenced by particular social conditions, technological literacy, and postmodern sensibilities.

Teaching this class, for me, is a personal adventure into the unknown narratives of others. But before the whole process begins in earnest, I stop in the middle of telling. Silence falls. For a moment all that can be heard is the howl of the winter wind as it whips around the old brick building, and though the steam radiator hisses warmly, a chill creeps in through the cracks in walls and floorboards. My mind is pulled back into memory as I recall a similar cold winter day over twenty years ago.

It's been a long journey from January 1982 in Maine to January 2003 in Wisconsin. Thousands of stories have been experienced, told, and written. Although my professional situation has changed to include a tenure-track job, publishing/research agenda, course load, committee membership, and the like, some of the underlying factors that led me to begin this life of storytelling remain. I still want to create theatrical opportunities for the next generation of artists and teachers, investigate through research what narrative tells us about social conditions, encourage the telling of stories in inner-city communities, and celebrate and discover the ways stories have meaning at a personal level.

This storied life isn't lonely anymore. As a storyteller in academe I've found a niche that seems to fit. I am enriched by telling within the context of higher education, where opportunities to combine the creative and analytical methodologies of performance and research come together. Finally, I've discovered that my three occupational roles—artist, teacher, and scholar—are linked through narrative, steeped in stories, and driven by curiosity, confusion, and epiphany. It feels much like Merlin waiting for release and enlightenment within his crystal cave.

Note

1. There are many versions of Merlin's story. Briefly, he was the greatest druid of his time and the mentor of King Arthur. His Machiavellian actions caused enmity between Camelot and the powerful sorceress Morgan La Fey. He now lives, studies, and contemplates the world inside a crystal cave, waiting for the return of Arthur, "the once and future king," at which time he will emerge to guide the world in a halcyon era of peace and prosperity.

CHAPTER 17

Silence of the Lambs: The Architecture of the Abattoir

Carla Corroto

As a young woman in architecture school in the early 1980s, I was uncertain of the cost of remaining silent. I was likewise unsure of the price of speaking my own truths and telling my own stories. This essay is derived from a longer autoethnographic study of architecture school that focuses on its attendant ideology and pedagogy (Corroto 1996). I employ retrospective participant observation to analyze the gendered organization and masculinist culture that sustains a resistance to women in architecture. The story is set in a graduate school program. In my last quarter of graduate school, the assignment was to design an abattoir in a rural area and a corporate headquarters for a meat company in a central business district. Somewhere between this lived experience and others' reactions to my depiction, my identity as a woman in the study and practice of architecture coalesced. This, then, is a story of a feminist identity that formed via responses to resistance and how feminist sociologists, in contrast, took my experience seriously and validated my identity.

Schools of architecture in the United States are organized around the "design studio." Design studio is a college course, a pedagogy, and a place. Typically, the course assignments in studio are drawings that represent the design of a building on a site. Through that architectural design work, knowledge garnered from all college coursework is supposed to be synthesized and made evident. Pedagogically, the studio is managed as a type of apprentice system, with students required to make public presentations. The instructor is an architect called the "studio crit"—short for "critic." The crit creates the assignments and then meets with each student at her or his desk, located in a campus building called the Studio. The institutional norm and expectation is for architecture students to work extremely long hours, frequently "pulling all-nighters," in these large, open-roomed studios. Pushing the body to the extremes of exhaustion is a badge of honor and a sign of commitment to the profession. Because students are expected to work in studio, they spend extended periods of time together, working at their individual desks on their individual designs, isolated from the rest of society.

After earning a bachelor's of science in architecture, I applied to a master's program in order to secure my professional degree. My goal was to become a licensed architect and someday design buildings. All told, I spent six years of long days and even longer nights toiling in design studios. But at the age of twenty-four, I felt as if two lifetimes had passed while I was entombed in studio.

While I had a deep appreciation for architecture and a true love of design work, I loathed architecture school. It was almost over. On the first day of the final quarter in Architecture Design Studio, our class of thirteen students learned that the assignment was to design two buildings. One was the urban corporate headquarters for a U.S. meat manufacturer, and the other was an abattoir. I had never heard the word *abattoir* and thought it was some sort of French prototype, perhaps like a Roman coliseum or Greek temple. I felt sick when I was told that it was a slaughterhouse. I had to repeat it to myself: The capstone or culminating quarter in architecture school was to be spent designing a *slaughterhouse*.

The studio crit arranged for us to take a bus trip downstate, into the heart of agriculture, to inspect an authentic functioning slaughterhouse. It was organized as a requirement of the course rather than an optional excursion. We had not gone to a school, a bathhouse, an arsenal, or a Lutheran church when we were assigned those design problems. Why the realism now?

The day we visited the killing floors, they were slaughtering hogs. The ordeal was as follows: Outside of the building the animal was stunned with an electrical shock to the skull so that the workers could clamp a hook and chain on the hog's back leg, lifting the squealing animal into the air and up into an opening in the structure, where another man with a knife waited to gouge a hole into the suffering animal's throat. As it bled to death, gravity took the animal down a line of assorted butchers who hacked off the limbs, the tail, the ears, the coat, the snout, and so on, until the live animal was carved into package-sized meat products or to a manageable-sized carcass for shipping.

Watching this carnage was horrific. Everything here was dreadfully wrong. Every one of my senses was shocked and sickened. Outside, the still live animals were being kicked and viciously prodded as they were forced into progressively smaller pens, funneled to their doom. Their shrieks of suffering grew louder and more pathetic, until the loudest one of all came as their throats were slit. The air smelled of cruelty and death and what I used to think of as manure. I was nauseous and my head was spinning. Could I believe my eyes? These poor creatures were treated as if they could not feel pain, let alone fear, treated as objects, as commodities, as products.

There were a hundred sheep that looked like fluffy stuffed toys in pens next to the hogs, awaiting their execution as well. They stuck their tongues out at us and made soft noises as we walked by. I thought they must be thirsty and looked around to get them some water. A fellow student said my actions were ridiculous, as the sheep were to be cut up the following day. Why bother with them? Was it that they should spend their final night suffering from thirst? I wanted to open the fences to set them free. It was too late for the hogs, but the sheep still had a chance. My mind was racing frantically as I tried to figure out what action to take to stop this extraordinary pain.

Inside the building, we watched as the laborers used huge knives to cut up the still warm and bleeding animals. Everything was blood red—blood saturated their aprons, splattered on the walls, and ran down the drains in the floor. All of the workers were men, and they were putting on a show for what was probably their first tour group. They smiled and leered at us as we gawked at their actions. One student, who thought of himself as an artist, detachedly took Polaroid photographs of the killing floor. What was he doing? He treated this like a field trip to see an architectural monument.

Radios blared rock-and-roll music from AM stations as the workers set about their tasks. We could still hear the doomed animals screaming above the din as they were being dismembered. When we walked by, the men whistled and hooted after the other woman in the class and me. They shouted that they liked "the one in the blue coat." "Look at her!" A student in my class thought it was funny to tell me, "That guy over there wants you." When I turned to look, I saw a man covered in blood and holding a knife, throwing mock kisses, making catcalls, and wiggling his hips in my direction. He was a gyrating Elvis, using the knife as a microphone. A partially vivisected animal swung between him and me, obstructing his view. He lunged at the creature with his butcher's knife, savagely slashing it. Men everywhere were laughing and looking for my reaction. There was no place to hide.

We were paraded into every nook and cranny of the slaughterhouse, as if the owners of the factory were our clients and we were really going to design one of these functioning buildings for construction. Most of my classmates took notes or made diagrams of the architecture in their sketchbooks. I walked around in a daze of sadness and horror. Heavy doors opened into freezer rooms stocked with hanging carcasses, smaller closets of assorted body parts, and long shipping docks with refrigerated boxes.

Our final stop was the suit-and-tie-wearing manager's office. Incongruously, the room had a carpeted floor, wood-paneled walls, and upholstered furniture. It could have been the manager's office at any white-collar office complex. A middle-aged white man asked us if we had any questions about the "plant," and several students seemed to need more details about square footage requirements and the like. My attention was riveted upon the framed "art" work that hung above his desk—a centerfold-type poster of a naked woman lying on her side. Her gaze was seductively aimed at the camera, but the photo of her body had been dotted off into parts. The sections were labeled, "flank steak," "shank," "rump roast," "breast," and so on. She too was just meat. My classmates chuckled at this representation, and the manager giggled too. It all seemed a conspiracy of men. Their machinations, their matrix of domination, the intertwined nature of control was somehow passed along as an inside joke.

In an instant, I came to the sick conclusion that I was next, that they would electrocute me and string me up and slit my throat. Many things that I already knew, that I needed to learn, and that I could not escape converged on that day at the abattoir.

I was told that if I wanted to graduate I had to design this building. So I set upon the task, trying unsuccessfully to block all my feelings of sadness. The project description did not give a literal or physical site upon which to place our buildings. I situated the slaughterhouse that I designed at an exit on a freeway that ran through a countryside only sparsely populated by humans. Surrounding a cloverleaf off-ramp "in the middle of nowhere," I positioned a farm at one corner, a cemetery at the other, and a McDonald's-type fast food restaurant across from the abattoir. This obvious and heavy-handed spatial metaphor was intended to reveal the socially constructed hierarchical relationships between man (literally) and nature and the economy. The slaughtered animals were abstracted as hamburgers sold for money at McDonald's to "man," who lived on the farm and raised the crops grown in the earth where humans were buried, decomposing into soil. There was no nature-civilization division, no man at the apex of the food chain at this highway exit. All sites and sides were of equal size, both symbolically and physically. It was the whole life continuum, tautologically speaking.

The abattoir itself was intended to be similarly representative, wherein people and animals had, broadly conceived, similar experiences. Animals were stunned; the workers punched the clock. The laborers were whole when they entered the workplace. Then their lives, as time, were reduced to a piece of abstracted monetary representation when they left: dollars and cents. The animals were living whole beings when they entered the building. Then they were reduced to abstracted pieces of meat when they left: hamburgers and bacon. Acknowledging the privilege of social class distinctions, the managers' offices were walled in glass and placed on the line across from the butchers dismembering the animals. The office workers were forced to face the "means of production." Every line that I drew representing architecture—a wall, a door, a floor, a window—fit into the story.

As the quarter progressed and I worked up this design scheme, I got nothing but negative reactions. The studio crit hated this design, telling me that it was an architectural one-liner. My classmates, who had never really taken my design work seriously before, took turns giving me advice. They alternatively told me that I was insulting them (because they were hunters and farmers or my concept was contrary to their religious beliefs) or that I should change my work because they were worried that I would fail the course. I was deeply offended by this sudden notice paid to my architecture. Having spent day and night for years in studio with these people, I mistakenly had thought that they would support me in whatever way I needed. I learned that challenging their belief system in this manner was not personal but political.

As one of only a handful of women in architecture, I had had my share of attention, but it was rarely paid to my course work. The other woman in the cohort, who was a wildly successful student (in the way that success was measured for women in architecture), took me aside and spoke to me about my attitude and my slaughterhouse design. She told me that as an older, wiser, more successful and experienced person in architecture, she recognized that I needed an attitude adjustment. She suggested that I was acting immature and "over the edge." She noted that my slaughterhouse was not functional, since I had not allotted proper drainage for the killing floor and certainly not enough refrigerator space. It was the very first time she had ever spoken directly to me, and I was under the impression that she thought women were in competition with each other. While I shared studio space with this woman, overall I did not understand her, although I understood her architecture. Her design work was always totally functional, well drawn, complete, and unassuming. She worked her slaughterhouse out in such painstaking detail that the Oscar Meyer Corporation could have taken her drawings and built a functioning house of pain. I could not have designed that building. I did not want to. For me, her work symbolized the maintenance of the status quo.

Disregarding all of this advice, I went ahead with my design and its associated story. Our final jury was, metaphorically speaking, a bloodletting. The esteemed panel of architects that was assembled to review the abattoir was particularly harsh in their criticism of my classmates' work. They publicly said that they had never seen such pedestrian and prosaic work. Architecture is a competitive field with a long history of in-fighting and manifesto generation that attempts to discredit established styles and personalities. Students often take the fallout from such posturing. The usual pattern was that the jurors would criticize the selection of the project itself, the studio crit's direction, and then the students' design solutions. This jury virtually followed the script.

My project was one of the last to be evaluated. I stood in front of these architects, all of whom were men (at this point I had never seen an architect who was a woman sit on a jury or teach an architecture course), expecting to hear disparaging comments. At the time I was unsure whether it was the passion with which I delivered my design concept, the work itself, the luck of the draw, or another extenuating factor, but these men had nothing but praise for my concept. They gave me advice to make the architectural design solution more effective. They provided the criticism that I had lacked all quarter. After the jury was completed, a couple of the architects offered me jobs that I did not accept.

In retrospect, I believe that they showed appreciation for my work because it served their need to discredit the somewhat famous and controversial architect who had directed our work that term. Because the other students took their designs in a different direction and my studio crit publicly expressed displeasure with my work, they essentially embraced my challenge to the project as their vehicle to denigrate the studio crit and the postmodern architectural style du jour that he promoted. At the time, however, I was just thrilled to get out of school alive.

For me, architecture school had been a long descent into a denial of fundamental aspects of the self. I embraced the masculine ethos and followed the institutional rules. Abandoning all social relations outside of architecture studio, working selfishly on my individual career aspirations, I tried to assimilate into the culture of architecture. For years in school I put up with a locker-room atmosphere in studio, malevolent critiques, gender harassment, and significantly, course content that privileged an exclusive Western/male perspective.

I present this particular evocative abattoir experience as evidence of how architectural designers are expected to ignore all that is not directly linked to building form. Form is not supposed to be political or personal for architects, as evaluation of design is based on aesthetics alone. Appearing apolitical and neutral is a position that is surely not conducive to a feminist interpretation of building. I am not precisely sure when an architecture student first realizes that although studio is intended to be a synthesis of all they learn in college, the institutional prerogative actually means "all that they learn in architecture classes."

Regardless of my acceptance of these disciplinary or institutional values, as a woman I was never fully admitted into the club. That realization came in small steps. I received more attention for my appearance than for my achievements. When I worked in architectural offices I was stereotyped and assigned lesser-prestige interior design projects. My classmates never asked me for a crit, although they asked my advice about personal issues. I was the cheerleader, the sex object, the den mother, the sister (Kanter 1977). But because I was a woman, I was never just the architect. At best, I was the woman architect.

My identity as a feminist in architecture was fomented not only in the tour of that abattoir but also in the retelling of the story of the tour. Subsequently, when I was working in various architecture firms, my office-mates would tell colorful stories about their experiences in school—tales about all-nighters in studio, humiliating juries, and eccentric studio crits. When I presented part of my graduate school narrative, it began with humor. I would say, "My class was assigned an abattoir to design, and I thought, 'Cool, a French building.'" Proceeding to what I thought was the punchline, that the manager had a poster of a naked woman dotted off for the butcher and that I thought they would kill me next, I naïvely expected responses of shock and consolation. Instead, most other architects laughed!

It was their reaction to my narrative that gave me some intellectual distance from the experience and from architecture. It took me some time to comprehend that I would never be "at home" in the cultural place that is the discipline of architecture and that I should keep my psychic guard vigilant. Or run away.

By the time I came to graduate study of sociology, I was considered a nontraditional student in age. My classmates often asked me how I could afford to resign from employment as an architect to become a full-time student. I knew that they meant afford the loss of prestige and identity. Initially I would respond with some sort of a joke or mumble something about gender and inequality. Eventually I told them many architecture stories, including the one about the abattoir. No one ever laughed. Everyone understood. I felt that a part of me had finally found a home, especially among my fellow feminist sociologists.

Several of my new friends and colleagues encouraged me to use my own experiences as the basis of an autoethnographic portrait of architecture school. Autoethnography, I subsequently learned, "would appear the perfect aegis under which every heretofore silenced group might enunciate, from its location and according to its own agenda, its vision of itself and the world" (Buzard 2003:61). The telling of one's story, however, is dependent on the way in which it is received, on others' appraisal of its meaning and significance. Most sociologists responded to my lived experience in a serious and thoughtful manner, letting me know that I had an important story to tell and thus validating my sense of self that had formed through many years of internal conflict.

I contend that our identities are informed as much by the stories we choose to share as by our audiences' responses to them. My autoethnographic work is about my existence as a feminist inside the professional culture of architecture and about architects' responses and resistance to difference. My perception of their reactions to my discomfort is as much "the story" as the original trip to the slaughterhouse. Finding a place and community with sympathetic women is part of the story as well. This is thus a tale of two responses.

Today, as I have reentered architecture school from the faculty side, where little of the culture has changed, I largely depend on like-minded women in sociology for ongoing support. I continue to confront issues of negotiating the culture as a lone feminist, and I fear giving voice to my concerns. Calling on my feminist friends, I often tell them stories of the trouble with institutional inertia, masculinity, and resistance. They usually respond by saying, "You are taking notes, aren't you?"

CHAPTER 18

Working-Class Heroes: Rinaldo Cappellini and the Anthracite Mineworkers

Robert P. Wolensky

Rinaldo Cappellini and his mine-working colleagues first captured my attention as I researched the sociology of work and labor-management relations in the anthracite ("hard coal") country of northeastern Pennsylvania.[1] The decade-long study taught me that severe conflict had plagued one of the country's largest industries from the post–Civil War years, when the coal corporations moved toward oligopoly, to the post–World War II years, when demand collapsed because of competition and corruption. However, the clashes between 1916 and 1936, when Cappellini was among the main actors, especially held my attention. Forget the unsuccessful strikes in 1868 and 1875, the former involving the infamous Molly Maguires and the latter the longest walkout to that date. Never mind the first significant labor victory under the banner of a new union called United Mine Workers of America (UMWA) in 1900, and forget the most famous strike of all in 1902, when President Teddy Roosevelt intervened, union president John Mitchell negotiated, and financier J. P. Morgan ordered his underlings (the coal company presidents) to settle. No, these labor actions did not demand my recognition as much as the tumult during the mid-1910s to the mid-1930s. At first I didn't comprehend the full depth of my captivity, but I believe I now understand.

While John L. Lewis ruled the UMWA on the national scene beginning in the 1920s, Rinaldo Cappellini, a charismatic figure, "young and boyish in look[s]" with "luminous dark eyes" and "a shock of black hair waving above a well-shaped brow," was the leader at the local level (Roller 1926:537). Born in Nocera Umbra in the central Italian province of Perugia in 1895, Cappellini immigrated to the United States with his mother and siblings in 1902, when he was almost eight years old. They settled in the city of Pittston, and shortly thereafter Rinaldo found work as a "breaker boy" for the Pennsylvania Coal Company (PACC), hand-picking rock waste out of freshly harvested coal. Within a few years he moved to an underground job as a mule driver. When he was fifteen (one year less than the legal age for mine work), a train of loaded cars ran over his right arm and left hand. Physicians amputated the arm, and the top parts of three fingers on the remaining hand were lost. A financial settlement brought nearly $10,000 and the promise of a "job for life" with the smallest of the region's seven major companies (Blatz and Wolensky 1999).

In 1919, at the age of twenty-four, the precocious Cappellini decided to run for the governing commission of a local municipality. Opposed by a company-sponsored candidate, he lost the primary amid cries of ballot fraud but won as a write-in during the general election. The victory cost him his job, according to his wife Marie Cappellini,[2] and the ill treatment turned him toward labor organizing.

> After he was elected commissioner, [Rinaldo] went back to work and he was discharged. . . . His family had a store in Hilldale and so he began to work in the store. One day there was a meeting right in front of their store and he went out on the porch to listen to the organizer talking to the miners. . . . He heard the organizer tell them that they better go to work because their [union] charter will be revoked and that they wouldn't have a job and they would starve to death. The organizer kept on repeating the same thing. He called the miners vile names.
>
> My husband couldn't stand it so he got on the [box]—at that time they just put a box in the middle of the road and a man would get up and talk. So he went and took the platform as you would, and he told the miners, "Do not pay attention to what the organizer was saying. You have your rights." The miners didn't go back to work. . . . And that's where he started. They went out and they began to organize. [Later] the people [mineworkers] elected him as their leader.

Although I had known about his work in anthracite, I first really "met" Cappellini during oral history interviews with Marie, his son Gifford, and several mineworkers and friends who knew the man and his movement. The oral histories were supplemented by documentary research, including the PACC Papers and existing scholarship (Blatz 1994; Bodnar 1983; Monroe 1976).[3] The more I learned the more I wanted to know. Moreover, as the story unfolded I became increasingly conscious of my own intimate relationship to it.

My mounting interest in Cappellini and his fellow workers had several sources. The first involved their heroism during the strikes of 1916 and 1920 (to be discussed later). The unanticipated but resounding success of the 1920 action propelled Cappellini into the presidency of District No. 1, the largest in the UMWA. Based in the cities of Wilkes-Barre, Pittston, and Scranton, as well as dozens of surrounding coal towns, this northernmost of three anthracite districts contained one half of all mineworkers, some 60,000 in number.

The second reason for my interest concerned their ethnic social status. These were working-class immigrants and their sons, with southern Italians and Sicilians representing the largest single group at PACC when Cappellini started his agitation. I wanted to learn more about these laborites, especially considering the commonly accepted view that "Italians consistently avoided underground [mining] work," but also because of the paucity of research on Italians in the anthracite fields (Golab 1977:61).

The third aspect related to the miners' resistance not only to a powerful coal company owned by a large conglomerate, the Erie Railroad, but also to an organized criminal gang composed of Sicilians. I was immensely attracted to a story that pitted Italian immigrant workers ("the good guys") fighting for a union against Italian immigrant mobsters acting in concert with the company ("the bad guys").

Yet that's not all. Not only did this apparently "good story" about Italian Americans grab my attention—after all, there are few such stories in the popular culture—but I had some very personal ties to the chronicle. I was born and raised in the anthracite region (near Wilkes-Barre), and my father, grandfathers, and several uncles worked in mining; the grandfathers and uncles participated in some of the strikes led by Cappellini. I am also of partly Italian (Sicilian) heritage, my maternal grandparents having sailed to the United States in the 1910s. In 1930 my Uncle Ludvico "Charlie" Siracuse was elected president of the mineworkers' local in our small town, where he was a supporter of Cappellini. Uncle Charlie also broke the coal company's control over local politics when he ran for city council in 1932 and won, becoming the first Democrat ever elected.[4] Unexpectedly, however, he died in 1933 at age twenty-nine (some relatives suspected foul play) in the midst of a historic rebellion led by Cappellini to establish an alternative union (also discussed later).

Therefore, my excursion into the life of "Cap" and his supporters became much more than a study of anthracite labor relations. It became a voyage with personal, familial, and class implications; a story about my own story. Moreover, I was able to use my status as a "local boy" to gain access to labor tales that were previously untold to outsiders. In this essay, I tell the story of Cappellini and his fellow labor activists and then make some self-reflexive observations about my research into this important period of U.S. history.

Fighting the Subcontract:
The IWW and the Strike of 1916

The prologue to the story begins in 1916 with the mineworkers' revolt against PACC's subcontracting system, a scheme whereby individual mining entrepreneurs secured agreements from the company to extract coal from relatively small veins. The subcontractor acted as an independent agent, employing a relatively large team (six to twenty) of laborers. Similar to the "putting-out" system common to early manufacturing, subcontracting was rejected by the mineworkers because it violated two tenets of the work culture: a miner should quarry only one vein at a time using one or two laborers, and production should be limited to two cars of coal per man per shift (Gutman 1976; Montgomery 1979). The men feared that subcontracting would speed up production and cheapen the workforce. They were also angered by the subcontractors' extraordinary earnings, which derived in part from their ability to secure the best mining places as well as a timely supply of empty cars from the company bosses. They were incensed by the monetary kickbacks that most demanded from their laborers. Finally, they resented the intimidation and antiunionism fostered by the company and the subcontractors, a grievance exacerbated by PACC's being the only one of the major companies without UMWA representation, despite over two decades of organizing.

Subcontracting had emerged as a grievance during the major strikes of 1900 and 1902, when the recently founded UMWA flexed its muscle and won major concessions. It became an issue again in 1905 and 1910, when PACC's employees walked out, the latter strike ending only after the Italian consul, Chevalier Fortunato Tiscar, helped broker a solution (Wolensky 2002).

When the Industrial Workers of the World (IWW or "Wobbly") decided to organize the hard coal fields in 1906, subcontracting emerged as the main issue. Wobbly membership in anthracite grew to between 5,000 and 10,000 by 1916, with PACC workers constituting the largest single contingent. Most prominent among them were the Italians, who vehemently opposed subcontracting because it kept laborers in a serflike position reminiscent of the hated padrone system, a bonded labor scheme prominent in late-nineteenth-century Italy that was particularly characteristic of the Mafia-infested sulfur mines of Sicily (Hobsbawm 1959). The resistance to subcontracting was built on what David Montgomery calls the workers' "sense of moral work relations" (1979:122).

The conflict peaked when the IWW called a series of strikes between February and October 1916, under the leadership of the multilingual Louis Galleani, a top IWW organizer. Violence marred the actions. Police arrested dozens of strikers, and the courts dispensed harsh penalties.

The combination of failed strikes, opposition by the UMWA and the companies, and negligible community support shattered the dual union. Despite having been defeated, the IWW's opposition provided a foundation for insurgencies in the 1920s and 1930s, when Cappellini, who was a PACC employee in 1916 and at least an observer of the strikes (no evidence of his participation was found), would be in a leadership position (see Mangione and Morreale 1992).

A Second Revolt: Cappellini and the Strike of 1920

The subcontracting system was built around a small group of southern Italian immigrants, mainly Sicilians, who hired their compatriots and drove them with "pushers" and "hustlers." Known organized criminals were among the leading subcontractors, a reality that the company chose to ignore publicly but encourage privately.[5] One of PACC's last surviving officers, E. Stewart Milner, later said that company officials knew they were dealing with known organized gangsters but no one asked questions: "I never heard any comment on it. No one really commented on it. I suppose it was probably well known throughout the region and everything, but you just kept your mouth shut or you were in big trouble." Milner rationalized the dealings as "strictly a business relationship."[6]

Cappellini, who had become a UMWA organizer at PACC in 1920, emerged as the leader of a movement to eradicate the plan and move the workforce into the union. Despite a national recession, nearly 10,000 PACC employees, about one-third of them Italian Americans, took strike action on July 16, 1920, accusing their employer of being the "worst offender in the operation of the [sub]contract system" and insisting that "the principal fight now is for the abolishment of the system" (*Scranton Times*, September 7, 1920). Though only 100 belonged to the UMWA, they held firm under Cappellini's leadership as well as that of another labor activist, Alex Campbell, a second-generation Scotsman who was chairman of the union's general grievance committee at PACC. Cappellini had originally organized the grievance committee, which was a powerful worker-elected body made possible by the labor-management agreement of 1912. Cappellini expressed his revulsion toward subcontracting in an address at the District No. 1 convention in 1921:

> [Subcontractors] were not satisfied to put you in the mines and make you load six and seven cars a day for the 40 and 50 dollars in two weeks, . . . no, they even wanted your dear wife and daughter to play with while you were working nights. They wanted your very flesh and blood and they wanted the honor of the poor innocent daughter and wife, which has been proven in different hotels in Lackawanna and Luzerne counties where they slept.
>
> In the Pittston District you had no organization. Your organization was only in existence to this extent that the President of the Local would be an assistant foreman; the Secretary of the Local would be a [sub]contractor; the Vice-president of the Local was a driver boss and the committee all politicians.

> [A] man would have to go to the foreman and say, "Mr. Man please give me a job,—please,"—after giving 15 or 20 years of his life to the company; or go to the [sub]contractor and "please, have you got a job for me." And their earnings, 45 or 50 [dollars] for some, but others 60 or twice as much because he stood in with the boss. (*Proceedings* 1921:156–157)

During the shutdown, Pittston detective Sam Lucchino, who had uncovered corruption within the subcontracting order, was murdered. One news report stated that he was ambushed "presumably because of his success in fighting Italian outlaws to justice" (*Wilkes-Barre Record*, December 1, 1920). Before dying this working-class hero told police, "A stranger shot me, but it came through the hands of Charles Consagra." A prosperous Sicilian subcontractor with ties to the region's criminal gang, Consagra was arrested, and police found a key witness against him, who later changed his

Courtesy of F. Charles Petrillo

story so the charges were dropped. Over 6,000 people marched in Lucchino's funeral procession, Cappellini among them. According to one report, "the homage paid the dead detective this morning was by far the greatest ever given a citizen of Pittston" (*Pittston Gazette*, July 24, 1920).

Citizens and mineworkers alike knew that subcontractors like Consagra, and, more important, Santo Volpe, who was the area's crime boss, wielded a strong hand in securing and dispensing the subcontracts (see note 4). Volpe had been a sulfur mineworker in Montedoro, Sicily, before emigrating to Pittston in the 1880s. He was known as "King of the Night" for his propensity for nocturnal violence. With fellow Montedoran Stefano LaTorre, he established the second oldest crime "family" in the United States (Fox 1989; Sondern 1959). The Pennsylvania Crime Commission referred to Volpe as the "first boss of the northeastern Pennsylvania Cosa Nostra family . . . [who] began as an impoverished coal miner but, through manipulation, obtained an interest in a number of coal mines" (1980:50). Like other criminal gangs, the Pittston mob made its way by "feeding off the common laborer's honest toil and claiming to serve as a means of easing adjustment to American society" (Nelli 1976:136). Volpe's archenemy became Rinaldo Cappellini.

Lucchino's death only hardened the strikers. Despite entreaties by President Woodrow Wilson's Anthracite Wage Commission, Pittston city officials, and the UMWA, Cappellini and his supporters persevered. Among their backers were clergymen such as Rev. R. D. Jordan, a Catholic priest, who provided moral legitimacy to the action. The *New York Times* reported that the strike at PACC "was the keystone in the situation surrounding labor unrest in the northern field" (September 13, 1920).

Growing public pressure, coupled with promises to rectify the system's abuses, finally brought an armistice. Cappellini joined some 6,000 marchers in a victory parade through downtown Pittston. Coal production commenced on September 27, 1920. However, many judged the episode a failure because subcontracting had survived. Within days complaints began to mount. After only one week, Cappellini, Campbell, and the general grievance committee called for another shutdown.

After one failed earlier attempt, in October 1920 Cappellini led a second negotiating committee to New York for a meeting with PACC's board of directors. To their immense surprise, the board agreed to eliminate the subcontracting system. On October 7 thousands of elated workers resumed mining. The cumulative influence of strong leadership, worker and ethnic solidarity, Lucchino's death, and a supportive public had had their effect. The company returned all coal chambers to the regular miners, who worked them in the traditional manner with one or two laborers. Production stayed at two cars per person. The determined and united employees had apparently achieved a momentous triumph. With subcontracting seemingly defeated and the workers triumphant, over 12,000 PACC employees at last joined the UMWA.

The celebration proved short-lived. Only three months later, in January 1921, some 1,000 colliers at one PACC colliery walked out when thirteen hustlers and pushers were reinstated. Stoppages continued at PACC operations throughout 1921, 1922, and 1923. Indeed, between 1919 and 1923, the company's Pittston-area facilities worked for no longer than four months without a strike. The agitation carried over into the 1921 union elections, when antisubcontracting candidates William J. Brennan (a PACC employee) and Enoch Williams were swept into the top posts of District No. 1. Although Cappellini supported the insurgent ticket, he soon split with Brennan and was fired as an organizer. He then defeated Brennan for the presidency in the next (1923) election, becoming the first Italian American to hold the position.

The Return of Subcontracting

A fall in demand for coal raised unemployment and exacerbated the antagonisms between labor and management during the early 1920s. Pittston police had become more critical of union-related violence following Lucchino's death and moved to break up several union meetings during 1922 and early 1923. Mayor P. R. Brown banned Cappellini from entering the city, even stopping cars at the city line to search for him. The union leader defied the order on one occasion, secretly entered a rally, and began speaking, whereupon the police arrested and jailed him. The organizing drive nevertheless continued, and the persecution probably helped Cappellini win the presidency in June 1923.

His election did not bring an end to the subcontracting debate. Indeed, in late 1924, 12,000 PACC mineworkers in ten union locals agreed with their general grievance committee's call for a strike after they discovered attempts to "smuggle" the system back in. President Cappellini, however, had begun to alter his views on unauthorized strikes. Undoubtedly feeling pressure from Lewis and coal company officials, he criticized the action as an attempt to undercut the labor-management agreement that forbade unauthorized strikes. When he demanded that strikers return to work and file grievances through established procedures, they refused. A split opened between Cappellini and his earliest grassroot advocates. Tensions remained high during a strike in early 1925, and Cappellini offered to resign at a meeting of 3,000 PACC boycotters:

> You men of Pittston made me and you men of Pittston can break me. You made me District President and Cappellini is big enough and honest

> enough to acknowledge that. . . . Cappellini does not want to stay where
> he is not wanted. If you men of Pittston are tired of me I will give you the
> opportunity now to get rid of me. Some one of you get up and make a
> motion that Rinaldo Cappellini resign January 7, 1925 and put it to a vote.
> If a majority wants Cappellini to quit, Cappellini will step down and out.
> (*Scranton Times,* January 7, 1925)

The men rejected the proposal, but the rift between the president and his
hometown supporters widened. He nevertheless retained broad support
throughout District No. 1 and won reelection in 1925 and 1927.

In January 1928, following two more years of persistent conflict, the
full reintroduction of subcontracting closed PACC's most rebellious operation, the No. 6 Colliery, Cappellini's former workplace and Campbell's current workplace. The company's new chief executive, Michael Gallagher,
argued that technical and managerial imperatives forced the decision. He
said that the recently installed mechanical loaders required labor crews of
up to twelve men who were better supervised by subcontractors. Why subcontractors? Because they could secure greater discipline and output from
the workers. "The simple fact is that the company can't get the men to work
eight hours and the subcontractor can," said one supervisor (Selekman
1928:193).

About 36 percent of the No. 6 Colliery's 1,700-person crew had immigrated from Sicily and elsewhere in southern Italy. Although they were the
largest contingent, all workers including those with Welsh, Irish,
Lithuanian, Hungarian, Polish, and other backgrounds remained in solidarity throughout the strike. In January and February 1928, "the Feud at No. 6"
turned murderously violent. Six men, all current or former union officials,
were killed in a spree of murder and retaliation between mob assassins and
angry mineworkers. Among the victims was Alex Campbell, the acknowledged leader of the insurgents following a rift with Cappellini.[7]

The strife at No. 6 disabled the whole of Pittston. One national reporter
described the city as the scene of riots, mob violence, and hand-to-hand
fighting (Selekman 1928). Mayor William H. Gillespie appealed for peace
but to no avail. He beseeched John L. Lewis to help restore order, but
Lewis declined the invitation, blaming the unrest on communists.

Given his prominent role in the controversy, Cappellini was at high
risk of becoming the next victim. Indeed, a lottery conducted at a local tavern predicted his demise: "It was significant that the man who drew the slip
with Cappellini's name was congratulated as being the certain winner"
(*New York Times*, March 4, 1928). Marie Cappellini recalled receiving
numerous phone threats around this time: "We had to get a trained police
dog to protect our children because we got threats" (see note 2).

The insurgents who now opposed Cappellini had gained an areawide
following, so they called a rump convention in Scranton in March 1928.

They impeached Cappellini and the other officeholders and elected a new slate that included a rejuvenated William J. Brennan as president. Lewis and Cappellini refused to accept the results, but the upheaval forced Cappellini's resignation on July 20, 1928. The three-term president said he resigned because of poor health, but in reality he was caught between the status quo intentions of Lewis and the companies on the one hand and the reformist purposes of rank-and-file mineworkers on the other. Cappellini secured a position as a section foreman for the Glen Alden Coal Company and stayed away from union politics for a short time.

The Return of Cappellini:
The United Anthracite Miners of Pennsylvania

In a sudden turn of events, the former District No. 1 president reemerged in 1929 as the head of the very militants who drove him from office. When the union and companies approved a new contract in 1930, a large organized group of dissidents, with Cappellini and Thomas Maloney at the helm, did not accede to it. They began in May 1931 by running a slate of candidates for the District No. 1's offices. When that strategy failed, they called a series of selected strikes. The operators and the UMWA mounted a countercampaign, leading the rebels to organize a paralyzing general shutdown in March 1932 (*New York Times*, March 19, 1932).

Banned from the UMWA and excluded from the district's convention in 1933, Cappellini criticized the union's leadership: "Lewis is not interested in the anthracite fields. . . .We are going to organize the anthracite union and we are going to have a rump convention. We are going to parade after they are through. If they will give me 15 minutes on the floor of the convention hall, that whole gang will have to resign" (*Wilkes-Barre Record*, July 21, 1933).

Maloney, a miner at the Glen Alden Coal Company and head of the grievance committee, joined his colleague in calling a convention in Scranton on August 7, 1933, in which over 600 representatives took the revolutionary step of forming a new union called the United Anthracite Miners of Pennsylvania (UAMP). Cappellini chaired the gathering but declined to run for president. The body elected Maloney to the top position and Cappellini as state chairman. In his featured speech, Cappellini urged conventioneers to champion their innovative organization. "You must remember we are no longer rumpers," he exclaimed:

> [But] neither are we members of the United Mine Workers of America. We will have our own laws and we will establish the right rates. It is up to

you to lend your support to your officers for as soon as the convention adjourns the coal companies and district officers will start to work and attempt to discourage the movement. It is up to you to show your colors and enlist the membership of every miner in the district. If you lose heart the old conditions will continue for many years to come. (*Wilkes-Barre Record,* August 10, 1933)

Although Cappellini played a pivotal role in establishing the UAMP, his participation diminished due to personal and legal problems. Charged and convicted of arson to his own home, he was sentenced on February 2, 1931, to serve two to four years in Philadelphia's Eastern State Penitentiary. His wife and allies claimed that he had been framed because of insurgent activities. Realizing the questionable nature of the conviction, Governor Gifford Pinchot pardoned the union leader on March 25, 1932. Following his release on parole, he rejoined the UAMP campaign.

He was again indicted in August 1933 for allegedly passing a counterfeit ten-dollar bill, the arrest carried out on the platform of the inaugural UAMP convention. Again the insurgents cried foul. A grand jury found insufficient evidence to press charges, so Cappellini returned to union organizing (*Wilkes-Barre Record*, August 15, 1933). The stress of the movement took its toll, however, and Rinaldo and Marie were separated. Five months later, on the eve of a major UAMP strike, he was arrested and charged with causing a disturbance at her home. Within days a stunned Cappellini was on his way back to the state prison for violating parole. He served the remaining thirteen months of his jail term (*New York Times,* January 17, 1934).

The new organization was built on a foundation of cultural and worker solidarity. It precipitated an extremely high level of industrial conflict, as violence and death tormented the region between 1933 and 1936. Despite broad support, in the end the upstart could not stand against the UMWA, the coal companies, and even the Roosevelt administration, which saw it as a detriment to New Deal recovery programs. The deepening depression and climbing unemployment worsened its mission. By the fall of 1935, after four years of internecine warfare, the UAMP had been beaten (*New York Times*, October 27, 1935). Its demise ended twenty years of insurrection against the subcontract. The rebel union came to a tragic symbolic end. On Good Friday, April 10, 1936, Maloney and his young son were murdered by a cigar-box bomb evidently mailed by a disgruntled UAMP member (Spear 1999).

Following his prison release in 1936, Rinaldo and Marie got back together, and he became the manager of an Italian-language newspaper for a brief period. He made peace with John L. Lewis and was hired as an organizer for the newly founded Congress of Industrial Organizations

(CIO). Marie and their two sons joined Rinaldo on the organizing trail, later recalling that "he ran and organized steel, gypsum, paper, cement, anything that came along. We traveled to Niagara Falls, Buffalo, New York, Detroit. We were at the automobile strike in Detroit in 1936 . . . Then we went to Youngstown on a steel [strike] in '37" (see note 2).

Cappellini continued with the CIO until he became disillusioned with the movement. Returning to northeastern Pennsylvania, he and his wife operated a popular restaurant in Wilkes-Barre called Villa Cappellini. He enjoyed a celebrity status throughout the coal region until his death in 1966 at age seventy-one.

In the meantime subcontracting continued. Moreover, at PACC—the leader in fostering tenancy structures—a new putting-out scheme was instituted called the leasing system. Under this plan, the company leased entire collieries (mines, buildings, equipment) to independent entrepreneurs like Santo Volpe who paid a per-ton royalty. Volpe enjoyed a meteoric rise from a subcontractor in the early 1920s to one of PACC's premiere leaseholders. Between 1934 and 1948, he secured a total of fifty-six leases, the most of any person, which provided access to five collieries and 14.4 million tons of coal.[8] By 1940 PACC had leased virtually all of its operations. To remain competitive, the other major coal corporations followed suit.

One PACC leaseholder, the Knox Coal Company, mined unlawfully under the Susquehanna River in 1959, causing a catastrophic breach that drowned twelve men, flooded miles of workings in the area, and facilitated the industry's demise. The company began leasing in 1943, under the partial ownership of then crime boss Joseph Sciandra (Volpe's successor). When it reorganized in 1950, District No. 1 president August J. Lippi, who had been brought into the district organization by Cappellini, became a silent and illegal partner. He and two other owners were sent to prison for their association with the Knox Coal Company (Wolensky, Wolensky, and Wolensky 1999).

Doing Anthracite History: Personal Reflections on Ethnic and Class Narrative

My research into Cappellini and the anthracite mineworkers helped me claim an important part of my ethnic working-class story, one that had been obscured by consistently negative characterizations. For example, consider the following three items.

Because many Italian-American stereotypes deal with organized crime, Item 1 relates to the popular television series *The Sopranos*, which represents all of the ever-popular Mafia productions. According to one hurtfully satirical author:

That's right, I'm pinning the ethnic tail right on the depraved donkey. Defenders of the good name of Italian-Americans, the anti-defamation crowd—and more power to them—will tell you that Mafia gangsters are just gangsters who happen to be Italian. Not for me. If they weren't Italian through and through, from the cut of their suit to the cut of their pasta, I wouldn't be interested. . . . A wiseguy always knows who he is, where he comes from, and whom he serves—the boss, the family, the Italian-American way of life. (Rucker 2001:2–3)

As in the straitjacketing roles available to African Americans in the popular media, it seems that Italian Americans (especially males) have been able to find an overabundance of mob-related (or at least tough-guy) television and film roles. But where are the other representations that speak to the diversity of occupational and class positions held by this group?

Item 2 addresses the social humiliation Italian Americans have regularly experienced. Maria Laurino writes that New York governor Mario Cuomo once pointedly asked her, "Were you always an Italian?" "With childlike guilt, I shook my head no" (2001:37). She had been ashamed of her heritage even as an adult because of the ridicule it typically engendered. "I know all about ethnic self-hate," the governor told her. Indeed, Laurino had spent years trying to overcome the junior high invective that she was "that smelly Italian girl" who was fundamentally different from her "white" suburban New Jersey colleagues. She became anxious about her smell because "body odor suggests that you are ill bred, a member of the lower class." She remained perennially repulsed by her own dark body hair and detested the "Guidos," the Italian working-class boys depicted in films such as *Saturday Night Fever*. Like the women in Azar Nafsi's bestselling book *Reading Lolita in Tehran* (2003), Laurino had seen her ethnic narrative and personal identity denied, taken away not by a regime of fundamentalist clerics but by a homogenizing society possessing a significant prejudice toward one of its largest ethnic groups (Stanfield 1998).

Item 3 concerns sociology, specifically Edward Banfield's classic case study *The Moral Basis of a Backward Society* (1958). Known for a strong tilt toward cultural interpretations, Banfield concluded that the residents of his southern Italian town were imprisoned by "amoral familism." To wit: "It is not too much to say that most people of Montegrano have no morality except, perhaps, that which requires service to the family." The pull of family so constrained the townsfolk, he found, that it prevented them from "act[ing] concertedly or in the common good," and it became "a fundamental impediment to their economic and other progress" (pp. 134, 155). In other words, these Italians were at best hopelessly tribal amoral villagers who were, by logical extension, their own worst enemy in the Old World and the New. Of course the emergence and persistence of the Mafia can be completely understood in light of these clannish values!

A reexamination of Montegrano by Filippo Sabetti (2000) brought one of the few challenges to Banfield's conclusions. Sabetti found that the work actually presented a caricature of the real community. He criticized the original study for ignoring the possibility that cultural patterns are themselves a result of structural factors such as unfair land tenure systems, underdeveloped social institutions, biased government policies, and systemic inequalities. Unfortunately, the academic damage had been done, so authors like James Q. Wilson and Robert Putnam, in *Making Democracy Work: Civic Traditions in Modern Italy* (1994), could highlight the civic values of northern Italians and the amoral individualism of southerners.

As this sampling suggests, Italian Americans are probably the most negatively viewed European group. It should thus come as no surprise that in 1992 the federal courts placed Italian Americans on the list of "protected groups" at the City University of New York because of the long-standing pattern of discrimination in hiring and promotion. No other European group is on the list.

Given that I was raised in a community and a society with numerous destructive conceptions about people like my grandparents, aunts, uncles, cousins, neighbors—and by extension myself (even though my Ukrainian last name has provided some insulation)—it is no mystery that I am drawn to Cappellini's story. While I want to emphasize that the saga included colliers from eastern, southern, and western Europe as well as the British Isles, I was impressed that Italians were in the forefront of the antisubcontracting movement beginning with the IWW, and that Cappellini was its leader during most of the fifteen-year challenge to the system. I was equally impressed that, rather than being members of the mob as typically portrayed, these working-class Italian heroes fought the organized criminals who, with tacit company consent, upheld the system.

Justice was theirs, for at least a time. It was an example that Italian Americans and others who have experienced harmful images, words, and structures should consider. It is a history that workers from all sectors of the contemporary working class should examine and learn from. After all, as Michael Zweig (2000) has reminded us, when workplace *power* (rather than income, status, or consumption) is the signature criterion, the vast majority of us are members of the working class.

Because I subscribe to the view that biographies are necessarily "fictions" or creations of authors who are writing in certain periods, drawing on certain ideologies, and predisposed to certain perspectives, I have brought my perspective to this story (Denzin 1989). I have attempted to give my subjects a voice and, at the same time, to present a constructive narrative as an antidote to the many negative ones that abound. My presentation is intended to lift the often-cast miscreants of popular discourse into a position they have not been accustomed to, that of heroes. Like all good narrative research, therefore, this story is intended to provide my subjects (and myself) with an opportunity to imagine a different sort of truth that provides "better . . . endings for [our]selves," our traditions, and our history (Taylor 2001:73; Travisano 2002).

Notes

1. I would like to thank Richard Stanislaus and Perry K. Blatz for information on Rinaldo Cappellini, and F. Charles Petrillo for the Cappellini photo.

2. Testimony from Marie Cappellini is from a videotaped interview at Coughlin High School, Wilkes-Barre, Pennsylvania, conducted in the late 1970s and from taped oral interviews I conducted for the Northeastern Pennsylvania Oral and Life History Project (NPOLHP) in 1988.

3. While these authors provide a solid background on Cappellini and the labor troubles of the period, they ignore the role of organized crime, which is essential to the story here.

4. This is from a taped oral history interview with Angelo Siracuse for NPOLHP in 1989.

5. This is from a taped oral history interview with William Hastie for NPOLHP in 1989.

6. The quote comes from a taped oral history interview with E. Stewart Milner for NPOLHP in 1994.

7. The murders are discussed in the *New York Times* (April 15, 1928) and Rochester (1931). Hired assassins with mob connections were convicted and electrocuted in the Campbell murder.

8. Volpe's leases were found in the PACC Papers, Pittston Co. and Canceled File, Contracts 1867–1969, in the Pennsylvania Historical and Museum Archives.

CHAPTER 19

A Road Less Traveled

John Horton

Once upon a time, a twenty-seven-year-old sociology instructor at UCLA took a "road less traveled by, and that has made all the difference."[1] His journey as an outsider—my journey—is about that difference, and about the rewards and repercussions of not following the good old boys down their road of careerism. In the 1960s, a budding "commie fag," I really had no choice. I didn't fit the establishment mode of the time. I had faculty supporters to be sure, but the upholders of the reigning empiricism dismissed me as an ideologue "who eschewed empirical evidence." One colleague with a fundamentalist bent confessed that he literally saw me as the devil. Another simply "felt uncomfortable in my [queer] presence." Some even held me responsible for rebellious students and advised new faculty to "avoid Horton." Quite a reputation for a shy guy from Milwaukee who as a college student hid in the back of classrooms.

My major sins at UCLA were teaching about social inequality, exploring the intellectual and methodological basis for a Marxist sociology, addressing progressive concerns that did not fit into the professional establishment, and not publishing enough of the right things in the right places. My passion was teaching and mentoring graduate students, especially those who otherwise might have fallen through the cracks because of their ideas or minority identities. I chaired the committees of forty-five Ph.D.s in sociology and was a member of over a hundred graduate committees in sociology and other departments. Because of my work with minority students, I served on the faculty advisory committees of the African American, Chicano, and Asian American studies programs and of Lesbian/Gay/Bisexual/Transgender studies. Most of my students now teach in liberal arts and state colleges or work in private and public sectors where they use their values and sociological skills to advance social justice. I remember an exception: a gay man, who went on to study the family at an Ivy League school and disappeared. I asked him, "Why this particular field?" He said, "Because I'm not interested in the family and can therefore be objective and more scientific."

In my early years at UCLA, I was in fact a good boy who wrote several well-received, if not mildly irreverent, articles published in "acceptable" journals, started a book, and got tenure in 1966. But by 1993, when I retired from UCLA at age sixty—never promoted to full professor—I was quite estranged from the department and the university, which seemed to have gone full circle from discord and democratization to business-as-usual careerism and petty empire building, far removed from the explosive energies of multicolored Los Angeles.

Now forced by this writing exercise to make something of myself, I realize that my story is not primarily about alienation in the workplace but about *de*alienation, resistance, excitement, experimentation, hope, working collectively, and living moments of empowerment and social change. My work was not just a job; it was my life and mission. The people I met as a professor, the relationships I made, became my supportive family and my comrades in our (sometimes misguided) battles to change the world. We talked a lot, studied together, planned, and organized. We listened to and helped each other to navigate, cross, and sometimes alter the boundaries that kept us apart. Most of us still believe in what C. Wright Mills famously called the "sociological imagination," making connections between personal troubles and public issues. Like Marx, we also believe that the purpose of making these connections is to change them.

From Nerd to Nutty Professor

I had a loving, supportive, unprejudiced family who would do anything for their Jack. They pinched pennies so that my sister and I could live on the fringes of the middle class and attend "good public schools" like Shorewood High School in the suburbs of Milwaukee. There I avoided "manly" pursuits like competitive sports and embraced Latin, writing, and listening to the rich sound of Paul Robeson's voice in music appreciation class. I clearly was not a proper male, and I was also a failure as a WASP (white Anglo Saxon Protestant), that is, as a true American.

One day, while still in grade school, I ran through a neighbor's yard, and a woman yelled out of her window, "Get out of my yard, you little kike!" I asked, "What's a kike?" After we established the definition, she told me, "If you're not a kike, behave like a gentile." I had black hair and a hooked nose, so something must have gone wrong. Eventually I decided that maybe I was indeed a "Jew," if that meant being like those immigrants who escaped Nazi Germany, read books, and listened to classical music.

The high point of high school was being appointed managing editor of our newspaper. My best assignment was to interview and write about a very gracious and inspiring Eleanor Roosevelt. Already imagining myself a "world federalist" and a pacifist, I was no doubt pushed further left by that unforgettable encounter and moved on to the University of Wisconsin–Madison, a bright light in those dark McCarthy days and a place removed from my WASP environment.

In Madison I studied history and dreamed about living in eighteenth-century England or maybe ancient China. I washed dishes for my board on campus and in the summer labored in a deafening can factory. A busy loner, I had neither girl nor boy friends. My goal was to study hard, get As, and cash them in for a fellowship to some distant graduate school and, perhaps, a job in a college or university where nerds and wimps might thrive. My only act of defiance was to join the marching band in order to avoid compulsory ROTC. My punishments: having to watch football games and being sentenced to hours of sorting sheets music when I refused to march on Army Day.

My reward for collecting As was a Fulbright to the College of Europe in Bruges, Belgium. That year, 1954–1955, was profoundly liberating. It opened me up to first love, a multinational community of friends, and traveling across Europe and North Africa. I desperately wanted to stay in Europe, a fantasy of Fulbrighters who wanted to keep their distance from "ugly Americans."

The next year, penniless, I accepted a fellowship to study sociology and anthropology at Cornell University. Ithaca was a shock after living in Europe, as was the department's fascination with Talcott Parsons and survey research. Somehow I managed to get by with the help of my friends and a young professor, who brought me into his family, worked with me on a study of alienated voters, pushed me to coauthor two articles, and even arranged an interview that got me my first and only job. I could not have made it without him. He was an exemplary mentor, a model that I have tried to emulate. However, after four years of endless Ithaca winters and trying to pass as a nice straight guy with a girlfriend, I fled west to the unfamiliar shores of the Pacific, frightened but ready for some mischief. UCLA was the gateway to a new home, a new life. I complained a lot but never left.

The 1960s: Moving Left and Building a Family

In the fall of 1959 I arrived at a quiet, picture-perfect, white middle-class UCLA basking in the end of ideology. Sociology meant learning about the concept of culture, how society (idealized American) was ordered by consensual values. The social structure was divided into institutions that served the functional prerequisites of society, like the family, where proper husbands and wives played different but complementary roles. As for undergraduate-professor relationships on campus, students waited reverently for appointments outside of their professors' doors and generally accepted their subservient role. Graduate students conformed by writing dissertations about professionalization from social psychological and functional approaches.

However, the times they were a-changing. In the early 1960s, the free speech movement came from Berkeley to UCLA, and students began to liberate the campus in peaceful and not-so-peaceful ways. The immediate student demand was for the right to organize politically on campus, set up tables, and express popular and unpopular ideas about control and empowerment. They learned the slogans and songs of the times, like—to the tune of "Jingle Bells"—"Pompon girls, pompon girls, UC all the way, oh what fun it is to have your mind reduced to clay-ay." When their opinions were ignored, students quickly learned to occupy buildings and set up tent cities. Meanwhile, they just took over campus space. Lawns, previously not for walking, became places for meetings and recreation. Babies and dogs began appearing in classrooms.

As the 1960s heated up with demonstrations, police violence, and political assassinations, a more militant civil rights movement came banging on campus. Shortly after the Watts Riot, there was a heated confrontation between black men from off campus and sociology professors. They wanted to know why they were not represented. By 1969 African American, Asian American, Native American, and Chicano studies were established on campus. Women's studies would soon follow. The excluded had intervened in the curriculum, the objective and traditional disciplines established by white men.

We were not unaffected. A growing minority of students and professors, still mostly white and middle class, were beginning to question the relevance and objectivity of sociology and the social order. It didn't help us understand imperialism, the Vietnam War, why we had to kill people of color abroad and at home. We were not so much trashing sociology as refashioning it as a tool for understanding and revolutionizing the "system," meaning variously, capitalism and imperialism, class, racial, gender, and heterosexist domination. By the late 1960s, sociology actually had a wide intellectual and political appeal among rebels, not only in the United States but also in Britain, Latin America, and certainly France, where it was integral to the thinking of the student/worker rebellion of 1968.

Interviewer: Well, Doctor Horton, your observations are interesting in a general sort of way, but what role did you in fact play in the left movement?

DR. HORTON: Well, during a free speech rally, I gave my first political speech at the newly inaugurated and restricted free speech area. I don't even remember what I said; I do remember that after I had prepared meticulous notes, it all just came out spontaneously from the heart. I was hooked.

Later, when Angela Davis, a member of the Communist Party, was unsuccessfully fighting the University of California regents to keep her job in the Philosophy Department, I spoke on a local radio station in support of her. Fighting against the McCarthy legacy, I also tried to bring on campus Dorothy Healey, formerly head of the Southern California branch of the party, as well as the left historian Herbert Aptheker. All were good Americans who had advanced labor and minority struggles.

I confess that I was a minor actor. I wanted to have my cake and eat it too. The university was, as Henry James so famously said about America, "a terrible place not to be." I wanted to get tenure and just made it before the shit hit the fan. Afterward I was suspect. I remember Ralph Turner talking to me before the 1969 meetings when he was the president-elect of the American Sociological Association (ASA). Probably he hoped I could have some influence on radical students who might disrupt the convention. He didn't realize that I had much less influence than was rumored at the time. I certainly attended the Counter-Convention of Sociology Liberation Movement, but I wasn't involved in the spontaneous plans to demand that a memorial to Ho Chi-Minh be held before Turner's presidential address. However, I did approve of the guerrilla theater tactics of leftist students. They caught attention for really important issues not addressed by the ASA. Silence on the war was complicity with war.

What I did do was give encouragement and provide safe haven to radical students. I also did my best to expose and attack the establishment ideology of sociology. The titles of my articles tell the story: "The Dehumanization of Anomie and Alienation," or how American sociologists defanged these critical concepts. "The Fetishism of Sociology," or how sociologists turn the political domination of capitalism into facts of nature. "Order and Conflict Theories of Social Problems as Competing Ideologies," or a liberal and conservative versus radical approach to the race problem. I also wrote "Time and Cool People," about the meaning of time for young black guys who hung out in the street in Venice Beach. One colleague called it "monkey sociology."

INTERVIEWER: Heavy stuff, man. But were you having a good time?

DR. HORTON: A wonderful time! I arrived on the scene mildly left, single, lonely, and just young enough not to be invisible. The social networks within and extending out from the university provided me with my life partner of almost forty years, Patrick, and friends and comrades for years to come.

My coconspirators in nonprofessional behavior were a few maverick professors who never got tenure and graduate students both older and younger than I. I was too green to have been part of the old left and too gray to be a trusted member of the under-thirty generation. I got my political and cultural education from both sides.

On the old left side, I hung out in the early 1960s with Count, an anthropologist who did not get tenure. He introduced me to what he called "beautiful people"—offbeat types from all walks of life. Traditional sociologists would call them "deviants," improperly socialized to the cultural norm of success or to the legitimate means to achieve it. Count was definitely "beautiful people." He knew how to cross social boundaries to survive and have fun. Bisexual and biracial, he had passed his way through Ivy League schools and then, like the civil rights movement, got bolder and blacker in the 1960s. Fifteen years older than I, he was a free spirit of the times, and I admired him greatly.

Then there was my first teaching assistant, Audrey, twenty years older than I, and my closest friend. She had eloped to the USSR in the 1930s, moved to Los Angeles in the 1940s to raise kids, and got involved in the left labor movement. With her knowledge of the working class, she wrote a dissertation critiquing Seymour Martin Lipset's concept of working-class authoritarianism and went on to be a founder of women's studies at California State University, Long Beach. She gave me my first lessons in feminism.

Audrey was tough, outspoken, and outrageous. She was given to swearing in Russian and greeting people with "All power to the Soviets." The USSR was part of her colorful history, not her idea of political utopia. Together we explored Los Angeles, attended rallies and love-ins, argued politics, and in quieter moments cooked gourmet dinners and listened to Bach's unaccompanied cello pieces. Audrey liked to give advice. Each semester when I fretted over not being able to teach or write, she would say, "Horton, you always go according to pattern—complain, and then do the work." I wish she were here now to help me with this assignment. On my birthday in 1967, she gave me Webster's *Third International Dictionary* with the inscription "For John. So when I'm dead you'll think of me." I do, often.

In retrospect I can't really separate my left journey from the students I knew and the events we experienced together. They were very much involved in fighting for my tenure. Two of my students accompanied me in the spring of 1965 to Montgomery, Alabama, the destination of the historic march from Selma. We got on a plane packed with assorted priests, nuns, ministers, and mostly white integrationists. On our arrival, police corraled us in a muddy lot. Finally, we joined the march, black and white together, singing and chanting, as we walked like a liberating army past cheering black residents to the massive rally at the capitol. I remember less about what Martin Luther King said than the feeling of being in an integrated movement united in a just cause. After the rally the police made sure that we got on the plane and went back where we came from. But President Johnson signed the Voting Rights Act the same year. It was a high point in the civil rights movement. When I got back to Los Angeles I got involved in projects in Watts and Venice and began to write with passion about what I believed.

The 1970s:
From Academic Marxism to Party Building

In the spring of 1970, in reaction to the U.S. invasion of Laos and Cambodia, strikes and demonstrations broke out at universities and colleges across the country. When I heard the news, I rushed from home to find the UCLA campus encircled by police cars and helicopters. The administrators had called them. It was domestic war—in the quads, skirmishes between radicals and "pigs" in riot gear; elsewhere, uninvolved students going about their business until targeted by the police and instantly radicalized. Some joined the fray; others retreated to buildings and threw bottles and whatever they could grab out of the windows. It was real, not another Hollywood movie being filmed on campus. The police ignored me; maybe they thought I was one of those sociologists taking notes on campus unrest for the FBI. In the end, we were lucky—nobody got killed. Students at Jackson and Kent State were shot to death.

The next day was not business as usual. Most classes were suspended, and we came together to make sense of the event. The Sociology Department held its first and last genuinely democratic meeting, where for the moment everyone—professors, students, and secretaries—had an equal voice. We even discussed new forms of governance. It didn't happen. The radical secretaries, being the most vulnerable, got the boot. Students got token representation on committees. Today professors, wondering how students got on committees in the first place, are discussing how to remove them in the name of professionalism and efficiency.

It's difficult to relive those times. They are so far away. Revolution was in the air. Then radicals lumped liberals and conservatives together as different faces of the same oppressive capitalist system. Now conservatives praise capitalism and the free market as the foundation of freedom and democracy, there are really no "radicals," and liberals are "very liberal leftists" (whatever that means).

Persuaded by the argument to fight for change from my workplace, I remained on the academic road. In the 1970s I chaired the committees of nineteen Ph.D.s, including four African Americans, two South Americans, an Iranian, a Puerto Rican American, and an assortment of Anglos. I encouraged students to follow their own bliss, and their progressive topics varied widely: art, South African and Caribbean literature, theoretical Marxism, and studies of race and social movements.

I wrote a lot those days, but mainly in radical newsletters and journals. Most of my articles were theoretical, oriented to analyzing positions and ideologies on the left and struggling to legitimate Marxism as a social science. Reflecting the internal battles among progressives, some of my articles were downright sectarian, with titles like "Contribution to the Critique of Academic Marxism" and "What the Friends of the People Are and How They Fight the Marxist-Leninists."

I also began to travel more and make contact with other radicals. I gave innumerable lectures at California universities and never missed a chance to intervene in sociological conferences, for example, by helping to found a new Marxist section and later becoming its president for a year. Like others, I also traveled abroad in search of models of socialist construction. Less than a year before the violent, U.S.-supported coup that overthrew the democratically elected left government of President Salvador Allende, I made a field trip to Chile. My Latin American friends supplied family contacts. I brought a copy of a UCLA sociology dissertation on the Chilean military requested by someone in the president's office. In return, I was given tours of socialist experiments in improving and politically organizing lives in the *campamentos*, poor neighborhoods that were springing up through the city of Santiago. I also observed some of the progressive and community-oriented changes being introduced in the universities. Needless to say, I was naïve about the political situation and horrified by the brutality of the coup. It was another lesson in imperialism, and I carried it to my classes and later to solidarity work with the progressive movements in Nicaragua.

Meanwhile, at UCLA, to the consternation of some of the faculty, my office with its revolutionary posters became a hub of activism: students coming in and out, meeting to discuss new teaching methods, planning courses and study groups, intervening in professional conferences, and building the Union of Marxist Social Scientists (UMSS). In all these activities, there was a strong sense of collective energy.

In 1972, with strong support from graduate students and a young Marxist professor then in the department, I tried with some success to move the graduate program in a more progressive direction. Challenging the "scientific" core of our professional establishment, we proposed a new course, "Marxist Methodology," and requested that it be listed among the courses that would fulfill the two-course methodology requirement. The idea came from my seminar "The Sociology of Science." We addressed the criticism that radical sociology needed to move beyond ideological and political criticisms of bourgeois scientism to a scientific viewpoint of its own. With readings on all sides of the question, we hotly debated whether Marxism had a scientific method and whether its unit of analysis was the individual, the concrete human subject, or the mode of production that gives it historical shape. We split. Following Jean-Paul Sartre, one of the few women in the seminar—the rabid scientific Marxists tended to be men—argued for a humanist base for Marxism. Following Louis Althusser, a male student shouted in his Persian accent, "I hate the human subject. This is not a theoretical category." We never achieved consensus on the point, but agreed strongly on the merits of a course that seriously investigated the theoretical and philosophical basis of a Marxist methodology.

Usually the chair, perhaps with the executive committee of the department, approves a course. In this case the matter was so controversial that it was discussed and voted on in a full department meeting. To my surprise, after much debate, the majority voted to include "Marxist Methodology" with an eclectic group of courses that included "Demographic and Ecological Analysis," "Measurement of Sociological Variables," "Ethnographic Methods," and "Ethnomethodology." The vote illustrated the importance of alliances. I may have been a Marxist, but I was not the only outsider in favor of pluralism. Ethnographers and ethnomethodologists also had to fight for a space in sociology, and like the Marxists, they looked beyond the taken-for-granted "facts" of society to find the practices that created and supported them.

The catalog described the new two-quarter seminar. "*Marxist Methodology:* Practice in the dialectical method of attaining scientific knowledge about society as a process and mode of production. A critical examination of methodological issues and techniques, and practical field researches."

The seminar was immensely popular, drawing students from fields outside sociology, from people like us who were in search of a method for knowing and changing the world. Once I had retired, I was not allowed to teach graduate courses and therefore had little contact with graduate students. However, to the displeasure of the chair, students, finding the course still in the catalog, petitioned for the course. I taught it, my last seminar. A few years later the course was removed. The new chair told me that somebody wanted my course numbers! As Lenin said, "one step forward and two steps backward."

Spring 1973, "Introduction to Sociology": John Horton, two teaching assistants, and thirteen volunteer graduate students confronted some 300 undergraduates. The syllabus gives a sense of what we were trying to do: "The course is an introduction to sociological reasoning. . . . To think sociologically is to think critically—to question the 'facts' of your immediate experience by placing them into the larger context of their social organization and production. Sociology is not another complicated word for commonsense. In our society, commonsense means to think in individualistic and psychological rather than sociological terms . . ."

The theme of the class was power and the inequalities of racism, sexism, imperialism, and class domination. Each of these themes was discussed from contemporary liberal, conservative, and radical perspectives. The class met for three hours weekly: one session devoted to individual sections with separate reading lists, the other to lectures and panels of people who represented socially conscious minorities.

In designing the class our first assumption was that learning sociology means learning the sociological method, reasoning about concrete events and problems as they relate to experience, not memorizing concepts. Another assumption was that learning is most effective when students are collectively and actively involved in the process. Therefore, we emphasized small study group discussions and writing journals (no other exams) that required students to relate theory to what they learned from class, readings, and panels. Also students participated in field projects designed by them, such as visiting a prison and comparing shopping in Beverly Hills with shopping in Watts.

The class required a gigantic and collective effort on the part of instructors. Students polarized on every issue, especially in relation to the controversial panels. At the end of the semester, based on a lengthy survey, we estimated that slightly more than half of the class really began to understand that learning is not simply a matter of memorizing; it involves them in a process of social change.

It was impossible to repeat this class on such a scale again. However, it was a model for radical teaching. I followed it in other courses, most particularly the popular "Sociology of Deviant Behavior." The title, focusing on the deviant, came right out of the 1950s. I reinterpreted it to mean the social and political construction of deviance under capitalism.

As the movement grew, radicals and students and professors began to struggle more among each other. In 1974, still convinced that Marxism was a social science, together with comrades in Canada, Southern California, Berkeley, and Oregon, we proposed that we come together under the banner of the Union of Marxist Social Scientists (UMSS). UCLA was active in writing newsletters and reporting and analyzing conferences and local struggles to hold on to academic jobs. My office at UCLA was busier than ever with students trying to extract information from chapters and put out the newsletters.

For four years we held conferences and cavorted in the woods of California during Labor Day weekend. Like professional conferences, ours were half serious and half fun. Unlike them, we had caucuses as well as lectures and panels, and we organized into teams to help cook, serve meals, and clean up. Up to 300 people attended—"heavies" from Berkeley and Oregon, "middleweights" like me from UCLA, a diverse group from state and community colleges and organizations. The first UMSS newsletter described us as "a loose confederation of some 250 students, teachers, and intellectual workers . . . both employed and increasingly unemployed."

The third conference ended in confrontation and change. Those representing the various causes of women, third world people, and gays and lesbians attacked the "elitist" leadership for marginalizing them and their concerns. There was truth in their charge. Men and the heavies had organized the conference along the established professional lines, meaning a lot of theoretical discussion and no mechanism for teaching, let alone communicating with the base. One of the feminist leaders drove a wedge in the proceedings by demanding that women and other underrepresented groups organize the next conference. Later, after much screaming and yelling, the ratio was reduced to 50-50, with equal representation from the caucuses. The in-charge males felt trashed.

I was caught in between. On the one hand, I had organized and participated in an abstract session on Althusserian Marxism. On the other hand, I stood with the caucuses. Pushed by gay and straight students, I "came out" at the conference as gay and understood what was left out from macho Marxism. Graduate students had also insisted that I come out in my "Sociology of Deviance" class. Could I really raise issues about gays and lesbians and not include myself? So I spoke out, and you could have heard a pin drop.

Other students dragged me to the Gay Pride March. I joined a short-lived organization called the Lavender and Red Union, fearfully went through the door of the Lesbian and Gay Center, and ran some consciousness-raising groups there. However, I had been too long in the closet to really feel a genuine sense of pride and militancy in being gay.

Meanwhile, back at UCLA, the powers of the department were not happy. Rumors spread about my "unprofessional" (i.e., political) behavior and the poor quality of my students. Years later, an excellent student of mine who did her dissertation on Marxist and Jungian interpretations of Chicano murals, was told that she really didn't have a Ph.D. because Horton had been her chair. But Horton was fortunate to have tenure, although at the cost of isolation and containment. A department committee was formed to standardize and oversee doctoral field exams, making it less possible for students to carve out their own fields. Two young Marxist professors did not get tenure. This was a national pattern: liberal pluralism rarely applied to Marxists, especially if they had any influence. The most egregious case of repression in California occurred in 1975, when UC Berkeley closed down its School of Criminology. Its crimes: too many popular and productive Marxist professors, too many "third world" students, and worst of all, a program dedicated to community service and studying the social construction of crime and criminal justice in a society characterized by class and racial inequality. At its height the student struggle to save the "Crim School" involved 3,000–4,000 people, a scale of militancy not seen since the massive protests against the 1970 Cambodia invasion.

During the fourth UMSS conference, a former student recruited me to a small left political party. She said, "John, I have a formation for you to join." I was ready to move toward activism and away from the discussions, debates, and showmanship to a disciplined organization dedicated to training cadre for the transition to socialism.

So in 1978, there is aging John selling a workers' newspaper on the street: It's only fifty cents, in Spanish and English. The well-dressed woman says she doesn't have enough money. The poor black woman is interested in the article on union organizing and slowly counts out her small change. We are a proletarian group and hate the petit bourgeois liberals (like many of ourselves).

Now there's John standing in the front of a bus, facing the seated passengers, and delivering a quick speech about supporting a referendum to increase taxes on corporations. A man tries to shout him down, "Goddamned Commie!" But others say, "Let him talk," and he finishes his pitch, passes out some literature, and disappears into the street.

We all were trained to be community activists. Valued as the university-link, I also edited our journals, did research on contemporary issues, and taught party classes to motivated cadre. The experience is another story for another time. The negative parts were the almost complete control over our lives and endless meetings that invariably included brutal criticism sessions. As the general secretary once told me, "it takes a little carrot and a lot of stick." There was also dogmatism. The first internal political campaign I remember was "Combat Lesbian Chauvinism." The primary contradiction was class, so don't bring your queer self to the working class. The positive part was working in the trenches with a very talented group of people—lots of women in leadership, mostly white, but also black and Latino, to say nothing of straight, gay, and lesbian members. We fought in the trenches together in our imaginary war, but with real sacrifices and injuries. The experience created lasting bonds, definitely additions to my human family. I don't regret my involvement and what I learned about poor people and those who think they can lead them.

One thing I do regret is the negative effect of my party affiliation on my graduate students. I never gave them political litmus tests. They didn't have to toe my line, but some, believing that this could be the case, fled to other mentors. Worst of all, the party told me that I could not work with a friendly collective of students who were writing a textbook about deviance influenced by the approach in my course at UCLA. The motive for controlling me was no doubt fear that I would get a big head and a sense of independence from the party. A big head I didn't have.

Back to the Grassroots

For five months between 1981 and 1982, I was on a Fulbright teaching in a graduate institute in Rio de Janeiro. The distance gave me new perspective on leftist politics. In the 1960s, a U.S.-supported right-wing military coup had brutally repressed the Brazilian left movement, led in part by an idealistic cadre of intellectuals without mass support. Twenty years later, Brazil was moving toward democracy under the leadership of a labor leader, Luiz Inácio Lula da Silva, with a strong working-class and intellectual base. Lula, as he is called, later became president of Brazil.

Applying the lessons of this history to the United States, I concluded that it was a fantasy, a misreading of history, to think that we in the United States were in a revolutionary situation. Within our disciplined miniparty, we were in fact isolated, irrelevant, and dogmatic, and we eventually self-destructed. I left and turned to research and activism around local issues of social injustice.

In 1989 an unexpected opportunity led me to become part of a national research team, the Changing Relations Project. With support from the Ford Foundation, our charge was to study relations between immigrant newcomers and established residents in five ethnically diverse cities. One of my graduate students, an activist living in Monterey Park and a leading opponent of the local English-Only movement, suggested that this was the place to do a study of the politics of diversity. I assembled a multiethnic team of Latino, Japanese American, Anglo, and Chinese students. Together we descended on the city and observed and even became part of local politics. This was what I always wanted—progressive, collective, relevant community research. We all learned politically and published the results (Horton 1995).

Monterey Park forced me to think about myself, who I was. For the first time, I had to confront my whiteness. The old-timer Anglos we studied, *the Americans,* were being replaced by Chinese immigrants. Moreover, the newcomers were often entrepreneurs with money and a strong sense of themselves, not at all the poor, grateful immigrants they were supposed to be. I recognized in the Anglos the people I had wanted to get away from in Milwaukee, and I looked like them and was taken for them.

One day a student from Monterey Park introduced me to a Latina activist. She said, "Is he *de la raza?*" The student replied, "No, but he is friend of the *raza.*" She wasn't impressed.

In another incident, when I went to check out a polling place, the elderly white woman in charge said, "They are voting for the chink."

Then when I was walking precincts with a Latino student, a Chinese American boy answered the door and said to his mother, "Barry Hatch is here!" Hatch was an archconservative and advocate of language and other legal restrictions on immigrants. He disliked the UCLA "pinkos" and Chinese lovers. Yet Barry and I were both white.

Later when I talked to a Latino student about this, he said that whatever you think, just being Anglo is sort of a class status; that's the way it is. Now being the "other," the minority/majority, I finally began to understand the contradictions built into my position. Still, I wasn't entirely white. I made friends and alliances on the basis of my difference.

When I retired in 1993, my Latino students organized a surprise party for me at La Golondrina restaurant on Olivera Street in the Mexican heart of Los Angeles. Over 100 people attended—students, a few radical women professors, and community people of all colors. It wasn't the only "Goodbye, Mr. Chips" celebration. The chair of the Sociology Department also gave me a farewell party. The gift was two crystal martini glasses instead of the usual suitcase—an idea of MJ, a member of the staff and one of my favorite people. This, then, is the social history of an outsider on a road less traveled by, who found a home in a time and place, where difference is no longer deviant but has become the norm.

Note

1. The title, which is adapted from Robert Frost's "The Road Not Taken," was aptly suggested by my poetic partner, Patrick.

CHAPTER 20

It Means Something:
The Ghosts of War

William B. Brown

For me, war stories are born of arrogance, and they reek of insolence. Stories about war are another matter. They demand reflection on the past and offer an insight into the insanity of war. This is a story about war. It is a story about Vietnam.

In a nameless location somewhere in the central highlands of the former South Vietnam, a young Vietnamese girl was killed. She was in the presence of an older man, quite possibly her father. He was killed too. They both died on the earthen floor of a smoldering hootch that offered the briefest of shelter. Their killer was rewarded with a three-day R&R at Vung Tao. In 1968 "rest and relaxation" on the South Vietnamese coast was the reward for killing gooks. Killing the young girl and her father had contributed to the Fourth Battalion's monthly body count.

The dead were left where they died. Their bodies were left to rot. Over the years the killer has gazed at the dead girl's face, a face without individuality. It is a face without expression. Sometimes he longs for forgiveness, forgiveness from the girl and forgiveness from himself. Other times his rage and hatred are directed toward the girl or others around him. Attempts to reconcile with the memory and image of the slain girl have been a series of struggles over the past thirty-five years.

This is a story about life, death, and an ongoing struggle of survival. This story is about the futility of war—yesterday, today, and tomorrow. It is a story that examines participation in the carnage of war. It is a story about escape—escape from the memories of the carnage of war. This is my story.

"Brown, fall out of that line and assume a front-leaning rest position," screamed the drill sergeant.

"Yes, drill sergeant," I screamed back.

As quickly as possible, I got out of the chow line and assumed the front-leaning rest position: both palms flat on the pavement, toes touching the pavement, elbows and knees locked. Here I was, in a front-leaning rest position in Ft. Polk, Louisiana. The rain was coming down in buckets. I had absolutely no idea why I was in this particular situation.

"What in the fuck did I hear you say a few seconds ago?" the drill sergeant asked.

"I don't know, drill sergeant," I replied.

"Are you a fucking moron, troop?" he asked.

"No, drill sergeant," I insisted.

"I distinctively heard you say 'Vietnamese.' Did you say 'Vietnamese,' troop?" he asked.

"Yes, drill sergeant, I said 'Vietnamese,'" I yelled.

"Well, troop, there ain't no such thing as Vietnamese. Do you understand that?" he continued.

"No, drill sergeant, I don't understand," I replied. I thought, "If there aren't any Vietnamese, then who is the enemy in Vietnam?" It seemed to be a legitimate question to me. It was not a legitimate question.

"There is no such thing as a Vietnamese. They are gooks—fucking gooks. Do you understand that, troop?" he asked.

"Yes, drill sergeant," I lied. I did not understand what he said. I did understand that my arms were getting tired, though.

"Troop, give me fifty push-ups. Each time you count, I want you to count off, 'One gook, drill sergeant,' 'Two gooks, drill sergeant,' and so on until you give me all fifty," he said.

He got down on both knees and put his face about an inch from my face. "From now on it's going to cost you fifty gook push-ups each time you are in my fucking chow line. Do you understand that, moron?" he asked.

Yes, the moron understood, and answered, "Yes, drill sergeant."

The military machine had successfully initiated the process of programming me for Vietnam. At Ft. Polk, during my second week of infantry AIT (Advanced Individual Training), the word *Vietnamese* had successfully been extracted from my vocabulary. The term *gook* replaced *Vietnamese* in my mind. There were no such things as Vietnamese. There were only gooks. Gooks were not human. I embraced this notion as I stepped off the aircraft the first time in Vietnam. The inhuman status of gooks was reinforced as I saw a woman urinate on the tarmac as I walked down the ramp of the United Airlines flight from Ft. Lewis, Washington.

At the time, of course, I was not aware of the policy that gook civilians working at the airfield were not allowed moments of privacy or seclusion. My time in Vietnam reinforced the notion that gooks were not human. It was convenient. It was easier to participate in the carnage of a country filled with nonhumans. The programming process that I experienced was so successful that I would not regain consciousness for more than twenty years. For more than twenty years Vietnam would mean a war that we were not allowed to win. For more than twenty years Vietnam remained nothing more than a land filled with nonhumans. For more than twenty years I was unconscious. For more than twenty years I struggled with dreams that offered no explanations and no answers. The struggle continues, but now I am able to talk with some of my ghosts of war.

The date was June 19, 1968. I will always remember this day. It was a day like so many other days. We had no way of knowing what the temperature on this day was. The blistering heat was almost unbearable. Sometimes the heat would divert our attention from the weight of our rucksacks. Sometimes the heat would allow us to ignore those straps that cut into our shoulders and the pus-filled, infected sores that developed from the cuts. Other times the heat and the discomfort of our rucksacks would simply join forces and make our circumstance a living hell. The faded OD (olive drab) green towel that draped across the back of my neck was completely saturated with sweat. Sometimes I would place a corner of that towel in my mouth and recycle the salty liquid. It was a way to conserve water. It was a distraction from the misery. It sharpened the senses. It stabilized the concentration.

We had been following a blue line for about two hours—a tiny curled blue line on the military map that I carried. On the ground the stream was a filthy rust-colored liquid that was confined to the grade and natural restrictions of the terrain. It was only good for GIs to walk through and animals and gooks to drink from. The terrain to our right was steep. To our left, about 150 meters below us, ran that filthy shallow stream, snaking through rocks and clusters of vines and around an occasional clump of green bamboo.

Each man struggled to maintain his balance while walking along the steep hillside. It is very difficult to balance a heavy rucksack on one's back when the body is forced to maintain an unbalanced posture. The remedy for discomfort was often allowing one's thoughts to drift back to a more pleasant place or experience—the wife, the girlfriend, the parents, the children, and the car you wanted to order as soon as you got back to "the world." I wondered if it would be easier if one leg were shorter than the other. Mostly I wondered how long it would take to break into the clearing ahead of us.

I signaled for the man behind me to stop. The whole column stopped. I told my point man, "Hold it up."

I wanted to check our direction. I knew we should be paralleling the blue line, but I wanted to be certain. I also wanted to stop and rest for a moment. I opened my compass, made certain that the cover was perpendicular to the case, and aligned the center of the sighting groove with the sight wire and a large tree several hundred meters to my front. I glanced down at the dial and noted an azimuth of 240 degrees. We were headed southwest. Perfect. I checked my map. We had about one click (one kilometer) to go before we would break into open terrain. There was not much vegetation along our course of travel. Aside from some typical wait-a-minute vines and a modest crop of low-level vegetation, it was pretty good humping. We would probably beat Second Platoon to the clearing. They were walking on top of the ridge along our right flank.

I didn't want everyone exhausted and complaining when we broke into the clearing. I told the man behind me to pass the word that we were "taking five." Everyone could adjust the straps on his rucksack, have a drink of water, have a cigarette, and take the opportunity to vent his frustration with the orders to hump nearly six clicks (6,000 meters) to the base of some obscure hilltop. Since I had been in the country, it had been a ritual to complain about orders to move from one point on a map to another. I could hear the "fuck this" and "fuck that" behind me. I turned my head and told the man behind me, "Pass it back to shut the fuck up." I knew "Fuck you" would be passed forward up the column, then back to me. After eleven months in the field, some things never changed.

The only exception was last November. I closed my eyes. There had been no complaints when we were ordered to hump our asses off to Hill 875 and help Second Battalion. I spent a lot of time reflecting on the events that took place on Hill 875. I still do.

In November 1967 two battalions of the 173rd Airborne Brigade fought for a piece of terrain known only as Hill 875. Hill 875 was located near Dak To—close to the Cambodian border. The 173rd had been in the Dak To region all month. The First Battalion had been hit really hard earlier in the month. The other battalions had experienced significant amounts of contact. On November 19 the Second Battalion waited at the base of Hill 875. They waited, poised and ready to advance. They waited for the conclusion of the ongoing air strike.

When the last canister of napalm tumbled from the wing of an aircraft, floating to its target on the military crest of the hill, and the pilots pointed their planes toward base, two companies from Second Battalion advanced on Hill 875. In a matter of minutes the fighting became intense. The North Vietnamese were dug in. At 1900 hours Second Battalion's radios were silenced. During a late bombing run against NVA (North Vietnamese Army) positions on the top of Hill 875, a U.S. Marine pilot accidentally flipped his toggle switch early and dropped two 500-pound bombs. One hit an NVA position, and the other one landed on the center of Second Battalion's aid station. Dozens of U.S. paratroopers died in a matter of seconds. They died in the wake of a mistake.

Fourth Battalion was given orders to rush to Hill 875 and assist Second Battalion. Their precise situation was not known. What was known was that they were in deep shit and needed help. Each man carried 600 rounds of M-16 ammunition, five to ten fragmentation grenades, and at least one 60-mm mortar round. Some carried additional M-60 machine gun ammunition. I am certain my rucksack weighed nearly ninety pounds—the two 60-mm mortar rounds that I carried weighed nearly twenty pounds each. The machine gunners carried more than 2,000 rounds of ammunition.

Bravo Company left FSB (fire support base) 16 about 0700 hours. We arrived at Hill 875 around 1430 hours on November 20. We advanced about 100 meters up the hill. We stopped. There were body parts strewn everywhere—heads, arms, feet, legs, intestines. A tree had been uprooted by the bombs and artillery. It was decorated with intestines. They reminded me of Christmas-tree tinsel. Today, tinsel hanging on a Christmas tree reminds me of intestines hanging from that uprooted tree.

I am not aware of any words that can describe the blood-soaked landscape. The ground itself had been plowed with bombs and artillery to the extent that mortar rounds often couldn't detonate because the ground was too soft. Up the hillside, thousands of trees had been uprooted and dropped randomly. Movement up that hill inevitably required exposing oneself to enemy fire coming from above. The smell was nauseating.

The survival of those who were not placed in body bags on Hill 875 can probably be linked to the grunts' philosophy: "Fuck it. It don't mean nothing." This philosophy proved valuable to many grunts in Vietnam. Subscription to this philosophy allowed us to detach ourselves from any type of emotion. In some cases it was possible to detach ourselves from the actual event we were engaged in. "Fuck it. It don't mean nothing" became a rational response to our participation in the carnage of that war. Oftentimes the carnage was camouflaged with terms such as "domino theory," "anti-communism," "fight for democracy," "for the people of South Vietnam," and other bullshit slogans that were designed to make certain that we did not open our eyes and see what the carnage actually was: the carnage of war is the useless slaughter of human beings on all sides. After many years of observation one thing is clear: the slogan makers are not the ones who die. They simply remain busy manufacturing more slogans so others can die.

Several days later, on Thanksgiving Day, we took Hill 875. The NVA had already fled by the time we reached the top. An ARVN (Army of the Republic of Vietnam) unit was supposed to block the NVA escape route. I guess they forgot. We began dragging the bodies of paratroopers off of that fucking hill. In many cases we placed body parts in ponchos and dragged them down the hill. Second Battalion lost 87 men killed in action; 130 men had been wounded, and 3 were missing. Many of Second Battalion's deaths were results of that marine pilot's apparent hurry to get back to his base. Fourth Battalion lost 28 men killed, 123 wounded, and 4 missing.

We killed a lot of the "enemy." The general and his colonels said we killed hundreds of NVA. But there were only a few NVA bodies on the ground when we took the hill. The NVA retrieved most of their own. The senior officers wanted body counts. Who cares whether they were real or invented? Fuck it. It don't mean nothing. What did mean something was the fact that we were leaving this nightmare. Of course, we simply exchanged this nightmare for a bunch of bad-dream events in the months to come. On November 25 the helicopters arrived. We were extracted from Hill 875. Sometimes I wish I could extract the memory.

I adjusted the straps to my rucksack and said to the man behind me, "Pass it back, we're moving out."

I could hear the rattling of gear, the muffled complaining, and other sounds that are common for grunts humping the boonies.

I looked at the point man. He looked exhausted. He looked so young. He was green. "Get behind me. I am going to take point for a while," I told him.

I had twenty-six days to go before DEROS (date of estimated return from overseas). In twenty-six days I would leave this fucking place. But first I had to survive. I did not want to be walking behind this FNG (fucking new guy) when we broke into that clearing up ahead. I started walking toward the tree that I had used earlier to determine my azimuth. It was about 200 meters ahead. We had covered about one-half that distance when we heard a distinct "crack." It was an AK-47. It came from our left, somewhere down along the blue line.

I dropped to the ground and yelled for everyone in the platoon to take cover and watch our flanks. I gave a series of instructions. One of those instructions included paying close attention to our right flank. I knew Second Platoon was up on the hillside to our right somewhere. I did not want anyone shooting our own men. Our platoon leader did what he did best. He stayed in the center of the column and did not lead. He had been in the field about ten days—maybe there was hope for him after all. I told the M-60 gun team to find a position and cover an opening along the blue line below us. I sent word down the column for the other M-60 gun team to cover our rear.

I finally glanced at the man behind me. He was dead. The FNG was dead. I was alive.

I spotted a hootch along the bank of the stream below us. I told Delbert to pass up the M-72 LAW (light antitank weapon) he was humping. I pulled the pin, extended the tube of the launcher, and aimed at the hootch. It was about 150 meters away from my position. I depressed the firing mechanism. The rocket found the target. The hootch burst into flames.

Within five minutes after the rocket left the M-72 tube, we were crossing the stream toward the burning hootch. We were alert. We were ready. We had not seen any movement. Lighting up the hootch provided no guarantees that we had killed the gook who killed the FNG. Slowly, we continued walking. The hootch was still smoldering when we arrived. I set out defense positions facing the tree line along the other side of the hootch. We began kicking away some of the debris.

There were two bodies under the debris. Ryan turned one body over with his foot. It was the body of a young girl.

"Look at the bitch. She's got no fucking face," Delbert said.

"She must have caught the fucking rocket with her mouth when it came in," Ryan observed.

Delbert looked over to me. "That was a great fucking shot, Sarge."

I looked down at the girl. She was maybe twelve years old. She could have been fifteen. Who knows? Who cares? Delbert and Ryan were right. She didn't have a fucking face anymore. Hell, she didn't even have brains anymore. The brains were exposed from the front of her skull and already turning gray. Brains did that after a while. I assumed that it had something to do with the air hitting them. Plus, these brains had to contend with the heat of the burned-out hootch. Her right arm had been ripped from its shoulder socket. The socket was blackened, but there was a shiny red gooey substance that seemed to coat the cuplike socket where her arm once had been attached to her body. I don't recall ever seeing the arm. Her right leg was twisted into some grotesque position, sort of like a twisted piece of licorice. I wondered how that leg got so twisted. What difference did it make? She was dead.

I glanced at the body on the other side of the girl. A man lay on the ground. His face was ground into the dirt. The rest of his body was twisted and mangled. There was a gaping hole on his left side. Several of his ribs had actually been ripped away from his torso, and some of his intestines had spilled onto the ground beside him. His dick and balls had been blown off.

"Fuck the gook—he's lucky that he's dead," I said to myself.

We found an AK-47 a few feet away from where he died. He had killed the FNG, and now he was dead. I glanced again at the girl. I remember saying, "*Xin loi*, no more boom-boom Victor Charlie (VC) for you."

But I really wasn't sorry. I did not care one way or the other. She was dead. That is all that mattered. Fuck it. It don't mean nothing.

Walking back across the stream, I took a couple of minutes to reflect and summarize the recent events. A few minutes earlier a round had left the muzzle of the AK-47 we found lying next to the dead gook. That round had passed through the head of the man behind me—the FNG. I knew the FNG was dead. After a while you can just tell the way a guy lies on the ground after he has been hit. Three people had died. I was responsible for all three deaths. I depressed the firing mechanism on the M-72 LAW that killed the two gooks, and I gave the order for the FNG to get off point and get behind me. If I had left him on point *I* would be dead now. Fuck the FNG—he was dead and I was alive. Fuck the dead gooks. We would have to pack the FNG body out to the clearing. I would have to call for a chopper to come and pick him up. First I had to notify the CO (commanding officer), through our new platoon leader of course, that we had a man down. Fuck it. It don't mean nothing.

We made the clearing without further incident. Seven days later I caught a ride back to the rear on the resupply chopper. It never occurred to me that I would not be returning to the platoon. I had been the platoon sergeant for about two months now. Survival through the attrition process was the key to my success. My senior NCOs (non-commissioned officers) had simply rotated back to the States, had been wounded, or had been stuffed into body bags.

A few days later I was notified that I was going to Vung Tao for three days of in-country R&R—my reward for killing the little girl had come through. Now the army was sending me to spend three days in a place where there were wall-to-wall MACV-approved little girls engaged in prostitution. Apparently Military Assistance Command, Vietnam, felt it was all right to kill them and fuck them. Fuck it. It don't mean nothing.

I left Tuy Hoa in my clean boonies fatigues and the same boots I had worn for the previous three months. I honestly do not remember a thing about my brief stay in Vung Tao. I do know that by the end my fatigues were completely covered in vomit and drenched in an assortment of alcoholic beverages. Five days after I arrived at Vung Tao, I sat on the chopper heading back to the base camp at Tuy Hoa. I sat in the door of the slick with my feet dangling just above the skids. The thought crossed my mind to simply lean forward, let go, and exit the aircraft. Such an act was not part of my programming.

When I arrived at the company orderly room, the XO (executive officer) started asking me why I was late getting back from Vung Tao. I told him the truth. "Sir," I said, "I just don't remember."

He told me that he wanted me on the next chopper back to the field. A few minutes later, the first sergeant came out of his hootch.

"Brown, I want you to supervise the shit-burning detail," the first sergeant said.

"Hell, Top, I'd rather go back to the field until I start processing. I certainly don't want to hang around that chicken-shit XO for two weeks," I replied.

He looked at me and said, "You dumb fuck, I am already processing you, and you are not going back to the field. You are going home to that wife of yours. I already have orders for you to be assigned to a training company at Ft. Lewis, Washington. You're going to be a fucking drill sergeant."

I placed my heels together, stood as straight as I possibly could, and looked directly at him. I said, "Airborne, First Sergeant."

He smiled, reached out, shook my hand, and said, "Airborne. Now get the fuck out of my sight for a week."

I started to walk away but stopped. I turned around and asked, "First Sergeant, what about the shit-burning detail?"

"Don't fuck with me, Brown. I do not want to see you until next week," he said as he walked away.

Seven days later I showed up at the door of his hootch. I knocked on the door. The first sergeant opened his door and handed me my orders to report to Cam Rahn Bay and then on to Ft. Lewis, Washington. We said nothing to each other. Several months later I heard that a chopper the first

sergeant was riding in was hit by an RPG (Russian-made 82-mm antitank rocket). There were no survivors. "Airborne, First Sergeant." Fuck it. It don't mean nothing.

It has been on my mind—my story. Several years ago I attempted to address the issues surrounding my participation in the killing of the Vietnamese girl who died in the hootch along the blue line. However, it was little more than an attempt. Sitting in a small café in Saigon more than twenty years after the killing, I found myself searching a sea of faces, trying to determine what she would have looked like if I had not killed her. That sea of faces brought me to the topic of reconciliation, reconciliation with Vietnam, with the little girl, and with myself. The past cannot be undone. I know. I have spent most of my life attempting to undo my own past. I was a participant in the carnage of war in Vietnam. The programming began wearing off in the early 1980s, and my vision was improving.

In 1982 I walked into the Vietnam Outreach Center (VOC) in Las Vegas, Nevada. The environment was rather calm. There were several guys sitting in the front office. The secretary, who had stopped typing, asked if she could help me. I said, "No, I just wanted to stop and see what this place is."

"Go ahead and make yourself comfortable," she said. She returned to her typing, and I continued looking around the front office.

I heard some noise in the back of the building. I looked around the corner and noticed several other guys milling about in a back room.

The secretary looked at me, smiled, and said, "There is coffee and some snacks for you guys in the kitchen back there. Please, go help yourself."

I walked into the kitchen and looked around. It looked like a miniconvention at the Salvation Army. These guys all looked homeless. Some looked as if they had been out on the street for a long time. I turned around and walked out of the kitchen, into the front office, and headed toward the door. I wanted no part of this.

"You come back anytime you want," the secretary said. She added, "Pick up some of those brochures if you want."

I looked at the rack of brochures on the wall next to the door. I grabbed a few and walked out the door. I did not look at the brochures until I parked my car in front of my house. One pamphlet was titled "PTSD: Post-Traumatic Stress Disorder." I remember thinking, "This is certainly a bucketful of shit. The last thing I need is to hang around a bunch of homeless street derelicts down at some Vietnam center."

Two months later I was a full-time client at the VOC. Within six months I had committed myself to group therapy, more commonly referred to as "rap groups." I learned that limiting one's sleep to three hours per day is not normal. Working until you drop is another habit that may need some work. Ignoring emotional demands from your family is not a decent thing to do. Being afraid to get close to people is not healthy. Telling my daughters that I love them does not necessarily mean I am going to lose them. I also learned that the memories I had of Vietnam were probably not going to go away. I would have to learn to make peace with the characters in those memories.

Three and one-half years after stepping across the threshold of the Las Vegas VOC I received my bachelor's degree in social work from the University of Nevada–Las Vegas (UNLV). I was going to help Vietnam veterans. The next year I was accepted into the graduate program in sociology at UNLV. I received my M.A. in 1987 and treated myself to a graduation present. I bought a round-trip ticket to Nicaragua. It is necessary, however, to stop at the island of Grenada before we move on to Nicaragua.

On October 25, 1983, the U.S. military invaded the Caribbean island of Grenada. It was Ronald Reagan's first attempt to demonstrate that he was more than a second-rate Hollywood actor. He was now America's commander-in-chief. He had defeated Grenada with his military might. Most Americans had no idea where Grenada was, but it seemed all right to invade it.

I remember sitting in a "Social Problems" class at UNLV at the time. The instructor asked for a show of hands from all those who supported the invasion. I did not raise my hand. However, as I looked around the classroom, nearly everyone had their hand waving in the air above their head. The hands looked like little five-fingered flags fluttering in their own breeze of patriotic bullshit. I was thirty-eight years old. I had already started to accept the idea that I was weird in comparison to many of the other students.

The instructor then passed out a blank map of the world. He said, "I want you to mark, within the circumference of a half dollar, Grenada. You do not need to write your name on the paper. I am not going to grade you on this exercise."

A few minutes later he collected the papers. Standing at the front of the class, he began sorting them. Only three students had placed Grenada in the correct hemisphere, and these were the only students who had not indicated that they were in favor of the invasion of Grenada. The other students had placed this little island in Africa, the Middle East, Europe, and yes, some had placed it close to Southeast Asia.

The exercise was brilliant. I was dumbfounded. All of these people who were in favor of war didn't even know where Grenada was, but they supported an invasion there. Of course they were sitting in this class-room—their asses were not out in the boonies.

That simple classroom survey sparked the beginning of my critique of the Vietnam War. The danger to society from the hegemonic control of political leaders became crystal clear to me. Imagine going to war without any supportive concrete evidence. The programming machine used at Ft. Polk, Louisiana, must have escaped the boundaries of U.S. military training installations. That simple survey was instrumental in the removal of my own blinders. I eventually turned my head to Nicaragua.

In 1987 the United States was deeply involved in a military action against Nicaragua. The short version of this policy was that America was once again fighting communism. Grenada had quickly escaped the minds and imaginations of most Americans. After all, only nineteen American sol-diers had died, compared to deaths of twenty-nine Cubans and forty-nine Grenada soldiers. Moreover, the event was over in a matter of two months. Nicaragua would be different. Nicaragua had been linked to the revolution in El Salvador, and if Nicaragua was not stopped, the commies would even-tually cross the Rio Grande River and invade the United States. Fuck it. It don't mean nothing.

When I arrived in Nicaragua, I did not speak any Spanish, I knew no one at all, and I had no idea what I was going to do. The officials checking baggage at the airport in Managua hurried me through the inspection process. Passport was American. They smiled. I was finished. In a matter of minutes I was on the street flagging down a taxi.

The driver began talking to me. I assume he was asking me where I wanted to go. I didn't speak Spanish, so I had no idea what he was saying. Even if I had spoken or understood Spanish, I did not know where I wanted to go. The driver became frustrated. I tried telling him to take me to a hotel. Instead he dropped me off at what appeared to be some kind of monastery. He pointed to the large wooden doors. It was my cue to grab my bag, get out of his taxi, and walk over to that large wooden door. He knocked on the door. It opened. A very religious-looking man opened the door and patient-ly listened to the driver for several minutes. Finally, he gave the driver a hug and handed him some money, and the driver turned and left. The reli-gious-looking man, who as I learned later was a Jesuit priest, turned toward me and asked, "Won't you enter, please?"

"Sure," I said, as I followed him down a rather wide hallway that had very little lighting.

He stopped in front of another large door, turned the handle, and opened it. He held his hand toward the doorway and said, "Enter."

I entered the room. It was very dark. Its only light source appeared to be a small window behind an oversized wooden desk. The Jesuit pointed toward a chair. I sat down. My face was the target of that tiny ray of window light.

"Now, what brings you to Managua?" the Jesuit asked.

"I'm not certain," I said. Then I looked and asked him, "Okay, what do I call you? Do I call you Father?"

"That is up to you. I am just curious as to why you are here," he said.

I looked at him. I did not know where to begin. I did know one thing. He obviously spoke English, so I figured I better take full advantage of that luxury. "I came to Nicaragua because I did not like what I was hearing at home about the Contras and the war down here."

"And you came to Nicaragua to see the war?" he asked.

"No, I did not come down here to see the war. I've seen war before. I came here to understand the war and to see if there is anything I can do to help," I said.

He invited me to share a snack and some very strong tea with him. I accepted. I was hungry. He was a craftsman in the art of extracting information. Within a few minutes he discovered that I was an American, was married, had two daughters and a black dog, and that I was trying to find a niche in the world where I could use my newly acquired M.A. degree. He also discovered that I had been in Vietnam. We talked for what seemed to be several hours.

"You have come to Nicaragua to wash your conscience," he said.

I started to object, but he was not finished.

"Please, what I said was not a criticism. It is simply a fact. I have seen several Vietnam veterans from America come to Nicaragua," he said. "They arrive with an agenda, like you, but they are not certain what their agenda is. They are impassioned by the resistance movement."

Finally, the Jesuit told me that he was going to contact someone he knew and help me find a place to discover my agenda. He provided me with a room to stay the night.

At 5:00 A.M. there was a knock on my door. I woke up.

"Hurry, we must go to the airport now." It was the Jesuit speaking.

I got out of bed. "What the hell is going on?" I wondered. "What is the deal with the airport? Are they kicking me out of the country?" Quickly, I got dressed.

I opened the door. The Jesuit was standing in front of me.

"I am sorry to wake you so early, but there is little time. We must go to the airport right away. Your flight to Puerto Cabezas leaves at 6:15 A.M."

I wondered, "What is Puerto Cabezas?" I asked the Jesuit, "What is going on?"

"I will explain everything to you on the way to the airport. Let us go now," he said.

On the way to the airport, the Jesuit explained that his friend was involved with various informal international groups that formed teams that went into the countryside to help the peasants. "They build schools and aid stations, and sometimes they help with the harvest. The work is hard," said the Jesuit.

Going out into the countryside to help the peasants sounded a bit like going out to hump the boonies. There was one significant difference—this time I felt as though I might actually be going out to help the peasants. Not like the bullshit stories about our helping the Vietnamese. For whatever reason, I trusted the Jesuit. I wanted to trust him. I needed to trust someone.

When we arrived at the airport, he retrieved my ticket, handed it to me, and said, "I believe I am doing the right thing." He gave me a hug and said something that sounded like a prayer.

"Thank you, Father," I said. I had finally managed to say the word *Father*. He walked me to the gate, and then he was gone.

The flight to Puerto Cabezas was uneventful—there were no shots fired at the aircraft from the ground. Web-type seating went along both sides of the fuselage. Luggage was piled in the center aisle between the two rows of seats. The aircraft appeared to be some sort of military transport. The prospects of building schools and aid stations occupied my mind for the duration of my flight. All of a sudden the nose of the aircraft pointed down, and in a few minutes we were disembarking.

I was greeted by someone named Jonathan. "Excuse me. Are you William Brown?" he asked.

"Yes," I answered.

"I am Jonathan, and I will take you to your room and introduce you to the group you have been assigned to," he said.

"Sounds great to me; let's go," I said.

I slung my bag over my shoulder and followed Jonathan. We approached a white four-wheel-drive vehicle and got in. About a mile down a dirt road we stopped in front of an old building. It was a hotel. I followed him up the wooden steps and entered the building. There were no luxuries here. There were no showers or toilets in this hotel. The outhouse was in the back, without toilet paper. It was Vietnam revisited.

Over the course of the next few months I became very close to most of the group members. There was Mark from West Germany, Rolf from East Germany, and the Russian who taught me the advantages of drinking warm vodka. There also was the Cuban who always talked about his family, and Peter the Frenchman. Peter and I shared a common thread—we both came from countries that had been defeated and forcibly removed by the Vietnamese.

Some of my fondest memories are set in the countryside outside Puerto Cabezas. I have pleasant memories of sitting on the ground at night engaged in conversations about people, living conditions, politics, and war with my international friends. Many times they would ask me about Vietnam. Often I would evade their questions or pretend that I didn't understand. Unlike many meddlesome Americans, my international friends did not pry. One of the highlights of my experiences in Nicaragua was watching the peasants as we built schoolhouses and aid stations. At first the peasants would look concerned and inquisitive. This was typically replaced with smiles as the job progressed, and the shedding of a tear or two was not uncommon when we completed our project and moved on. I thought the tears were products of gratitude. Perhaps they were. They may also have been expressions of fear.

Over the course of about six months I became educated in what I called the "Reality of Nicaragua," or RON (also for Ronald Reagan). The Contras came along behind us and destroyed the schoolhouses and aid stations. Sometimes they would not wait for the buildings to empty before detonating their bombs. They would kill everyone inside the structure.

Geography can change and time can change. Some things do not change. To me, Americans seem to be obsessed with the murdering of peasants. If *obsessed* is incorrect, then the word *indifferent* certainly applies. For centuries white Americans slaughtered indigenous people, commonly referred to as "Indians," and in the name of democracy Americans slaughtered tens of thousands of peasants in the Philippines. Hundreds of thousands of Vietnamese peasants were murdered by Americans in order to "help" them. Americans were supporting the slaughter of tens of thousands of peasants in El Salvador. Now, under the direction of Reagan and Oliver North, Americans were supporting the murder of Nicaraguan peasants through our Contra proxies. I use the term *supporting* to highlight the fact that U.S. tax dollars support U.S. political leaders who use those dollars to kill peasants around the world.

One day as we were returning to Puerto Cabezas, our pickup came to an abrupt stop. Everyone got out. There by the side of the road was the body of a young girl. She had been raped, urinated on, and decapitated. It was the work of the Contras—that group of thugs Reagan and North referred to as "freedom fighters."

Several members of the group broke down and cried openly. At first I did not cry. Instead I envisioned what I wanted to do to those who had left this girl by the side of this road. I tried to detach myself from what I was witnessing. I thought about how great it would be to pick up the head of this girl, place it in a box, and send it to Ronald and Nancy Reagan. I would include a card, "Just Say No." I was thinking like those who had committed this atrocious act.

Then I thought about the conversation with the Jesuit months earlier. I began to cry. I fell to the ground and cried uncontrollably. The Jesuit had perceived that I had come to Nicaragua to cleanse my conscience. He was right. I had come to Nicaragua to find forgiveness. Well, that forgiveness was not Nicaragua's to give. The forgiveness had to come from me.

I left Puerto Cabezas a few days later. Two days after that, I left Nicaragua. I never saw the members in the group again. As with guys I knew in Vietnam, I could only hope that they made it out in one piece. If they didn't, then they at least died knowing they were helping the poor peasants. I never saw the Jesuit again either. I heard later that he had traveled to Puerto Cabezas and was killed. I have no way to verify this. I had never even bothered to ask him what his name was—I didn't want to know at the time. If he was killed, I hope that at least it was very fast and he did not suffer. He was a good man.

In my reflections on my experiences in Nicaragua, the phrase "it don't mean nothing" was replaced with the realization that the loss of human life does mean something. The little girl's death in Vietnam means something. The girl by the road to Puerto Cabezas means something. Their deaths cannot be trivialized, nor can the behaviors of those who took their lives be rationalized or minimized with some simple phrase.

The Jesuit helped me discover my agenda. I would always stand in opposition to war. I would battle the state's programming machines, and I would struggle to maintain my own consciousness. On the way back home, I decided to continue my education and go into the sociology Ph.D. program at UNLV.

I returned to Vietnam in 1990. I returned as a member of a delegation sponsored by the Indochina Reconciliation Project, an organization that has struggled for reconciliation between America and Vietnam. Its participants have had a very difficult struggle. America does not like to accept defeat— even when that defeat is considered legitimate by most countries of the world. Many Americans continue to believe that we should have won the Vietnam War. Sadly, the programming machines have limited people's ability to question the legitimacy of American intervention in Vietnam. Perhaps this is why America was able to support the Khmer Rouge throughout much of the 1980s and early 1990s. The Khmer Rouge were mass murderers of more than one million Cambodian people. We shared a common enemy with the Khmer Rouge during this period—the Vietnamese.

I lived with several Vietnamese families during the early 1990s. I taught at Open University in Ho Chi Minh City (Saigon), and I shared bottles of rice wine with war vets on a wooden floor in a veterans' hospital north of Saigon. We exchanged stories. We engaged in healing. Strange, to Americans it is the Vietnam War, but to the Vietnamese it is the American War. While in Vietnam, I spent a lot of time looking at the faces of

Vietnamese women who might have been between twelve and fifteen years old in 1968.

"What would she look like today?" I wondered. I continue to wonder.

Hate and suffering clutter my story. Hate and suffering are a combination of the emotions and the experiences of the victims of war. There are only victims in my story. Some victims are buried beneath the ground, and others bear the burden of living with the memory of those they have buried or those they have helped to bury. The accumulation of victims continues today in Iraq. At present, my story seems to have acquired a life of its own—it continues on and on. With new victims entering my story, there is no end in sight.

There is a black wall in Washington, D.C. It is called the Vietnam Veterans Memorial—the Wall. I have not been to the Wall. On its face, on individual marble panels, are inscribed the names of more than 58,000 Americans who died in Vietnam. I knew some whose names appear on the Wall. For me the significance of this Wall is perhaps found in that which is *not* inscribed on its marble surface. The Wall does not mention the estimated several million Vietnamese, Laotians, and Cambodians who died in that war. The Wall does not include the names of those Americans who, for very personal reasons, perished by their own hand after returning from Vietnam. The Wall does not make reference to depleted veterans' benefits since the Vietnam War. Since 1981 hospitalized soldiers wounded in action must reimburse the government for their food while in the hospital. The Wall does not contain the name of the young Vietnamese girl whose expressionless face continues to interrupt my sleep. The Wall should provoke critical thoughts about American intervention in Vietnam. It should rouse critical dialogue about all forms of American military interventions. Yet the Iraq War was launched and continues.

Where are those weapons of mass destruction in Iraq? Where is the link that connects Iraq to the horrific destruction of September 11, 2001? These are questions that I expect Americans to ask right now. Perhaps my expectations are too high. Only a few people are asking these questions.

Five more American soldiers died in Iraq the other day. Two more died a couple of days later, another one died the next day. Near the end of July 2003, American soldiers killed eleven Iraqi civilians. Two were children, and one was an old man in a wheelchair. Thirty-five years have passed since my encounter with the Vietnamese girl with no face. Today the soldiers rationalize and justify their actions. Tomorrow they will remember. My story continues.

On August 1, 2003, a young soldier serving with the 173rd Airborne Brigade was killed in Iraq—thirty-six years after the battle for Hill 875. Young men from my old unit are still dying. My story continues.

The Iraqi families who bury their dead add pages to my story. The pain in the hearts and minds of the family and friends of that young paratrooper are cause for recollection. "Why did he die?" I wonder. How would my first sergeant explain his death?

"First Sergeant," I would say.

"Yes, Brown. What do you want now?" he would ask.

"A young man in the 173rd died the other day in Iraq," I would respond.

"Brown, where in the fuck is Iraq? And what was that trooper doing there in the first place?" he would bark.

The first part of his question would be an examination of my geographical knowledge, not a reflection of his ignorance. It would be a test. I would try to provide him with the coordinates of Iraq and a brief description of the terrain features. Then I would answer the second part of his question: "He was in Iraq because George W. Bush ordered him there."

"Who the hell is George W. Bush?" he would ask.

"He is our president, First Sergeant." I would take pride in offering an endnote to my initial statement, knowing the response that would follow. "He was in the Texas Air National Guard during the war."

"You mean to tell me that we have a president that was once a fucking draft-dodging weekend warrior?" he would scream.

"That's right, First Sergeant. Also, he was AWOL for almost a year," I would note.

"And you elected him president?" the first sergeant would ask.

"Well, I didn't vote for him. He wasn't exactly elected by anyone, First Sergeant. The Supreme Court appointed him president," I would respond.

With his jaw set firmly, he would look at me at this point and say, "Brown, what in the fuck are you talking about? Are you trying to fuck with me?"

Following a most emphatically stated, "No, First Sergeant," I would briefly explain what happened in Florida during the 2000 presidential election.

"So tell me about this Iraq war. How did we get there?" he would ask.

"The public was told that Iraq had weapons of mass destruction and that we had to go and get them from Saddam Hussein, the leader of Iraq," I would respond.

"How many did we find?" he would ask.

"None, First Sergeant," I would answer.

"Who in the hell is in charge of this cluster fuck operation?" he would scream.

"Well, First Sergeant, I guess you could say the president is in charge," I would answer.

"Are the hippies and hair-heads demonstrating at home about this?"

"Not exactly, First Sergeant. We have a situation where if people demonstrate they are considered traitors and can be sent to jail and held in detention," I would answer.

"Brown, that is the same way it was in the 1960s. The cops busted their heads, but they kept on protesting. Those hair-heads were persistent," he would say.

"It's different now, First Sergeant," I would say.

"Bullshit. It is not any different now than it was in Vietnam. War is war. You have young men dying and getting shot up. You got people on the other side getting fucked up and dying. You have people getting promotions. You have people making money on this Iraq thing. You have a president who doesn't know shit about war. It is no different now than it was back in the 1960s," he would state.

"Maybe you are right, First Sergeant," I would say.

"I am right, Brown. There's no maybe about it. Now I have to get back to that card game and a fresh bottle of Cutty Sark. I'm going to keep my eye on you, Brown. You just tell your story and make them listen," he would order, turning and starting to walk away.

"First Sergeant," I would yell.

"What is it, Brown?" he would ask.

"There was a young Vietnamese girl, and I was wondering . . ."

"Yes, Brown. I know who you are talking about. She is fine. Someday the two of you will sit down and talk. But now, go and find a way to close this story," he would say.

"Airborne, First Sergeant," I would say.

"Airborne, Brown," he would respond.

As of this writing, April 7, 2004, more than 10,000 Iraqi civilians have died as a result of U.S. military action (including American allies). More than 10,000 U.S. military personnel have been evacuated from Iraq for wounds and other medical reasons. There have been 620 Americans, 103 coalition troops, and more than 20 journalists killed. The loss of these lives means something to me. My story continues the search for an ending.

PART 4

The Passing of Time

Earlier we wrote that we intended this book of self-reflexive narrative inquiry to tell a story about the life course, about the writers' familial and spatial/temporal roots, about the ways in which the social is embedded in their skin and bones, about the writers' entrances and exits and time spent within various institutional worlds. We hoped to advance a *storytelling sociology* that would be theoretically minimalist, seeking meaning in the stories themselves and encouraging readers' active engagement with the material. We have trusted readers to bring their own interpretive and emotional sensibilities to bear on the tales being told. What different persons take away from this book may vary, but we hope there's been a sociological payoff for everyone, for the narratives are all sensitive to the sociological contexts that shape the stories we are able to tell.

In this concluding section of the book, we contemplate the final stage of the life course. We recognize that life is in many respects nothing more than the passing of time. And from the passing we attempt to redeem ourselves from insignificance, to paraphrase W. H. Auden. At various points in our life, and especially toward its end, we think a lot about where we've been, what our life has been about, what we're leaving behind. We may wonder whether we have a story to tell, whether anybody has cared that we were here or will care when we are gone.

Richard Quinney has traveled widely and accomplished much throughout his life. But upon retirement from his professorship at Northern Illinois University, he wanted to move closer to home, to spend more time at the Wisconsin family farm of his birth, a farm that has belonged to his family for generations, a place "where there is life among the ruins." He has also been living with chronic lymphocytic leukemia, an illness that requires ongoing treatment.

In "The Glowing of Such Fire," with its title taken from a Shakespeare sonnet, Quinney offers the closing essay, a poignant meditation that captures the ineffability of life, that expresses a profound reverence for the importance of living in the moment, of appreciating the everyday, of being "a witness to a time and place." Writing and keeping a journal has been part of Quinney's life for years. Photography, too, has been a way to capture the passing moment, preserving it in a human artifact. This essay, which is accompanied by some photographs taken at the Quinney farm, is an abbreviated chronicle of what he calls "the odyssey of 2001." It is in part about living "in the middle of a storm," about "seeking a reordering" of his life. Quinney no longer searches for absolute truths, as perhaps he once did. He simply wants to encourage us "to live in the glowing of such fire," in the hope that we too will leave behind a story of a life that was worth living, one that will help others live their stories as well.

CHAPTER 21

The Glowing of Such Fire

Richard Quinney

That time of year thou may'st in me behold
When yellow leaves, or none, or few, do hang
Upon those boughs which shake against the cold,
Bare ruined choirs, where late the sweet birds sang.
In me thou seest the twilight of such day
As after sunset fadeth in the west,
Which by and by black night doth take away,
Death's second self that seals up all in rest.
In me thou seest the glowing of such fire
That on the ashes of his youth doth lie,
As the death-bed whereon it must expire,
Consumed with that which it was nourished by.
    This thou perceiv'st, which makes thy love more strong.
    To love that well which thou must leave ere long.
                    —*William Shakespeare, Sonnet 73*

That time of year, that time of life. Shakespeare's narrator is in the autumn of a life. At the beginning of the sonnet, the speaker is in a dark mood, likening life at this twilight stage to a ruin, to the "bare ruined choirs" of destroyed churches that dot the landscape. But presently, in a change of mind, the narrator senses a glowing of a fire that comes out of the ashes of the aging life. Upon these ashes—as a consequence of living—the true and present reality rests.

As a witness and participant, I keep a close watch on my life at this time. Writing—especially the fairly regular keeping of a journal—has been a part of my life for years. Early in my adult years, I developed the need to make sense of life as lived daily. Important also has been the use of photography to see and understand the world within which I move and have my being. Stories are always being told and revised to make sense of this changing life. Each of us is on an odyssey in our own time.

The turn of the new century brought me a retirement from one way of life, from a life of professing in the university. At the same time, a chronic illness, lymphocytic leukemia, which had been dormant for a decade, reached a critical stage that required hospitalization, intensive care, and continuing treatment. Moreover, I was about to make a physical move from one place to another. As the new year began, I started to keep a record of what I would regard as the odyssey of 2001. In fact, over the year I often thought of myself as a modern-day Odysseus, as one on a long journey with the hope of someday returning home.

As the year progressed, I spent more of my time at the farm. This is the farm that has belonged to my family for generations. First settled by my great-grandparents fleeing the potato famine in Ireland, it is the farm of my birth and early years. It is a place that I have never been able to leave completely, the place that I continue to call home. As summer came, and as I went to the farm weekly, I photographed this place "where yet the sweet birds sing." Although there were many strong and constant reminders of the

past—from the rot and rust of decaying buildings to aging artifacts found in drawers and trunks—I was transported by the wonders of the present in this much-loved place. Even with the coming of fall and winter, solace was found in that which is near and now.

The account that follows is a chronicle, and an abbreviation, of the year of the odyssey. As the tale ends, my wife and I are settling into a life in a new place. The farm remains, of course, the place where yet the sweet birds sing and where there is life among the ruins. I will speak in the present tense—as the life was being lived.

January

The thermometer outside the kitchen window has hovered around zero the last several days. My health—or my lack of it—has kept me indoors. On Christmas morning, I opened the front door and with my back to the sun, pointed the binoculars toward a sheet of white paper. An image of a partial solar eclipse formed before us. Solveig and I watched as the moon's shadow passed over the face of the sun. For a few moments, the sparkling snow blanketing the front yard turned blue.

The night before winter solstice—a night with a wind chill of minus 40 degrees—a small screech owl fell down the chimney and into the burning fireplace. Immediately it flew out of the flame and into the living room, landing gracefully on the stairway banister. For a long time we gazed carefully at each other. Eventually Solveig and I coaxed the owl toward the doorway, and it flew out the opened door. We wondered later why we had not spent more time together. We had wanted, I suppose, to see the owl safely returned to the night.

On a morning of the new year, we woke up in the bedroom of the farmhouse in Wisconsin. We watched the sun rise over wooded hills and snow-covered fields. Long icicles were hanging from the roof of the barn. The branches of the trees surrounding the house, covered with an icing during the night, glistened in the morning light. For a good part of the day, driving in all directions, we meandered over snow-packed back roads that finally led south toward home.

At the end of my street there is a river and a lagoon lined with willows. From my window, I see a bridge, a tree in which a lone crow is perched, and a frozen river covered with snow. The pilgrimage now is near at hand.

February

Another blast of arctic air surges across the northern plains and down to the Wisconsin and Illinois border. Here in our home in DeKalb, west of

Chicago, it is too cold to take a morning's walk downtown. Again, my travels must be close to home.

The ways are many in the keeping of a journal. The motivations and the needs are various. But at the heart of my effort is a single reason—a paradox, seemingly, at first: to study oneself is to forget oneself, to become part of that which is larger than the individual self. This is the insight of Buddhism that informs my life daily. Expressed concisely by Shunryu Suzuki in *Zen Mind, Beginners's Mind*: "When we forget ourselves, we actually are the true activity of the big existence, of reality itself."

With a change in my antibiotic prescription, I now can have a bottle of beer during a noontime visit to the Twins Tavern. Tables and booths are filled with lunchtime customers. I seat myself on one of the tall chairs at the bar that runs the length of the room, and I exchange a few words with fellow customers. The sign over the bar sends the familiar greeting: "Beer—So Much More Than A Breakfast Drink." Ornate handles for the dispensing of draft beer line the counter. New Glarus Spotted Cow is the latest addition to the selections. Packages of potato chips and salted nuts are displayed along the edges of the mirror. Antique fishing tackle, bottles of liquor, and knickknacks of all kinds are displayed on the back wall. The news from WGN plays on the television set at the end of the bar. Colored neon lights give a warm glow to the room. A good place on a winter's day.

March

On the first day of March, my mother used to tell me that on this day in earlier times the country roads would be traveled by wagons piled high with furniture and trunks as tenant farmers and their families moved to "the new place." It seemed that the first of March would always be stormy and that the roads would be filled with snow. Today, at the beginning of a week's visit to Florida, we walk a beach on the Gulf of Mexico. The sun glistens on the water's surface, shore birds run ahead of us, and we gather rocks and shells from the sand.

This month marks the anniversary of my father's birth over a hundred years ago. He died at the age of sixty-nine, in the sixty-ninth year of his life. My father never suggested that I continue in his path as a farmer. He knew that I was not fit for the life of hard work, and perhaps he thought that I might pursue the life he had dreamed of when young.

Later in the month, after supper, I stand on the back porch of the farmhouse, looking out the window into the dark night. The yard light on the corner of the barn cuts through the darkness and casts shadows over the driveway and along the sides of the outbuildings. I know that no matter how much I might try to bring a life back to the farm, the life I once knew here can never be restored. What is gone is gone forever. A lone opossum crawls through the crack of the barn door. During the night, while we are sleeping, a dusting of snow will cover the land. In the morning, I await the results of a lab test and CT scan.

Much of my inspiration for writing comes from listening to music. The country voices of Willie Nelson, Merle Haggard, and Dolly Parton go round my brain as I sit at my desk and write. Songs of the highway, of leaving home, of missing the ones you love make up my repertoire—along with the classical nocturnes of Chopin and the requiems of Fauré, Brahms, and Mozart. Sounds and sensibilities for a lifetime.

A line from a poem by Charles Wright will end the month: "Buds hold their breath and sit tight."

April

Amid patches of snow, bluets are dotting the lawns in town. Clusters of daffodils have started to bloom. A warm wind blows all day long. After yesterday's thunderstorm, green grass is beginning to appear from under winter's musty mats of brown. The golf course at the country club has turned completely green.

My brother and I have met at the farm to make plans for spring planting. We sit at the kitchen table talking to the district conservationist and to a wildlife biologist from the Department of Natural Resources. In a few weeks we will be planting trees and prairie grasses under the Conservation Reserve Program. Soon the old grasses—primarily reed canary—will be burned around the pond at the old place. Eventually the ecosystem around the pond will be restored and will provide a rejuvenated brooding habitat for water birds. Someday—years from now—the black oaks and bur oaks that we're planting will give shelter and sustenance to other life.

A long time ago, I left rural Wisconsin with thoughts and desires for a life in the larger world. Here I am back on the land that once was my home and from which I sought my escape. And here I am now trying to preserve and protect the land—but happy that I have also had a life elsewhere.

When in Madison last week for what I thought was a routine appointment with my hematologist, I was asked if the removal of my spleen had been mentioned yet. The problem is that my white blood counts are low again, with neutrophils below 500. I must begin the four infusions of Rituxan. With low counts, there is the danger of infection, especially of fungal pneumonia. I wonder and worry about the invasion of the aspergillus fungus, which comes with the spring winds that blow over these midwestern fields.

After the infusions, I am relieved to learn that my neutrophils have risen to 2,500. My daughter and I celebrate with an early dinner at a Turkish restaurant on Monroe Street.

On the high shelf of my closet, I store boxes of family letters that have accumulated over the last fifty years. Last week in the top drawer of the desk at the farm I found some of the letters that I wrote home in the 1950s. In one letter to my parents, I tell about my first experience of teaching. I had been sent by Kimball Young, whom I was assisting in graduate school, to the Chicago campus of Northwestern University to administer an examination to a sociology class. My assignment was also to deliver a ten-minute lecture—my first lecture ever—to a class I would find seated in a large auditorium. Later that evening, after returning to my room at the Evanston campus, I wrote to my parents that I had made the long walk up to the lecture table. I ended my letter, "The evening is over and I feel that at last there is something I can do." For the next thirty-two years I would do what I had found that I could do. And the letters home continued to be written until there was no longer any reason to write.

May

The sweet birds have returned to the farm for another season. I have assisted their return and reproduction by nailing bluebird houses to posts and hanging a wren house on the limb of the lilac bush. Upon these boughs this season, birds will sing their songs. Already, from the kitchen window, I watch as twigs are brought to the nest.

On the floor of the attic of the farmhouse, in a broken cardboard box, I have found a few trinkets and artifacts rescued from the old house when it was torn down in the 1940s. Among the items is the black-glass rosary that belonged to my father's Aunt Kate. A gray clay pipe rests in the bottom of the box, the pipe that I have seen my great-grandmother Bridget holding in an old photograph. My father told me that she brought the pipe with her from Ireland and smoked it regularly. More of the past can be found in the attic when I am of a disposition to look. Soon I will begin to photograph the ruins on the farm, including the buildings that have deteriorated during my own lifetime.

While gathering wild asparagus along the road for last night's supper, I stood motionless and watched a fox run across the tilled land east of the barn. A weasel scurried into the ditch. A marsh harrier, in sleek silhouette, glided over the stubbled field. Thrushes and thrashers were feeding under the brush in the aging orchard. Invading honeysuckle bloomed profusely along the roadside. Chorus frogs sang in the evening from the pond down at the old place. In the morning, after my night of restful sleep in the room in which I was born, goldfinches gathered for thistle seed at the feeder beyond the kitchen window.

We attend Memorial Day services in Delavan. The war dead are remembered with a parade through town and a service on the hill at Spring Grove Cemetery. Not since 1952, when I played in the high school band for the last time, had I been a part of the procession to the cemetery. After the service of speeches, prayers, musical numbers, and the firing of guns, Solveig and I walk to the graves of my ancestors to check on the progress of the flowers we planted beside the stones.

The days of summer are about to begin. I shall take my doctor's advice and "make hay while the sun shines."

June

Let June begin with an early morning welcome. I rise to Dawn's rose-red fingers, as in Homer's *Odyssey*. For weeks I have been reading the classical tale, and I envision myself daily on a wine-dark sea as I cross the prairie on my way to the farm. Some mornings I think of myself rising handsome as a god.

Dawn's lovely locks stream through layers of fog as I stand looking over the fields to the hills east of the barn. Later in the morning a crew of archaeologists will arrive to make systematic probes into the oak knoll that rises from the marsh. The objective is to document the occupation of the land around the marsh by the Potawatomi before European settlement. Someday the archaeologists plan to document the settling of the farm by generations of my family. It is my wish that these acres become a public preserve for others to enjoy and appreciate in the future. Someday we will be among the old ones who once lived on this land.

On another morning we take our folding chairs and sit again behind the barn to watch the rising goddess of morning and listen to the early morning sounds. Barn swallows swoop around us. A great blue heron flies gracefully out of the tamaracks on the edge of the marsh. Songbirds are awakening in the trees surrounding the house. A Baltimore oriole emerges from its basket-nest in the Chinese elm. We hear pheasants calling and cackling from the far end of the field across the road. Two sandhill cranes are pulling sprouted corn from the planted rows and sending deep-throated rattles into the morning air. A crescent moon with bright Venus to its left hangs in the eastern sky above the old, empty corncrib. To our backs, red Mars sinks below the western horizon.

My neutrophils are on the rise with the summer solstice, as the sun reaches its highest point above the earth's equator. The corn has grown at least eight inches during the last week of this month. Sky-blue blossoms of chicory stand tall along the sides of the road. Large clusters of white flowers cover the elderberry bushes. Ripe mulberries are dropping to the ground. This is the day that we will attempt to remove accumulated dust and dirt from the basement floor. An overture by Aaron Copeland plays on the classical music station. On the front porch, I sit in the rocking chair between trunks that came generations ago from the old country.

July

Two woodchucks stand upright, looking toward the house. I stand in the shadows of the kitchen so that I will not be seen. A young woodchuck peers from the hole in the granary door. The standing adults soon resume their four-legged posture and return to the culvert under the driveway.

I am here alone for a day or two to get some idea of what living in the farmhouse was like for my parents. They lived in this house from the time of their marriage in 1930, having built it during the previous year for the life they would create together. Although the house has been cleaned and halfheartedly rearranged since my mother died two years ago, it remains pretty much the way she kept it during the thirty years she lived here alone after my father died. I sense in this house a presence other than my own.

I cannot be at the farm long without imagining that I am a character in Anton Chekhov's play *Uncle Vanya*. The Russian estate on which the drama takes place belongs to the old order that is fading. I, too, am of a passing order, and I am not certain of my place in the coming order. Repairs are being made on the house; the land is rented out to pay the taxes; trees and native grasses are being planted on previously tilled land, and some of the fields are returning to their native state. I am a caretaker with little notion of what is to come.

I have found the deeds to the lands that make up the farm. Acres of land have been acquired by generations of my family over the last 130 years. The first deed is for the few acres purchased by my great-grandfather John Quinney in 1868. He and Bridget settled forever into a house over-

looking the marsh and muskrat pond. Beside his name on the deed is his substitute for a signature—a large X. Oh, pioneers!

My photography this summer is taking a new and unexpected turn. I had thought that I would be roaming the byways of the county, finding and photographing the remains—the ruins—of another time. Instead, I am on pathways I make by foot around the boundaries of the farm. My photographs are of landscapes seen from a distance and from very near. I now see more clearly the place where yet the sweet birds sing. At the same time, all signs are pointing to the cresting of summer. In the humid haze of a summer's evening, we drive through the small towns of southern Wisconsin. A summer night such as this we could wish to last forever.

August

The dog days of summer are evident as the month begins. The early Egyptians believed that the appearance of Sirius, the Dog Star, rising with the sun intensified the heat of the day. Warm and humid southerly winds prevail. A year ago at this time, I was in a hospital with life in the balance. A year later after treatments and experiments of various kinds, my disease has stabilized, and I am feeling much better. In mysterious ways, I know that I am blessed.

We are beginning to prepare the ground for next year's garden. It will be the first garden we have planted on the farm, except for this year's three tomato bushes, which are struggling beside the sheep shed. Beyond the farm buildings where once cows grazed, now at sunset a lone deer forages in the field of corn.

What advice would you give to someone beyond middle age? I am not thinking about absolutes, truths that might apply to everyone under all circumstances, but about something that might be a guide under relative conditions. Is not my own keeping of a journal an attempt to tell others—to show others—how one life is being lived with some intention? I hope that I might give inspiration to others in the course of finding and examining my own life. No absolutes, but encouragements to live in the glowing of such fire.

We sit at the kitchen table over a late supper, listening to a hard rain. All afternoon the sky was dark, interspersed with sun-laced cumulus clouds. We watched a large yellow butterfly with wings edged in black fly back and forth over the timothy field. Crickets are already jumping in the grass. On the radio, we are listening to a program of blues music being broadcast from Memphis. Jerry Lee Lewis is interviewed ever so briefly, and a recording of his song on the night train to Memphis is played. The lyric is repeated: "Singin' hallelujah all the way." Solveig tells me I am looking the best I have looked all year. Nothing to be blue about tonight. Hallelujah.

Odysseus still has not made his identity known to his wife. Penelope, as night comes, retires to her bedroom to take some rest. The goddess Athena, daughter of Zeus and patron of human resourcefulness, gives her comfort. As Homer assures us, "Athena sealed her eyes with welcome sleep." And so to bed for welcomed sleep at the end of a day of a summer that is fast fading.

September

A full moon rises above the racetrack and climbs the far end of the grandstand as night falls and the show begins. George Jones, with a fanfare from the Jones boys, walks onto the stage to the enthusiastic applause and cheers of the crowd. We secured our seats early and waited as the grandstand filled and the time neared for the appearance of the country star. All the years of writing songs, performing, and living a life were before us as the lights above the stage flashed from one color to another, ending in blue for the start of another slow song. The aging singer gracefully, and humorously, acknowledged his advancing years, working his life into the themes of the long list of songs for which he is known.

As we slowly walked down the steps of the grandstand and left the fairgrounds, I commented to our friends that we invest our heroes with qualities that we cannot entirely embody ourselves. The last days of the county fair—coming on Labor Day weekend—always meant that fall was about to begin.

We listen to the radio, watch the television coverage, and read the newspapers following the destruction of the towers of the World Trade Center in New York—and wander about in great sorrow for the lives that have been lost and for the families that are mourning the loss of loved ones. The most that I can do at the moment, here at home so far from the events, with blood that will not be accepted for donation, is to share compassionate concern. I listen to the majesty of Verdi's "Requiem," music that expresses the range of emotions in a time of grief. And I will do all I can in support of the banner that is displayed across the street from the National Cathedral in Washington as services for a day of prayer and remembrance take place: *No war. No retaliation. Stop the violence.*

Later we stare into the dark sky and look briefly through the edge of our Milky Way galaxy. A coyote howls in the night.

We wake to cool mornings and the yellowing light of fall. I go down the road, along the fence line to the bottom of the hill, and photograph goldenrod in bloom. This time of year, when I was growing up and working in the fields, my father would recite the poem that begins, "The goldenrod is yellow." I remember lying in a field nearby, when I was eight or nine, looking into formations being created by the white clouds, suddenly seeing clearly the face of George Washington, and knowing then that I had been chosen to do good works in my life. Sixty years later I look into the sky of billowing clouds and simply entertain the mystery of existence.

October

The legendary harvest moon rises as scheduled shortly after sunset: a *harvest* moon because it is the closest full moon to the autumnal equinox, and because the moon furnished light for farmers before tractors with headlights came to the harvest. All year I have waited to record in my journal a few lines from the poem by John Keats titled "To Autumn": "How beautiful the season is now—How fine the air."

We have spent a day in Madison with a realtor, looking for a house that we might buy. We have entertained the prospect of leaving DeKalb and living in Madison for some time. Today I am checking on the financial possibilities of such a move, which would place us closer to the farm and at the same time in a larger city, the state's capital. Thirty sandhill cranes circle high above the farm, gathering in a flock for their fall migration to the south. Thirteen wild turkeys cross the road and walk into the woods that leads down to the marsh.

The Nobel Peace Prize has been awarded to the United Nations and its secretary general, Kofi Annan. The Nobel committee noted that it "wishes in its centenary year to proclaim that the only negotiable route to global peace and cooperation goes by way of the United Nations." In the wake of the attacks on the World Trade Center and the ongoing military response being waged by the United States, this recognition of the international organization is important. I await the morning mail for the arrival of a United Nations flag that I have ordered. I have heard recently the quote from Socrates: "I am not a citizen of Athens or Greece, I am a citizen of the world."

Our offer to purchase a house in Madison is accepted. We will be starting a new life as this year ends and the new one begins. This town on the prairie in northern Illinois has been a nurturing source for a significant portion of our lives. We will be certain to sustain our friendships and family relations as we move.

Before dawn the planets Mercury and Venus, within a degree of each other from our perspective here on Earth, accompany one another in the eastern sky. We will arise to a new month and to All Saints Day, a day traditionally celebrated as a reminder of the hope of entry into heaven.

November

This little household is on the move. Before the month is over, the contents of our house in DeKalb must be packed, labeled, and made ready to transport north to the farm and to Madison. As the month ends, if all goes well, we will be living in a different house in a different place. The mind is scattered, as the belongings of a lifetime are being scattered.

Most hardcover books I will save and pack into boxes for the move north. Paperbacks, which age faster than hardcover books, even paperback editions of my own books, I place in the discard pile, which is fast growing on the basement floor. Academic books are more likely to go into the discard pile than literary works. I save most biographies and memoirs. Nature books have a good chance of surviving the cut. There are the books of sentimental value that will be saved, books given to me as gifts by friends and family. And there are the books that have been crucial to me at various points in my life. The discarded books will go to public libraries for their collections or annual fund-raising sales. Each book has played its part in my life. Books discarded are given my blessing as they enter the cardboard box.

The corn has been picked on the farm. The fields are now in stubble. An antlered deer stands tall on the hill at the far end of the harvested soybean field. We have gone to the woods to post No Hunting signs, since the bow-and-arrow season for deer is now in full swing.

We set the alarm clock for 4:00 in the morning. When it rings, we slip on our clothes and make our way to the far side of the barn, where there is darkness away from the yard light. The Leonid meteor shower is just beginning. Meteors, which are actually pieces of the comet Tempel-Tuttle, flash across the sky. More than the occasional shooting star we sometimes see in the night sky, we see several streaks of light each minute. We lean against the silo as a fresh breeze rises out of the south. Condensation from the night's dew drops from the high eaves of the barn. After half an hour of gazing and delighting, we return to the kitchen for a cup of coffee, and then go to bed for another four hours of sleep—the soundest sleep of the night.

I continue my night reading of V. S. Naipaul's new novel *Half a Life*. This half a life is the life of a great part of the world's population. Whether you are a refugee, a migrant to another land, class, or culture, or from one town to another, you are experiencing half a life. In an interview, Naipaul said that he escaped some of his half-life by being a writer. A writer invents a life in the process of imagination and the construction of a narrative. In the writing, one is creating a life.

Cool, windy, scattered showers, a possibility of snow flurries—the forecast for the day. There is nothing like a move to make you realize how precious is this life and how precarious our existence. We travel with car-

tons of breakable treasures from what once was our home to the place that we hope will eventually become familiar. Solveig and I both remark that we feel like aliens from another world.

December

The month begins in a mist, but there is promise of sunshine later in the day. A redheaded woodpecker searches for insects on the bark of the Chinese elm next to the farmhouse. We move back and forth between the three places in a camping mode, from a near-empty house in DeKalb, to the farmhouse now packed with boxes, to the house in Madison, which is slowly beginning to look like what may be a home.

The main roads into Kandahar, in Afghanistan, are being cut off by troops supported by U.S. air power. The front page of the morning newspaper carries a color photograph of refugees gathered around small tents set in sand. I clip the photograph from the paper, fold it, and place it in my bill-fold as a reminder of those who travel under circumstances much less fortunate than ours.

Three camels with riders dressed as the magi lope down the streets of Elkhorn in the annual Christmas parade. Floats, ponies hitched to carts, and marching bands fill the streets for over an hour on this cold, windy, sunny day. Early in the evening, back at the farm, we light a candle and for the first time talk about the uncertain wisdom of our move. Already we are missing the company of friends, particularly remembering their visits to our house during the critical times of my illness. We promise that we will give care to others as care is needed.

As a graduate student in the 1950s at the University of Wisconsin, I would walk along State Street, passing used bookstores, newsstands, men's clothing stores, art supply stores, groceries, and movie theaters. Once on a winter night, I walked in a snowstorm to hear Bob Scobie and his Dixieland band play into the night. In recent years, Solveig and I have driven to Madison to gather provisions at the farmers' market held on Saturdays around the Capitol Square. The day we were married, we drove to Madison to spend the weekend.

Yesterday, before catching the number 7 bus for my return home from a stroll along State Street, I stopped for lunch at a Himalayan restaurant. I purchased a small Buddha statue as a gift for one of my daughters. In a bookstore window, I saw displayed a copy of my recently published book *Borderland*. I had a cup of coffee at a café before the bus pulled up at the station. I got off the bus a half block from my house, a senior citizen returning from an outing.

I do sense that I am in the middle of a storm, that I am all shook up. Certainly I was seeking a reordering of my life. But I had forgotten about the pains that come with change. There is a price to be paid in the attempt to find new—or renewed—interest and meaning in life.

Finally a sense that a cloud may be lifting after the travails of moving. I awake in the morning at the farm, with an inner peace that has been escaping me these last few weeks. Sunlight streams through the lace curtains in the south window of the farmhouse, making patterns on the living-room wall. A prism high in one of the windows sends rainbow colors dancing on the ceiling. I will take a walk along the fence line and make my way to the stone pile in the far corner of the field to fetch a rock that I can take back with us to Madison.

In order to avoid having to "dodge the bullet," as my doctor puts it, I must have another round of Rituxan infusions after the holidays. In the meantime, the snow has come in the night, and to the farm we must go to photograph the coming of winter. With the temperature well below freezing, the shutter drops slowly. Chickadees, nuthatches, and a red-bellied woodpecker are eating from suet blocks on the trees. I make a photograph of the ice-filled birdbath.

Back on the island of Ithaca, after his return, Odysseus is gradually recognized by his son, his old dog Argos, and his nurse Eurycleia, who identifies him by an old scar. Penelope finally welcomes her husband to the bed, and Odysseus, with his wife in his arms, knows joy: "Joy, as warm as the joy that shipwrecked sailors feel when they catch sight of land." In the morning, Dawn with her rose-red fingers shines upon their happiness.

To be a witness to a time and a place is a calling of sorts. And as twilight comes and the bare ruined choirs appear, may there be—with some grace— a glowing of the fire. A fire that will light the way as boughs shake against the cold, as night comes. That we may rejoice in the mystery of both the light and the darkness.

References

Adler, Patricia A., and Peter Adler. 1987. *Membership Roles in Field Research.* Newbury Park, CA: Sage.

Agger, Ben. 2000. *Public Sociology: From Social Facts to Literary Acts.* Lanham, MD: Rowman and Littlefield.

Alinsky, Saul D. 1971. *Rules for Radicals: A Pragmatic Primer for Realistic Radicals.* New York: Vintage.

Anderson, Nels. 1923. *The Hobo.* Chicago: University of Chicago Press.

Ansay, A. Manette. 2001. *Limbo: A Memoir.* New York: HarperCollins.

Anzaldúa, Gloria. 1987. *Borderlands/La Frontera: The New Mestiza.* San Francisco: Aunt Lute.

APA (American Psychiatric Association). 1994. *Diagnostic and Statistical Manual of Mental Disorders.* Washington, DC: APA.

Austin, James, and John Irwin. 1994/2001. *It's About Time.* Belmont, CA: Wadsworth.

Balkan, Sheila, Ronald J. Berger, and Janet Schmidt. 1980. *Crime and Deviance in America: A Critical Approach.* Belmont, CA: Wadsworth.

Banfield, Edward. 1958. *The Moral Basis of a Backward Society.* New York: Free Press.

Barone, Thomas. 1995. "Persuasive Writings, Vigilant Readings, and Reconstructed Characters: The Paradox of Trust in Educational Storytelling." *Qualitative Studies in Education* 8:63–74.

Barrett, Michele. 1991. *The Politics of Truth: From Marx to Foucault.* Stanford, CA: Stanford University Press.

Barth, John. 1968. *Lost in the Funhouse: Fiction for Print, Tape, Live Voice.* New York: Doubleday.

Befu, Harumi. 2001. *Hegemony of Homogeneity: An Anthropological Analysis of Nihonjinron.* Melbourne, Australia: Trans Pacific.

Bell, Michael Mayfield. 1997. "The Ghosts of Place." *Theory and Society* 26:813–836.

Benson, Jackson J. 1996. *Wallace Stegner: His Life and Work.* New York: Penguin.

Benson, Michael L. 2002. *Crime and the Life Course: An Introduction.* Los Angeles: Roxbury.

Berger, Ronald J. 2004. "Pushing Forward: Disability, Basketball, and Me." *Qualitative Inquiry* 10: in press.

Blatz, Perry K. 1994. *Democratic Miners: Work and Labor Relations in the Anthracite Coal Industry, 1875–1925*. Albany: SUNY Press.

Blatz, Perry K., and Robert P. Wolensky. 1999. "Rinaldo Cappellini, the Knox Mine Disaster, and the Decline of the Anthracite Coal Industry." In *Keystone of Democracy*, ed. Howard Harris and Perry K. Blatz. Harrisburg: Pennsylvania Historical and Museum Commission.

Blinde, Elaine M., Diane E. Taub, and Lingling Han. 2001. "Sport Participation and Women's Personal Empowerment: Experiences of the College Athlete." In *Contemporary Issues in Sociology of Sport*, ed. Andrew Yiannakis and Merrill J. Melnick. Champaign, IL: Human Kinetics.

Bochner, Arthur P., and Carolyn Ellis, eds. 2002. *Ethnographically Speaking: Autoethnography, Literature, and Aesthetics*. Walnut Creek, CA: AltaMira.

Bodnar, John. 1983. *Anthracite People*. Harrisburg: Pennsylvania Historical and Museum Commission.

Bornoff, Nicholas. 1986. "The Harpo Marx of Media Japanology." *PHP Intercept* 2:33–36.

Bottigheimer, Ruth. 1987. *Grimms' Bad Girls and Bold Boys*. New Haven, CT: Yale University Press.

Brown, Rita Mae. 1973. *Rubyfruit Jungle*. Plainsfield, VT: Daughters.

Bruner, Jerome. 1990. *Acts of Meaning*. Cambridge, MA: Harvard University Press.

Buber, Martin. 1923/1976. *I and Thou*. New York: Simon and Schuster.

Butler, Judith. 1999. *Gender Trouble: Feminism and the Subversion of Identity*. New York: Routledge.

Buzard, James. 2003. "On Auto-ethnographic Authority." *Yale Journal of Criticism* 16:61–91.

Camilleri, Joseph M. 1999. "Disability: A Personal Odyssey." *Disability and Society* 14:845–853.

Campbell, Joseph. 1990. *Transformations of Myth Through Time*. New York: Perennial.

Chekhov, Anton. 2001. *Five Plays*. Trans. Ronald Hingley. New York: Oxford University Press.

Church, Kathryn. 1995. *Forbidden Narratives*. London: Gordon and Breach.

Cigarroa, Maria-Isabel. 1991. "George Washington's Birthday Festivities in Laredo: A Celebration of Community." Master's thesis, University of Texas.

Clandinin, D. Jean, and F. Michael Connelly. 1998. "Personal Experience Methods." In *Collecting and Interpreting Qualitative Materials*, ed. Norman K. Denzin and Yvonna S. Lincoln. Thousand Oaks, CA: Sage.

———. 2000. *Narrative Inquiry: Experience and Story in Qualitative Research*. San Francisco: Jossey-Bass.

Clifford, James, and George E. Marcus, eds. 1986. *Writing Culture: The Poetics and Politics of Ethnography*. Berkeley: University of California Press.

Coles, Robert. 1989. *The Call of Stories: Teaching and the Moral Imagination*. Boston: Houghton Mifflin.

Cook-Lynn, Elizabeth. 1996. *Why I Can't Read Wallace Stegner and Other Essays*. Madison: University of Wisconsin Press.

Corroto, Carla. 1996. "Constructing Architects: A Critical Ethnography." Ph.D. diss., Ohio State University.

Crittendon, Anne. 2001. *The Price of Motherhood: Why the Most Important Job in the World Is Still the Least Valued*. New York: Metropolitan.

Dai, Sijie. 2001. *Balzac and the Little Chinese Seamstress*. New York: Random House.

Dale, Peter. 1986. *The Myth of Japanese Uniqueness*. New York: St. Martin's.

Davis, Kathy. 1997. "Embody-ing Theory: Beyond Modernist and Post-modernist Readings of the Body." In *Embodied Practices*, ed. Kathy Davis. Thousand Oaks, CA: Sage.

Davis, Leonard J. 1997. "Constructing Normalcy: The Bell Curve, the Novel, and the Invention of the Disabled Body in the Nineteenth Century." In *The Disability Studies Reader*, ed. Leonard J. Davis. New York: Routledge.

Dégh, Linda. 1979. "Grimms' *Household Tales* and Its Place in the Household: The Social Relevance of a Controversial Classic." *Western Folklore* 38:83–103.

Dennis, Dion. 1997. "Washington's Birthday on the Texas Border." *CTHEORY*, February 17, www.theory.net.

Denzin, Norman K. 1989. *Interpretive Biography*. Thousand Oaks, CA: Sage.

———. 1997. *Interpretive Ethnography: Ethnographic Practices for the Twenty-first Century*. Thousand Oaks, CA: Sage.

———. 1998. "The New Ethnography." *Journal of Contemporary Ethnography* 27:405–415.

———. 1999. "Interpretive Ethnography for the Next Century." *Journal of Contemporary Ethnography* 28:510–519.

Denzin, Norman K., and Yvonna S. Lincoln, eds. 2003. *The Landscape of Qualitative Research: Theories and Issues*. Thousand Oaks, CA: Sage.

DePauw, Karen P., and Susan G. Gavron. 1995. *Disability and Sport*. Champaign, IL: Human Kinetics.

De Waal Malefijt, Annemarie. 1968. "Homo Monstrosus." *Scientific American* 219:112–118.

Doniger, Wendy. 1998. *The Implied Spider*. New York: Columbia University Press.

Dorst, John D. 1999. *Looking West*. Philadelphia: University of Pennsylvania Press.

Dunbar, Paul Laurence. 1913. *The Complete Poems of Paul Laurence Dunbar*. New York: Dodd, Mead.

Duncan, Margaret Carlisle. 1998. "Stories We Tell Ourselves About Ourselves." *Sociology Sport Journal* 15:95–108.

Durkheim, Émile. 1912/1965. *The Elementary Forms of Religious Life*. New York: Free Press.

Eiseley, Loren. 1975. *All the Strange Hours*. New York: Charles Scribner.

Elder, Glen. 1985. "Perspectives on the Life Course." In *Life Course Dynamics*, ed. Glen Elder. Ithaca, NY: Cornell University Press.

———. 1994. "Time, Human Agency, and Social Change." *Social Psychology Quarterly* 57:4–15.

Ellis, Carolyn. 1995. *Final Negotiations*. Philadelphia: Temple University Press.

———. 2004. *The Ethnographic I: A Methodological Novel About Autoethnography*. Walnut Creek, CA: AltaMira.

Ellis, Carolyn, and Arthur P. Bochner, eds. 1996. *Composing Ethnography: Alternative Forms of Qualitative Writing*. Walnut Creek, CA: AltaMira.

Ewick, Patrick, and Susan S. Silbey. 1995. "Subversive Stories and Hegemonic Tales: Toward a Sociology of Narrative." *Law and Society Review* 29:197–226.

Faley, Jean V. L. Hector. 1990. *Up Oor Close: Memories of Domestic Life in Glasgow Tenements, 1910 to 1945*. Oxford: White Cockade.

Fausto-Sterling, Anne. 2000. *Sexing the Body*. New York: Basic.

Feiler, Bruce S. 1991. *Learning to Bow: Inside the Heart of Japan*. New York: Ticknor and Fields.

Feinberg, Leslie. 1996. *Transgender Warrior*. Boston: Beacon.

Fine, Michelle, and Adrienne Asch. 1988. "Disability Beyond Stigma: Social

Interaction, Discrimination, and Activism." *Journal of Social Issues* 44:3–21.

Fine, Michelle, and Lois Weis. 2002. "Writing the 'Wrongs' of Fieldwork: Confronting Our Own Research/Writing Dilemmas in Urban Ethnographies." In *The Qualitative Inquiry Reader*, ed. Norman K. Denzin and Yvonna S. Lincoln. Thousand Oaks, CA: Sage.

Foucault, Michel. 1973. *Madness and Civilization*. New York: Mentor.

———. 1978. *The History of Sexuality*, vol. 1. New York: Random House.

———. 1979. *Discipline and Punish: The Birth of a Nation*. New York: Vintage.

Fox, Stephen. 1989. *Blood and Power*. New York: Penguin.

Frank, Arthur W. 1995. *The Wounded Storyteller: Body, Illness, and Ethics*. Chicago: University of Chicago Press.

———. 2002. "Between the Ride and the Story: Illness and Rememoralization." In *Ethnographically Speaking*, ed. Arthur P. Bochner and Carolyn Ellis. Walnut Creek, CA: AltaMira.

Frank, Gelya. 2000. *Venus on Wheels: Two Decades of Dialogue on Disability, Biography, and Being Female in America*. Berkeley: University of California Press.

Frey, Lawrence R., Gary L. Kreps, Paul G. Friedman, and Carl H. Boton. 1992. *Interpreting Communication Research: A Case Study Approach*. Englewood Cliffs, NJ: Prentice-Hall.

Friedan, Betty. 1964. *The Feminine Mystique*. New York: Norton.

Frisch, Michael. 1990. *A Shared Authority: Essays of the Craft and Meaning of Oral and Public History*. Albany: SUNY Press.

Fryer, Paul. 1984. *Staying Power: The History of Black People in England*. London: Pluto.

Gamson, Joshua. 1998. *Freaks Talk Back: Tabloid Talk Shows and Sexual Nonconformity*. Chicago: University of Chicago Press.

Geertz, Clifford. 1988. *Works and Lives: The Anthropologist as Author*. Stanford, CA: Stanford University Press.

Gergen, Mary M., and Kenneth J. Gergen. 2003. "Qualitative Inquiry: Tensions and Transformations." In *The Landscape of Qualitative Research*, ed. Norman K. Denzin and Yvonna S. Lincoln. Thousand Oaks, CA: Sage.

Goffman, Erving. 1963. *Stigma: Notes on the Management of Spoiled Identity*. New York: Simon and Schuster.

———. 1967. *Interaction Ritual: Essays on Face-to-Face Behavior*. New York: Pantheon.

———. 1971. *Relations in Public: Microstudies of the Public Order*. New York: Harper Colophon.

Golab, Caroline. 1977. *Immigrant Destinations*. Philadelphia: Temple University Press.

Gordon, Lewis R., T. Denean Sharpley-Whiting, and Renee T. White, eds. 1999. *Fanon: A Critical Reader*. Malden, MA: Blackwell.

Green, Stan, ed. 1999. *A History of the Washington Birthday Celebration*. Laredo, TX: Border Studies.

Gubrium, Jaber F., and James A. Holstein. 1997. *The New Language of Qualitative Method*. New York: Oxford University Press.

———. 1998. "Narrative Practice and the Coherence of Personal Stories." *Sociological Quarterly* 39:163–187.

———. 1999. "At the Border of Narrative and Ethnography." *Journal of Contemporary Ethnography* 28:561–573.

Gutman, Herbert G. 1976. *Work, Culture, and Society in Industrializing America:*

Essays in American Working-Class and Social History. New York: Alfred A. Knopf.

Hales, Diane. 2003. "Who Says You Can't?" *Parade Magazine*, July 27, 16–17.

Hall, Stuart. 1988. "New Ethnicities." *ICA Documents* (Institute of Contemporary Arts, London) 7:27–30.

Haraway, Donna. 1988. "Situated Knowledges: The Science Question in Feminism as a Site of Discourse on the Privilege of Partial Perspective." *Feminist Studies* 14:575–599.

Harding, Sandra. 1991. *Whose Science? Whose Knowledge? Thinking from Women's Lives*. Ithaca, NY: Cornell University Press.

Hayano, David. 1979. "Auto-ethnography: Paradigms, Problems, and Prospects." *Human Organization* 38:99–104.

Hedrick, Brad, Dan Byrnes, and Lew Shaver. 1994. *Wheelchair Basketball*. Washington, DC: Paralyzed Veterans of America.

Hobsbawm, Eric J. 1959. *Primitive Rebels: Studies in Archaic Forms of Social Movement in the Nineteenth and Twentieth Centuries*. New York: W. W. Norton.

Hobsbawm, Eric J., and Terrence Ranger, eds. 1983. *The Invention of Tradition*. Cambridge: Cambridge University Press.

Hochschild, Arlie. 2002. *The Time Bind: When Work Becomes Home and Home Becomes Work*. New York: Metropolitan.

Holstein, James A., and Jaber F. Gubrium. 2000. *The Self We Live By: Narrative Identity in a Postmodern World*. New York: Oxford University Press.

Homer. 1996. *Odyssey*. Trans. Robert Fagles. New York: Viking Penguin.

Horton, John. 1964. "The Dehumanization of Anomie and Alienation." *British Journal of Sociology* 15:283–300.

———. 1965. "Order and Conflict Theories of Social Problems as Competing Ideologies." *American Journal of Sociology* 71:701–713.

———. 1967. "Time and Cool People." *Transaction* 14:5–12.

———. 1971. "The Fetishism of Sociology." In *Radical Sociology*, ed. J. David Colfax and Jack L. Roach. New York: Basic.

———. 1972. "Combating Empiricism." *Insurgent Sociologist* 3:24–34.

———. 1976. "What the Friends of the People Are and How They Fight Marxist Leninists: A Polemic Against Paul Piconne." *Synthesis* 1:22–27.

———. 1977. "Contribution to the Critique of Academic Marxism." *Synthesis* 2:78–104.

———. 1995. *The Politics of Diversity: Immigration, Resistance, and Change in Monterey Park, California*. Philadelphia: Temple University Press.

Hovey, Diane. 2003. "Once upon a Time: The Power of Storytelling." *The Muse* (newsletter of Family Institute for Creative Well-Being) 2, no. 2:1, 3.

Huber, Joan. 1995. "Centennial Essay: Institutional Perspectives on Sociology." *American Journal of Sociology* 101:194–216.

Hutchison, Gerard, and Mark O'Neill. 1989. *The Springburn Experience: An Oral History of Work in a Railway Community from 1840 to the Present Day*. Edinburgh: Mainstream.

Ionesco, Eugene. 1997. *The Chairs*. London: Faber and Faber.

Irwin, John. 1970. *The Felon*. Englewood Cliffs, NJ: Prentice-Hall.

———. 1980. *Prisons in Turmoil*. Boston: Little, Brown.

———. 1985. *The Jail*. Berkeley: University of California Press.

Irwin, John, Vincent Schiraldi, and Jason Ziedenberg. 2000. "America's One Million Nonviolent Prisoners." *Social Justice* 27:135–147.

Jackson, Michael. 1998. *Minima Ethnographica: Intersubjectivity and the Anthropological Project*. Chicago: University of Chicago Press.

Jaggar, Alison M. 1983. *Feminist Politics and Human Nature*. Totowa, NJ: Rowman and Allanheld.

Jones, Richard S., and Thomas J. Schmidt. 2000. *Doing Time: Prison Experience and Identity Among First Time Inmates*. Stamford, CT: JAI Press.

Kanter, Rosabeth. 1977. *Men and Women of the Corporation*. New York: Basic.

Kesey, Ken. 1963. *One Flew over the Cuckoo's Nest*. New York: Penguin.

Kiesinger, Christine E. 2002. "My Father's Shoes: The Therapeutic Value of Narrative Reframing." In *Ethnographically Speaking*, ed. Arthur P. Bochner and Carolyn Ellis. Walnut Creek, CA: AltaMira.

Klein, Alan M. 1997. *Baseball on the Border: A Tale of Two Laredos*. Princeton, NJ: Princeton University Press.

Kushner, Tony. 2002. *Homebody/Kabul*. New York: Theatre Communication Group.

Laing, R. D. 1964. *The Politics of the Family*. New York: Vintage.

Laing, R. D., and A. Esterson. 1964. *Sanity, Madness, and the Family*. London: Tavistock.

Laslett, Barbara, and Barie Thorne. 1997. *Feminist Sociology: Life Histories of the Movement*. New Brunswick, NJ: Rutgers University Press.

Laurino, Maria. 2001. *Were You Always Italian?* New York, W. W. Norton.

Lawrence-Lightfoot, Sara, and Jessica Hoffmann Davis. 1997. *The Art and Science of Portraiture*. San Francisco: Jossey-Bass.

Lemert, Charles. 1997. *Postmodernism Is Not What You Think*. Malden, MA: Blackwell.

Lepenies, Wolf. 1988. *Between Literature and Science: The Rise of Sociology*. New York: Cambridge University Press.

Lincoln, Yvonna S. 1997. "Self, Subject, Audience, Text: Living at the Edge, Writing in the Margins." In *Representation and the Text*, ed. William G. Tierney and Yvonna S. Lincoln. Albany: SUNY Press.

———. 2002. "Emerging Criteria for Quality in Qualitative and Interpretive Research." In *The Qualitative Inquiry Reader*, ed. Norman K. Denzin and Yvonna S. Lincoln. Thousand Oaks, CA: Sage.

Lincoln, Yvonna S., and Norman K. Denzin. 2003. "The Seventh Moment: Out of the Past." In *The Landscape of Qualitative Research*, ed. Norman K. Denzin and Yvonna S. Lincoln. Thousand Oaks, CA: Sage.

Lincoln, Yvonna S., and Egon G. Guba. 2003. "Paradigmatic Controversies, Contradictions, and Emerging Confluences." In *The Landscape of Qualitative Research*, ed. Norman K. Denzin and Yvonna S. Lincoln. Thousand Oaks, CA: Sage.

Lipman, V. D. 1954. *Social History of the Jews in England, 1850–1950*. London: Watts.

Lopate, Phillip, ed. 1995. *The Art of the Personal Essay: An Anthology from the Classical Era to the Present*. New York: Random House.

Lorber, Judith. 1994. *Paradoxes of Gender*. New Haven, CT: Yale University Press.

Maines, David. 1993. "Narrative's Moment and Sociology's Phenomena: Toward Narrative Sociology." *Sociological Quarterly* 34:17–38.

———. 1999. "Information Pools and Racialized Narrative Structures." *Sociological Quarterly* 40:317–326.

Malcolm X, with Alex Haley. 1975. *The Autobiography of Malcolm X*. New York: Random House.

Mangione, Jerre, and Ben Morreale. 1992. *La Storia: Five Centuries of the Italian American Experience*. New York: Harper Perennial.

Manning, Peter K., and Betsy Cullum-Swan. 1998. "Narrative, Content, and Semiotic Analysis." In *Collecting and Interpreting Qualitative Materials*, ed. Norman K. Denzin and Yvonna S. Lincoln. Thousand Oaks, CA: Sage.

Maugham, William Somerset. 1944. *The Razor's Edge*. Garden City, NY: Doubleday.

May, William F. 1991. *The Patient's Ordeal*. Bloomington: Indiana University Press.

Mayer, Karl U., and Walter Muller. 1986. "The State and Structure of the Life Course." In *Human Development and the Life Course*, ed. Aage B. Sorenson, Franz E. Weinert, and Lonnie R. Sherrod. Hillsdale, NJ: Lawrence Erlbaum.

McKay, James, Michael A. Messner, and David Sabo. 2000. *Masculinities, Gender Relations, and Sport*. Newbury Park, CA: Sage.

McKee, Robert. 1997. *Story: Substance, Structure, Style, and the Principles of Screenwriting*. New York: ReganBooks.

McVeigh, Brian J. 2000. *Wearing Ideology: State, Schooling, and Self-Presentation in Japan*. New York: Berg.

McWhorter, Ladell. 1999. *Bodies and Pleasures: Foucault and the Politics of Normalization*. Bloomington: Indiana University Press.

Mello, Robin. 2001. "Cinderella Meets Ulysses." *Language Arts* 78:548–555.

———. 2002. "Collocation Analysis: A Method for Conceptualizing and Understanding Narrative Data." *Qualitative Research* 2:231–243.

Mendelsohn, Joyce. 2001. *The Lower East Side: Remembered and Revisited*. New York: Lower East Side.

Miller, Arthur. 1949. *Death of a Salesman*. New York: Viking.

Miller, Laura. 2000. "Media Typifications and Hip *Bijin*." *U.S.-Japan Women's Journal* 19:176–205.

———. 2003a. "Mammary Mania in Japan." *Positions: East Asia Cultures Critique* 1:271–300.

———. 2003b. "Male Beauty Work in Japan." In *Men and Masculinities in Contemporary Japan*, ed. James E. Roberson and Nobue Suzuki. New York: Routledge.

Mills, C. Wright. 1959. *The Sociological Imagination*. New York: Oxford University Press.

Mitchell, W. J. T., ed. 1981. *On Narrative*. Chicago: University of Chicago Press.

Moeran, Brian. 1990. "Introduction: Rap Discourses." In *Unwrapping Japan: Society and Culture in Anthropological Perspective*, ed. Eyal Ben-Ari, James Valentine, and Brian Moeran. Manchester: University of Manchester Press.

Monroe, Douglas K. 1976. "John L. Lewis and the Anthracite Miners, 1926–1936." Ph.D. diss., Georgetown University.

Montgomery, David. 1979. *Workers' Control in America*. New York: Cambridge University Press.

Murphy, Robert. 1987. *The Body Silent*. New York: Henry Holt.

Nafsi, Azar. 2003. *Reading Lolita in Tehran: A Memoir in Books*. New York: Random House.

Naipaul, V. S. 2001. *Half a Life*. New York: Alfred A. Knopf.

Nelli, Humbert. 1976. *The Business of Crime*. New York: Oxford University Press.

Neuman, W. Lawrence. 2003. *Social Research Methods: Qualitative and Quantitative Approaches*. Boston: Allyn and Bacon.

Newbold, Greg. 1989. *Punishment and Politics: The Maximum Security Prison in New Zealand*. Auckland: Oxford University Press.

O'Brien, Tim. 1990. *The Things They Carried: A Work of Fiction*. Boston: Houghton Mifflin.

Ochiai, Emiko. 1997. "Decent Housewives and Sensual White Women: Representations of Women in Postwar Japanese Magazines." *Japan Review* 9:151–168.

Ochs, Elinor, and Lisa Capps. 2001. *Living Narrative: Creating Lives in Everyday Storytelling*. Cambridge, MA: Harvard University Press.

Oliver, Michael. 1990. *The Politics of Disablement*. Basingstoke, UK: Macmillan.

Orlie, Melissa. 1997. *Living Ethically, Acting Politically*. Ithaca, NY: Cornell University Press.

Owen, Barbara. 1998. *"In the Mix": Struggle and Survival in a Women's Prison*. Albany: SUNY Press.

Pathas, George. 1995. *Conversation Analysis: The Study of Talk-in-Action*. Thousand Oaks, CA: Sage.

Paul, Kathleen. 1997. *Whitewashing Britain: Race and Citizenship in the Postwar Era*. Ithaca, NY: Cornell University Press.

Pennsylvania Crime Commission. 1980. *A Decade of Organized Crime*. Harrisburg: Commonwealth of Pennsylvania.

Pierce, Jennifer. 2003. "Traveling from Feminism to Mainstream Sociology and Back: One Woman's Tale of Tenure and the Politics of Backlash." *Qualitative Sociology* 26:369–396.

Pinker, Steven. 1994. *The Language Instinct: How the Mind Creates Language*. New York: HarperCollins.

Polkinghorne, David E. 1995. "Narrative Configuration in Qualitative Analysis." In *Life History and Narrative*, ed. J. Amos Hatch and Richard Wisniewski. Washington, DC: Falmer.

Pollack, William. 1998. *Real Boys: Rescuing Our Sons from the Myth of Boyhood*. New York: Henry Holt.

Pomeroy, Earl. 1957. *In Search of the Golden West: The Tourist in Western America*. Lincoln: University of Nebraska Press.

Portelli, Alessandro. 1991. *The Death of Luigi Trastulli and Other Stories*. Albany: SUNY Press.

Potok, Andrew. 2002. *A Matter of Dignity: Changing the World of the Disabled*. New York: Bantam.

Proceedings of the Nineteenth Successive and Fourth Biennial Convention of [United Mine Workers of America] District No. 1. 1921. July.

Quinney, Richard. 1994. "The Lightness of Being: A Visual Sociology of Human Existence." *Sociological Imagination* 31:130–148.

———. 1998. *For the Time Being: Ethnography of Everyday Life*. Albany: SUNY Press.

———. 2000. *Bearing Witness to Crime and Social Justice*. Albany: SUNY Press.

———. 2001. *Borderland: A Midwest Journal*. Madison: University of Wisconsin Press.

Reinharz, Shulamit. 1992. *Feminist Methods in Social Research*. New York: Oxford University Press.

Rich, Adrienne. 1980. "Compulsory Heterosexuality and Lesbian Existence." In *Blood, Bread, and Poetry: Selected Prose, 1979–1985*. New York: W. W. Norton.

Richards, Stephen C. 1990. "Sociological Penetration of the American Gulag." *Wisconsin Sociologist* 2:18–28.

———. 2003. "My Journey Through the Federal Bureau of Prisons." In *Convict Criminology*, ed. Jeffrey Ian Ross and Stephen C. Richards. Belmont, CA: Wadsworth.

Richardson, Laurel. 1996. "The Political Unconscious of the University Professor." *Sociological Quarterly* 37:735–742.

———. 1998. "Writing: A Method of Inquiry." In *Collecting and Interpreting Qualitative Materials*, ed. Norman K. Denzin and Yvonna S. Lincoln. Thousand Oaks, CA: Sage.

———. 2002. "Skirting a Quilted Pleat: De-disciplining an Academic Life." In *The Qualitative Inquiry Reader*, ed. Norman K. Denzin and Yvonna S. Lincoln. Thousand Oaks, CA: Sage.

Rochester, Anna. 1931. *Labor and Coal*. New York: International.

Rodriguez, Richard. 1982. *Hunger of Memory: The Education of Richard Rodriguez*. Boston: David Godine.

Roller, Anne H. 1926. "Wilkes-Barre: An Anthracite Town." *The Survey* 55:534–537.

Rosenhan, David L. 1973. "Being Sane in Insane Places." *Science* 179:250–258.

Rosenwald, George C., and Richard L. Ochberg, eds. 1992. *Storied Lives: The Cultural Politics of Self-Understanding*. New Haven, CT: Yale University Press.

Ross, Jeffrey Ian, and Stephen C. Richards. 2002. *Behind Bars: Surviving Prison*. New York: Alpha.

———, eds. 2003. *Convict Criminology*. Belmont, CA: Wadsworth.

Rothman, Hal K. 1998. *Devil's Bargain: Tourism in the Twentieth-century American West*. Lawrence: University of Kansas Press.

Rubin, Gayle. 1993. "Thinking Sex: Notes for a Radical Theory of the Politics of Sexuality." In *The Lesbian and Gay Studies Reader*, ed. Henry Abelove, Michèle Aina Barale, and David Halperin. New York: Routledge.

Rucker, Allen. 2001. *The Sopranos: A Family History*. New York: New American Library.

Ryan, William. 1971. *Blaming the Victim*. New York: Vintage.

Sabetti, Filippo. 2000. *The Search for Good Government: Understanding the Paradox of Italian Democracy*. Montreal: McGill-Queen's University Press.

Said, Edward. 1979. *Orientalism*. New York: Vintage.

Schatzman, Merton. 1973. *Soul Murder: Persecution in the Family*. New York: Random House.

Scheub, Harold. 1996. *The Tongue Is Fire: South African Storytellers and Apartheid*. Madison: University of Wisconsin Press.

———. 1998. *Story*. Madison: University of Wisconsin Press.

Scholinski, Daphne. 1997. *The Last Time I Wore a Dress*. New York: Riverhead.

Schullery, Paul. 1997. *Searching for Yellowstone: Ecology and Wonder in the Last Wilderness*. Ithaca, NY: Cornell University Press.

Scotch, Robert K. 1988. "Disability as the Basis for a Social Movement: Advocacy and the Politics of Definition." *Journal of Social Issues* 44:159–172.

Sebald, W. G. 1996. *The Emigrants*. London: Harvill.

Sedgwick, Eve Kosofsky. 1993. "Epistemology of the Closet." In *The Lesbian and Gay Studies Reader*, ed. Henry Abelove, Michèle Aina Barale, and David Halperin. New York: Routledge.

Seidman, Steven. 1996. "The Political Unconscious of the Human Sciences." *Sociological Quarterly* 37:699–719.

Selekman, Ben. 1928. "Miners and Murders." *Survey Graphic* 60:151ff.

Shaffer, Marguerite S. 2001. *See America First: Tourism and National Identity, 1880–1940*. Washington, DC: Smithsonian Institution Press.

Shah, Idries. 1983. *The Pleasantries of the Incredible Mullah Nasrudin*. London: Octagon.

Shakur, Sanyika. 1993. *Monster: Autobiography of an L.A. Gang Member*. New York: Penguin.

Shapiro, Joseph P. 1993. *No Pity: People with Disabilities Forging a New Civil Rights Movement*. New York: Times.

"Shavers Demanded for Detainees." 2002. *Japan Times*, July 3.

Shaw, Clifford. 1930. *The Jack Roller*. Chicago: University of Chicago Press.

Shelden, Randall. 2001. *Controlling the Dangerous Classes: A Critical Introduction to the History of Criminal Justice*. Boston: Allyn and Bacon.

Shirer, William. 1960. *The Rise and Fall of the Third Reich: A History of Nazi Germany*. New York: Simon and Schuster.

Shôgakukan. 2001. *Dêtaparu: SaishinJjôhô,Yyôgo Jiten* (DataPal: Up-to-Date Information and Encyclopedia of Terms). Tokyo: Shôgakukan.

Silverman, David. 1991. *Interpreting Qualitative Data: Methods for Analyzing Talk, Text, and Interaction*. Thousand Oaks, CA: Sage.

Simmel, Georg. 1971. "The Transcendent Character of Life." In *Georg Simmel on Individuality and Social Forms: Selected Writings*, ed. Donald N. Levine. Chicago: University of Chicago Press.

Sobol, Joseph. 1999. "The Storytelling Revival." In *Traditional Storytelling Today*, ed. Margaret Read MacDonald. Chicago: Fitzroy Dearborn.

Sondern, Frederick, Jr. 1959. *Brotherhood of Evil*. New York: Farrar, Straus and Cudahy.

Spalter-Roth, Roberta. 2001. "Pathways to Scholarly Productivity: Differences Among Moms and Dads, Childless Men and Childless Women in a Feminizing Profession." Paper presented at American Sociological Association annual conference, Anaheim, CA.

Sparks, Andrew C. 2002. "Authoethnography: Self-Indulgence or Something More." In *Ethnographically Speaking*, ed. Arthur P. Bochner and Carolyn Ellis. Walnut Creek, CA: AltaMira.

Spear, Sheldon. 1999. *Chapters in Northeastern Pennsylvania History*. Shavertown, PA: Jemags.

Spiegelman, Art. 1973, 1986. *Maus*, vols. 1–2. New York: Pantheon.

Stanfield, John H. 1998. "Ethnic Modeling in Qualitative Research." In *The Landscape of Qualitative Research*, ed. Norman K. Denzin and Yvonna S. Lincoln. Thousand Oaks, CA: Sage.

Stegner, Wallace. 1943. *The Big Rock Candy Mountain*. New York: Doubleday.

———. 1962. *Wolf Willow: A History, a Story, and a Memory of the Last Plains Frontier*. New York: Viking.

———. 1979. *Recapitulation*. New York: Doubleday.

———. 1987. *Crossing to Safety*. New York: Random House.

———. 1992. *Where the Bluebird Sings to the Lemonade Springs: Living and Writing in the West*. New York: Random House.

Stich, Sally S. 2002. "Stories to Keep." *Time*, November 11, A1–A3.

St. John, Warren. 2003. "Professors with a Past." *New York Times*, August 9, A13–A14.

Stone, Kay. 1998. *Burning Brightly: New Light on Old Tales Told Today*. Peterborough, ON: Broadview.

Strong, William E. 1876. *A Trip to the Yellowstone National Park in July, August, and September, 1875*. Norman: University of Oklahoma Press.

Suzuki, Shunryu. 1970. *Zen Mind, Beginner's Mind*. New York: Weatherhill.

Szasz, Thomas. 1970. *The Manufacture of Madness*. New York: Delta.

———. 1974. *The Myth of Mental Illness*. New York: Harper and Row.

Taylor, Daniel. 2001. *Tell Me a Story: The Life-Shaping Power of Stories*. St. Paul: Bog Walk.

Taylor, Ian, Karen Evans, and Penny Fraser. 1996. *A Tale of Two Cities: Global Change, Local Feeling, and Everyday Life in the North of England*. London: Routledge.

Terry, Charles M. 2003. *The Fellas: Overcoming Prison and Addiction*. Belmont, CA: Wadsworth.

Theroux, Paul. 1979. *The Old Patagonian Express: By Train Through the Americas*. Boston: Houghton Mifflin.

Thomas, W. I., and Florian Zaniecki. 1918–1920. *The Polish Peasant in Europe and America*. Chicago: University of Chicago Press.

Thompson, Paul. 1986. *The Voice of the Past: Oral History*. Oxford: Oxford University Press.

Thoreau, Henry David. 1849/1995. *Walden*. Minneola, NY: Dover.

Thrasher, Frederick. 1927. *The Gang*. Chicago: University of Chicago Press.

Travisano, Richard V. 2002. "On Becoming Italian American: An Autobiography of an Ethnic Identity." In *The Qualitative Inquiry Reader*, ed. Norman K. Denzin and Yvonna S. Lincoln. Thousand Oaks, CA: Sage.

Tregasis, Claire. 2002. "Social Model Theory: The Story So Far . . ." *Disability and Society* 17:457–470.

Treviño, A. Javier. 1996. *The Sociology of Law: Classical and Contemporary Perspectives*. New York: St. Martin's.

———. 1999. "Baseball, Nationalism, and the Two Laredos." *Qualitative Sociology* 22:269–274.

———, ed. 2001. *Talcott Parsons Today: His Theory and Legacy in Contemporary Sociology*. Lanham, MD: Rowman and Littlefield.

———, ed. 2003. *Goffman's Legacy*. Lanham, MD: Rowman and Littlefield.

Vendler, Helen. 1997. *The Art of Shakespeare's Sonnets*. Cambridge, MA: Harvard University Press.

Wendell, Susan. 1995. *The Rejected Body: Feminist Philosophical Reflections on Disability*. New York: Routledge.

White, Hayden. 1973. *Metahistory: The Historical Imagination in Nineteenth-century Europe*. Baltimore: Johns Hopkins University Press.

Whyte, William F. 1943. *Street Corner Society*. Chicago: University of Chicago Press.

Williams, Terry Tempest. 2000. *Leap*. New York: Vantage.

Wilson, James Q., and Robert Putnam. 1994. *Making Democracy Work: Civic Traditions in Modern Italy*. Princeton: Princeton University Press.

Wolensky, Robert P. 2002. "The Subcontracting System and Industrial Conflict in the Northern Anthracite Field." In *The Great Strike*. Harrisburg: Pennsylvania Historical Museum Commission.

Wolensky, Robert P., Kenneth C. Wolensky, and Nicole H. Wolensky. 1999. *The Knox Mine Disaster*. Harrisburg: Pennsylvania Historical Museum Commission.

Wolf, Naomi. 1992. *The Beauty Myth: How Images of Beauty Are Used Against Women*. New York: Anchor.

Wright, Charles. 1990. *The World of Ten Thousand Things: Poems, 1980–1990*. New York: Farrar Straus Giroux.

Young, Elliot. 1998. "Red Men, Princess Pocahontas, and George Washington:

Harmonizing Race Relations in Laredo at the Turn of the Century." *Western Historical Quarterly* 29:48–85.

Zeitlan, Steve, ed. 1997. *Because God Loves Stories: An Anthology of Jewish Storytelling*. New York: Touchstone.

Zinsser, William, ed. 1998. *Inventing the Truth: The Art and Craft of Memoir*. Boston: Houghton Mifflin.

Zipes, Jack. 1995. *Creative Storytelling* New York: Routledge.

Zweig, Michael. 2000. *The Working Class Majority*. Ithaca, NY: ILR Press.

The Contributors

Ronald J. Berger is professor of sociology at the University of Wisconsin–Whitewater. He is the author of ten books in the areas of sociological criminology, feminist theory, and Holocaust studies, including *Crime, Justice, and Society* (with M. Free and P. Searles), *The Sociology of Juvenile Delinquency, Rape, and Society* (with P. Searles), *Feminism and Pornography* (with P. Searles and C. Cottle), *Constructing a Collective Memory of the Holocaust*, and *Fathoming the Holocaust*. He has received his university's highest honors in both teaching and research, as well as the Wisconsin Sociological Association's William H. Sewell Award for outstanding scholarship.

Richard Quinney is professor emeritus of sociology at Northern Illinois University. He is the author of over twenty books in critical criminology and sociological theory, including classics such as *The Social Reality of Crime; Critique of Legal Order; Class, State, and Crime;* and *Criminology as Peacemaking* (with H. Pepinsky). His autobiographical writings include *Journey to a Far Place, For the Time Being, Borderland,* and *Whete Yet the Sweet Birds Sing*. He has been a Fulbright lecturer in Ireland and has received the American Society of Criminology's prestigious Edwin H. Sutherland Award for his work on criminological theory.

Sheila Balkan is a criminologist in Santa Monica, CA.

William B. Brown is assistant professor of sociology at Western Oregon University.

DeWitt Clinton is professor of languages and literatures at the University of Wisconsin–Whitewater.

Carla Corroto is assistant professor of architecture at Mississippi State University.

Norman K. Denzin is professor of sociology and communications at the University of Illinois, Urbana-Champaign.

Jean V. L. Hector Faley is associate professor of sociology at the University of Wisconsin–River Falls.

John Horton is professor emeritus of sociology at the University of California, Los Angeles.

Robin A. Mello is assistant professor of education and theatre arts at the University of Wisconsin–Milwaukee.

Laura Miller is associate professor of anthropology at Loyola University, Chicago.

Nelia Olivencia is director of Latino Student Programs at the University of Wisconsin–Whitewater.

Tony Platt is professor of sociology at California State University, Sacramento.

William E. Powell is professor of social work at the University of Wisconsin–Whitewater.

Stephen C. Richards is professor of sociology and criminology at Northern Kentucky University.

Marga Ryersbach is a doctoral student in education at the University of West Florida.

Diane Schaefer is assistant professor of sociology at Eastern Michigan University.

A. Javier Treviño is associate professor of sociology at Wheaton College, Massachusetts.

Darcie Vandegrift is assistant professor of sociology at Drake University.

Robert P. Wolensky is professor of sociology at the University of Wisconsin–Stevens Point.

Index

Abattoirs, 169, 207–212
Abrazos, 43
Abstracted empiricism, 2
Academia: felons in, 168, 183,
    190–193; Marxists in, 231, 234–244;
    people with disabilities in, 104; pre-
    sixties, 233–234; pregnancy in, 88,
    119–127; in the sixties, 234; story-
    telling in, 168–169, 203–204
Academy of Criminal Justice Sciences,
    191
Aesthetic salons, 107–109
Afghanistan, 280–281
Agger, Ben, 2
Aging, 109, 116, 267, 276–277
Agnew, Spiro T., 40
Alcoholism, 179–180
Allende, Salvador, 238
Althusser, Louis, 239
America (rock group), 37
American Correctional Association, 191
"American Pie" (McLean), 37
American Psychiatric Association, 133
American Society of Criminology, 191
American Sociological Association
    (ASA), 235
Amoral familism, 227
Analytic inquiry, 9
Animal suffering, 208–209
Annan, Kofi, 278
Ansay, A. Manette, 165
Anthracite Wage Commission, 221
Anthropology, 7

Anti-racism, 66
Anti-Semitism, 65–70
Anzaldúa, Gloria, 136
Aptheker, Herbert, 235
Architecture schools, 169, 207–214
The Art of the Personal Essay (Lopate),
    11
Arthurian myth, 203
Aspergillus, 271
Atahualpa, 75–76
Auden, W. H., 265
Aunt Nancy stories, 199
Auschwitz, 16, 74–86
Austin, James, 191
Authenticity, 9
Autobiography, 8
Autoethnography, 7–8

Back-close patois, 57
Balkan, Sheila, 167–168, 171
Banfield, Edward, 227–228
Bank robbery, 179
Barber, Eric, 161–163, 165
Barker, Pat, 63
Barone, Thomas, 9
Barth, John, 4
Beauty, concepts of: and age, 109, 116;
    breast size, 108, 113–114; feminist
    approach to, 114–116; hair, 110–114;
    nose size, 111; and sales pressure,
    109, 115–116; weight, 107
"Being Sane in Insane Places"
    (Rosenhan), 93

Belloc, Hilaire, 65
Bergen, Candice, 174
Berger, Ronald J., 1, 89–90, 153
Bicultural identities, 14–15, 26–31
"Big Rock Candy Mountain," 19–20
Biography, 132
Biracial people, 102
Birkenau, 74
Bisexuality, 89, 129–136
Black Panthers, 27, 39
Bleile, Amy, 154
Body image: disability and, 89–90; disease and, 88; drug use and, 89, 139–151; ideal form, 87; in Japan, 88; pregnancy and, 88, 119–127; sexual expression and, 89
Borderland (Quinney), 281
Borders, 15
Bosch, Hieronymus, 21
Boundaries, 129–130
Bowling alleys, 141
Brahms, Johannes, 271
Brazil, 243
Breasts, 108, 113–114
Brecht, Bertolt, 63
Brennan, William J., 222, 224
Briscoe, Dolph, 42–43
Brown, P. R., 222
Brown, William B., 170, 245
Bruner, Joseph, 195
Brunstrom, Jan, 165, 166*n*4
Bryant, Kobe, 154, 166*n*2
Buber, Martin, 73
Buchenwald, 73
Bush, George H. W., 19
Bush, George W., 262
Butler, Judith, 130–131

The Call of Stories (Coles), 9
Cambodia, 260
Campamentos, 238
Campbell, Alex, 219, 221, 223, 229*n*7
Campbell, Joseph, 202
Canícula, 37
Cappellini, Gifford, 216
Cappellini, Marie, 216, 225–226
Cappellini, Rinaldo: as CIO organizer, 225–226; conflict within the union, 222–224; criminal charges against, 225; early days of, 215, 218; as labor leader, 169–170, 228; loss of arm, 216; as restaurateur, 226; strike of 1920, 219–222; UAMP role of, 224–225
Carnivals, 40
Censorship, 199–200
Cerebral palsy, 153, 165
Changing Relations Project, 243
Chavez, Cesar, 39, 176
Chekhov, Anton, 275
Chicago (rock group), 41
The Chilam Balam of Chumayel, 75
Child labor, 141
Children's patois, 57
Chile, 238
Chopin, Frederic, 271
Chronology, 4
Church, Kathryn, 8
Cinderella syndrome, 134
Civil rights movement, 234
Civilian Conservation Corps (CCC), 141
Clandinin, D. Jean, 4
Class, 228
Cleanliness, 53–56
Clinton, De Witt, 16, 71
Closes, 57–58
Clouds, 278
Coal miners: early labor activities among, 141, 215, 218; interunion conflict, 217, 224–225; Italians as, 169, 217–218, 228; leasing system, 226; Sicilian mobsters against, 217, 219–221, 223; strike of 1916, 217–218; strike of 1920, 216; subcontracting, 216–223, 228; as working-class heroes, 170, 228
Coles, Robert, 9
Colombia, 189
Colton, Reggie, 160
Communal life, 175–176
Communicative bodies, 90, 165
Communism, 256
Communities, tenement, 49–62
Community activism, 242
Compassionate release, 180–181
Composting, 135–136
Confession, 132, 134
Congress of Industrial Organizations (CIO), 225–226
Connelly, F. Michael, 4
Consagra, Charles, 220–221

Conscientious objectors, 102
Conservation Reserve Program, 271
Contras, 257, 259
Conversion, religious, 72, 74
Convict criminologists, 168, 183, 190–193
Cook-Lynn, Elizabeth, 17, 23
Copeland, Aaron, 274
Corroto, Carla, 169, 207
Cosa Nostra, 217, 219–221, 226–227
Costa Rica, 119
Cota Valdez, Maria Antonia, 112
Coyote (trickster), 75, 199
Cremins, Bobby, 164–165
Criminal justice: academic studies of, 176, 191–192; compassionate release, 180–181; ex-convicts as professors of, 168, 183, 190–193; Federal Sentencing Guidelines, 181; humanization of defendants, 177–181; reform movements, 168
Crittendon, Anne, 125
Crossing to Safety (Stegner), 123
Cult of youth, 88

Davis, Angela, 235
Davis, Jessica Hoffman, 9
Davis, Leonard, 87
Deafness, 100
Death of a Salesman (Miller), 14, 18
Demonization, 231
Denzin, Ken, 18–21
Denzin, Norman K., 9, 13–14, 17
Descartes, René, 87
Design studios, 207–208
Dialects, 56–60, 95
Disabilities: attitude, 155–156, 163–164; being young with, 93–101; and the Hunchback of Notre Dame, 91–93, 99–100; living with, 87–88, 91; physical and psychological pain of, 102–103; potential of people with, 104–105; rights of people with, 156–157; social model, 156–157; "supercrips," 89, 157; wheelchair sports, 89, 154–165
Discrimination: against bisexuals, 130–136; against ex-convicts, 191; against gays, 242
Diversity, 191, 243–244
Draft card burning, 178

Dr. Seuss, 129
Drug Enforcement Agency (DEA), 188
Dualism, body-mind, 87
Dunbar, Paul Laurence, 104
Durant, Ariel, 172
Durant, Will, 172
Durkheim, Émile, 35
Dyadic bodies, 90, 165

Echeverría, Luis, 43
Education: and family, 167–168; of felons, 190; as liberation, 174; of orphans, 168, 185–186; of storytellers, 196, 203–204; storytelling curricula, 198
Einerson, Allen, 159
Eiseley, Loren, 102
El Salvador, 256, 259
The Elementary Forms of Religious Life (Durkheim), 36
Ellis, Carolyn, 7
Ellis, Havelock, 64
Emerson, Ralph Waldo, 145
Emplotment, 4
Empowerment, 182
Endo, Shusaku, 112
English-only movement, 243
"Epistemology of the Closet" (Sedgwick), 134
Erie Railroad, 217
Ethic of inspiration, 153
Ethnic studies, 234
Ethnography, 7, 239
Ethnomethodology, 239
Ewick, Patricia, 6
Ex-convicts, 168, 183, 190–193
Exhaustion, 121
Exodus, Book of, 71–72, 74

Faley, Jean Hector, 15, 49
Family: and education, 167–168; father-son relationships, 17–23, 97; husband-wife relationships, 171–172; isolated, in suburbia, 173; morality of, 227; mother-daughter relationships, 28–34; and narcotics addiction, 140–143, 145–146; and place, 13–16; sibling relationships, 28–29, 32–33; in Sicily, 227; as social construction, 13
Fanon, Franz, 27

Farm Bureau Life Insurance Company, 21
Fauré, Gabriel, 271
Fausto-Sterling, Anne, 133
Federal prison system, 188–190
Federal Sentencing Guidelines, 181
Feiler, Bruce, 110
Feminism: and architecture, 169, 207–214; and concepts of beauty, 115; and pregnancy, 122; role in changing sociology, 3
Ferber, Max, 63
Fine, Michelle, 7
Ford, Jack, 68
Ford Foundation, 243
Foreigners in Japan, 109–113, 117n2
Foucault, Michel, 3, 132, 134–135
Frank, Arthur, 4–5, 90, 153
Free speech movement, 234
Freedom, 136
French student/worker rebellion (1968), 234
Friendly fire casualties, 248–250
Frisch, Michael, 60
Frogley, Mike, 163–165
Fulbright scholarships, 233, 243

Gaijin, 109–113, 117n2
Gallagher, Michael, 223
Galleani, Louis, 218
Gamson, Joshua, 133
Gays, 131–132, 241–242
Gender, 130–131
Gender identity disorder (GID), 133
Gender roles, 176, 232
Gender Trouble (Butler), 131
Genealogy, 8
Gillespie, William H., 223
Glassford, George E., 45
Glen Alden Coal Company, 224
Global culture, 116
God, 200
Goffman, Erving, 39, 46, 134
Gold Cup championships, 156, 160–161
Golden Spurs, 39–40
Gonzalez, Ruben, 44
Grenada invasion, 255–256
Grief, 49–51, 60–62
Grimm's tales, 199
Gubrium, Jaber, 5
Guerrilla theater, 235

Haggard, Merle, 271
Hair, 110–114
Half a Life (Naipaul), 279
Harvest moon, 278
Hatch, Barry, 244
Hayano, David, 7
Healey, Dorothy, 235
Hedrick, Brad, 159–160
Hegemony, 131–133
Hendrix, Jimi, 173
Hermaphroditism, 133, 137n3
Heroin, 139, 147–150
Herscher, Uri, 70
Heterosexuality, 132
Hierarchies: in sexuality, 131–133; and socially structured trauma, 89, 151
Higher education. *See* Academia
Hitler, Adolf, 66, 69–70
Ho Chi-Minh, 235
Hochschild, Arlie, 122
The Holocaust, 16, 73–74, 185
Holstein, James, 5
Homer, 273, 277, 282
Homosexuality, 131–132, 241–242
"A Horse with No Name" (America), 37
Horton, John, 170, 231
Hugo, Victor, 87, 91–93, 99
The Hunchback of Notre Dame (Hugo), 87, 91–93, 99–100
Huntington Library, 68–70
Hypermasculinity, 164

Identity, 129–132
Immigrants: grief of, 15, 49–51, 60–62; Italians, 217; Jews in England, 63–64; and September 11 attacks, 26
Imperialism, 234
Incarceration rates, 192
Indians, 14, 17, 22–23
Indochina Reconciliation Project, 260
Industrial Workers of the World (IWW), 217–218, 228
Institutions, 132
Intersexuals, 133, 137n3
Intifada, 67
Iraq, 261–263
Irwin, John, 191
Italian Americans, 169; prejudice against, 226–229

James, Henry, 235
Japan, 88, 107–117
Japanese language, 115
Jataka tales, 199–200
Jewishness, 16, 63–70
John, Elton, 44
Johnson, Lyndon B., 237
Johnson, Trooper, 160
Jones, George, 277
Jones, Rev. Jim, 95
Jordan, Michael, 162
Jordan, Rev. R. D., 221
Journal writing, 267, 270, 276
Juette, Melvin, 154–155, 157–162, 165
Juvenile delinquents, 177

Kaddish, 81–82
Keats, John, 278
Kegirai, 111
Kemp, Evan, Jr., 166*n3*
Kennedy, John F., 172
Kenyatta, Jomo, 66
Khmer Rouge, 260
Kindness: inability to respond to,
    144–145; as response to pregnancy,
    121, 123–124, 127
King, Martin Luther, 237
Klein, Alan, 36
Knowledge, 3
Knox Coal Company, 226
Kristallnacht, 73
Kushner, Tony, 67
Kyphosis, 98, 104

Labor unions: CIO, 225–226; farm-
    workers, 176; Industrial Workers of
    the World (IWW), 217–218; Molly
    Maguires, 215; oral history,
    169–170; United Anthracite Miners
    of Pennsylvania (UAMP), 224–225;
    United Mine Workers of America
    (UMWA), 170, 215–219, 221–225
Language: of children, 57; foreigners
    speaking Japanese, 115; social levels
    and, 56–60
Lao Tzu, 74–77, 86*n1*
Laredo Times, 40–41, 43
Laredo, Texas, 35–46
LaTorre, Stefano, 221
Laurino, Maria, 227
Lawrence-Lightfoot, Sara, 9

Leal, Raul, 44
Leasing system, 226
Lemert, Charles, 3
Leukemia, 265, 268, 271–272, 281
Lewis, Jerry, 156
Lewis, Jerry Lee, 276
Lewis, John L., 215, 222–225
Liberation movements, 187
Life course, 167
Lippi, August J., 226
Lipsit, Seymour Martin, 236
Longoria, Dennis A., 44
Lopate, Phillip, 11
Lorber, Judith, 130
Lordosis, 98
Lost in the Funhouse (Barth), 4
Lucchino, Sam, 220–222
Lykins, Ron, 158

MacVeigh, Brian, 116
Mafia (Cosa Nostra), 217, 219–221,
    226–227
Magnon, Alberto, 43
Maines, David, 4
*Making Democracy Work: Civic
    Traditions in Modern Italy*, 228
Malcolm X, 39
Maloney, Thomas, 224–225
Marginalized groups, 6
Marijuana, 188–189
Marxism, 2, 67, 231, 234–244
Massage parlors, 175
Maternity leave, 124
Mathematization of sociology, 2
Matrix of intelligibility, 131
Maus (Spiegelman), 73
McLean, Don, 37
McWhorter, Ladelle, 132–133, 135–
    136
Mein Kampf (Hitler), 69–70
Mello, Robin A., 168–169, 195
Mental illness, 176–177
Merlin, 203, 205*n1*
Methodicalness, 54–55
Mexican Americans, 35–46
Mexico, 15, 36, 40, 43–44, 187–188
Miller, Arthur, 14, 18
Miller, Laura, 88, 107
Mills, C. Wright, 2, 8, 13, 49, 232
Milner, E. Stewart, 219
Milwaukee Bucks NWBA team, 161

Milwaukee Jewish Children's Home, 185
Mitchell, John, 215
Moeran, Brian, 109
Molly Maguires, 215
Montgomery, David, 218
The Moral Basis of a Backward Society (Banfield), 227
Morality, 227–228
Morgan, J. P., 215
Morning sickness, 120–121
Moving house, 279–280
Mozart, Wolfgang A., 271
Multiculturalism, 191
Mundane charisma, 153
Myasthenia gravis, 97

Nader, Ralph, 140
Nafsi, Azar, 227
Naipaul, V. S., 279
Narcotics addiction: culture of, 139, 147–149; family and, 140–143, 145–146; isolation and, 146–147; self-esteem and, 89, 145; sexual abuse and, 143–144; transformation out of, 150–151
Narrative: analytical approach to inquiry, 9; authorial strategies and obligations, 5; conversational analysis in, 5–6; diversity in thinking about, 3–4; as method of inquiry, 4; oral, 52–62; and plot, 4; storied approach to inquiry, 9. *See also* Storytelling
Narrative practice, 5–6
Nasrudin tales, 199–200
National Endowment for the Arts, 196, 202
National Wheelchair Basketball Association (NWBA), 156
Native Americans, 259, 274
NBC Sports Fantasies, 162
Nelson, Willie, 271
New Deal, 225
Newbury, Terry, 44
Nicaragua, 238, 255–260
Nixon, Richard M., 38–39
Nobel Peace Prize, 278
North American Free Trade Agreement (NAFTA), 46
North, Oliver, 259

Nuevo Laredo, 36
Nuyoricans, 14, 26

Obon odori, 110
O'Brien, Tim, 1
Occidentalism, 109
Ochiai, Emiko, 113
Odyssey (Homer), 273, 277, 282
Olivencia, Nelia, 14, 25
Oppression, 175
Oral history, 52–62, 169–170
Orientalism, 109
Orlie, Melissa, 129–130, 136
Orphans, 168, 185–186

Padrone system, 218
Parades, 41–44
Paralympics, 156, 159
Parenting, 126
Parsons, Talcott, 42, 233
Parton, Dolly, 271
Paso libre, 40
Passing of time, 265–266
Patois, 56–60, 95
Patton, Gen. George, 69–70
Peasants, 259
Penn, William, 102
Pennsylvania Coal Company (PACC), 215, 217–219, 221–223; Papers, 216
Performance artists, 196–197
Performance texts, 10
Personal essays, 11
Philippines, 259
Photography, 148, 266–267, 276
Physical attractiveness, 87
Pinchot, Gifford, 225
Pizarro, Francisco, 75
Place(s): Auschwitz, 16, 74–86; borderlands, 35–46; English Midlands, 63–67; and family, 13–16; New York, 25–34; Scotland, 49–62
Platt, Tony, 15–16, 63
Portelli, Alessandro, 60, 62
Positivist sociology, 1–2
Post-Traumatic Stress Disorder (PTSD), 254
Postmodernism, 3, 7, 46
Poverty: among coal miners, 141; in Laredo, Texas, 45; in Mexico, 187; of orphans, 186; respectable, 53,

55–56; shame of, 56; and social inequities, 95–97
Powell, William, 87–88, 91
Pregnancy: attitude changes toward, 126–127; early, 120–121; and feminism, 122; kindness as response to, 121, 123–124, 127; lack of institutional support for, 125; lack of role models for, 119; and race, 122; seen as impediment to work, 122–124; and sexuality, 122; society's ambivalence toward, 88
Prejudice, 111; anti-Semitism, 65–70; against Chinese, 244; against Italians, 226–229; in the Vietnam War, 245–246; against whites, 244
Prison system, U.S., 188–190
Puerto Ricans, 25–34
Putnam, Robert, 228

Quakers, 102
Qualitative inquiry, 7
Quantitative sociology, 2
Quasimodo, 87–88, 91–93, 105
Quetelet, Adolphe, 87
Quinney, Bridget, 272, 275
Quinney, John, 275–276
Quinney, Richard, 1, 35, 265–267
Quinney, Solveig, 269, 273, 276, 281

Race, 122
Racism, 66–67, 175
Rape, 143–144
La Raza Unida Party, 39
Reading Lolita in Tehran (Nafsi), 227
"Reading the Tao at Auschwitz" (Clinton), 75–85
Reagan, Ronald, 255, 259
Rehabilitation Institute of Chicago (RIC), 157, 161–163
Relations in Public (Goffman), 46
Religion: Auschwitz and the Tao, 76–86; and Jewish identity, 67–68, 185; Mayan, 75; Methodist, 71; Quaker, 102; Sufi, 199; and umbilical cords, 35
Religious Society of Friends, 102
"Requiem" (Verdi), 277
Respectability, 53, 55–56
Richards, Stephen, 168, 183
Richardson, Laurel, 10

The Rise and Fall of the Third Reich (Schirer), 73
Ritual face-work, 39
Rituxan, 271, 281
Robeson, Paul, 232
Rodriguez, Richard, 42, 46
Roosevelt, Eleanor, 233
Roosevelt, Teddy, 215
Rosenhan, David, 93
The Royal Commentaries (Garcilaso de la Vega), 75
Rubin, Gayle, 131
Russell, Bertrand, 64, 172
Russia, 202–203
Ryersbach, Marga, 89, 129

Sabetti, Filippo, 228
Said, Edward, 109
Sartre, Jean-Paul, 8, 239
Saturday Night Fever, 227
"Saturday in the Park" (Chicago), 41
Schaefer, Diane, 89, 139
Schatzman, Merton, 146
Scheuerman's disease, 88, 93, 98, 104
Schirer, William, 73
Scholinski, Daphne, 133
Schullery, Paul, 21–22
Sciandra, Joseph, 226
Scobie, Bob, 281
Scoliosis, 161
Scotland, 15
Seders, 71–72
Sedgwick, Eve Kosofsky, 134
Self-esteem, 142, 145
September 11 attacks, 33; effect on the border of, 46; and identity as New Yorker, 14, 25–26, 28; Iraq linkage question, 261; viewed from the farm, 277–278
Sexism, 175, 209–213
Sexual abuse, 143–144
Sexuality: boundaries in, 89, 129–136; hierarchy in, 131–133; and pregnancy, 88, 122
Silbey, Susan, 6
Silva, Luiz Inácio Lula da, 243
Simmel, Georg, 129–130
Siracuse, Ludvico "Charlie," 217
Sister-City Exchange Program, 202
Sisyphus, 203
Skirball, 70

Skotheim, Robert, 69
Slaughterhouses, 169, 207–212
Smuggling, 188
Social closure, 103
Social inequities, 95–97, 101
Society of Martha Washington, 45
The Sociological Imagination (Mills), 2
Sociology: emergence as discipline of,
    1; feminism's role in changing, 3;
    and immersion in the world, 126;
    Marxist, 231, 234–244; positivist,
    1–2, 6; quantitative, 2; role in social
    change of, 234; self-reflexive, 8; sto-
    rytelling, 8–11; as vehicle for libera-
    tion, 170; and Vietnam War, 234;
    writing style in, 10–11
Sociopoetics, 10
Socrates, 278
Soldiering, 170
The Sopranos, 226
Soul murder, 146
South Africa, 199
Soviet Union, 202–203, 236
Spastic diplegia, 153
Spector, Dave, 110
Spiegelman, Art, 73–74
Spiegelman, Vladek, 74
Spinoza, Benedict de, 172
Sports 'N Spokes magazine, 160
Spousal abuse, 173
Stairheid politics, 55
State of Maine Arts Commission, 196
Stegner, Wallace, 13, 17–18, 22–23, 123
Storied inquiry, 9
Storytelling: in academia, 168–169;
    class and ethnicity in, 226–229; cur-
    ricula for, 198; education for, 196,
    203–204; and entertainment, 10;
    itinerant, 197; through journal writ-
    ing, 267, 270, 276; as performance
    art, 197–198; revival of, 8; and
    social change, 199–201; by teachers,
    198–199; as truth, 9, 195; in the
    USSR, 202–203; as witness to time
    and place, 265–282. *See also*
    Narrative
Strong, Gen. William, 17
Students for a Democratic Society
    (SDS), 186
"Studio crit," 207–208
Subcontractors, 216–223

Suburbia, 173
Sufiism, 199
Suicide, 150
"Supercrips," 89, 157, 165
Suzuki, Shunryu, 270
Systems-functionalism, 42

Talk shows, 133–134
Tao de Ching (Lao Tzu), 74–76, 78–85,
    86*n1*
Teaching, 272
Tenement communities, 49–62
Tenure, 242
Terry, Chuck, 191
Theroux, Paul, 35
Thompson, Paul, 52
Thoreau, Henry David, 145, 147, 151
Three-up patois, 57
Thrift, 53, 56
Time, 265–266, 282
Tiscar, Chevalier Fortunato, 218
Tocqueville, Alexis de, 151
Trangendered people, 136*n1*
"The Transcendent Character of Life"
    (Simmel), 129
Transsexuals, 136*n1*
Trauma, 89, 151
Treviño, A. Javier, 15, 35
Truesdale, John, 158
Truth, 3, 9
Turner, Ralph, 235
Tutoring, 175
Twin Towers, 14, 25–26, 28, 32–33
Two-up patois, 57

Ubuge, 111–112
Umbilical cords, 35
Uncle Vanya (Chekhov), 275
Union of Marxist Social Scientists
    (UMSS), 238, 240–242
United Anthracite Miners of
    Pennsylvania (UAMP), 224–225
United Mine Workers of America
    (UMWA), 170, 215–219, 221–225
United Nations, 278

Valdez, Martina Felicidad, 112
Values, social: among Scottish tene-
    ment-dwellers, 53–56; ritual face-
    work, 39; work ethic, 20, 121,
    163–164

Vandegrift, Darcie, 88, 119
Vega, Garcilaso de la, 75
Vietnam Outreach Center (VOC), 254
Vietnam War: conscientious objectors
    during, 102; the draft, 172–173;
    killing of children, 245, 250–252;
    meaning of, 170; prejudice against
    Vietnamese, 245–246; protest
    against, 186–187, 237; sociology
    and, 234; U.S. defeat in, 260;
    Veterans Memorial, 261
Villarreal, Joe, 42
Volpe, Santo, 221, 226

Waller, Darryl "Tree," 160
War: in Grenada, 255–256; in Iraq,
    261–263; meaning in, 170; in
    Nicaragua, 256–260; opposition to,
    102; victims of, 261; violence
    against women in, 245, 250–252,
    259. *See also* Vietnam War
Washington, George, 15
Washington's Birthday Celebration,
    Laredo, Texas, 36–46
Watts Riot (1965), 234
"We Wear the Mask" (Dunbar), 104
Weber, Max, 103
Weil, Berta, 73
Weil, Hermann, 73
Weis, Lois, 7
Wesley, John, 72
Wheelchair basketball, 89, 154,
    156–165
Wheelchair sports, 154–156
White, Hayden, 4
Wiesel, Elie, 1
Williams, Enoch, 222

Williams, Terry Tempest, 21
Wilson, James Q., 228
Wilson, Woodrow, 221
Wobblies (IWW), 217–218, 228
Wolensky, Robert, 169–170, 215
Wolf Willow (Stegner), 17
Women: abuse by partners of, 173, 179;
    in architecture schools, 169,
    207–214; body image, 107–117;
    criminal justice and, 176; harass-
    ment of, 25; mother-daughter rela-
    tionships, 28–34; violence in war
    against, 245, 250–252, 259
Woolf, Virginia, 1
Work: of housewives, 173; power and
    class at, 228; pregnancy seen as
    impediment to, 122–124; for psycho-
    logical sustenance, 142
Work ethic, 20, 121, 163–164
Works Progress Administration (WPA),
    140
World Trade Center, 14, 25–26, 28,
    32–33
Wright, Charles, 271
Writing, as part of research processs, 10

Yellowstone National Park, 14, 17–18,
    20–22
Young, Kimball, 272

Zen Mind, Beginner's Mind (Suzuki),
    270
Zero drag, 122–123
Zinn, Howard, 67
Zionism, 63
Zúñiga, Josephine P., 45
Zweig, Michael, 228

About the Book

This exciting new book is about the narrative turn in sociology, an approach that views lived experience as constructed, at least in part, by the stories that people tell about it.

The book is organized around four themes—family and place, the body, education and work, and the passage of time—that tell a story about the life course and touch on a wide range of enduring sociological topics. The first chapter explores some of the theories of narrative that mark contemporary social analysis. Introductions to the four sections identify the sociological themes that the essays reflect. The heart of the book, however, is not *about* narrative but *of* narrative: scholars who have been involved in class, racial/ethnic, gender, sexual orientation, and disability studies compellingly write about their own life experiences.

Storytelling Sociology is essential reading for all those who want to learn about narrative inquiry, teach about it, or develop a "storied" approach in their own work.

Ronald J. Berger is professor of sociology at the University of Wisconsin–Whitewater. He has published extensively in the areas of criminology, feminist theory, and Holocaust studies and is now working on *Wheels of Fortune: Gangs, Disability, and Basketball.* **Richard Quinney** is professor emeritus of sociology at Northern Illinois University. Author of such classics as *The Social Reality of Crime* and *Class, State, and Crime: On the Theory and Practice of Criminal Justice*, his recent publications include *For the Time Being: Ethnography of Everyday Life* and *Borderland: A Midwest Journal.*